(SPOKANE POET)

THE ROOF OF STONE

THE ROOF OF STONE

Poems by Franz Schneider

TEMPORAL ACUITY PRESS

Temporal Acuity Press
  a division of Temporal Acuity Products, Inc.
1535-121st Avenue S.E., Bellevue, WA 98005

Acknowledgement is made to the following publications in which
some of these poems first appeared: *Charter, Columbia River Watch,
Copula, Eads Bridge, Fresco, Hudson Review, Italian Americana, Literary
Arts Press, Northwest Arts, Poetry Northwest, Poetry Seattle, Portland
University Review, Puget Sounder, Raindance, Reflection, Slackwater
Review,* and *Willowsprings.*

Design: Leo Aspenleiter
Printer and binder: University Press, Spokane, Washington

LIBRARY OF CONGRESS CATALOGING IN PUBLICATION DATA

Schneider, Franz, 1928-
    The roof of stone.

    I. Title.
PS3569.C5224R6   1983   811'.54   83-629
ISBN 0-911723-00-5

For Ann and the Six

CONTENTS

I Prologue

CANTO

In this locust summer
Of the middle life,
I rehearsed the moments
Of my going.

Some doors were open,
Some were shut.

But the fragrance
Of a thousand flowers
Could not stay the cat
Lusting for the blood
Of the woodpecker.

II Seasons

PALM SUNDAY AT SALISHAN

At night a wind began to blow
from west-north-west
that rocked the cedar house
and made the shingles rattle.
Old trees shook with
the breakings of the sea.

The wind-tossed surf crashed
booming down on lava beds
and flushed the scoured funnels clean,
until fossil clams—
stone dead these 20 million years—
thought it was time to wake
to salt-washed life again.

While the wind raked
bone dry winter grass away,
the tavern drunks at Lincoln City
argued over DNA and
watched "Jesus of Nazareth"
in magicolor on TV.

FISHING

Water stirs gently:
New light cascades
From the morning sun.

In the wake of my boat
A mallard dives:
Silence over emptiness.

Circular waves recede
And vanish in the stillness:
A fish jumps.

A splash from my oar:
Slowly a heron rises
On blue wings.

Shrill cries disturb the sky:
The brawling voices
Of herring gulls.

Trout do not talk.
I cast another line
Upon the waters.

Fighting and leaping,
A fish smashes through
Watery mirrors.

In the blue haze,
The heart stops
For one terrible moment.

On the trout,
Coruscations of rainbows,
Suns and stippled stars.

Speak but one word, oh fish,
And I put down
My gear forever.

THE VASE

Rounding the globe
of this earthenware vase
and sorting the colors
One by one
In the evening twilight,
I suddenly recall
A bend in the river
Where a clump of willows
Mark the bank
(it was spring time).

Their bark gleamed yellow
With the rising sap,
And at sunset felt moist
To the touch of the hand.

The mallard's wake
Traced a sign on the water,
Its secrets lost
In up-river darkness:

There would be basswood
And mint in the summer,
Sweet taste, and the tender
Scent of the bergamots.

THE HAWK

Do you see him on his perch,
The hawk, in his prideful ease?
Even at rest his eye is far away,
Concentration intent.
Detached and inhuman,
He is without tenderness
While he watches his prey.
(I fear for you, my daughter;
Some men are that way.)

Now he is roused, instant and keen;
The eye glittering, glad and aflame.
A quick contemptuous toss of his head,
And he is launched. Master of air—
Stooping, swooping,
Suddenly striking hard—
He takes the squealing hare.
(I pray for you, my daughter,
And your beauty so unaware.)

SUMMER IDYLLS
(from the German of Karl Krolow)

Floating Leaves

Trapped snake!
Noon holds her captive
In his hands
Until she grows still.
With clippers
He cuts from hedges
Boats for the old stream.
True to ancient design,
Swans and carnations drift by
With curved necks.

Then a flotilla of leaves.
The fishes are silent.
Their mouths pull
The green keels
To the bottom of the garden.

Sky

Arena of paper cut-outs!
They battle
To become snowflakes
Or larks.

Summer lets nostalgic
Blue ships sail in it.
They grow lighter and lighter
On their trip to the zenith.
With lights underneath eye-lashes,
The angels of the horizon
Are already waiting.

The River

When he carries barges,
Smoke and whistles on his face,
He is a man.
But by the willows
He turns into woman
Whispering to
Leaves and goldfinches—
Or into a girl, silver
In her mouth.
Bridges break down
From the light of the water.

River, with violin music
And bicycles along the shore;
Supple body
Caressed by sloping banks:
Admit that you use
Changing mirrors
Where the sky reads
Of airplanes.

Drifting downstream you speak,
Leaving alms along the way
For fishermen, and tear your hair.
Algae quietly
Conceal your age.

SUMMER INSOMNIA

Hoping for sleep,
I listen to my breath.
Counting sheep hadn't worked,
Nor had rehearsing again
And again, the lustful outrage
I saw in Satyricon committed
On the body of a woman
Who has nothing in common
With my wife who is asleep.

Breath conjures words to exorcise
The demons flesh and death,
Unrhyming the rest I need
To purify the care
At least of this one day
So I can watch in awe
And with the clear eye of morning
The skin of my children
Assume the patina of hazelnut.

My meditation fails.
Perhaps I should try prayer:
"Veni creator spiritus . . ."
But the paraclete comes only
To the pure in heart.

SEPTEMBER NIGHT
(for Norine McRea)

While we sleep in milky moonlight,
Tomatoes ripen in their skin.
The rocky soil exhales diurnal heat.

Like acolytes bearing lanterns,
Sunflowers guard the garden walls.
The house glows safely in the dark.

I dream of children in tall corn
Leafing, hidden, through dog-eared books.
Their father's voice is lost among the husks.

HUNTING INTERLUDE

Moving downslope toward water,
Dry milk-weed crackling underfoot,
We spooked three deer where
The creek cuts into the gulley floor.

The big buck broke first,
Panic carrying him through the brush.
His fierce rush made the sticks rattle.
The noise startled us.

The fawn was next.
It blundered into the clearing
And stared with doleful eyes.
Suddenly it bolted
And vanished among the trees.

Only the doe retained her poise.
Never losing cover,
She vaulted gracefully over the browse,
Her white brush flickering.

For a long time I had dreamed
About a clean kill
And the leaping deer transfixed in mid-air.
Now I felt hot and small,
Shamed by love put to flight.

Turning toward high ground,
My pride snuffed out and smoking
Like a wick,
I was glad my friend was there
To go before me up the slope.

HUNTING SEASON
(for John Logan)

After a red-berried summer,
The snows have come.
Darkness has fallen on the hillside.

The tongue is silent, lest it raise
Ghosts waiting for ambush
In the thickets of the heart.

Regarding the dog's sharp tooth
And the wailing of the wind,
A unicorn steps from the frozen dawn.

AUTUMN

(from the German of Karl Krolow)

The wind answers unasked.
Maple and birch leaves die of it.
Everywhere there is death,
But nobody talks of it.

O Mort, vieux capitaine—
The cold composure,
Considering the fate of others.

A child sings of the passing year.
In the open mouth shines
The rose-colored palate.

DECEMBER

Hoarfrost covers the world.
In the fog, houses move quietly
Like men-of-war riding at anchor.
Telephone poles are a forest of masts.

A woman appears through the misty shrouds.
Her black hair reminds me of those wigs
Ceremonious ladies wear in Japanese prints
When bidding their Shogun lovers good-bye.

With a few measured strokes,
She scrapes the ice off the car window.
Her stiff coat brushes against shrubs
Now and then.

Strands of frozen web
Fall noiselessly to the ground.
A door slams shut.
The car begins to move.

A PRAYER IN WINTER

In the summer I made him run
(the sun, I mean);
Ate strawberries and drank wine
At the fair, and wore
The clothes of a clown.

In the autumn, I wept much
Under the moon, and watched
The leaves come down
In the cold night air.

In winter,
All trees are bare
And the heart is a stone.

God, give us back your flesh
And clothe the bare bone.

III *Italian Poems*

VALDARNO
(for Kitty Whelan)

We love the pools
And the river
Where the willows touch
Reeds and deep water
At the edge of the wall
Along the road
To Pontassieve.

Our gaze follows
A goldfinch skipping
From branch to branch
As we eat our bread and fruit
Listening to fish
Jump for their lunch.

In the heat
Upriver, a poacher
Furtively works
His hidden lines.
The nervous shade
On the brocaded white sand
Pulses
Like a network of blood vessels.
The hard-rock thunder rolls
High in the air.

We pretend to read
But soon flee across a field
To escape the downpour
Seeping into our bones.

THREE FLORENTINES SUMMONED
(for Tom Rukavina)

1. *Savonarola*

Last night I dreamed
Another man's dream
And drank the milk
Of his word
In the morning.

At noon I will die.
For what is written
Won't be torn up.
I have an argument
With the truth.

2. *Leonardo*

The tiger of thought
Paces silently
In jungles of concentration.
His luminous eyes
Convert distance into imagery.
Without malice,
He stalks black voids
Between stars.

3. *Michelangelo*

The word hovers
Above the world
Of my thought
Like a dove.

A lost trail,
Meaning winds
Its hidden way
Through memory.

The evening flows
Sweet and low,
A melodious darkness.

VALLOMBROSA

Bone-dry are the slopes
Of Vallombrosa in summer.
Brooks without water run
Thick with crackling leaves,
Filling the rocky pools
High overarched with shade.
A veil of dust cannot hide
The scent of pines, nor the
Fragrant red of strawberries
Scattered through the forest.
Across the valley, I hear
The teeth of a saw bite through
The wood of the morning.
We sit down to eat.
While we watch monks
Walking the roads below,
Trees die in the mountains.

SUMMER STORM: ALPE DI SAN BENEDETTO

In the rain
I hear the driving
Surf of time,
The wet progression
Of a music older
Than the stones
Marking the road.

I pick my way with care
Along the hills
That shun
Illusions of ambition.
They have a saying here:
You must drink both,
The water and the wave.

DEATH IN PISA

He looked at me
With dumb eyes,
A blood clot under one lid
Hard and round like a pebble.

He stood there
Like a starving steer
Rattling around in
The hoops of his ribs.

But pigeons were
Playing in the grass,
And across time I heard
The cry of the she-wolf
Calling the twins.

IN THE APENNINES

The moon,
Round and yellow
Like the yolk
Of an egg,
Rises slowly
From black trees
Along the way.

The voice
Of the stranger
Flowed softly
Like a river
At night, cooling
The fire and wound
Of the heart.

Beyond
Laughter and tears,
Hunger pursues us.
We will be lucky
To be on time
For a late meal
Of bread and wine.

TITIAN: LADY IN A MIRROR
(for Walter Ong, S.J.)

The mirror doubles her image
And brings distance to the space
Between reflection and true form
So that the eye in bold comparison
Can make a vision of mere sight
And build a bridge from soul to self.

Yet these encounters in the glass
By which a mask defines its face
Are wavelike, twinning circumstance;
For fusion of two separated worlds
Bent on confirming bone and blood
Is twice the certainty of death.

And so the mirror's outer dark
Refracted from some dark within
Shows beauty a divided thing
Except that fancy seize these mortal shapes
And unify the desperate halves
Through love transparent and fantastical.

IV Carry-overs

AT NIGHT
(from the German of Kirt Sigel)

In your iris
The sky turns into a spacious land.
Exotic birds begin to move their wings
Underneath your temples.
Come!
I will hide myself in your voice.

Your hair
Casts a net of shadows over the fields.
The night waits in astonishment
And my dreams
Have come ashore in your mouth.

The river kindles
His fires from the light of our eyes.
The wind climbs down from the hills
And shyly
Touches your forehead
With chilly hands.

LOVE POEM
(from the German of Karl Krolow)

I speak to you with a low voice:
Will you hear me
Behind the bitter herb-face of the moon
Which decays?
Beneath the heavenly beauty of the air,
When the day comes,
And the dawn is a reddish fish with quivering fins?

You are fair.
Cool and dry is your skin.
Your gaze—gentle and sure as that of a bird.
I tell it to the whirling wind.
Your nape—do you hear—is of air
That slips through the mesh of blue leaves like doves.

You lift your face.
On the brick wall it shows once more as shadow.
Fair you are. You are fair.
Cool as water was your sleep by my side.
I speak to you with a low voice.
And the night crumbles like soda crystals, blue and black.

SONG
(from the Italian of Guiseppe Ungaretti)

Again I see your slow mouth
(At night the sea moves toward it),
And see the mare of your thighs
Fall dying
In my arms that sang once,
And see that sleep brings you
New coloring again and new dying.

And the cruel loneliness
Found by all who love,
This infinite tomb,
Now keeps me from you forever.

Beloved, far away as in a mirror . . .

ORPHEUS, EURYDIKE, HERMES
(from the German of Rainer Maria Rilke)

This was a miracle, a mine of souls.
Like silent silver ore that runs in lodes
They flowed as veins through darkness. Between roots
Arose the blood that then goes forth to man.
And it seemed heavy as porphyry in that gloom.
Otherwise, nothing was red.

Rocky slopes were there
And lifeless forests. Bridges over nothing.
And that large grey blind pond,
Floating there above its distant bottom,
Hung like a rain-filled heaven over landscapes.
Between the meadows, smooth and full of forbearance
Ran the one pale strip of path
Like a spread ribbon of bleached linen drying.
And on this path they came.

In front, the slender man in a blue garment
Who looked impatiently, silently before him.
Without nibbling, his feet tore at the path
In great devouring bites. His hands hung down,
Taciturn, heavy from the falling folds
And could no longer know the weightless lyre
Which, rooted in his hand, had grown
Like climbing roses grown to olive trees.

His senses quarrelled in dissension:
And while his gaze ran like a dog ahead,
Turned round, and came, and always stood to wait,
Guarding the next turn of the road,
His hearing like a smell remained with him.
It sometimes seemed to him as if it reached
The steps of those two other walkers
Who were to follow this entire ascent.
But no; it was the echo from his climb
And from the wind stirred by his coat behind him.
But yet, he told himself, they would be coming,
Said it aloud and heard it fade away.
They would be there, the two of them
Who walk with dreadful softness. If only
He could turn (would looking back
Not mean destruction of this giant task
That had to be accomplished) he would see
The quiet pair that followed him in silence:

The god of news, conductor of the dead,
His hood of travel over brilliant eyes,
Bearing the slender staff before his body,
With beating wings on his talaria.
And given to his left hand: She.
She so beloved, that mourners never wailed
So loud as did this one complaining lyre;

That once again a world of threnody was built
In which all things exist: the woods and valleys,
Roads and towns, fields, rivers, and the beasts;
And that around this mournful world revolves
A sun, as round the other earth it goes,
And too, a star-thick, silent sky,
A heaven of lament with mutilated stars—:
She, so beloved.

But she walked on at the hand of that god.
Bound in her step by the long winding palls,
Uncertain, gentle, and without impatience.
She was lost in herself as one high with child.
Not thinking of the man who walked before her
Nor of the way that rose up to the living.
She was lost in herself, and her death
Filled her with abundance.
She was full of her great death
As a fruit is full of sweetness and of darkness,
A death so new she could not comprehend.

For she was hidden in a new maidenhood,
Untouchable; her very sex was closed
As a young flower closes towards evening.
Her hands were weaned away so far from marriage
That the immensely tender leading touch
Even of the nimble god could cause her pain;
Offended her with too much intimacy.

She was no longer that blonde woman now,
Who had sometimes echoed in the poet's song;
Of the wide bed no longer was she scent and island,
And of that man no longer property;

Already she was loose like her long hair,
Given away once more like fallen rain,
Scattered about like rich grain from a hoard.

She was already root.
And when the god abruptly
Stopped her, calling out to her in pain
The words: But he has turned around—
She did not understand and asked him softly: Who?

Far away, dark, in front of the cleared entrance
Stood someone with a face
Not to be recognized. He stood and saw
How on the strip of path along the meadow,
Sorrowing in his gaze, the god of errands
Turned in silence, to walk behind the shape
That walked already back the self-same path,
Bound in her step by the long winding palls
Uncertain, gentle, and without impatience.

(Translated by Franz Schneider and James Wright)

ELIS

(from the German of Georg Trakl)

1

Complete is the quiet of this golden day.
Under ancient oaks
You appear, Elis, resting with round eyes.

Their blueness mirrors the slumber of lovers.
At your mouth
Their rosy sighs were silenced.

At nightfall the fisherman hauled in the heavy nets.
A good shepherd
Leads his flock by the forest's edge.
O! how just, Elis, are all your days.

Quietly,
The olive tree's blue silence seeps down barren walls;
An old man's dark song dies away.

A golden boat,
Elis, your heart rocks in the lonely sky.

2

A gentle ringing of bells sounds in Elis' breast
At nightfall
When his head sinks into black pillows.

A blue deer
Bleeds quietly in the thorny briars.

A brown tree stands alone and dead;
Its blue fruits fell from it.

Signs and stars
Sink quietly in the evening pond.

Behind the hill winter has come.

Blue doves
Drink at night the icy sweat
Which runs from Elis' crystal brow.

Forever on black walls
Sings God's lonesome wind.

CHOPIN
(from the German of Gottfried Benn)

He never talked much.
Thinking was not his strong point.
Opinions are indefinite.
When Delacroix started theorizing
he became embarrased; for his part
he could not explain the Nocturnes.
Weak lover;
Shadow at Nohant
where George Sand's children
would not take his advice.
In his chest he had the disease
that causes hemorrhages and scars
and drags on and on;
quiet death
in contrast to one
with paroxysms of pain
or by volleys of guns;
they pushed the grand piano (Erard) to the door
and Delphine Potocka
sang to him at the hour of death
a song about violets.
He had gone to England with three grand pianos:
Pleyel, Erard, Broadwood,
had played evenings for 20 guineas
a quarter of an hour
at the Rothschild's, Wellington's, at Strafford House
and before numerous Garters;
eclipsed by fatigue and the nearness of death
he had returned
to d'Orleans Square.

After that he burns his sketches
and manuscripts,
no fragments, notes
or revealing remnants—,
said at the end:
My efforts have reached perfection to the degree
possible for me to achieve.
Each finger was supposed to play
with the strength corresponding to its structure,
the fourth one is the weakest
(being only the Siamese of the middle finger).
When he began, they lay on e, f-sharp, g-sharp, b, c.
Whoever has heard
certain preludes of his,
whether in manor houses or
on a hillside
or from open terrace doors—
for instance at a sanatorium—
will hardly forget it.
Never wrote an opera,
no symphony,
only these tragic progressions
out of artistic conviction
and with a small hand.

THE SCREAM
(from the Spanish of Federico Garcia Lorca)

The elipsis of a scream
echoes from mountain
to mountain.
Near the olive trees
it turns to a black rainbow
above the blue night.
   A . . .Y!
The long strings of the wind
vibrate under the scream
as if touched by a fiddlebow.
   A . . .Y!
The people in the caves
show their bronze lamps.

THE SILENCE

Listen, my son, to the silence.
It is a silence rising and falling,
A silence
Through which glide valleys and echoes—
Which presses the foreheads
To the ground.

ST. AUGUSTINE'S FIRESONG TO GOD

(from the Latin of the Confessions*)*

Fire rises, a stone falls.
Impelled by their weight,
They seek their own places.
Oil poured beneath water
Is raised above the water.
Water poured on oil
Sinks down beneath the oil.
Impelled by their weight,
They seek their own places.
Not put in proper order,
They are without rest;
When set in due order,
They are at rest.
My love is my weight.
It carries me wheresoever I am borne.
By your gift we are enkindled,
And we are borne upwards.
We glow with inward fire,
And we go on.
We ascend steps within the heart,
And we sing a gradual psalm.
By your fire, by your goodly fire
We glow with inward flame,
And we go on, for we fly upwards
To the peace of Jerusalem.
There, good will find us a place
So that we may wish no other
But to abide there forever.

V *Places*

LITTLE SPOKANE RIVER: INDIAN PAINTINGS

Rocks rise from the hill
And wall the river forever.
The swirling eddies
Shake the guardian trees
That mark the sacred place.
There the center is still.
The sun runs faster in its track.

Cleaving resistant waves,
A man made land by the rocks.
He painted this red sign
When the deathbird called:
Here by the thundering water
I am safe in the circle of earth.
We are each other's work.

LITTLE PEND OREILLE RIVER

I watched them come back
Laughing through the tall grass.
Their fishing poles rattled
In the haze of late afternoon.

Diving from the bridge,
A couple of cliff swallows
Took advantage of a timely hatch.

My sons keep coming,
Their faces hidden now and then
Behind green walls.

MOYIE RIVER: WELCOME RANCH

At noon
I stopped fishing
And went back
To the log cabin
Among the elms.

I returned
By way of the meadows
Along the river bank.

Through the window,
I noticed our red-head
Resting on her cot:
A beam of light
Had set each curl ablaze
Until the child's hair flamed
And seemed to crackle
Like a burning bush.

As I worked the latch,
My wife opened the door:
She complimented me
On the morning's catch.

MOYIE RIVER

I

Along the river
Only single trees
Stand straight.
The aspen of this grove
Lean slightly forward,
Their trembling shade
Moves slowly on hard ground.
I sit and watch
A leaf against the sky
Until its heart shape
Has become a tongue
That speaks in silver-green
And silence.
I breathe and listen.

II

When evening comes,
Great hills are rising.
Land turns casual.
Each stone is what it is.
Even the trees relax
In lean resiliency.
Silence is clean as a bone.
The horizon's edge shines green
After sunset.

The air feels warm
Like a well-worn coat
Until the night dew falls
And a breeze blows ice-cold
Off the slopes.

III

During sleep,
I hear water run seaward.
The voice of trout talks in the river.
I dream of the sound of shadows
On green leaves.

BEAR GULCH: HOME PLACE

You threw a bright stone,
Shattering light above the pond.
From the center of the pool,
Dazzling wavelets rippled off
Until they died away
In ever widening circles.

Beating his wings slowly
In the morning sun,
A crane rose from the water
By the farthest bank
And disappeared without a sound
Between the trees.

The stone lies on the bottom
In the dark.

CAMP FIELD: ICICLE RIVER

Corona rides golden and bareback,
Spurring the flanks of Mt. Cashmere.
The dipper tilts steeply
Toward northern horizons.

Gasping from sudden blows
Of night falling early,
I know in my autumn heart:
Some losses are permanent.

Brown leaves collect in the pools.
The river-bed blooms saffron
With a myriad of reflected stars.
I am not afraid of winter.

HOME PLACE: BEAR CREEK IN AUTUMN
(for Rojer McRea)

Fall rain has filled the creek bed full.
Now mist hangs in the windless dawn
Above the teeming gravel shoals
Where salmon spawn. The hen fish roll
From side to side in rhythmic pain.
Attendant cocks in deadly labor caught
Cast jets of fertilizing sperm
On eggs that stain the water brown.
The salmon know exuberance in death;
The current sets them gently down.

The journey here was arduous,
Too steep for some the arcs of breaking waves.
They floundered in the tumult of the tides
Or fell to predators an easy prey.
Only the final mastery
Of white swirls in the roaring surf
Allowed the strong in muscled light
To turn their shoulders toward home
And flash like arrows up the stream
Where the ancestral urge abides.

From here the parent fish depart.
Their souls ride on the water back to sea.
The red-fleshed bodies rot and stay
As food to feed the orphaned young—
Now mere translucent pearls, their faces blind,
But marked already by a hint of eyes.
For life lives in these spheres so left behind
And will assert its ancient way:
The salmon in his selfless liturgy
Speaks to our destiny.

THE SECULAR CITY

In the city by the sea,
Golden girls climb
To steep-staired apartments
Like a choir of angels
Ascending to heaven
Over Jacob's ladder.

Their arrival is past treetops
Where congregating in cages
They warble their hosannas over
Scotch from Waterford glasses
Before they feast on breaded
Lamb, cabob and rice pilaff.

For dessert: Black espresso
And slides taken in Europe
Which throw on pale walls
Seas, sunsets, and drunken boats
Crashing through blood-red
Barricades in the sky.

Compline surprises them in bed,
Their temporal thighs tucked in
Well out of harm's way
(How sweet the moonlight
Sleeps upon this bank)
And hairdos glowing in the dark
Like a thousand crowns of life.

FISHING AENEAS CREEK
(for Grace Potochnik)

I cursed my city greed
And let the cut-throat go.
He threw a gravel-wake
And vanished in the flow

Of water plunging deep
And riffles not too warm.
The shade of bank and stone
Keeps him from further harm.

So dive we into God,
Released by death from pain.
The waters of His love
Will make us whole again.

MT. STUART: NORTH WALL IN OCTOBER

Rockfalls drive me into myself.
Jack Lake below is a dream.
I lift my head and wait.
Only the runes on the north wall stare back.

The icy downdraft blows snow in my eyes.
I think of eagles and hawks.
All day I have not seen a bird.
Why did I come here?

Now I am stopped by glacier and wind.
The frost has swept the granite clean.
I close my eyes:
Upon what signal will the rock wall crumble?

THE WHALER'S LANDFALL:
SANDWICH ISLANDS
(for Roger and Diane)

After heaving swells
And riding the surf into harbor,
We dropped anchor in the tranquil bay.
Now I walk on black sand under palms
Past orchids and anthuriums.

Behind us are the wind-tossed waves,
The curls, the foaming into spume,
The thudding crests that beat like whale flukes
On the ocean's drum.
Only a spouting horn
Plays now its spindrift tune.

The island shore is balm to salt-stung eyes.
Steep falling slopes hold us in awe.
Some cliffs rise green and vertical.
Only my gaze can force the lava slides
Or scan Lehua groves above
Where mists bar it from access to the top.
There earth bleeds through a crater's wound
And stains with red the mother clouds
That wash the jungle clean. Nurse
Of hibiscus and the banyan tree,
The rain feels good upon my skin.

To-morrow in the quickening dawn
Our budding sails will bloom again
Because we chase the humpback in his road.
Then winds crest waves with manes of foam
As we run joyful to the open sea.

The winds! The clarion winds!
What trumpet will announce the storm
When all the straining sheets will snap,
Booms sweep the deck like scythes,
And pounding seas sink our gallant prow?

The island paradise is mute: Death is not now.

VI *Communications*

BEACH IDYLL

The surf is high
And rolling in, advancing
In straight lines
Before it leaps into change
And the rushing foam
At sun-down.

"No one can tell when
Life really ends, can they?"
Asks the child, looking
With eyes opened wide
And steadily at the sparkling
Terror of the sea.

An old man walks his dog
Hard by the water's edge.
They need no help
In their old age
And steady progress
Toward evening.

THE GARDENER'S LETTER
FROM STALINGRAD

Ajax is writing
This letter for me.
His real name isn't Ajax,
But Lachmann,
And he comes from Königsberg.
But we call him Ajax.
My arm is propped up
And wrapped in thick bandages,
So I cannot write.
I'll soon be home,
The doctor says,
And I am looking forward to it
Very much.
The doctor is a good man.
There is a little piece
Missing from my arm.
Only the funny thing is
That I cannot move my fingers.
I need my fingers
To dig in the dirt.
The soil here is very rich and soft.
We sure could use some of that
In the sandy flowerbeds at home.
There is snow outside.
You can't see the soil.
Four days ago I lay

In a hole a yard deep,
And all day long
I looked at the soil;
Good soil for wheat.
Naturally there was no trace
Of fertilizer.
The steppes produce their own.
I got scared in that hole.
Today I laugh about it.
I don't have a very comfortable bed,
But once I am home
I'll laugh about that too.
And all of you will laugh with me.

THE ANALYST'S REPORT ON HIS CONVALESCENT PATIENT

He looks at his left hand,
Every day, waking from sleep
And the steady drip of grief.
Moving his fingers he wonders:
Is this the hour of stone
Or are the teeth of sorrow stayed
Once more at the heart's edge?
He watches the weather for portents
And consults his dreams: When will
The rigid stare thicken the blood
With cold?

Today, like every day
Since going back to work
He must pass the drinking fountain again
Where, explosion in his brain,
He went down like a bull.
His last thought had been of his wife.
And, when he fell, the words:
Seated at the right hand
Of the Father.

Now he yearns for the light outside
And the trees in his yard.
Tall in their upright beauty,
They keep roots deep in the soil and drink
Long of the pure water of morning.

He remembers his mother's voice
In the orchard in spring.
Even then, a single blossom
Could break his heart.

He talks to his death as the days gather.
Whatever happens is almost acceptable.
Still, some fears remain of a net
Poised in the cool air of nightfall:
Will it drop from the shade of the sycamore,
Or snare him in pools of moonlight
By the road where he walks?

LAST LETTER OF A CONDEMNED PRIEST

(Alfred Delp, S.J., executed by the Nazis
in the Plötzensee prison on February 2, 1945.)

Already
Black wagons
Are rolling
To take
Our corpses
Away.

Last night
I dreamed
Of a loaf of bread
And a basket
Of bleeding fish.

When I awoke,
The dawn swam
In the sky,
Moving gently
Her reddish fins.

THE TERMINAL PATIENT TO HIS WIFE

Please, let us make an epilogue,
So we can say our dignified farewells
To what we love: The forested plateaus on
Fierce basaltic buttes; the grassy clearings
Ringed by guardian rocks; the granite
Sentinels along the singing streams.
Thereafter, let the sun and stars go down.

Meanwhile, I wear the tender names
I gave to you in secret places
As amulets against the eye of time:
Long legs   golden mouth
Mind and body loyal friend woman
Sister of the ample air
And the spare pine boughs of winter.

I know I whistle in the wind
(A scythe has scant respect for grass).
It does not matter.
Where aquifer and river intersect,
And scores of springs regenerate the water,
There I would like to die,
By that large fir, do you remember?
Where once we watched a red-tailed hawk
Teach her three branchers how to fly.

THE EDITOR'S REPLY

I would want to read your lines
As I tend my carrot rows in spring:
First, a careful thinning;
Then, some skirmishing with weeds.
At times they'll want some water
Or the two-pronged hoe
To cultivate a too substantial soil.

But it is fall already.
The maple crowns glow red among the pines.
Their leaves begin to fall,
Dropping like harvest hands
Palm open and resigned,
As broad-leafed tongues of swiss chard
Clamor in the cold
And late tomatoes try to save their skins
From the advancing frost.

Only the bristling marigolds,
So spiny tough they challenge the first snow,
Burn steadily their yellow flame
To light the way
When worn from work the sun comes in.
The only lines that autumn replicates
Are furrows plowed across the stubble fields.

LAND SPECULATOR

Though the roof sags at the eaves,
I covet my neighbor's house.
I have plans for his unplanted garden.

To his wife I say: "Sign the paper.
The option will keep your place from harm
And is a hedge against his stroke
That almost spelled catastrophe."

Nightfall suggests a different plot:
Three   by   eight   by   six.
That house has a roof of stone.
It is acreage enough.

VII *Epilogue*

ST. AUGUSTINE'S PRAYER
TO GOD, THE FATHER

We talk of time and time
And times and times.
But not in time you come before the time:
Else you would not precede all times.
Therefore, the willow planted at my birth
Will give no pain, though hollowed
By the hammering birds,
It creaks and cracks in storms.

You came before past time,
Eternally sublime and new,
And you surpass all future times
Because they are to come.
And when they come, they shall be passed.
The river, therefore, does not make me cry
Though I can't drink the self-same water twice
Or stop the changing twilight between trees.

For you are always Self-same, you are here.
Your years shall never fail.
Your own years neither come nor go,
But our years will come and go—
The flowers that adorn the spring,
Birds in the air, beasts in the field—
So that the other years may come
And all your years stand up at once.

For you said: "I am steadfast.
I give you sunshine, earth and rain.
Departing years are never turned away."
Therefore our years shall all forever be
When time and times shall be no more,
Nor gold crysanthemums burn bright
Their votive lights in late November days.

Your years are like one day.
Your day is not each day but now.
Today does not give way to other days,
Nor will it follow yesterday.
With you one day is an eternity,
An everlasting burst of light
Like radiance in fields of snow
When sunlight strikes high mountain peaks.

Therefore you loved the Word and said:
"To-day I have begotten you.
For you have made all times
And you have come before all times
And not at any time was there no time."
The cataracts are plunging down,
The foam-froth will be blown away.
Your water innundates forever living stone.

THE CATHOLIC LITERARY REVIVAL

Calvert Alexander, S.J.

The

Catholic Literary Revival

Three phases in its
development from
1845 to the present

The Bruce Publishing Company
Milwaukee

TO
MY MOTHER AND FATHER

Preface by The General Editor

The interest displayed in Catholic literature is unquestionably greater today than in any other period during the past few centuries. The significance and extent of that literature, as evidenced by the present volume, is even more remarkable, and will doubtless prove a revelation to many.

Naturally, in a book of this kind, the problem of selection and stress is one on which no two persons can ever hope to agree entirely. It suffices that the main points are made to stand out clearly and the whole range of subject matter is revealed to the reader, who can then carry on his own researches in a field now rendered familiar to him.

Not merely is the reader made more fully acquainted here with the Catholic literature written in English-speaking countries, but a still wider view is given him, however briefly, of the Catholic literary revival elsewhere, particularly in France. Thus the full truth and magnificent vitality of the resurgent Catholic movement in its onward sweep over the earth today is brought home to him in a manner equally informative and inspiring. It is the latter quality, especially, which distinguishes this volume and should make it a vital force in the Catholic literature of today.

What is more, the author teaches us to see how, in the scales of reason and experience, the old materialism has been weighed and found wanting. Men are reaching out once more after the things that were of old their Catholic heritage, but which they and their sires have foregone so long that now they fail to recognize them. Old familiar Catholic thoughts are vaguely echoing in their minds, but these, too, seem new and strange to them. And yet all such facts render them more receptive to

Catholic truth, or more curious at least to learn about it. In doing so they are making discoveries which they had not thought possible before.

Naturally, under such conditions, the forces, too, of chaos and materialistic superstition have become aroused and are putting forth their strongest opposition. Their attacks are more extreme than any that have taken place in previous periods. Never before in the history of the race was religion itself attacked as it is today, and that with a hatred and astuteness rarely witnessed. Communism, in particular, among the several counter-revolutionary forces is everywhere making its organized attempt to outlaw and ban it from the face of the earth. Hence all the more reason for supporting with our combined powers the Catholic revival which the author vividly portrays. We have here the one true revolution which alone can reach deep enough to renew mankind, and so to reshape more closely after the divine plan our entire social order.

But attention should be called, in fine, to certain features found in this volume which are of the utmost practical importance. They concern the bibliographies at the ends of the various sections. These have been compiled with a set purpose in view, and should prove most helpful to the reader in whatever further study of Catholic literature he may care to undertake. They not merely contain a select list of the works of the various authors treated, but also references to books and magazines where critical and biographical matter can be found. Besides the writers dealt with in the text, the names and works of others are added to supply, in part at least, for the many omissions necessitated by the very nature of the present work.

A brief search into the field of Catholic literature will disclose the fact that lists of books by Catholic authors have seldom been selective, while critical references and short biographical sketches of modern Catholic writers are exceedingly rare. Apparently, no published bibliographies actually contain all this necessary matter. To supply it would have been a task well-nigh impossible had the author not been aided by the pioneer labors of the Rev. Arnold J. Garvy, S.J., who after years of patient and scholarly effort has produced a monumental codification of source material in this field. Through his kindness the author was enabled to utilize this valuable work, as yet in manuscript, and with it as a starting point has followed up references and carried further his own original research.

While the entire bibliography is of interest to every reader, it has a particular value for directors of study groups and teachers in high-school classes or colleges. Thus, the first reference given for an author furnishes biographical and critical material that is brief and not too difficult for the beginner. With a single volume by a Catholic author and this single reference, the student is enabled to prepare a fairly complete paper. The other biographical and critical references are then of service for more advanced readers. The material itself has been successfully tested out in educational institutions in many parts of the country, while nation-wide interest was created in it by the Sodality campaign.

Most appropriately does this book appear in the Science and Culture Series, which is neither more nor less than an authentic expression of the international Catholic literary revival now taking place over the earth. Authors of practically every English-speaking country are here grouped into an organized and concerted movement which cannot fail to impress upon the consciousness of men the extent and significance of the new Catholic awakening in science, art, and letters. England and Ireland, Australia and New Zealand, Canada and the United States are all contributing to this undertaking, which thus becomes itself a flowering and a fruitage of the Catholic Literary Revival.

Joseph Husslein, S.J., Ph.D.,
General Editor, Science and Culture Series

St. Louis University,
January 8, 1935.

Acknowledgments

The author wishes to express his thanks to the following publishers for permission to quote from books published by them:

George Allen and Unwin — *The Free Press*, by Hilaire Belloc.

Burns, Oates and Washbourne — "St. Catherine of Siena," "The Young Neophyte," "Renouncement," "The Unknown God," and "A General Communion" from *Poems of Alice Meynell;* several selections from *May Carols*, by Aubrey de Vere.

Coward-McCann Inc. — *The Stuffed Owl, an Anthology of Bad Verse*, edited by D. B. Wyndham Lewis and Charles Lee; *The Complete Poems of Francis Ledwidge.*

Dodd, Mead and Company — "A Last Word," "Carthusians," and "Non Sum Qualis," from *Poems of Ernest Dowson;* "Race Memory," selections from "Lepanto"; and "Ballad of the White Horse," from *Collected Poems of G. K. Chesterton.*

Doubleday, Doran and Company — *Poems, Essays and Letters of Joyce Kilmer; The Romantic '90's*, by Richard Le Gallienne.

Alfred A. Knopf, Inc. — "St. Valentine's Day," from *Poems* by Wilfrid S. Blunt; *The Eighteen Nineties*, by Holbrook Jackson.

Gerald Duckworth and Co. — *Lambkins Remains* and *Ladies and Gentlemen*, by Hilaire Belloc.

J. B. Lippincott Company — *Cranmer* and *Wolsey*, by Hilaire Belloc.

Harcourt, Brace and Company — selections from *Poems of Coventry Patmore.*

Houghton Mifflin Company — selections from *Happy Endings*, by Louise M. Guiney.

Little, Brown and Company — *The Puppet Show of Memory*, by Maurice Baring.

Robert M. McBride and Company — *How the Reformation Happened*, by Hilaire Belloc.

Oxford University Press — "The Habit of Perfection," "Pied Beauty," "God's Grandeur," "The Windhover," and Robert Bridges Dedication from *Poems of Gerard Manley Hopkins.*

The Macmillan Company — "Maternity," from *Poems of Katherine Tynan;* "Our Lady of France," "Robert S. Hawker," "Dark Angel," and "The Precept of Silence," from *The Poetical Works of Lionel Johnson; Winchester Letters of Lionel Johnson; Essays in Order No. 1* (Maritain, Wust, Dawson): "The Plougher," "A Poor Scholar of the Forties," "The Wayfarer," "The Cradle Song," "Old College of the Irish," "Odysseus" from *Poems of Padraic Colum.*

Frederick A. Stokes Company — selections from *Watchers of the Sky, The Book of the Earth*, and *The Last Voyage*, by Alfred Noyes.

Sheed and Ward — selections from *The Making of Europe* and *The Modern Dilemma*, by Christopher Dawson; *Broadcast Minds*, by Ronald Knox; *The*

Nature of Sanctity, by Ida Coudenhove; and *The End of Our Time,* by Berdyaev.

Charles Scribner's Sons — "To the Dead Cardinal of Westminster," "Sister Songs," "Kingdom of God," "Ode to the Setting Sun," "Hound of Heaven," "Orient Ode," "Lily of the King" from *Works of Francis Thompson;* "St. Catherine of Siena," "The Young Neophyte," "Renouncement," "The Unknown God," and "A General Communion," from *Poems of Alice Meynell; Art and Scholasticism,* by Jacques Maritain, and *Alice Meynell: A Memoir,* by Viola Meynell.

The author also herewith expresses his thanks to Mr. G. K. Chesterton for permission to quote from some of his poems, to Mr. Gerard Hopkins for permission to quote from the collected poems of his uncle, and to Rev. Arnold J. Garvy, S.J., of Chicago, Rev. Daniel A. Lord, S.J., Miss Josephine Gratiaa, of the St. Louis Public Library, Mr. Benjamin Masse, S.J., of Denver, Sister Mary Joseph, librarian of Webster College, Rev. Cornelius Shyne, S.J., Rev. John A. Weiand, S.J., Mr. Norman T. Weyand, S.J., and others for assistance rendered.

Contents

We gladly echo the words of the revolu-
tionary song, "Down with the old world!"
But we understand by that term the doomed
world of modern times.

— NICHOLAS BERDYAEV

... Generations have trod, have trod, have
        trod;
    And all is seared with trade; bleared,
        smeared with toil;
    And wears man's smudge, and shares
        man's smell; the soil
  Is bare now, nor can foot feel, being
      shod.

  And for all this nature is never spent;
    There lives the dearest freshness deep
        down things;
    And though the last lights off the black
        West went
    Oh, morning, at the brown brink
        eastward, springs—
  Because the Holy Ghost over the bent
    World broods with warm breast and
        with ah! bright wings.

— GERARD MANLEY HOPKINS

Introduction

Although the "three phases" of modern Catholic literature we are about to consider cover the entire history of that literature, this volume is to be regarded as something less than a complete history of modern Catholic letters. It is an attempt rather to trace the development of Catholic literature through three successive and rather well-defined stages in its growth from the middle of the nineteenth century to the present day.

The partition of these approximately ninety years into three divisions is not an arbitrary one. The three phases (the first or Victorian phase from 1845 to 1890, the second or middle phase from the 1890's to the World War, and the third or contemporary phase from the World War to the present) will be found to correspond rather accurately with three generations of Catholic authors. They will be found to tie up even more accurately with the same number of stages in the cultural history of Europe, in as much as the decisive downward movement of that culture is reflected in the non-Catholic literature of English-speaking countries. The middle years of the nineteenth century, the 1890's, and the World War are each critical moments in the descending action of modern history; and they play no less significant a part in the rising action of the Catholic Revival. The numerous changes brought about in what we may call the non-Catholic world determine the characteristics taken on by Catholic literature in each of these phases. Moreover they determine the position of importance or unimportance it holds in the eyes of men. Hence the necessity of understanding the relation between the Catholic Revival and the secular history with which it is everywhere in contact.

This relation is primarily one of revolt. Catholic literature, when we discover it coming into being in the mid-nineteenth century, is a literature of protest against the course being followed by European society. Its writers then were not very numerous, nor did the typical Victorian man see any particular significance in their opposition to Liberalism, the anti-intellectual Romantic aesthetic, scientific naturalism, and the other institutions of a social order that seemed firmly established and destined to endure indefinitely. The criticism advanced by men like Arnold or Ruskin against the mechanization of life would be understood and even accepted by some because it came from a philosophy that was a part of the world it essayed to criticize. But not so the fulminations of Newman and Patmore; the position from which they launched their anathemas seemed remote and very far away, either in the dead past or in the unborn future. Thus, too, a Catholic like Gerard Hopkins could write supreme lyric poetry in the nineteenth century which would not be recognized or even published until after the World War, and then it would be regarded as contemporary poetry. Catholic literature was dwarfed into insignificance by the towering prosperity and confidence of this bourgeois world against which it rebelled.

With the advent of the 1890's, however, a distinct turn for the better is observable. Alice Meynell, Lionel Johnson, Francis Thompson, and other Catholics who wrote during this period receive recognition and are even accorded a measure of leadership by those who are rapidly losing their faith in nineteenth-century civilization. But that recognition is a restricted one. Catholic literature does not occupy a position of importance in the non-Catholic world until after the Great War, that is to say, in the third of the three phases.

This phase goes under the name of "post-war," although it has been evident for some time that the term has ceased to mean anything in modern literature. It was invented by that elder generation of Liberals that caused the war to designate the unsteady state of soul of the generation that had borne the brunt of it. And it was full of hope. The hope was that all these manifestations of a youthful sickness and rebellion were temporary; they would pass and men would return again to the buoyant, confident rhythm of pre-war days. That war generation, the object of so much solicitude, is today no longer young. It talks of returning to many strange things, to the Elizabethans, to the philosophy of Aquinas, to the classics, to monarchy, to baroque mysticism, to a healthy barbarism — but not to democratic Liberalism, nor to the promises of Science and Progress, nor to the parousia of Big Business and Industrialism, nor to reverent Rationalism, nor to charming bourgeois letters, nor to any of the other happy institutions and splendid ideologies of the society into which its members were born.

There survive, of course, not a few who still hold on to the externals of this old order, the majority because of the binding force of established conventions, but some because they sincerely believe in it. These latter are for the most part old men, grandfathers some of them, who committed themselves in the nineteenth century of their youth to bad guesses, already in those days prosperous conventions. They do not understand the pronounced impiety of the younger generation. They still diagnose it as a post-war malady and think, like H. G. Wells, that they may tease the young man out of his sickness by dangling before his tired eyes bigger and better promises and all the shining mechanical toys of the world to come.

But the sickness is not a heritage of the World War. It is the heavy sense of being wholly without a heritage that sickens him, of being obliged to face the uncertainties of the future with empty hands because he has been bequeathed nothing worthy of transmission, nothing but "the accumulated rubbish of three centuries of cracked-brain revolt and faded dreams." Not even the impious joy of turning upon this old world of his fathers and rending it is now left him; for that also today has taken on many of the futile characteristics of beating a dead horse.

For the majority of these "post-war" writers whom the years have made mature and thoughtful, and for many older ones too, there is no longer any question of bemoaning the passage of this order or of celebrating the magnificence of its demise.

> *This is the way the world ends,*
> *This is the way the world ends,*
> *Not with a bang but with a whimper*

sings T. S. Eliot. They accept the fact, evident enough in itself and confirmed by the mass of evidence patiently collected and arranged by such philosophers and critics of culture as Oswald Spengler, Nicholas Berdyaev, Christopher Dawson, Wyndham Lewis, and others. They are already concerned with the problems of a new world which they see emerging "from the obscure chrysalis of history."

The choice of the modern man in this new world, says J. Middleton Murry, lies between Communism and Catholicism; he chooses Communism. The Russian Nicholas Berdyaev sees the choice as between a militant Catholicism and a militant atheism, between Christ and anti-Christ, and he chooses Catholicism. Evelyn Waugh, whose accession to the leadership of London's young intelligentsia has given rise to the "pre-Waugh and post-Waugh" designation of the new alignments, announced in 1930 when he was received into the Church that the modern artist must make a brave and disjunctive choice between Rome and Moscow. In America, Eugene O'Neill has recently fixed the points of the modern dilemma even more sharply in his play *Days Without End;* the choice, as he sees it, seems to lie between the Catholic Church and suicide. Even those who do not admit that "the hour of decision" is immediately at hand, see the dilemma in much the same terms. Thus the late Irving Babbitt:

The choice to which the modern man will finally be reduced, it has been said, is that of being a Bolshevist or a Jesuit. In that case (assuming that by a Jesuit is meant the Ultra-montane Catholic) there does not seem to be much room for hesitation. Ultra-montane Catholicism does not, like Bolshevism, strike at the very roots of civilization. In fact, under certain conditions that are already partly in sight, the Catholic Church may perhaps be the only institution left in the Occident that can be counted upon to uphold civilized standards.

In this third or "post-war" phase of the Catholic revival, then, we discover the Catholic Church firmly established in the modern consciousness as one of the alternatives which the modern artist recognizes he must choose between. We may assert, as we shall, that this same dilemma existed in the middle of the nineteenth century. But we should find difficulty in showing that any, except a very few, recognized it in these present terms. Catholicism in those days was not a recognized choice for the modern artist. It was considered the choice of the illiberal, the mentally warped, of him who loved the darkness better than the light. In other words, it was no choice at all.

II

The history of the Catholic Revival during the past three or four generations presents a number of sharp contrasts such as this, which to those who have not followed its development must seem almost unbearably abrupt. Dean Inge, for instance, announced several years ago, with the air of one who had discovered a plot, that instead of the contempt felt for the Roman Church in England a hundred years ago, it was now "the fashion for popular men of letters to become Romanists." What he had in mind was not the conversion of the poet, Alfred Noyes, or that of the novelist, Sheila Kaye-Smith, which occurred about this time, but the rather long list of writers who since the beginning of the World War have come into the

Church, including Compton Mackenzie, Ronald Knox, Christopher Dawson, D. B. Wyndham-Lewis, Christopher Hollis, Bruce Marshall, Evan Morgan, Francis Stuart, Algernon Cecil, together with disquieting rumors of others. This, however, had not seemed anything worthy of remark until the advent of the centenary of the Oxford Movement caused him to catch the contrast between this state of affairs and that which prevailed in 1833.

These contrasts are particularly startling and inexplicable to those who have got into the habit of thinking of the world and of the Church in terms of the nineteenth century. Such contemporary phenomena as the blasphemies everywhere being hurled at that Liberalism against which the early Catholic revivalists rebelled, the popularity of Thomistic philosophy among intellectuals, the respect in which pagan litterateurs hold the mystical wisdom of St. Teresa and St. John of the Cross; the spectacle of an ecclesiastic like Martin D'Arcy being looked up to as an important philosophical leader, of a man with so outstanding an evangelical name as Knox, now a Catholic priest and one of England's first satirists, of a radical exponent of modern art like Eric Gill laying down a Catholic aesthetic, of Christopher Dawson's importance as a critic of culture — all these and numerous other phenomena which are a part of the modern scene are, according to the philosophy of the man in question, things that should not have happened, and since they have happened, must be a temporary something or other, appearing from nowhere and likely at any moment to go back there — a fashion.

According to this philosophy, for instance, it was inevitable that the world should go on developing along the lines laid down for it by Thomas Huxley in England and by Ernest Renan in France. Today, however, the grandson of Thomas Huxley, Aldous Huxley, is found damning his grandparent's dialectic in terms much stronger than those used by any of the nineteenth-century popes; while in France the grandson of

Ernest Renan, Ernest Psichari, killed in the World War after his conversion to the Church and whole-hearted repudiation of everything his grandfather stood for, has become the symbol of a Catholic intellectual and literary revival that has given to France its most outstanding modern novelists, critics, poets, and philosophers.

It is not only non-Catholics, but Catholics too, who are not infrequently surprised when they discover many distinguished modern authors not only professing Catholicism but writing under the influence of the full spirit of the Church. They are surprised because they also have been accustomed to think of the Church as it existed in the nineteenth century, when, as Paul Claudel has said, "by losing its envelop of Art . . . it became like a man stripped of his clothes; in other words, that sacred body, composed of men, believers and sinners alike, displayed itself for the first time materially before the eyes of the world in all its nakedness, in a kind of exhibitionism and permanent translation of the wounds and infirmities." Those were the days of the great schism between the artist and Catholicism when it seemed that art and sanctity must be forever separated. One thinks of the convert J. K. Huysmans standing among the crowd of pious pilgrims at Lourdes, his soul harassed by the observation that, although Mary had chased the devil from the rocks of the shrine and the hearts of the pilgrims, he was still there blaspheming her and her Son by the "hideous" architecture of the place. He distinctly hears the devil say to Mary: "I shall dog your footsteps, and wherever you stop, there I shall establish myself; you may have at Lourdes all the priests you please, but art, which is the only worth-while thing on earth after sanctity, not only will you not have, but I shall so effect that it will unceasingly insult you by the prolonged blasphemy of its ugliness. . . . All that represents you and your Son will be grotesque. . . ."

Catholics have come to look upon bad art almost as one of the "notes" of the Church by which men might know that she

was of Christ — a kingdom not of this world. In many ways
this was not a situation wholly to be deplored. For one thing
it was a guarantee that those who did come to her then, came
because they placed a higher value on the supernatural life than
upon their art. To the nineteenth-century convert it seemed that
he was making a disjunctive choice between art and religion,
and having chosen the new supernatural life on this basis, his
art also was renewed. But he was surprised that this should be
so. "You thought you were giving up poetry, Giovanni!" ex-
claimed the Danish writer, Johannes Jörgensen, after his con-
version at La Rocca. "Behold, she is coming to you and she is
fairer than ever before." Today, however, it is impossible for an
author to think there can be any conflict between his Catholi-
cism and his art. Indeed there is some danger that he may make
his art the chief reason for becoming a Catholic.

The intellectual and artistic position of the Catholic Church
today — stronger, it is asserted, than at any time since the
Middle Ages — is a fact that no one denies, although one does
find at times the rather subtle effort to explain it away by re-
garding this resurgence as a phenomenon of great suddenness
sprung unexpectedly and full-armed out of a chaotic situation
from which anything bizarre might be expected. The expo-
nents of this view, it is significant, invariably take the same at-
titude toward the collapse of the "old world of modern his-
tory"; they were given no warning; the firmament of the old
values suddenly came rattling down about their ears. But, as a
matter of fact, neither of these events came about unexpectedly.
They were both a matter of slow and certain evolution. Any-
one familiar with the events that were taking place within the
Church during the last half of the nineteenth century could not
have failed to notice the awakening and consolidation of forces
that were bound to make their internal position more powerful
with the years. So, too, one has only to read the history and the
literature of the world outside the Church during the same
period to perceive the inevitable operation of an opposite proc-

ess, the languishing of spiritual energies, the deep-down decay of the props upon which the huge apparatus of material culture rested, the sense of uneasiness, revolt, and frustration that gripped men's minds. Such a world was bound to decrease because its inner life was withering; and in proportion as it did decrease, in proportion as it lost its ascendency over the best intelligences, the allegiance of these intellects would be given to the Catholic Church, not only because of the increased life of the latter, but because of the very different sort of culture for which it stood. Complete loss of faith in the old secular world would mean a renewed faith in the new supernatural world. It would either mean that or abysmal despair. So true was this that a wise nineteenth-century man could have predicted with accuracy that when the consciousness of the old world's death became widespread, equally widespread would be the turning of men to Catholicism.

This process becomes quite apparent when one examines the nature of the "old world" in which men have ceased today to believe. The philosophers and critics of culture are virtually unanimous in designating it as the world that began at the Renaissance. It was a humanistic world, a world with a splendid confidence in the autonomous natural man and in the ability of his spirit to rule and enrich the earth. The culture which the Renaissance had inherited and from which it separated itself had been built upon a different principle. It was humanistic, but its humanism was that of the Christ-man and not of the natural man. It was a supernatural culture; it drew its strength from and founded its achievement on the fact of the Redemption. Yet it was also, as Etienne Gilson remarks, "the heir of Athens no less than of Bethlehem and of Rome, Western thought in its most complete form," determined to sacrifice nothing that might give the supernatural man of the Redemption, "more truth, more beauty, more love and order."

It may seem too simple a statement of the project of post-Renaissance history to say, with Berdyaev, that it attempted to carry forward this culture without its supernatural foundation; that in breaking with this energizing source its career has been one of extravagant spending in which the natural man has squandered the cultural capital accumulated by the supernatural man, and that he has at length climbed to the summit of the modern period weak and exhausted, stripped of his own and the cultural capital he originally inherited. Yet it is a good general statement of what has happened. Progressively, if not all at once, the society of the modern world has come to be one built upon the natural man, and its failure is unmistakably the failure of that natural man.

Man, says Aldous Huxley, has sunk toward a kind of "sub-humanity," and his advice is that we try to live "superhumanly." Gorham Munson, the American critic, after rejecting as inadequate the program of the American Humanists to revive a dying world by a return to the well-springs of the Renaissance, opines that the situation would seem to call for nothing less than "a science for divinizing man." "For here is man, the prey of innumerable illusions, stunted in psychological growth, spiritually inert, bewildered by himself, discordant in behavior, perhaps incurably paralyzed in will. Will anything but the tremendous means metamorphose him into a falconer of reality, an experiencer of bliss and ecstasy, a doer of deeds on the fighting edge of the cosmos?"

Some may choose to see in the rather general feeling we find around us today that one cultural order has perished and man is in labor until another shall be born, merely a recurrence of what took place in the early Romantic years of the nineteenth century, or what occurred again and with greater violence in the closing years of the same century. But there is an essential difference between these periods of disillusionment and our own which must not be overlooked. The blasé, skeptical citizen of the 1890's, for instance, had lost faith in Victorian civilization but not in the natural man that had produced that civilization. He still believed in him; and the numerous renaissantial movements on which he squandered his enthusiasm all postulated a naïve belief in that lay creature, and in his inherent powers of recovery and expansion. But the thoroughgoing skeptic of our own day has lost his faith not in any particular culture or civilization, but in man himself, in the natural man which Europe for the last four centuries has worshiped. The culture of the modern world is decadent because that man is dead. Its renovation demands nothing less than that "tremendous means" of man's rebirth. He must be born again.

"How can these things be done?" This question put by Nicodemus to Christ in a famous midnight interview of long ago has become a modern question. And Christ's answer to it is a modern answer. Yet all do not accept it. There is something terrifying in the radicalism of this Christian rebirth. It seems almost too "tremendous a means"; it demands the abandonment of so many familiar ideas, conventional ways of acting, and uncritical beliefs which are, for all that, none the less dear to one.

Yet many have accepted it, and this is especially true of modern artists and writers. It is they who constitute modern Catholic letters. I speak here not only of converts *to* Catholicism but of converts *from* a certain type of bourgeois Catholicism which has been willing out of an absurd deference to a prosperous humanistic world to deprecate the supernatural content of their faith. Yes, Catholic literature is entirely a literature of converts. It is written from a new aesthetic based on a new concept of man. One does not hesitate to call the genuine Christian today a *novus homo*. In a world which for centuries has known only the natural man or a weak parody on the Christian one, the truths of Christ's redemption and elevation of human nature have all the newness and freshness they had to the man of the old Roman world. These truths are new in an absolute sense, too; for man is older than the Redemption, and it is only through Christ that anything that might be called new has entered into this very old world.

III

No survey of contemporary literature can call itself complete today which ignores Catholic literature. And this not only because of the promise it holds out for a complete renovation of the arts, but also because of its many distinguished writers and its not inconsiderable critical and creative work in all departments of literature. Yet this is precisely what is frequently done. Not that Catholic writers are neglected. That would be perhaps the better part. But they are bunched indiscriminately with those authors and movements which belong either by choice or by convention to the "old world."

Thus it is customary today to speak of prominent Catholic authors as belonging to what is called the Classical Revival, just as forty years ago it was customary to speak of them as belonging to the neo-Romantic revival. Because the philosophical and historical criticism of men like Christopher Dawson, Douglas Woodruff, E. I. Watkin, Jacques Maritain, and Henri Massis, is one that calls for a return to order, they are classed *in globo* with all proponents of "law and order"; they are Conservatives. Catholic poets and critics are labeled "anti-Romantic" or "Romantic"; they are conceived as belonging to the "Revolutionary Right" as opposed to the "Revolutionary Left," and so on.

But, in all truth, none of these designations fits Catholic literature. One even wonders whether they fit anything any more. They are all the worn-out counters of that old world which for generations has kept itself alive by a series of reactions, of rebellions, and inevitable returns to "order," of rationalism and anti-rationalism, of romanticism and conservatism, and of numerous other oscillations in all human fields. That pendulum of reaction today swings in an increasingly small arc; it has almost reached dead center. The difference between Capitalism and Bolshevism, between the "classicism" of Ezra Pound and that of the loosest Romantic, is almost entirely a matter of words.

All those vital differences that once gave a semblance of life have disappeared, leaving only monotonous uniformity from which little notable vitality results.

Catholic literature is written by those who intellectually have stepped clear of this "waste land" into a world full of an abundant and varied life. Physically they still remain in the old order that lingers on about them, and it is, I suppose, inevitable that the numerous schools, tendencies, individual artistic preferences existing among modern Catholic authors should be called "romantic" or "classical" or "traditional" or "modernist." But these terms must be applied with a difference. And that difference is fundamental and of great importance.

First
Phase

> *The motto shows the feeling of both Froude and myself at the time; we borrowed from M. Bunsen a Homer, and Froude chose the words in which Achilles, on returning to the battle, says, "You shall know the difference, now that I am back again."*
>
> NEWMAN, *Apologia*

1

John Henry Newman

I

The Catholic Literary Revival belongs in its remote historical origins to what historians have agreed to call the Romantic Movement. Most people today have come to look upon Romanticism as a flash in the pan, a movement that promised much for the renovation of the arts and ended by debasing them immeasurably. So the movement might have turned out as far as the Church and her artistic and intellectual renaissance were concerned had not the wisdom of certain of her leaders, at a very early date, definitely cut the Revival free from official Romanticism. This was an important step. The modern Catholic Revival cannot be said to have begun until it was taken.

The term "Catholic Revival," which we shall have occasion to use frequently hereafter, is a wider one than Catholic literature, since it embraces not only the literary revival, but also the philosophical or Thomistic revival, and the liturgical revival, as well as other Catholic activities which began to manifest themselves in the nineteenth century, indicating that the Church had recovered from the effects of the Reformation and was beginning to return to the intellectual and artistic councils of Europe. All of these manifestations of the new life of the Church came in contact with and were stimulated by Romanticism. It even appeared for a time they would become permanently identified with it. However, this danger was averted, not without considerable resistance, by those who insisted on stressing not the similarities but the differences that separated the Catholic Revival from this effort of the "old world" to renew itself by a compromise with its Catholic origins. These men have since been looked up to as founders of the various activities of the revival. In the Liturgical Movement, for instance, there is Dom Guéranger, the iconoclastic abbot of Solesmes, who ruthlessly smashed the early medieval predispositions of the movement and is thus justly credited with having saved it from the romantic dilettantism and subjectivism which might otherwise have been its lot.

Thus, too, Newman is usually regarded as the founder of the literary revival in England, although the revival had already begun before his entrance into the Church. The two Cambridge converts, Kenelm Digby and Ambrose Phillips de Lisle, as well as the founder of modern Gothic architecture, Augustus Welby Pugin, were doing literary and artistic work in the Church a full decade and more before Newman's conversion. The renewed interest in things medieval, effected by Romanticism, had played a large part in their entrance into the Church, and indeed sustained them after they were within the fold. They seemed rather to have been converted to the medieval Church than to the Catholic Church of the nineteenth century. This is not to say they were insincere. It is merely to point out what is very obvious, that in their artistic work it is somewhat difficult (not impossible, however) to see the essential *difference* which made the Catholic Revival, not a part of the Romantic Movement, but something quite separate from it. Digby wrote glowing and rather unreal pictures of medieval life, de Lisle was an enthusiastic medievalist, Pugin a bigoted one, yet quite stimulating withal. Of the cupola of St. Peter's in Rome he said that it was "a humbug, a failure, an abortion, a mass of imposition, and a sham constructed even more vilely than it was designed." There is nothing worth living for, he is quoted as saying, "but Christian architecture [meaning Gothic architecture] and a boat!"

Quite apart from all this was George Spencer. No hallowed medieval light had shone upon him in the proper Whig home of his father, Earl Spencer, nor did the interest in Gothic castles and chivalry with which he must have come in contact at Cambridge turn his mind and heart toward Catholicism. Romanticism played no part whatsoever in his conversion to the Church in 1830. Although on intimate terms with Digby, de Lisle, and Pugin, he saw no connection between Catholicism in the nineteenth century and the revival of the Middle Ages. For him the Church did not mean the Gothic architecture or Gothic vestments which the spirit of the times admired so much, but only the living Christ and His gift of a supernatural life which all England needed. Pugin's scornful exclamation, "What! convert England in a cope like that?" was addressed to him when, as Father Spencer, he was spending himself in the great work of his life, an international crusade of prayer for the conversion of his native land. The importance of this crusade in founding the Catholic Revival can hardly be underestimated. It was the year following its inception, during the summer of 1839, that there came across the mind of Newman the first doubt as to the tenability of Anglicanism and his *Via Media*. By the end of August, he records he was "seriously alarmed."

Spencer, however, was not a literary man and hence does not properly belong to the history of Catholic literature. Newman was a literary man, one of the greatest of his century. Moreover, in his work before and after his conversion the *essential difference* between the Catholic Revival and the Romantic Movement is strikingly manifest. It is this aspect of his influence on Catholic literature that will be stressed here, rather than his importance as a litterateur.

II

Newman may be said to have been born into the Romantic revival. The date of his birth, 1801, was twelve years after the French Revolution, eleven years after the publication of Blake's "Prophetic Books," three years after the *Lyrical Ballads* of

Wordsworth and Coleridge, and one year before Chateau-briand's *Le Génie du Christianisme.* All Europe was feeling the profound stirrings of renovating forces which seemed to promise much not only for the renewal of the arts but for the revival of religion.

A reaction had set in against the hard Deistic Rationalism of the previous century. On the Continent the brilliant negations of Voltaire were no longer *a la mode;* men had turned from the coldness of the Enlightenment to warm their spirits at what fires the ecstatic religiosity of Rousseau had set burning. The transition from the destructive philosophical criticism of religion to the positive assertion of belief in the supernatural, the momentary eclipse of the classical ideal in the arts in favor of the medieval, was bringing into the Church notable intellectual and literary converts and was lifting to prominence Catholic apologists whose writings sparkled with all the fine confidence of the new spirit. In Germany and Austria the movement would bring forth such champions as Brentano, Werner, the Schlegels, the Count of Stolberg; in France, Chateaubriand, De Maistre, De Bonald, Lamartine, Montelambert, Lacordaire; in Italy, Alexander Manzoni; in Spain, Balmes and Donoso Cortes.

England was not unaffected by this return to religious feeling. Indeed the new temper had begun at an earlier date there than on the Continent, but because of the absence of a living Catholicism, did not result at once in those notable conversions among the literati which Wilfrid Ward has called "the halo of the Romantic Movement, the nineteenth-century Renaissance — too-short-lived of Christianity. . . ." But the pulse of Protestant Christianity was quickened; John Wesley's Methodist revival belongs to this spirit as well as the prose and verse of Joseph Warton, Edward Young, Blair, Collins, and Thomson, which began to ooze religious sentiment at every pore. The Middle Ages, its art and its faith, also took on a new significance and glamour with Horace Walpole, with Bishop Hurd, who opined that "the philosophic moderns have gone too far in their perpetual ridicule and contempt" of Gothic romance, and with Thomas Chatterton, who forged medieval documents to satisfy his own and the people's taste for the ancient spirit.

This rebirth of religious feeling and the nostalgia for the Middle Ages were concurrent phenomena and in most instances definitely associated one with the other, especially in literature. The common cause of both was the disgust and tedium which began to manifest itself over the excessive rationalization of art and life effected by the previous generations. The flight to the Middle Ages has been accurately called "a re-awakening of a former state of the national mind."

Two centuries of intellectualism had produced such an intolerable state of society that there occurred a spontaneous insurrection against all its works and an equally spontaneous turning to a social order and art which an integral Christianity had produced. It was in many ways a blindly popular return to the Catholic Church of their ancestors. But the point must not be pushed too far. William Cobbett, who traveled the length and breadth of England observing conditions, did indeed make his generation ring with the comprehensive curses he hurled at the Protestant Reformation for having brought about the numerous social abuses. John Wesley, who made the same circuit and saw the same conditions, drew a different conclusion.

Newman, who had read Walter Scott's medieval re-creations in prose and verse in his Calvinistic youth, would not have considered all this pother about an antique state of things a return to Catholicism. As a matter of fact, it was not such a return either in England or on the Continent. The high promise held out for a religious revival began to melt with the appearance of the second generation of Romantics who displayed definite anti-Christian, amoral, and anti-social biases which had only been hinted at in the works of the earlier revivalists. With Shelley and Byron, with George Sand and Victor Hugo,

Romanticism stood revealed not as the prelude of the return of the West to the ancient Catholicism, but as a movement that would stand on its own feet and which would move decisively away from the religious and intellectual bases on which Europe had been built.

There is a temptation, even today, to read into the Romantic Movement a spirit which, if it existed at all, was not very widespread. That spirit is the spirit of repentance, the acknowledgment by the majority of men that the course of history since the Renaissance and Reformation, when Europe broke with the Catholic Church, had been a mistake and that civilization must be revived by a return to these origins. This spirit belongs to a much later date. What gives rise to the belief that it existed then is the contempt in which such typical products of Post-Reformation culture as Rationalism and pseudo-Classical art were held by the Romantics, and their enthusiasm for all things medieval. The current medievalism is especially deceptive unless it is recalled how much real superficiality there was involved in it; how from Horace Walpole, the skeptic who took delight not only in Gothic castles but in the pomp of Roman ritual, all the way to William Morris, who had to be chiseled out of a suit of armor an Oxford blacksmith had made for him, the taste for the medieval was for many merely a sentimental dilettantism naïvely happy in the possession of Gothic melodrama, Gothic art, Gothic chivalry, and other historical trinkets. "I approve of your taste for the pageantry of the Roman religion," wrote Walpole to a young lady agitated by the new spirit, "and I ask myself if the world has not lost something of imaginative joy by the extinction of that religion just as it lost it in the decline of chivalry and the proscription of the pagan divinities."

Even on its more serious side the flight to the Middle Ages did not mean to the average Romantic a return to Catholicism. It meant the effort to revive the shriveled culture of the non-Catholic world by contact with a Catholic culture without any disposition to reaffirm belief in the supernatural principle that had produced that culture. Romanticism was a movement within the Renaissance-Reformation civilization by men who still believed in its postulates.

The part played by Romanticism in continuing the course of this civilization can be seen to even better advantage in another of its characteristics, one which was much deeper than its medievalism. I mean its anti-intellectualism, its intransigent opposition to reason, which profoundly modified its artistic and religious programs. In one sense this detestation of reason was the very laudable outgrowth of reaction against the super-intellectualism of the "age of prose and reason." In another and truer sense it was but the perpetuation of the supreme accomplishment of this super-intellectualism. For that former age had put the climax to generations of furious philosophical speculation by finally destroying the intellect, erasing the metaphysical order, admitting in a Hume that the intellect was an inept instrument for the attaining of spiritual and religious truth. The Romantics accepted this contribution as final and definitive. They made it the cornerstone, the point of departure for their efforts to restore religion and revive the arts. They would, with William Law, desert "the bare and swept temple of reason" and amid the universal ruin of reason and metaphysics rest their case on the "inner light," feeling, intuition. "Does a firm persuasion that a thing is so make it so?" asks William Blake of the Prophet Isaias in the *Marriage of Heaven and Hell*. To which the prophet sagely responds, "all poets believe that it does." The non-Catholic world having lost its structure of truth through too great a trust in reason now attempted to validate what was left of the edifice by a repudiation of reason and by a positive affirmation based for the most part on pure emotion.

The natural man of the Renaissance, who had come down through the centuries so confidently, was being torn asunder, and this dismemberment of humanity would go on until the end of the century when Nietzsche would declare that he could see about him, not men, but only parts of men.

For the moment, however, Romanticism succeeded. There

was a revival of religion, a revival of poetry. But it could not last on so insecure and slippery a basis. Very soon there began to appear those ominous symptoms of an interior sickness, want of balance, eccentric radicalism which made a conservative of Wordsworth, drove Coleridge to German metaphysics, and forced the English middle-class mind into an indiscriminating opposition to it.

III

Already, at the time Newman was a shy and awkward undergraduate at Oxford, a new intellectual atmosphere was in process of preparation which would be hostile to Romanticism, and it would be this attitude that would persist throughout the greater part of the century. We may today sympathize with and even applaud the manner in which the Catholic Church anathematized the Romantic Movement in its condemnation of the attempts of Lamennais and Bonald to construct a Catholic apologetic on the central doctrine of the movement. She condemned Romanticism for the precise reason we condemn it; because, namely, it attempted to dethrone the intellect. Among moderns, however, there is less sympathy for the manner in which the religious middle class in England attempted to freeze it out. They entered into an alliance with the scientific Rationalists. Of the two, Rationalism or Romanticism, it is difficult to say which was the more anti-intellectual. The Rationalists had certainly cut reason's throat, and, as Professor Whitehead remarks, Rationalism has continued to be "an anti-intellectual movement based on a naïve faith." Still, in those days, as now, it leaned heavily upon reason, not the reason that deals with final causes, which puts order into spiritual chaos, but the reason which is concerned with the present, with the collection and correlation of material facts, with the advancement of the physical sciences and industry, with the business of imposing upon society a mechanical rather than a spiritual order. Thus the alliance did meet the rebellious challenge of the Romantics by a return to order but to an order that would be a continual torture to all except those who were perfectly willing to barter religion and art for bourgeois prosperity and a conventional morality.

Newman was a product of this religious middle class and we know from his own confession that he was at first powerfully drawn to the side of the Rationalists. His Evangelicanism melted away before the criticism of Arnold and Whately in the Oriel Common Room. But despite the awakening to the inadequacy of the religion of his youth, and despite his personal admiration for Whately, this liaison with Rationalism was only temporary. Very soon he came to join hands with a group which held very different views in religion — with Froude, with Keble, with Pusey. The issue in the controversy between Rationalism and Romanticism was still at that time in doubt. And Newman, in rejecting the program of the Oriel "Liberals" and going over to the group which would begin the Oxford Movement, placed himself definitely on the Romantic side.

In his *Apologia* Newman quotes from an article of his in the *British Critic* by way of showing that the Oxford Movement was not an isolated phenomenon but really a part of the Romantic revival. The article, he says, accounts for the movement by considering it as "a re-action from the dry and superficial character of the religious teaching and the literature of the last generation, or century, and as a result of the need which was felt both by the hearts and the intellects of the nation for a deeper philosophy, and as the evidence and as the partial fulfillment of that need, to which even the chief authors of the then generation had borne witness. First, I mentioned the literary influence of Walter Scott, who turned men's minds in the direction of the Middle Ages. . . . Then I spoke of Coleridge. . . . Then came Southey and Wordsworth, two living poets, one of whom in the department of fantastic fiction, the other in that of philosophical meditation have addressed themselves to the same high principles and feelings, and carried forward their readers in the same direction!" The agitation stirred up by the Tracts, then, he said, was not to be considered the work of two or three individuals. "It is not so much a movement as a 'spirit afloat' . . . an adversary in the air, a something one and entire, a whole wherever it is, unapproachable and incapable of being grasped, as being the result of causes far deeper than political or other visible agencies, the spiritual awakening of spiritual wants."

The Oxford Movement was a late echo of the Romantic Revival. Coming as it did in 1833, at a time when popular opposition to the Romantic excesses had already begun to solidify, it was in the nature of a last brave attempt to realize for religion and art some of the early promises of the revival before English society had hardened into Victorianism. Because it was late, because its leaders had the advantage of the experience of the past thirty or forty years with their blunders and false starts, the movement was relatively free from the exaggerations of the previous manifestations of Romanticism. It was a revolt against contemporary society, but not a blind one. It saw clearly what it opposed, Liberalism, the name given to all those efforts, whether Rationalistic or Romantic, to whittle down the revealed truths of Christianity until only pure naturalism was left. It clearly saw what it wanted, the return, namely, of those truths of the Christian revelation which alone could satisfy the "spiritual wants" that lay at the bottom of the Romantic disquiet.

But it is in the *modus* of restoring Christianity it outlined for itself that we may see how the Oxford Movement belonged unmistakably to the Romantic Movement and was stamped with its essential deficiencies. History, antiquity, the past, were to play an enormous part in the enterprise. A feeling of almost unbearable homesickness filled the souls of these Oxford scholars when they contrasted the religion and life of the Middle Ages and the Primitive Church with that of nineteenth-century England. It was their conviction that all these glories might be brought forward to enrich the starved state of religion by what amounted to an historical and imaginative flight into the past, and by the imposition of a mind purified by these contacts on the present *milieu*. We may grant that the leaders of the movement were unlike most literary Romantics in the clear perception very nearly all of them had that the modern soul was starving for want of the genuine supernatural. But they were very much like them in imagining that the supernatural could be extracted like so much subtle juice from the flowers of past epochs. A decisive point was their attitude toward the Catholic Church of the nineteenth century. They swooned with joyous admiration over the Catholic Church of Augustine and Anselm, but the Catholic Church of the Council of Trent left them as cold as it did Horace Walpole. What saved them from Romantic dilettantism was their obvious sincerity and the subjective conviction that the English Church was actually a part of the supernatural order established by Christ. But objectively their program for the restoration of religion was as nostalgic, vaporous, and unreal as that of the Romantics in other fields, a truth that later history of the movement has amply demonstrated.

Newman, as is known, after ten years during which he exercised the chief leadership, abandoned the Oxford Movement. He left it because he saw that the revival of religion in England was not primarily a matter of historical re-creation and renewed contact with the past at all. It was first and foremost a matter of re-establishing contact with the authentic source of the supernatural in the present. He became convinced that the English Church had no real connection with the supernatural society Christ had founded to perpetuate His doctrines and to give to men of all ages the divine life to which He had elevated humanity.

After this discovery it was impossible for him to remain in the Anglican Church. The Oxford Movement became in his eyes just another of those many attempts to save religion and culture on what Coleridge called "man's defective dialectic."

It was a mere human project and despite the noble religious predispositions of its adherents was doomed to failure no less than was Rationalism. "Man is not enough." Newman had as firm a grasp on this principle at the enthusiastic dawn of modern human achievement as we have at its whimpering close.

None of the several attempts, including that of Mr. Paul Elmer More, to identify Newman with the typical mind of nineteenth-century Romanticism, have succeeded in adducing anything but superficial resemblances. He was anti-rational, it is asserted. Yet it is equally as obvious that his anti-intellectualism, if we may so call it, was not that of Blake, or Wordsworth, or William Law, or Coleridge. He was not a disbeliever in reason on criteriological grounds. "I have no intention at all of denying," he says in his *Apologia,* "that truth is the real object of our reason, and that if it does not attain to truth, either the premise or the process is at fault; but I am speaking here of right reason as it acts in fact and concretely in fallen man. I know that even the unaided reason, when correctly exercised, leads to belief in God, in the immortality of the soul, and in a future retribution; but I am considering the faculty of reason actually and historically" and from this viewpoint experimental evidence forced him to the conclusion that the tendency of un-aided human reason, especially in matters of religion, was toward simple unbelief, doubt, negation, and intellectual suicide.

If he was skeptical of reason he was none the less suspicious of the various substitutes for reason, on which the Romantics rested their case, feeling, intuition, the "inner light," the imaginative escape to past ages of faith and color. The glories of history did not warm or enlighten him; "they do not take away the winter of my desolation or make the buds unfold and the leaves grow within me, and my moral being rejoice." His skepticism embraced the entire gamut of man's efforts on the humanistic level:

"To consider the world in its length and breadth, its various history, the many races of men, their starts, their fortunes, their mutual alienation, their conflicts; and then their ways, habits, governments, forms of worship; their enterprises, their aimless courses, their random achievements and acquirements, the impotent conclusion of long-standing facts, the tokens so faint and broken of a superintending design, the evolution of what turn out to be great powers or truths, the progress of things, as if from unreasoning elements, not towards final causes, the greatness and littleness of man, his far-reaching aims, his short duration, the curtain hung over his futurity, the disappointments of life, the defeat of good, the success of evil, physical pain, mental anguish, the prevalence and intensity of sin, the pervading idolatries, the corruptions, the dreary hopeless irreligion, that condition of the whole race, so fearfully yet exactly described in the Apostle's words 'having no hope and without God in the world' — all this is a vision to dizzy and appal; and inflicts upon the mind the sense of profound mystery which is absolutely beyond human solution."

It demanded a divine solution, a Redemption, an extraordinary intervention of God in human affairs. Human nature must be liberated from "the terrible aboriginal calamity" in which it was involved, by the elevation of that nature to a higher level than the natural. This, as far as Newman was concerned, was the first principle, the first fact that must be grasped before anything could be done about reviving religion and culture. It was this principle, "broken in the soul of man as he passed through his later history," that must be restored. Other groups, other leaders in the nineteenth century were insisting on other remedies, the revival of the Middle Ages, confidence in science and progress, but only the Catholic Church insisted upon this. "Such truths as these she vigorously reiterates and pertinaciously inflicts upon mankind; as to such she observes no half-measures, no economical reserve, no delicacy or prudence. 'Ye must be born again,' is the simple, direct form of words she uses after her Divine Master; 'your whole nature must be reborn; your passions, and your affections, and your aims, and your conscience and your will, must be bathed in a new element, and reconsecrated to your Maker — and, the last not the least, your intellect.' "

Those who have represented Newman's accession to Rome in 1845 as a retreat — the passage of a beaten and discouraged man out of the most vital controversy of his day — have sketched more accurately than they were aware. It was just that. This man, in whom all had recognized the qualities of a great religious and cultural leader, had at first with a high courage placed these talents on the most constructive and valuable side of the debate between Romanticism and Rationalism. The issue of that debate was still then in doubt. But even after it had been decided and the battle was continued throughout the remainder of the century by those who belonged in various degrees to the same camp — Carlyle, Ruskin, Dickens — the side taken by Newman was still the side of the most precious spirits. It was the protest in the name of outraged art and despoiled religion, by those who all belonged to the earlier Romantic resurgence, against a strongly entrenched, complacent, and rationalistic Philistinism.

The decision taken by Newman on that memorable rainy night at Littlemore in 1845, did indeed remove him from the Romantic side, did indeed partake of a complete abandonment of the controversy between idealistic Romanticism and Utilitarianism. But it did not, as we may see clearly today, carry him out of that larger battle between the forces of civilization and those of disruption. It merely changed, for him, the state of the question. It lifted the controversy out of the confusion of its Victorian setting and placed it upon a basis it has taken seventy years of agonized European history to make clear. Men do not today hotly debate the opposing claims of Romanticism and Utilitarianism, for the intervening years have made them both stand forth as two sides, one "hard," one "soft," of the same uniform project, the effort, namely, of an anti-supernatural society to hold together a rapidly disintegrating culture that had been founded on a supernatural principle. The dilemma, as the modern man sees it, is between the supernatural order of the Catholic Church and the mechanical, cultureless order that now faces the natural man at the conclusion of his journey from the Renaissance. This was the dilemma as Newman saw it, cut free from all middle positions and accessory issues, in the twilight of Victorian confusion. And in so seeing it and in choosing one of the alternatives, he made himself a modern man.

IV

What concerns us chiefly here is the effect of this decision on that section of English literature which we have called the Catholic Literary Revival. Newman, although one of the foremost litterateurs of the nineteenth century, did not consciously form a new literary movement. That was rather the work of artists like Patmore, de Vere, Gerard Hopkins, and others who, following Newman, applied the inner connotations of this decision to letters, especially to poetry.[1] There was born with these men a group of English litterateurs who in the Victorian period had already faced and resolved the dilemma that the majority of artists would only begin to face in our own day, and who thus commenced seventy years ago to work out the implication of their decision to literary problems. That is their importance to us and to modern English literature in general.

------

[1]This is not to be construed as meaning that the work of Catholic writers in fields other than that of poetry was inconsiderable and had small influence on the Revival. It means merely that it is easier to get at the essence not only of the Catholic Revival but of any literary movement through its poets than through its prose writers. This principle has determined the selection of authors treated both in this phase and the subsequent one.

The first effect of all this was to cut the group off sharply from the official Romanticism of the day. They were from the beginning isolated, for it seemed at that time that such a severance also cut them off from the main stream of English letters. The reverse of this is what actually happened. For Romanticism itself, whatever may have been its goal in the beginning, did not, as a matter of fact, continue the best English traditions, but moved away from them. The philosophy upon which it was built would with the years carry it farther and farther away from the fundamental aesthetic which had informed not only the greatest English literature but the enduring literature of the ancient European world.

T. S. Eliot has said of William Blake that "what his genius required and what it sadly lacked, was a framework of accepted and traditional ideas which would have prevented him from indulging in a philosophy of his own, and concentrated his attention upon the problems of the poet. . . ." The concentration resulting from a framework of theology and philosophy, he says, is one of the reasons "why Dante is a classic and Blake only a poet of genius." The intellectual disorder of the nineteenth century gave the poet no such system, indeed it imposed upon him the necessity of being at once an artist and an original speculative thinker — an impossible combination. Thus the effort to construct for himself a workable plan out of the odds and ends of the wreckage of philosophical systems not infrequently resulted in grotesque and unsteady structures, the early collapse of which left him a prey to despair and frustration. If, on the other hand, he neglected the work of being a philosopher, and gave his attention to the specific problems of the artist, what he produced had polish but no body; he was a rhetorician.

The Catholic artist was in a large measure preserved from this double disillusionment. I say "in a large measure" because it is not true to assert that Newman or anyone else in those days

constructed a complete synthesis of the philosophical and the-
ological science of the times such as Aquinas gave to Dante.
But what Newman gave was the firm and secure foundation
on which such a synthesis could be constructed and which, as a
matter of fact, did preserve the artist from wrecking his genius
in philosophical blind alleys. He gave them the mind of the
Church. That mind, formed as it was on the best speculation
of the West, recognized the primacy of intelligence without
destroying the claims of the heart. It gave purpose and direc-
tion to the romantic emotional *élan* without trying to stretch
it upon the Procrustean bed of a dry and earth-bound Ration-
alism.

We shall have occasion to see how, precisely because the
Catholic Revival was disentangled from the conventional nine-
teenth-century Romanticism, it was able to preserve and perfect
what was really valuable in the artistic program of the early
Romantic artists. The renovation in diction and prosody begun
by Wordsworth and Coleridge will be continued by Patmore
and de Vere and will be elevated to new heights by Gerard
Hopkins; the Romantic sense of history, of affection for the
great past will be found without sentimental dilettantism in
these and in Robert Stephen Hawker; and all the primal fire
of Blake's mysticism will burn again but freed now of its first
turgescence, becoming in the incandescent verse of Patmore
and Hopkins a clear and mounting flame. All this renovation
will be possible because the mind of the artist has been re-born.

These men will fix a tradition in modern English verse that
will persist along the lines laid down by them until the present
day. It will be romantic (if you choose) and yet sharply sepa-
rated from historical Romanticism as we know it. Historical
Romanticism began with Rousseau's cry *Retournez a la nature*;
the watchword of this literature, we may say, paraphrasing a
remark of Karl Adam, will be "Back to the supernatural." This
cry will be a sign of contradiction and a symbol of derision in

its Victorian day. Only the passage of years will be able to make it stand forth clearly as the one path of deliverance from the desert in which the artist will find himself at the end of four centuries of too great a trust in the natural man.

2

Aubrey De Vere
R. S. HAWKER

One likes to remember Aubrey de Vere as the author of *Caedmon, First English Poet*. It is not perhaps his best poem, but there is a symbolism in it that is arresting. English poetry begins with the charming legend related by Venerable Bede of the swineherd, Caedmon, whom an angel had commanded to sing while he lay disconsolate and songless on the Saxon straw. His song that night was of God and creation. English poets had lost the meaning of this legend when de Vere came into the literary world. He gave the greater part of a long life to its restoration.

Had they lost it because they had wandered from the Church which had given inspiration and patronage to the first English poet? De Vere did not know. But, at any rate, Coleridge and Wordsworth had convinced him from the start that its meaning somehow must be recovered if the departing artistic soul of England would be stayed. Poetry was dying because religion was in decay, and secularism triumphant. He wrote later,

> *Roll on, blind world, upon thy track*
> *Until thy wheels catch fire,*
> *For that is gone which comes not back*
> *To seller or to buyer.*

Said Sara Coleridge of de Vere, "I have been among poets a great deal and have known greater poets than he is: but a more *entire* poet, one more a poet in his whole mind and temperament, I have never met." It was, perhaps, this which made him

see what ailed poetry deep down more clearly than greater
artists, like his friend Wordsworth. His life was spent in in-
timate contact with those who represented the glorious sunset
of Romantic poetry; and he may be said to have taken the torch
of poetic inspiration from their hands, and to have placed it
where the first English poet had found it.

Very early in life this young Irishman began to feel the
struggle upon which so much in his age depended — the
struggle between the cold materialism of Bentham, which was
crushing art and religion between the millstones of skepticism
and commerce, and the Romantic resurgence. "Benthamite or
Coleridgian in those days was the alternate description of every
thinking youth." He chose Coleridge. He had never met the
prophet of Highgate for he was dead before de Vere left
Trinity College, Dublin. But his message he had imbibed from
his friend and teacher, Sir William Hamilton, the philosopher,
and later from Wordsworth, Hartley, and Sara Coleridge, and
the group he visited so frequently at Rydal.

If de Vere was a disciple of Coleridge he was not a disciple
with a closed mind. He did not regard the conclusion of the
master as the final word any more than the master did himself,
or, for that matter, the master's wife, who is said to have in-
terrupted her husband during one of his philosophical séances
with the question, "Man, do you really understand yourself?"
So in the year 1838 he began a sort of pilgrimage which
brought him into contact with virtually all of the vital spirits
of the period. He was writing poetry the while and becoming
known as a poet, but his chief interest was in those problems,
philosophical and religious, which concerned most nearly the
future of all the arts and national morality. His mind was oc-
cupied with the theme that possessed the most thoughtful of
the day, "the religious revival which succeeded to the indiffer-
entism of the eighteenth century, and to the irreligious philos-
ophy which the pioneers of the French Revolution had made
popular, and its issue had discredited." To F. D. Maurice and

his circle at Cambridge, he went; to Newman and the Trac-
tarians at Oxford; to Tennyson, Hallam, Fitzgerald, and Mac-
aulay in London, and back again to the Lake country where
brooded the spirit of Coleridge, and where he paced beside the
aged Wordsworth and treasured each gem that fell from the
prophet's lips.

The solutions offered by these minds had very little in com-
mon. The impression they should have made upon de Vere was
that the problem was insoluble. Yet this was not the case. His
way was made light by single beams that shone from each of
these diverse sources and converged upon truth. His path, ob-
serves his biographer Wilfrid Ward, was a sunny one. *"Horas
non numero nisi serenas* might have been the motto of his
mental history," which explains why neither prejudice nor im-
mature judgment deflected him from his course, and also why
his poetry never reaches the highest levels of emotion. His was
not a turbulent soul.

He had that sort of philosophical mind which delights not
in differences but in similarities. Maurice, Wordsworth, New-
man, Keble, Tennyson, and the others, he saw, were in agree-
ment in their insistence that religion must be restored. But
how? And what religion? From Coleridge he had learnt to re-
gard Christianity highly as "the mind of regenerate man, as
something resting on wider or deeper experiences than belongs
to the life of one individual." He had learnt from him also to
distrust sectarianism, "the outcome of self-confident private
judgment, the attempt of the average individual man to con-
struct a religion by means of his own defective dialectic." Yet
this is precisely what he came to see that Coleridge himself was
doing, trying to erect a man-made system on what the eight-
eenth century had left of Protestantism. There was confusion
and misunderstanding and in the meantime the simple doc-
trines of materialism were carrying all before them. De Vere
was now prepared to go a step farther than his preceptor, for
he saw that private judgment even of the most profound and

sincere kind had broken up the ancient Christian Church in England, which Church seemed to him now "the only means of preserving among the masses, faith in the invisible world."

"Is it not the word *Religio* to bind again?" he asked, "and how can you bind except by Doctrines reduced to their orthodox form and Duties explained, applied and enforced. . . . St. Paul says that the Church is to be listened to and obeyed; a German philosopher would put it into his pipe and smoke it."

The climax of his "romance," as he called the journey which led him to Rome, was near. There came the Irish Famine of 1847 which sorely tried his soul; then the death of his father. He wrote to Sara Coleridge that he had been reading the *Summa* of St. Thomas. He was already an intellectual Catholic, overpowered by the spectacle of the concrete and united Church which met his gaze "when he lifted his eyes to the mountains." Newman had entered the Church, but it was not to Littlemore that de Vere went in this new state of mind, but to the grave of Coleridge and to the fresher one of Wordsworth (he had died in 1850) as to the soil from which his regeneration had sprung.

Early in November, 1851, he went with Manning on a journey to Rome. "I am going to Rome — I mean geographically," he wrote his friend, Miss Arnold. But he was baptized at Avignon on the fifteenth day of the same month.

De Vere, I think, is the only one of the early revivalists whose conversion occasioned no severance of the long-established ties of friendship. He retained his old intimacies, especially with the literary folk of the Lake country. Poetically he was still a romantic of the Wordsworthian school. All this is a tribute to the perennial sweetness of his disposition; but one cannot refrain from wishing there had been some sort of break, such as that which occurred in the case of Patmore or of Hopkins. It was invariably rewarded by a marked improvement in the subject's poetry. De Vere's verse needed something of this sort. It is too Wordsworthian, it wanted a renovation of diction and rhythm to fit the newness of inspiration.

But if he was content to continue the Romantic tradition in its established diction and rhythm he introduced important changes elsewhere, and it is these which constitute his best contribution to the Catholic Revival. Perhaps the greatest part of his work as a poet was, in the manner of Montalambert, to recapture the spirit of the Christian past and that part of the pagan past which the Church had made her own. His narrative poems on Ireland's heroic age and its Christian periods such as *The Foray of Queene Maeve, Legends of St. Patrick,* and *Innesfail* must be reckoned among the earliest beginnings of the Celtic revival; while his *Legends of Saxon Saints,* his drama, *St. Thomas of Canterbury,* his *Medieval Records and Sonnets* and others did much, as Woodbury remarks, to repair "the spiritual deprivation to the northern imagination" brought about by the Reformation.

It would seem at times, as one reads through de Vere's rather voluminous medieval re-creations, that he has fallen into the Romantic mistake of thinking the renewal of the artistic mind consisted simply in stocking it with a mass of vivid pictures taken from the high spots of the ages of faith. This, however, was not his intention. What he sought to make live again was not the Middle Ages or the early ages of the Church but the supernatural principle that had produced the glories of these times. Beneath the color and the romance, the heroism, the sanctity, the art, he saw only the Incarnation of Christ, God's own remedy for the broken humanity of all ages.

Pope Pius IX had asked de Vere as a convert and a poet to write hymns to Our Lady, whose Immaculate Conception he was shortly to define. The result was a volume called *May Carols* to the preface of which we may turn to discover de Vere's technique for renewing the artistic imagination. It is his important gift to the Revival, and since some may find it more pious than aesthetic, it is perhaps well to recall what Mary's inspiration meant to men like Dante, Guido Cavalcanti, and Chaucer, and how Giotto, Cimabue, and Raffael made themselves immortal by painting her with the Child. Mary loomed large in that springtime of art and letters, the Renaissance; she was to have no less an influence on artists in the "Second Spring."

Speaking of the early Renaissance, de Vere remarks that this period was rich in art because to the imaginations of a Giotto or a Fra Angelico had been present a glorious image of religion, an image not manufactured by man, but given by God Himself in the Incarnation. "Everywhere throughout the worlds of painting, sculpture, and architecture shone out that nobler beauty, severe at once and tender, mystic yet simple, gladsome yet pathetic. . . . The Holy Family was the center at once of things earthly and things heavenly; and art when it saw that vision wisely desired to build tabernacles in its light and whispered 'it is good for us to be here.' This was the true preaching of the Incarnation. The pictured prophet or the apostle might be honored only for the spoken word or the deed done; but that Infant on His mother's knee could have a significance for one cause alone, viz., because He was God."

"Art," de Vere observes as he passes from this state of things to the religion given to the artist of the nineteenth century, "grew neither more heroic nor more beautiful when it abandoned this earthly Eden and exchanged the higher for the lower knowledge." The "higher knowledge" of the eighteenth-century Deists had, by scorning the Incarnation, driven God from the world, had made Him an intellectual abstraction who had created the universe and abandoned it to the operation of general and impersonal laws. "Adore God and act like a gentleman," was the formula Kant had given to his generation. But this God was too far away, too infinite to be adored, so the eighteenth century ended by adoring the gentleman. The Romantic revolt had been an attempt to restore God to His world, not under the aspect of His creatorship, for the Deists had held that, but as a "sheathed Divinity diffused throughout the universe, its life, not its maker," an immanent something identified with and one with matter. This concept captured the fancy but left the deeper imagination untouched because it was but a vague and partial truth. Men might write verse about the Wood-God, the River-Nymph, and the World Soul, but they could not believe in these. So the Deists adored man, the Romantics adored nature, and in the meantime the transcendent God and His world still remained apart, as far as the poet was concerned.

"The whole truth, in the long run," de Vere continues, "holds its own better than a half-truth, . . ." and the whole truth after which the age was blindly striving was to be found in the Incarnation. "When the Word was made Flesh a bridge was thrown across that gulf which else had ever separated the finite from the Infinite," and for poetic minds to whom "the Infinite God had become either very finite or entirely indefinite," the objective fact of the Incarnation was the true remedy both for subjectivism and the worship of matter.

The preface to the *May Carols,* difficult reading as it is, stands as one of the most important critical documents of the century. It holds up to the artist the Incarnation as the primal font of the renewed poetry, and what is more practical, it shows him the manner in which he may best reach and understand the artistic significance of the Word Made Flesh. For de Vere's advice to the poet is not that he concern himself directly with the sublime theological truths of the Incarnation, but that he approach these truths as did the early Christian artists through "the lesser elevation" of the divine motherhood of Mary. "In the former case the higher elevation commands a wider field of vision and one 'sun-clad' with the glory of a stronger light. Yet for some purposes the lesser elevation and the fainter light are not without their advantages. We are not thus so much brought face to face with matter too awful for poetry. . . . Mary is the guard-

ian of all those sacred mysteries which relate to the Sacred In-
fancy; through her the Church keeps a perpetual Christmas,
rejoicing in mysteries which can never lose their objective char-
acter and historical attestation. Through Mary the palpable is
preserved in the spiritual and the truth of fact holds its own
against that subjective habit of the modern mind which 'with
error opposite to that of Narcissus,' to quote Dante, wastes away
because it imagines it sees but its own face in all things, believ-
ing in no other reality."

The first sentence in the Preface to the *May Carols* sum-
marizes de Vere's entire purpose when it warns the reader that
the work "must not be regarded as a collection of hymns but a
poem on the Incarnation, a poem dedicated to the honor of the
Virgin Mother, and preserving ever as the most appropriate
mode of honoring her, a single aim, that of illustrating Chris-
tianity at once as a theological truth and *as a living power,
reigning among the humanities and renewing the affections and
imagination of man."* The collection begins with the lines,

> *O thou whose light is in thy heart,*
> *Reverence, love's mother! without thee*
> *Science may soar awhile, but Art*
> *Drifts barren o'er a shoreless sea.*

His plans, then, for the renewal of the arts was Mary, whom
his friend Wordsworth had called "our tainted nature's solitary
boast." Through her, poetry might be saved from the curse of
an "abstract Christ," and nature, already withering under the
passionate kisses of the Romantics, might again magnify the
Lord:

> *Not less does Nature teach through thee*
> *That mystery hid in hues and lines;*
> *Who loves thee not hath lost the key*
> *To all her sanctuaries and shrines.*

If we look upon the Catholic revival of letters under the

aspect of its being a continuation after a breach of two centuries of that strain of English poetry that had died with Crashaw, we may see how singularly fitting it was that the Mother of God should play a large part in it. It was to the Marian shrine at Loretto that Crashaw, exiled from his native land, had gone; and he was buried there.

> *How well (blest Swan) did Fate contrive thy death*
> *And make thee render up thy tuneful breath*
> *In that great Mistress' arms, thou most divine*
> *And richest offering of Loretto's shrine!*

sang Abraham Cowley in his *Ode on the Death of Mr. Crashaw*. The revival of Catholic art in the nineteenth century was accompanied everywhere by a revival of devotion to the Mother of God, but most notably in England, "Our Lady's Dowry," as the island had anciently been styled. Thus Newman, returning from Rome to England after his ordination, went out of his way to pay a visit of devotion to the shrine at Loretto. Later, in a letter to Wilberforce, he says, "I have ever been under her shadow, if I may say it. My college was St. Mary's, and my Church; and when I went to Littlemore, there by my own previous disposition Our Blessed Lady was waiting for me." Robert Stephen Hawker, while still an Anglican, wore always about his neck a medal of the Immaculate Conception; Coventry Patmore at the age of fifty-four experienced a complete renewal of poetic inspiration as a result of a visit to Lourdes; Aubrey Beardsley, the *fin de siècle* artist, was discovered through his black-and-white sketch "Hail Mary"; Francis Thompson's first published poem, and the one, by the way, which was chiefly instrumental in reclaiming him from a life of sterile vagabondage, was "The Passion of Mary." And so on. There is no artist in the revival who has not left us in prose or verse some record of his literary debt to the Mother of God. It was inevitable that all this should be unintelligible to the nineteenth-century mind. Robert Bridges, for instance, in one of his frequently confused scholia on Gerard Hopkins' verse speaks of "the exaggerated Marianism of some of his poems." Not only the religious but the poetic value of this Marianism is entirely dark to him.

"Your place," says Paul Claudel to the somewhat skeptical Jacques Riviere, "is marked out along with Patmore, with Chesterton, and if I may say so, with me, among those whose role it is to create a Catholic imagination and a Catholic sensitivity which for four centuries has been withering away. . . ." Here, from the author of *The Tidings Brought to Mary,* is a modern echo of the doctrine contained in the preface to the *May Carols.* It is de Vere's specific and permanent gift to the Revival — Mary as the way to the Incarnation, and the Incarnation "as a living Power, reigning among the Humanities, and renewing the affections and imagination of man."

II

There is among modern artists, says Mr. Eric Gill, speaking principally of the sculptors and painters, but one binding idea, and that "the general enthusiasm for objectivity, and detestation of illusionism and representation and anecdotage." This passion for reality is the symbol of their rebellion against "the sentimentality and hypocrisy, the utilitarianism and smugness of the nineteenth century." It is what makes their art appear eccentric because the Victorian mentality still persists among the masses of those who look at pictures and sculptures.

These observations are applicable both to the life and the art of the little known but authentic poet and early Catholic revivalist Robert Stephen Hawker, whom Mr. Paul Elmer More has called "one of the most original and interesting personalities of the past century." To his own generation he was a hopeless eccentric, chiefly, I think, because of his queer realism. It neglected him, although it did confer on him a sort of anonymous celebrity by quoting, as did Walter Scott and Macaulay, one of his original ballads, *The Song of the Western Men,* as a genuine folklore relique. He, on his part, had the noblest sort of contempt for the period, and deliberately separated himself from its dismal commercialism by a wall of idiosyncrasies, preferring to live in the more integral world which he revived from the Celtic and Saxon memories of his native Cornwall.

We have already referred to Hawker as the Anglican clergyman who wore about his neck a medal of the Immaculate Conception. From his beautiful devotion to Our Lady there welled forth some of our most original and charming Marian poems. The boon so sought after by the saints, of dying on one of the Virgin's feast days, was bestowed on him — a fitting reward for such striking achievements in her honor as *King Arthur's Waes Hael* and *Aishah Schechinah.* And on the eve of the Assumption, 1875, as he lay on his deathbed, he was received into the Church he had loved so much from the outside.

From early youth Hawker displayed marked promise of poetic ability, having published his first volume of verse while yet in grammar school. At Oxford he won the Newdigate prize, but his bishop wanted pastors, not poets. After taking Anglican orders, he was hurried off to an obscure and dilapidated parish in Cornwall which had not had a resident vicar for a century. There he remained for forty years, a devoted pastor and father of the simple seafaring folk. To the world, or that part of it that had sensed his genius, it may have seemed a burial, but to Hawker it was the entry into a newer and fuller life.

Morwenstow, his charge, had been the ancient Saxon shrine of St. Morwenna. With the enthusiasm of St. Francis at San Damiano he set to work restoring its ancient grandeur in a spiritual way as well as materially; he dug up the forgotten Celtic and Saxon legends of the locality, revived the primitive flavor of the place, not in the temper of the antiquarian, but that he and his people might drink deeply the spirit of the faithful days when England had been reclaimed from a dark paganism to the light of Christianity. With the nation rapidly returning to something worse than this antique barbarism, he seemed determined to bring it about that at least in one spot the newer and more real spirit should flourish.

As the years passed, Hawker grew to love his Saxon shrine and its memories so deeply that it was with difficulty and repugnance that he could detach himself from it, long enough to make a short journey of twenty-five miles to attend the yearly archdeaconate conference. This affection illuminates his poem *Morwennae Statio:*

> *My Saxon shrine! the only ground*
> *Wherein this weary heart finds rest:*
> *What years the birds of God have found*
> *Along thy walls their sacred nest!*
> *The storm, — the blast, — the tempest shock*
> *Have beat upon thy walls in vain:*
> *She stands a daughter of the rock —*
> *The changeless God's eternal fane.*
> *They knew their God, those faithful men.*
> *They pitched no tent for change or death,*

> * * *

> *How all things glow with life and thought,*
> *Where'er our faithful fathers trod!*
> *The very ground with speech is fraught,*
> *The air is eloquent of God.*
> *In vain would doubt or mockery hide*
> *The buried echoes of the past;*
> *A voice of strength, a voice of pride,*
> *Here dwells amid the storm and blast.*

In *The Poor Man and His Parish Church* he records with bitterness his attitude toward a society which had deprived the poor man of his Church and given him the poorhouse in its place.

> *O! for the poorman's church again,*
> *With one roof over all:*
> *Where the true hearts of Cornish men*
> *Might beat beside the wall:*
> *The altar where in holier days*
> *Our fathers were forgiven,*
> *Who went, with meek and faithful ways,*
> *Through the old aisles to heaven.*

The contrast between the warmth of one culture and the coldness of the other sharpened his detestation for all that went on in the world outside his parish. The prospect of a visit to a neighboring town, he records, caused him sleeplessness, "a faint and sickening sensation which was humiliating and depressing indeed."

Among his more humorous animadversions was Victorian respectability, especially as expressed in the dress of the clergy. Whenever one of these visitors ("dressed like an undertaker, Sir") dropped in on him he would sometimes annoy him with the story of how his pet stag "Robin" had pinned another such "father of saucepans with a shirt-tail" to the ground. Hawker, by way of protest against what he considered a drab convention, affected a dress that has been described as "eccentric" but which was certainly symbolic and colorful. He sometimes wore red gloves like a cardinal even at services; a long purple cloak now and again served him for a cassock; under this he wore a fisherman's jersey "as befits a fisher of men," set off with a small red cross to mark the spot where our Lord's side had been pierced.

Besides the anti-Victorian stag, "Robin," Hawker had numerous other animal friends, including a very intelligent black pig, a dog, and nine or ten cats, all very much at home in the church. There was, indeed, something Franciscan in the familiarity between the Vicar of Morwenstow and the animal brotherhood. One time, in order to keep the jackdaws out of his peas and beans, he set up a scarecrow attired in one of his old hats and a cast-off cassock. But the birds took it for the Vicar himself, and gathered about looking up to be fed.

The Western County in which Hawker passed these curious but fruitful years is filled with monuments and memories of the great King Arthur and the heroes of Celtic romance. Headlands and sea and inland lakes within walking distance of Morwenstow speak of great loves and wars enacted in the twilight of history. There on the north coast is Tintagel where, it is said, Arthur was born and Tristam and Isolde loved; there, too, is Dozmaré Pool where Merlin took Excalibur from the white, samite-clothed arm, where the grieving Bedivere reluctantly returned the brand, and carrying his dying master from the near-by field where had raged the tragic last battle of the west, saw the black-draped barge and the three queens and the mystic passing of the King.

Hawker haunted these places and rebuilt the ancient scenes. In the year 1848 there occurred a meeting between him and one who had come to the Western County in search of material for a projected epic. It was Alfred Tennyson, and he and the Vicar sat on the historic rocks until dusk discussing King Arthur and the legends of the place. The meeting is particularly interesting because Hawker, too, wrote a poem on the Holy Grail which, when compared with that of the laureate, brings out some significant points. The Tennysonian achievement towers high above the other in verbal magic, in romance, in the mastery of music, although there is, as Mr. More points out, "a certain fine sonorousness in Hawker's measures." But the Vicar's true strength shines out clearly in a department where Tennyson and his brother poets of the second generation of Romantics are weak — in an inspiration that is firm and strong because it rises out of a solid and undeceitful realism. "I have read Tennyson's *Holy Grail* and Mr. Hawker's *Quest*," said Henry Wadsworth Longfellow, "and I think the latter poem far superior to the Laureate's."

Although Tennyson, no less than Hawker, had seen the real rocks and moorlands of this romantic stage, the locale of his *Idylls* bears no resemblance to it, but is a land "no eye has beheld, no human foot ever trod." Hawker, on the contrary, in his *Quest of the Sangrael,* makes real Celtic knights set out from an historic Tintagel in search of what is to them and to him a huge and needful reality. With Tennyson it is difficult to say just what the Holy Grail symbolizes; indeed its very symbolism seems to vanish in the thin air of the ideal; all we have left is knights who war with unreal elements, and wander aimlessly in quest of that which is vaguely conceived and impossible of attainment. It is very beautiful, very sad, and very unreal. The real tragedy and the true realism of the Tennysonian poem is to be looked for in the obscurity that grimly sits upon the poetic mind because of the absence of a faith and a philosophy that might enable him to pierce through the confusion of his times, that might give reality to these sincere longings for he knows not what.

Hawker's faith and his philosophy, too (he was a close student of the *Summa* of St. Thomas), had put him in contact with that groundwork of truth from which all great Christian poetry must rise. His *Sangrael* is not a tenuous ideal. It is the Eucharist and the Church which alone dispenses the Body and Blood of Christ. Arthur is no mere legendary figure but an historic king who sees faith leaving his land and wars to bring it back, and does not fail but succeeds in the success of Galahad who symbolizes for Hawker the coming of Augustine after the temporary havoc wrought by the barbarians. Once more —

— *fonts of Saxon rock stood full of God,*
Altars rose, each like a kingly throne,

Where the royal chalice with its lineal blood,
The glory of the presence, ruled and reigned.

＊　　＊　　＊

This lasted long until the white horse fled,
The fierce fangs of the libbard in his loins:
While ages glided in that blink of time.

The following years of England's history are read to us in
the light of what happened to the Blessed Sacrament — faith in
It growing cold by reason of clerical and political corruption,
then Protestantism, then scientific agnosticism, and finally in
his own day,

The shrines were darkened and the chalice void.

The poem ends with a plea from the lips of Merlin to nine-
teenth-century England to find again the Grail which means
so much to poets and people.

Ah! native England! wake thine ancient cry:
Ho! for the San grael! vanished vase of heaven,
That held, like Christ's own heart, one hin of blood.

Hawker's whole life at Morwenstow may be said to have
been a search for the Holy Grail which he found in a true sense
on the eve of the Assumption, 1875. He was a product of the
sacramental revival within the Church of England growing out
of the Oxford Movement. But long before his final conversion
it was evident that intellectually he had definitely turned
toward Rome, that he saw in the Roman Catholic Revival, the
revival of Newman, Wiseman, and Manning, the only authen-
tic hope that the Sangrael of Arthur and Galahad might be re-
stored to England again. Thus in his poem *Ichabod* he saluted

the dead Cardinal Wiseman in lines that might be applied to his own work also:

> *He, when the sage's soul with doubt was riven,*
>   *Smote the dull dreamers with the prophet's rod:*
> *He called on earth and sea to chant of heaven,*
>   *And made the stars rehearse the truth of God!*

3

Coventry Patmore

Returning from Rome in 1852, Aubrey de Vere fell in with Robert Browning at Florence. In a conversation which lasted well into the small hours of the morning de Vere made what appears to have been an heroic effort to communicate to his poet-friend his new-found enthusiasm, with the possibilities it held out for the revival of art and religion. Browning was interested but unconvinced. He wrote later: "I was interested by the hours you gave me on that last evening of yours in Florence, and grateful, too, and not 'tired.' . . . *I am never tired of sunrises.* . . . That I believe you mistaken in much is obvious. . . ."

This interest in sunrises was a characteristic of those who belonged to the sunset of the Romantic Movement. As late as 1871, Swinburne was writing *Songs Before Sunrise.* The dawn he celebrated came, disillusioning and without sun. The old inspiration had run down.

It is perhaps idle to speculate on what course the Romantic Movement might have taken had its leaders listened to what the Catholic revivalists were saying. Of course they did not. And so the work of the men we have been treating was done in a corner and without recognition or notable influence. If they were not great poets, their message at least was great. But the age was not ready for it; which also may explain why those of the founders who *were* unquestionably major poets, as Patmore and Hopkins, likewise went unnoticed.

The importance of these two men is just becoming generally recognized today by non-Catholic critics. Mr. F. R. Leavis has recently said of Gerard Manley Hopkins, who died in 1889 that "he was one of the most remarkable technical inventors who ever wrote, and he was a major poet. Had he received the attention that was his due the history of English poetry from the nineties onward would have been very different. But that is a fanciful proposition. . . ."[1] His literary executor, the late Robert Bridges, did not even dare to publish his poems until after the War. Nothing could have made Hopkins popular in his day. It was necessary that the old conventions be blown away, and a new generation of poets arise to absorb his message. Such a process is going on today. "He is likely to prove, for our time, and the future," continues Mr. Leavis, "the only influential poet of the Victorian age and he seems to me the greatest."

Although Coventry Patmore did achieve immense popularity in the Victorian period with his *Angel in the House,* he deliberately turned his back upon this popularity to follow another course. "No poet — indeed no personality of the whole period —" observes Mr. Herbert Read, "stands in such direct opposition to all its beliefs and ideals — perhaps we should say, finally stood in such opposition, for Patmore's settled attitude did not develop until the middle age."[2] He had become a Catholic, he had begun his mystical odes of which Mr. Read has said that "those who are braced to the highest levels of the art [of poetry] . . . will find in the best of the odes a fund of inspired poetry for which they would willingly sacrifice the whole baggage of the Victorian legacy in general."[3]

I

Coventry Patmore was born at Woodford, Essex, in 1823, a year after the death of Shelley, one year before that of Byron;

[1] *New Bearings in English Poetry,* by F. R. Leavis, p. 160 (Chatto & Windus).
[2] "Coventry Patmore," by Herbert Read, in *The Great Victorians,* p. 356.
[3] *Ibid.,* p. 368.

Keats had died two years earlier. The reaction against the political and spiritual radicalism of the Romantics of the second generation was well under way. The power of the middle class was being thrown on the side of economic stability and order in that compromise with scientific liberalism which fixed the character of the Victorian period. A new mental temper was in preparation, hostile to an uncompromising mysticism, which would divide and torture the artistic soul.

It was Patmore's achievement that he reconciled these two tendencies, mysticism and the scientific spirit. He did it, not like Tennyson, by accepting both into a grotesque and sterile union, but by rejecting both in their current acceptation, Romantic mysticism because it was confused and illusory, and the rational syncretism because it was unreasonable. The basis on which he worked out this fusion is interesting and explains why the modern artist today is turning to him.

Very early in youth he exhibited a keen interest in mathematics and the experimental sciences. His father, P. G. Patmore, who personally supervised his education, gave him a laboratory as a concession, no doubt, to the scientific amateurism of the day. There young Patmore claimed that he discovered, as a result of his researches, a new chloride of bromine. Edmund Gosse chooses to regard the claim as a typical Patmorean exaggeration. Perhaps he is right. But at any rate, the fact of an early and enthusiastic interest in science remains. There was the intellectual equipment, too, which would have fitted him for a career in science had not the elder Patmore deftly guided the young and inquiring intelligence into the way of letters. He himself was a literary man, an associate of Lamb, Hazlitt, and Barry Cornwall, but notorious rather than distinguished. He was somewhat blatant, a poseur, and had played an unfortunate part in a famous duel which had crystallized popular sentiment against him.

He was an agnostic after the prevailing fashion, and so raised his son. But at the age of eleven while reading a book he had picked up somewhere, Coventry records that it struck him "what an exceedingly fine thing it would be if there really was a God." Here was an intriguing hypothesis in an age of many hypotheses. At the age of sixteen we find him still at work on the question. He had just finished what he describes as an "exhaustive" study of Shakespeare's plays which called forth the following observation set down in his autobiography: "After much meditation on the idea of tragedy I came gradually to the conclusion that this idea [of tragedy] in order to constitute a just foundation for the highest kind of poetry, ought to present the solution rather than the mere conclusion by death of the evils and disasters of life. This set me inquiring whether there was such solution; and this train of thought brought me face to face with the idea of religion. . . ."

He speaks also of "illuminations" during his youth, "the earth lighted up with a light not of this earth," showing him, among other things, "that sin was an infinite evil and love an infinite good"; the discernment of sexual impurity and original purity, "the one as the tangible blackness of hell, and the other as the very bliss of heaven, and the flower and consummation of love between man and woman." More remarkable was the light that came to him on the Incarnation, of God made man, and the possibilities of intimate communion with Him. This idea he describes as having been thenceforth, "the only reality worth seriously caring for."

These "illuminations" are to be understood as interior things and unlike those of Blake who saw God at the age of nine and a treeful of angels a little later. Hence we have less cause to suspect their authenticity. Whatever attitude we may adopt toward them as well as toward his scientific leanings, it is difficult to exclude the intervention of a careful Providence which was saving at least one poet in a confused age from a quack mysticism, on the one hand, and a bland materialism, on the other.

The tendency of the artists of his own generation was toward the latter. Too naïve a trust in the prophetic powers of science was giving birth to the literature of Naturalism, which, in an extreme exponent like Zola, regarded a novel as a sort of laboratory experiment in which the action of the characters was automatically controlled by environment, heredity, and the iron laws of evolution; virtue and vice were explained biochemically. This liaison between the artist and science owed much to the conviction, then quite widespread, that the old order of things advocated by religion was demonstrably false, and that for a fresher grasp of reality, one must turn to the new concepts of man, God, and the universe being constructed by the scientists.

Even this, however, would fail to explain why litterateurs continued to find inspiration in a creed that was materialistic and joyless, and which tended to make of the poet a sort of "sonorous hardware man" as Huysmans called Leconte de Lisle. We must look to religio-scientists of the type of Thomas Huxley, who elevated the most tenuous hypotheses of scientists into solemn dogmas, covered the dry bones of research with a veil of prophecy, and with a genuine feeling for lucid prose, equal if not superior to that of Bishop Cranmer, converted the scientific movement into a religion, calling it very appropriately the "New Reformation." Huxley, though muddled, was, like many a reformer, quite sincere. His crusade for realism and intellectual honesty profoundly affected the course of literature, and still shows signs of life in isolated areas where firmly established convention has resisted the new solvents. Among the more advanced spirits, however (Huxley's grandson, Aldous, is one of them), there is the conviction that the "New Reformation" has failed quite as dismally as the old. The hope held out for a new order of reality has collapsed. The disillusioned artist finds himself left without any reality, or with a reality so bleak that the cork-lined room of Marcel Proust seems the only refuge left.

Patmore's contempt for the artistic and sociological products of this *scientisme* was forthright and undisguised. He lashed out against it as savagely as did the late D. H. Lawrence, or to take a man who was his contemporary, as savagely as Ruskin. Yet his protest was not made in the name of Romanticism or on the traditional Romantic basis. While it is true, as Mr. E. I. Watkin remarks, he "proclaimed the bankruptcy of analytic reason and the mechanical science as a philosophy for individual and social life," he did not, as did Ruskin, make the mistake of rejecting the intellect and objective metaphysics — a mistake common to both Rationalism and Romanticism. Thus, in his flight from the "reality" of the scientists, he did not fall into the bog of unreality into which so many of the Romantic rebels blundered. His first poems, however, which his father caused to be published prematurely in 1844, would seem to indicate the possibility of such a course. A reviewer in *Blackwood's Magazine* hailed them as "the life into which the slime of the Keatses and the Shelleys of former times have fecundated."

II

Shortly after the appearance of these poems, his father, because of financial difficulties, fled to the Continent, leaving Coventry to shift for himself. His existence in London until 1846, when he obtained the post of assistant librarian in the British Museum, was a hand-to-mouth affair, what support there was coming from occasional bits sent to the magazines. It was during this period that he first met Tennyson, spent much time with him in nocturnal discussions of poetic problems, and in many other ways looked up to him as a leader and inspirer. In later years he was wont to deplore the time he had wasted following Tennyson around "like a dog." He seems to have come to regard him as an empty idol much in the same manner as our modern anti-Victorians. Gosse and others have given ingenious explanations for the change of attitude. There was undoubtedly some of the Patmorean pride and haughtiness in it.

But that is not all. While paying due tribute to Tennyson's gifts as an artist, Patmore must have been acutely aware of his own superiority over his friend in things of the intellect.

His impatient search for reality was leading him in a direction opposite to that taken by Tennyson, indeed, in a direction opposite to that taken by any poet perhaps since Dante. He had been meditating an epic of love, and it may be seen in how far he departed from the honored traditions of his day when we learn that it was not the delirium of unfettered and extra-matrimonial love, the rights of the lover against God and society, that he thought of celebrating, but love within the bonds of matrimony. There is something really pedestrian in the very thought. Those bred on centuries of amorous poetry from Sappho to Keats, might conceive of this as a possible theme for a moral reformer but scarcely for a poet. Yet we must insist with Edmund Gosse that Patmore's "transcendental adoration of wedded love was originally neither a rule of theology nor an argument of morals, but was a symptom of purely individual lyricism . . . it was a fierce expression of personal instinct . . . the exclusively aesthetic idea of marriage inflamed his imagination with a noble excitement. He saw no difference between marriage and poetry."

In 1847 he had, after a brief courtship, married Emily Andrews, daughter of a non-Conformist minister, and a woman of celebrated beauty and charm. Ruskin, Carlyle, and the Pre-Raphaelite Brotherhood were captivated by her; the artists Millais and Woolner drew her portrait, as did Browning in the sketch "A Face" from *Dramatis Personae*. Patmore was a close associate and sympathetic friend of the Brotherhood. He induced Ruskin to assist them and supplied them with the motto "It is the last rub which polishes the mirror." He shared their reaction to the Philistinism of the times and their search for a naïve freshness of reality. But he was not a pre-Raphaelite. And so Emily Andrews did not suffer the fate of the beautiful and tragic wife of Rossetti, Elizabeth Siddall, the original of the Blessed Damozel who killed herself because of her husband's neglect. She became the "Angel in the House," the heroine of Patmore's epic of married love — "the first of themes sung last of all."

> *In green and undiscovered ground,*
> *Yet near where many others sing,*
> *I have the very well-head found*
> *Whence gushes the Pierian spring.*

Although he compared his wife and inspirer with Beatrice and told Rossetti he meant to make *The Angel in the House* bigger than the *Divina Commedia,* it falls, of course, considerably short of the Dantean achievement. No one realized this more in later life than Patmore himself, who was inclined to blame the failure on the Tennysonian influence, which had made the work, in the words of Ruskin, "one of the most blessedly popular poems" in the language. The poem, indeed, was cursed with the wrong sort of popularity; over half a million copies were sold, but principally to the curates and the old maids who were intrigued with the story and the more obvious aphorisms, but missed the philosophy. The cathedral close, the white-haired dean, a stolen glove, tea, and all the conventional accessories of a Victorian afternoon, which Patmore had intended to serve as a vehicle for what he considered a really audacious philosophy of marriage, caused many to see in the book a rather charming celebration of nineteenth-century respectability, and in the author "a kind of sportive lambkin with his tail tied in bows of blue ribband." Even the modern reader of this narrative of the love of Honoria and Vaughan must be warned that there is something more substantial than this in the tale if he is to be kept from classing it with the novels of Anthony Trollope and Miss Yonge.

It is only the modern reader, however, who can fully appreciate the fact that the epic contains high seriousness and a doctrine on marriage that is at once daring and original. We see in our own day the degradation of marriage as a sacrament. The same condition, contrary to the popular misconception, existed in the heart of the Victorian era. All we have done has been to remove the veil of respectability that hid the same inner corruption. For the age of Queen Victoria was not one in which the idea of marriage and the family was at its highest. On the contrary, as Mr. Chesterton has acutely observed, it was one at which domesticity was at its lowest. The Victorians had lost the sense of the sacredness of home — they believed in the respectability of home but had no reverence for it.

Although it was not Patmore's purpose to restore that reverence (he was merely writing out what to him was a sublime inspiration) the general effect of the poem, had its message been grasped, would have been just this. He proposes marriage, not as a *remedium amoris,* a compromise with man's frailty which works hardships on both parties but which is necessary for law and order and the comity of the state, but as an institution deeply rooted in the nature of man, the consecration of the highest human virtue and the prelude and necessary requirement for the perfect love of God, which is the supreme end of man on earth. Says Vaughan of Honoria,

> *I loved her in the name of God,*
> *And for the ray she was of Him.*

The mystical analogy between the love of man and wife and the love of Christ for the soul, *sponsa Dei,* which he developed later on, was at this time somewhat vague in his mind. Still, we may say that *The Angel in the House* and its sequel, *The Victories of Love,* contain the substance of the Church's ordinary doctrine on the sacrament of marriage. Both poems may be read and enjoyed as simple and interesting stories. They may also be read as a collection of profound meditations on the philosophy of love which recall at times the *Divina Commedia.* He is able to pass from touching portraits of the reverence that must exist between man and wife to passages of lyric beauty in which he sings the praise of the very things in the institution of marriage from which most of its difficulties arise — the restrictions it imposes, its bonds,

> *Nay, the infinite of man is found*
> *But in the beating of its bonds. . . .*

III

The death of Emily Patmore in 1862 brings to a close the first period in Patmore's poetic career. To him it must have seemed also the end of his career as a poet. She was his "angel" and inspiration. He found himself alone and abandoned, the incompetent father of six children. But yet another romance was waiting for this "consecrated laureate of wedded love."

Two years after his wife's death we find him on the way to Rome with his friend Aubrey de Vere. For several years he had been thinking seriously of entering the Church. Emily had seen the tendency and opposed it bitterly. On her deathbed she had said, "When I am gone they [the Catholics] will get you; and then I shall see you no more." What he saw of Catholicism in the Eternal City brought his meditations to a practical turn. But, while still in a state of indecision, he met and fell violently in love with an English convert, Miss Marianne Byles. Patmore had been led to believe that she was the impecunious traveling companion of a very rich lady. He proposed, was accepted, and then discovered that she, herself, was the wealthy lady. He fled in haste from Rome, but was overtaken by his friends who persuaded him to return. They were married by Manning in England the same year.

Marianne Byles may be said to have been the inspiration of his mystical odes just as Emily had been of his *Angel in the House.* The couple took up residence in an old estate in Sussex, which Patmore converted into a famous beauty spot. He had leisure, and he gave much of it to the study of the classical documents of mystical theology, those of St. Bernard, St. John of the Cross, St. Theresa, and St. Thomas Aquinas. Patmore now enters the second and greatest stage of his poetic career. Not that his subject changed. It was still the same — love. That is why he always insisted on the essential oneness of his inspiration. It was his manner of writing that was altered. He no longer wrote for the old maids and curates. He became mystical and difficult. His doctrine was deepening, for he had caught glimpses of great and awful truths. This was to be the period of his greatest triumph as an artist.

The simple, almost banal, narrative measure of his earlier work, he abandoned for the ode, but a curious and difficult form of the ode, the essential features of which some critics have traced to the Canzonieri of Petrarch, but which Patmore thought was an original discovery. "I have hit upon the finest metre that ever was invented, and the finest mine of wholly unworked material that ever fell to the lot of an English poet," he declared while preparing *The Unknown Eros*. The "mine" was Catholic mystical theology, especially the idea, so dear to the mystics, of setting forth the intimate union of the soul of the individual with Christ in the language of the most exalted type of earthly union — the soul as the spouse of Christ. But how express the secrets of the saints to the crowd? "How teach them what love meant, and what the Word Made Flesh implied." He saw, as the one great reality of life, the love of God, to which all other loves are tributary. He saw that this idea had fled from England,

> *O, season strange for song!*
> *And yet some timely power persuades my lips.*
> *Is't England's parting soul that nerves my tongue . . .?*

So he would,

> *Notes few and strong and fine*
> *Gilt with sweet day's decline*
> *And sad with promise of a different sun.*

He had early seen how, in the Incarnation, the Word had, by becoming Man, translated and brought closer to us the great and infinite love of God. He became weak that He might lift our weakness, He took flesh as a concession to our fleshiness. There was a lesson to the artist in this economy of the Incarnation, and especially to the artist who perceived that the highest mission of the poet was to speak in man's language of the love which dwelt in inaccessible heights. Patmore would, it seems, interpret this exalted love to England by a close and daring analogy between the love of God and another love his generation seemed so thoroughly to understand. The mystics had used this analogy — so would he. The technique we may see clearly stated in one of his best-known odes, *Prophets Who Cannot Sing.*

> *The holders of the Truth in Verity*
> *Are people of a harsh and stammering tongue!*

Earthly love and nature, which are but partial reflections of God's love, both have their great singers, but

> *Views of the unveiled heavens alone bring forth*
> *Prophets who cannot sing.*

*   *   *

> *At least from David until Dante none*
> *And none since him.*

Hear wherein they fail —

They think they somewhere should [sing] and so they try,
But (haply 'tis they screw the pitch too high)
'Tis still their fates
To warble tunes that nails might draw from slates,
Poor Seraphim!

He will learn wisdom from the "foes," the amorous secular and nature poets,

> *Therefore no longer let us stretch our throats*
> *With straining after notes*
> *Which but to touch would burst an organ pipe.*
> *Far better be dumb dogs.*

The somewhat voluptuous character of a few of the Psyche odes of the *Unknown Eros* were the occasions of scandal to some of his Catholic brethren, who thought the analogy between human love and divine love rather too vivid to be entirely effective. Aubrey de Vere was frank enough to urge the suppression of these particular odes, and Newman never became reconciled to "mixing up amorousness with religion." Some of his own dissatisfaction with the fruits of his experiment may be seen in the lyric, *Dead Language*:

> *Thou dost not wisely, Bard.*
> *A double voice is Truth's to use at will:*
> *One, with scorn of good for ill,*
> *Smiting the brutish ear with doctrine hard. . . .*
> *The other tender-soft as seem*
> *The embraces of a dead love in a dream.*
> *These thoughts which you have sung*
> *In the vernacular*
> *Should be as others of the Church's are,*
> *Decently clothed in the Imperial tongue.*
> *Have you no fears*
> *Lest, as Lord Jesus bids your sort to dread,*
> *Yon acorn-munchers rend you limb from limb,*
> *You with heaven's liberty affronting theirs!*
> *So spoke my monitor; but I to him,*
> *Alas, and is not mine a language dead?*

So it would seem. In 1868 he printed nine of these odes privately and sent them off to his literary friends, anonymously.

There was not a ripple of interest or reaction of any sort. He recalled the issue and threw it in the fire.

In 1875 he sold his seat in Sussex and removed to Hastings by the sea. The frigid reception of what he considered his greatest work when compared with the popularity of the *Angel in the House* was bitter to him and all but froze him into complete and morose silence.

> *Here in this little Bay,*
> *Full of tumultuous life and great repose,*
> *Where, twice a day,*
> *The purposeless, glad ocean comes and goes,*
> *Under high cliffs, and far from the huge town,*
> *I sit me down.*
> *For want of me the world's course will not fail:*
> *When all its work is done, the lie will rot;*
> *The truth is great, and shall prevail,*
> *When none cares whether it prevail or not.*

He was now fifty-four years old, an age when poetic inspiration is on the wane, if not in most cases entirely extinct. But it was at this time that Patmore experienced a complete renewal of enthusiasm. "He walked," says Gosse, "along the sea by Hastings or over the gorse-clad downs, muttering as a young man mutters, with joy up-lifting his pulses and song bursting from his lips."

It came about in this way. He reminds us, in his autobiography, that he had never been in entire sympathy with the mind of the Church in her insistence on devotion to the Mother of God. There was, he felt, something perfunctory in his own devotion to her. So he resolved to do a thing which, when we consider his haughty and aristocratic nature which frequently made him a most unlovely person, must have been hard and humbling in the extreme. He resolved to make a plebeian pilgrimage to the grotto at Lourdes. "On the fourteenth of October I knelt at the shrine by the River Gave and arose without any emotion or enthusiasm or unusual sense of devotion, but with a tranquil sense that the prayers of thirty-five years had been granted." He paid two subsequent visits in thanksgiving "for the gift which was then received and which has never since for a single hour been withdrawn."

The gift of renewed inspiration was accompanied by the vision of Mary as the essential type of womanhood "the symbol and prototype of humanity, nature, the body." He recognized that it was of her he had unknowingly sung "when clear my songs of lady's grace rang." The immediate fruit of the pilgrimage was the splendid ode, *The Child's Purchase,* in which he dedicates his artistic gifts to Mary and asks in lines of crystalline beauty her help and inspiration in his future work. It has the deep sincerity of a prayer, which of course it is, and stands as one of the finest Marian poems in the English language.

The thirty-one odes of the *Unknown Eros* were rapidly revised and published. They were not well received. They were for the future. "I have respected posterity," Patmore wrote in the front of the collected edition of his poems, "and, should there be a posterity which cares for letters, I dare to hope it will respect me."

In 1884, feeling that he had written all that he could give to poetry, he devoted himself exclusively to prose. Mr. Herbert Read complains that justice is not often done to Patmore's prose. He compares *The Rod, the Root, and the Flower* with Pascal's *Pensee* and declares that "no poet since Wordsworth and Coleridge, not even Matthew Arnold, has such a clear conception of the poet's function" as that displayed in the *"Religio Poetae."* Patmore, indeed, has not yet received his full recognition as a prose stylist. The content of this work, however, is of far greater potentiality. He has laid the deep foundation of modern Catholic aesthetic, and when the authoritative book on this subject comes to be written it will draw heavily on this prose contribution.

IV

Death came in November, 1896. The priest who was reading the prayers for the dying, being overcome with the emotion of the occasion and unable to continue, Patmore took the book and read the Latin himself. "Then lighting an imaginary cigarette," records Derek Patmore, "he spoke his last words, 'I love my God best.'" He was buried, like Dante, in the rough habit of the Franciscans in the Lymington Churchyard.

There is, indeed, something Dantesque about him, especially in his central theme, love, human and divine. Then, too, there is his love for the thought of St. Thomas which he said was "a huge reservoir of the sincere milk of the Word," and the result of studying the *Summa* seriously was that, in his own mind poetry began to grow "like the moonrise when the disk is still below the horizon."

The one important thing he attempted was the elevation of dogma to song. The Incarnation, especially as viewed through Mary, was to be the great and prolific font of poetry. "The Incarnation," he said, "is still only a dogma. It has never got beyond mere thoughts. Perhaps it will take thousands of years to work itself into the feelings, as it must do, before religion can become a matter of poetry." He viewed it as an almost impossible work amid the unbelief of his Victorian surroundings. "But impossibilities," as his friend de Vere once remarked, "will never get done if no one attempted them, and the attempt usually brings a good reward, be the failure ever so great."

Theodore Maynard has called Patmore the most considerable Catholic poet since Dante. He stands to our age much in the same position as Dante stood to his. He has not only pointed out the way for the regeneration of poetry, but has taken us a considerable distance along the road of achievement. He has dug again "the wells which the Philistines have filled" that we may drink the waters Chaucer drank.

"Wherever a critic of faithful conscience," remarks Mr. Read, "recalls the poets of this period — Tennyson, Arnold, Clough, Patmore, Browning, Rossetti — it is on the name of Patmore that he lingers with a still lively sense of wonder. The rest have been fully estimated, and their influence, if not exhausted, is predictable. Patmore is still potential. . . ."

4

Gerard Manley Hopkins

I

The lesson learnt by Patmore at Lourdes was picked up by another founder of the Revival at Oxford. The spirit of Newman still hung like a shield upon the gray walls when he was a student there in the sixties. And Newman had preached this doctrine; it is a fundamental one in the modern renovation of the arts. *Purify the source.* Jacques Maritain has thus expressed it. The renewal of the arts must begin with the artist himself. "If you want to produce a Christian work, be a Christian . . . do not adopt a Christian pose. . . . A Christian work would have the artist, as artist, free . . . as man, a saint."

Gerard Manley Hopkins put this doctrine into practice in a way more radical than any of the early revivalists, and so was the renovation of his art the most complete and revolutionary. He was born the year before Newman entered the Church and died as the nineties were in the offing. His work epitomizes and crowns the best efforts of the first phase of the Revival, and at the same time marks its transition to the modern period.

When, in 1868 he left Oxford and entered the Society of Jesus, the attitude of his friends who knew his ability and promise is perhaps best expressed in the statement made by Wordsworth when he heard that Frederick Faber, who had won the Newdigate prize at Oxford, intended to take orders: "I do not say that you are wrong, but England loses a poet."

"Poetry," the prophet of Rydal told Aubrey de Vere when they were discussing together Faber's action, "requires the whole man." Time, however, was to show that what poetry required more than "the whole man" was that the man be whole, that he be a complete and integral man, indeed that he be a superman — one of those men who, in the words of Gregory the Great, *Quia qui divini sapiunt videlicet supra-homines sunt.*

Hopkins, on retiring from the world, consigned his early poems to the fire. He decided to write no more. He would choose silence and the complete immolation of all the senses. He so expressed his intention in "The Habit of Perfection," written the year of his reception into the Church.

> *Elected Silence, sing to me*
> *And beat upon my whorlèd ear.*
> *Pipe me to pastures still and be*
> *The music that I care to hear.*
>
> *Shape nothing lips, be lovely dumb:*
> *It is the shut, the curfew sent*
> *From there where all surrenders come*
> *Which only makes you eloquent.*

* * *

> *Palate, the hutch of tasty lust,*
> *Desire not to be rinsed with wine;*
> *The can must be so sweet, the crust*
> *So fresh that comes in facts divine*

* * *

> *O feel-of-primrose hands, O feet*
> *That want the yield of plushy sward,*
> *But you shall walk the golden street,*
> *And you unhouse and house the Lord.*

Among the faculties which Hopkins does not list in this litany of renunciations was his will. But he gave it up none the less. And those to whom he had yielded it, his superiors, decided, sometime after his entrance into the Society of Jesus, that he ought to write and requested him to do so. He did, and in lines of such inspiration and newness that one cannot read them without thanks to the spirit that caused him to make so complete a renunciation. Their divergence from the then-prevailing fashion in Romantic poetry was so abrupt and startling that they were known only to the few and in fragments, and unappreciated fully even by these. Robert Bridges, his literary executor, feeling that they were too advanced for the taste of his generation, withheld them until after the World War. The lines he wrote in dedication are charged with misgivings.

> *Our generation already is overpast*
> *And thy lov'd legacy, Gerard, hath lain*
> *Coy in my home; as once thy heart was fain*
> *Of shelter, when God's terror held thee fast. . . .*
>
> *Yet love of Christ will win man's love at last.*
> *Hell wars without: but, dear, the while my hands*
> *Gathered thy book, I heard, this winter day,*
> *Thy spirit thank me in his young delight*
> *Stepping again upon the yellow sands.*
> *Go forth! amidst our chaffinch flock display*
> *Thy plumage of far wonder and heavenward flight.*

Comprehensible as these misgivings are in one of the late Poet Laureate's background, they proved to be without foundation. The "chaffinch flock," as he called the exponents of modern poetry, hailed them with delight, as belonging essentially to the new era, and as capable of giving intelligent direction to the search for a new technique and the effort to work out a new inspiration to take the place of the old. Modern poetry took Hopkins to herself. Mr. Herbert Read has recently said that "when the history of the last decade of English poetry comes to be written by a dispassionate critic, no influence will rank in importance with that of Gerard Manley Hopkins."

Those who are out of sympathy with what is called the "New Poetry" are, as a rule, dissatisfied with Hopkins' experiments in diction and meter. They wish he had been a bit more conventional. But to those who see in the modern complex an undoubted element of newness, who realize that an old artistic generation has died and another is in labor until a new man be brought forth, Hopkins is at once a portent and a sign. Many atrocities have been committed in the name of modern poetry. One is willing to put up with most of them provided he can convince himself that the eccentricities and incoherences arise from a yet unperfected attempt to express a new vision in a new way. It would, of course, be too wide a generalization to say that most of the eccentricity of modern verse is mere eccentricity, and is a vagueness that arises from an interior nothingness-to-say. James Stephens, however, has recently made such a statement. He believes (and he is not alone among modern poets in the opinion) that innovation in the mere mechanics of verse have not given us a new poetry, and that there will be no new poetry until a new inspiration appears, a new reality to take the place of that which served the Victorians but which has no validity for us.

There are difficulties in Hopkins. But the major ones, I think, arise from the fact that he has too much to say, rather than from his saying it in an unconventional manner. He has seen a vision so ineffably full and new that the traditional machinery of expression seems incapable of carrying it and he needs must invent a new one. With him the vision came first and the technique later. So while he is acclaimed as one of our greatest technical inventors by those whose principal interest is in the new machinery, he is of far greater importance to those who are in search of what is to them more vital — the new inspiration to justify the use of the new technique. We may mention among the latter Mr. T. S. Eliot, who studied Hopkins in preparation for his ode of regeneration, *Ash Wednesday.*

II

Ominous symptoms that he might develop into the conventional type of romantic genius of which the world is so weary, were manifested by Hopkins in early and later youth. The eldest son of the British Consul General of the Hawaiian Islands, he was born at Stratford in Essex. Precocity, that sickness of youth, set him apart from the crowd and exhibited him as one proficient in art and music beyond his years. At the Hampstead school to which he was first sent, and later at Highgate, we see him a frail lad, taking no part in football or cricket. His time was spent "dreaming and reading and chewing the cud of his gleanings from the world harvest of poetry, a fairy child in the midst of a commonplace, workaday world," says his biographer, G. F. Lahey, S.J. One of his juvenile poems, "Spring and Death," begins with lines heavy with the sort of adolescent melancholy we find in Keats and others whom a temperamental isolation from the world has made prematurely sad and introspective;

> *It was an evening in the Spring*
> *— A little sickness in the air*
> *From too much fragrance everywhere.*

He was not wanting in courage of a somewhat eccentric type, which spoke of a nature inherently rebellious. He was a fearless tree climber. Once he went without drinking for a week because he noticed his school fellows usually drank too much; and he fainted at drill. Salt was his next subject of abstinence, and for the same reason. He was extremely sensitive too, and had a highly developed faculty for observing and noting down changes, the most minute, in the world of nature. The faculty was not scientific but aesthetic. He had that gift of all the great lyric poets of the Romantic Movement, a supersensitivity amounting almost to hyperaesthesia. He was strongly religious; intellect, keen and penetrating. He won an exhibition for Balliol College and went up for the Christmas term, 1863.

Oxford was to determine the issue of these characteristics as it had in the case of Shelley. Hopkins underwent, through contact with undergraduates and teachers, the several streams of thought which reflected rather accurately the intellectual make-up of the England of his day. In Jowett, under whom he read Greek, he met with the powerful rationalistic current which was at work liberalizing religion through Kantian philosophy and German higher criticism. Jowett was impressed by the young man's proficiency in Greek, referred to him as the "star of Balliol" and one of the first scholars at the college. And Gerard must not have been unaffected by this. Another potent influence at whose feet he sat was Walter Pater. Gerard's fine Hellenic taste, his knowledge and love of the sacred word made him a fit subject for Pater's charming erudition and an apt disciple who might carry on the doctrine that sought to make of art a super-religion.

Finally, there was the remnant of the Oxford Movement, that splendid protest of exquisite scholars and artists against these liberalizing tendencies in an effort to save both art and scholarship by saving religion. Thirty years had altered many of its fortunes and hopes. Its leader, Newman, had gone, but Pusey was still there as were also James Riddell and Henry Parry Liddon.

William Addis, who with Robert Bridges was among the more intimate companions of Hopkins at this critical period, reports that Gerard was at first "a little tinged with the liberalism prevalent among reading men." There appears to have been a short period of indecision in which he might have thrown his talents into any one of these several currents. But it was a very short period. For in August, 1866, we find him writing to Newman, telling of his attraction for Catholicism and asking for an interview. He had already decided upon the step, but he was not received until the following October by Newman at Birmingham. His parents objected strenuously; Liddon, his confessor, tried desperately to prevent the act; and Pusey after it, refused to see him. He took his degree, nevertheless, in the Spring of 1867, spent the summer abroad, and then accepted a position as tutor in Newman's Oratory School.

Biographical data which might show the process of thought that led him to become a religious is wanting. We merely know that he had been thinking along these lines. His friend Addis, who later apostatized, had joined the Oratorians. His own decision was made in May, 1868. Newman wrote congratulating him: "Don't call the Jesuit discipline hard; it will bring you to heaven." He again spent the summer abroad and in the following September entered the Novitiate at Roehampton. From the first he made a complete oblation of himself, burning his poems and renouncing poetry.

How shall we explain this? We have seen three dominant loves at work in Hopkins, the undergraduate: a love for art which might have caused him to give himself to Pater's program, a love of scholarship which drew him mightily to the humanism of Jowett, and a love of religion. Did he believe it impossible to fuse all these into a synthesis? I think he did. But it was not his belief that art and scholarship had no place in the Church. He rather saw that nineteenth-century art and scholarship had no place in the Church; that the art of Pater drew one away from true religion, and the humanism of Jowett meant the apotheosis of mere man. The centuries had secularized both beyond redemption, except through that redemption that might come by a complete consecration to the principle from which European art and scholarship had originally sprung, namely sanctity — the sanctity of Augustine, of Jerome, of Boëthius, of Bonaventure, of Aquinas, and those who laid the deep foundation of Christian culture.

Whether or not Hopkins actually went through this reasoning process, we have no way of knowing. We only know the fact of his deliberate abandonment of the nineteenth-century world, his complete dedication of himself to truths rejected by this world, and his emergence some years later as a new poet, with a new diction, a new prosody, and a new inspiration. Literary history has few instances of so complete an alteration in style to record. One has only to compare one of his early poems, "The Habit of Perfection," say, with "The Wreck of the Deutschland" to see the amazing character of the changes in his own verse. Its divergence from the prevailing mannerisms of his times is still more striking. English Romantic verse was then experiencing a kind of renovation through the work of the pre-Raphaelites, a renovation which in the general collapse of ideas was obliged to restrict itself almost entirely to the business of polishing up what was old. The renovation effected by Hopkins was a deeper thing than that, which probably explains why even today after the lapse of a half century his poetry impresses us as something entirely new. One finds none of the *clichés* of Romanticism in his verse; there is a stimulating absence of the banal and the commonplace; he seems summarily to have rejected the poetic language of his day and to have invented a new one.

Much of the tantalizing newness of his diction, as well as its not-infrequent eccentricity, no doubt must be attributed to something Hopkins always had, a nature, namely, that took delight in "all things counter, original, spare, strange. . . ." As he says in one of his best sonnets, "Pied Beauty":

> *Glory be to God for dappled things—*
> *For skies of couple-color as a brinded cow;*
> *For rose-moles all in stipple upon trout that swim;*
> *Fresh-firecoal chestnut-falls; finches' wings;*
> *Landscape plotted and pieced—fold, fallow, and plough*
> *And all trades, their gear and tackle and trim.*

All things counter, original, spare, strange;
  Whatever is fickle, freckled (who knows how)
  With swift, slow; sweet, sour; adazzle, dim;
He fathers-forth whose beauty is past change;
                  Praise him.

But more important still in explaining the strangeness, the
surprise of Hopkins' dictional effects must be the fresh vision
he had obtained of the "uncreated light." His knowledge of
the supernatural extended beyond the intellectual definition of
dogma to something very close to that experimental knowledge
of the mystics, which even M. Henri Bergson now holds up to
the modern world as the door to all reality. His new diction
sprang spontaneously from a new grasp of the real.

"Gerard Hopkins was the only orthodox, and as far as I could
see, saintly man in whom religion had absolutely no narrowing
effect upon his general opinions and sympathies," remarked
Patmore of his friend in a letter to Robert Bridges. He had first
met Hopkins in 1883 during a visit to Stonyhurst College. His
respect for Hopkins' judgment as a critic was very high. The
story of how he burned the manuscript of his *Sponsa Dei* be-
cause of a misinterpreted remark passed on it by the priest is
well known. Yet he could never bring himself wholly to sym-
pathize with the latter's new prosody. To him it was as "hard
as the darkest parts of Browning." And he insisted that "to the
already sufficiently arduous character of such poetry you seem
to me to have added the difficulty of following *several* entirely
novel and simultaneous experiments in versification and con-
struction — any one of which novelties would be startling and
productive of distraction from the poetic matter to be ex-
pressed. . . ." While he later altered this opinion somewhat,
the chief objections remained. They survive today among those
who think that Hopkins would have been a better poet had he
dropped his new technique. Yet it is this same technique which

has caused others to place him among the first poets in the English language. There is some danger that he will become known today only as a great technical inventor.

This would be unfortunate. It is true that his prosody is inseparable from his poetry, that if one does not sympathize with it and understand it, one does not get at the essential Hopkins. Lahey rightly contends that a "preliminary ascesis," a sort of "ascetic aestheticism" is necessary to appreciate his poetry. There are difficulties, but after they have been overcome "what before seemed masses of impractical quartz may now become a jewel-case marvelously wrought and lovely to behold, a monstrance, as it were, for a Living Flame."

There is more than just a new technique in his verse; there are ideas. A criticism he himself advanced about some odes of Patmore's son may be applied to his — "they are strong where the age is weak — I mean Swinburne and the popular poets, and I may say, Tennyson himself — in thought and insight...."

III

In 1884 Hopkins was sent to Dublin to take the chair of Greek in the Royal University of Ireland. A general misunderstanding about this period in his life has recently been cleared up by Dom Wulstan Phillipson. It is not inaccurate to say that Hopkins' entire life in the Society of Jesus has been subject to the same misunderstanding. It is usually represented as one of dark and painful self-torture. Newman's remark, "you are leading a most self-denying life," is usually quoted as a fitting summary of it, or the following passage from Bridge's *Testament of Beauty:*

> *When the young poet my companion in study*
> *And friend of my heart refused a peach at my hands,*
> *he being then a housecarl in Loyola's menie*
> *'twas that he feared the savor of it, and when he waived*
> *his scruple to my banter, 'twas to avoid offense.*

Hopkins did take the religious life quite seriously but not without a certain grace. The story is told that once while passing through a village during a walk some miles from Dublin he called upon a curate friend of his, a Reverend Mr. Wade, who asked him in to dine. Hopkins refused, saying he had no permission. Father Wade expressed the willingness to take the responsibility on himself. "That is all very well," replied Hopkins, "you may be Wade but I should be found wanting."

We know from notes taken while in his course of studies that he at times indulged that gift of sensitive observation of nature we have previously mentioned, putting down comments on what he used to call the "inscape" and "instress" of objects from clouds and flowers and waves to the Castle-Rock at Edinburgh. We know also that he sometimes mortified himself in this direction. Thus an entry of 1869 says: "A penance which I was doing from January twenty-fifth to July twenty-fifth prevented my seeing much that half-year."

All this might seem hard and inhuman and prejudicial to the production of poetry. Still it must be admitted that his gifts of observation were not decreased but rather sharpened by this asceticism. The joy, too, he experienced in the wild and uncultivated landscape so dear to the early Romantic revivalists increased:

> *What would the world be, once bereft*
> *Of wet and of wildness? Let them be left,*
> *O, let them be left, wildness and wet:*
> *Long live the weeds and the wilderness yet!*

One feels that a little asceticism of this kind might have preserved the nature worship of the Romantics from turning sour. His own asceticism gave him and us the blessed technique for the poetic rediscovery of this nature which the modern world has largely lost. We find it in the sonnet *God's Grandeur:*

The world is charged with the grandeur of God.
It will flame out, like shining from shook foil;

It gathers to a greatness, like the ooze of oil
Crushed. Why do men then now not reck his rod?
Generations have trod, have trod, have trod;
*   And all is seared with trade; bleared, smeared with toil;*
*   And wears man's smudge and shares man's smell; the soil*
Is bare now, nor can foot feel, being shod.

And for all this nature is never spent;
*   There lives the dearest freshness deep down things;*
And though the last lights off the black West went
*   Oh, morning, at the brown brink eastward, springs —*
Because the Holy Ghost over the bent
*   World broods with warm breast and with ah! bright wings.*

From accounts given to us by Father Hopkins' contemporaries of his life in the Society of Jesus, we find little justification for the theory that he suffered much from isolation and loneliness. He took an active and interested part in various community celebrations, sometimes setting his lyrics to music and playing them. He found the companionship neither monotonous or intellectually beneath him. This is particularly true of his residence in Dublin where, says Dom Phillipson, he lived with men who might have been found among the dons of any of the Oxford or Cambridge colleges. The dean of studies, Father Joseph Darlington, had been his fellow undergraduate at Oxford, had had Walter Pater for his tutor, and like Hopkins was a convert. There was the Rector, Monsignor Malloy who was continuing Newman's ideals of making an Irish Oxford in Dublin, and associated with him Casey, Ormsby, Stewart, and Thomas Arnold, son of Arnold of Rugby. His teaching schedule was not particularly heavy (Greek to a class of five or six three times a week); Jowett's testimony to his proficiency in this branch makes it seem unlikely that he could have found the work trying or that it would contribute to the alleged "cru-

cifixion of spirit." Nor was he particularly interested in or an-
noyed by the political situation.

Yet he did suffer. His were spiritual sufferings, periods of
dryness and aridity which the mystics speak of — "the dark
night of the soul." He had chosen suffering. And it is well that
he had, for he was of that type of genius which must be torn
by the thorn of life. He gave to the world a wholesome example
of one who was neither rebellious nor neurotically defiant in
the face of what must be. Thus he was saved from the moral
failure of Keats and Shelley and Byron and a hundred other
romantic geniuses whose failure was one of will.

Not, I'll not carrion comfort, Despair, nor feast on thee;
Not untwist — slack they may be — these last strands of man
In me, or most weary, cry I can no more, I can.

In his sonnet "The Windhover" ("the best thing I ever
wrote") we catch a glimpse not only of the beauty, the fruit-
fulness, the effort expended in this task of mastering himself,
but also of the deep, divine source of his energy. It is dedicated
"to Christ Our Lord."

I caught this morning morning's minion, king-
*   dom of daylight's dauphin, dapple-dawn-drawn Falcon,*
*   in his riding*
Of the rolling level underneath him steady air, and striding
High there, how he rung upon the rein of a wimpling wing
In his ecstasy! then off, off forth on swing,
*   As a skate's heel sweeps smooth on a bow-bend: the hurl and*
*   gliding*
*   Rebuffed the big wind. My heart in hiding*
Stirred for a bird, — the achieve of, the mastery of the thing!

Brute beauty and valor and act, oh, air, pride, plume, here
*   Buckle! and the fire that breaks from thee then, a billion*

Times told lovelier, more dangerous, O my chevalier!
  No wonder of it: sheer plod makes plough down sillion
Shine, and blue-bleak embers, ah, my dear
  Fall, gall themselves, and gash gold vermillion.

Hopkins died in 1889. The last words he was heard to utter
were, "I am so happy, I am so happy."

"Christianity does not make art *easy*," says Jacques Maritain.
"It deprives it of many facile means, it stops its progress in
many directions, but in order to raise its level. In the very crea-
tion of these salutary difficulties, it elevates art from within,
brings to its knowledge a hidden beauty more delightful than
light, gives it what the artist needs most, simplicity, the peace
of reverent fear and love, such innocence as makes matter docile
to men and fraternal."

BIBLIOGRAPHY

DE VERE, AUBREY (1814–1902)
  Brégy, Katherine, *Poet's Chantry* (St. Louis: Herder), p. 52.
  Ward, Wilfrid, *Aubrey deVere: a memoir* (New York: Longmans,
    1904).
  Woodberry, George, *Studies of Literature* (New York: Harcourt,
    1921), pp. 159–180.
  WORKS
  Innisfail, Miscellaneous and Early Poems (London: Macmillan, 1897).
  Legends and Records of the Church and the Empire (London: Burns,
    Oates, 1898).
  Legends of St. Patrick (London: Kegan Paul, 1884).
  May Carols and Legends of Saxon Saints (London: Burns, Oates,
    1907).
  Medieval Records and Sonnets (London: Macmillan, 1893).
  Woodberry, George, *Selected Poems of Aubrey de Vere* (New York:
    Macmillan, 1894).
HAWKER, ROBERT STEPHEN
  More, P. E., *Shelburne Essays* (Fourth Series), "The Vicar of Mor-
    wenstow," pp. 1–34.
  Ave Maria, January 4, 1930.
  Byles, C. E., *Life and Letters of R. S. Hawker* (London: Lane, 1905).

WORKS

Cornish Ballads and Other Poems (London: John Lane, 1905).

Poetical Works of R. S. Hawker (London: Kegan Paul, 1879).

PATMORE, COVENTRY (1823–1896)

Read, Herbert, "Coventry Patmore," in *The Great Victorians,* H. J. and Hugh Massingham, editors (New York: Doubleday, 1932).

Brégy, Katherine, *Poet's Chantry,* pp. 89–119.

Burdett, Osbert, *The Idea of Coventry Patmore* (New York: Oxford Press, 1921).

Gosse, Edmund, *Coventry Patmore* (New York: Scribners, 1905).

Page, Frederick, *Patmore: A Study in Poetry* (New York: Oxford U. Press, 1933).

WORKS

Champneys, Basil, *Poems by Coventry Patmore* (complete edition), (London: Bell, 1906).

Courage in Politics and Other Essays (New York: Oxford Press. 1921).

Patmore, Derek, *Selected Poems of Coventry Patmore,* with introduction (London: Chatto & Windus, 1931).

Principle in Art and Other Essays (London: Bell, 1912).

"Religio Poetae" (London: Duckworth, 1893).

The Rod, the Root and the Flower (London: Bell).

HOPKINS, GERARD MANLEY, S.J.

Downside Review, April, 1933, p. 326.

Lahey, G. F., S.J., *Gerard Manley Hopkins* (New York: Oxford Press, 1930).

Phare, Elsie E., *The Poetry of Gerard M. Hopkins* (New York: Cambridge University Press, 1934).

Read, Herbert, *Form in Modern Poetry* (London: Sheed & Ward), pp. 44–55.

WORKS

Poems of Gerard Manley Hopkins, edited by Robert Bridges (New York: Oxford Press, 1930).

Letters of Gerard Manley Hopkins, edited by C. Collier Abbott, 2 volumes (New York, Oxford Press, 1935).

The
Middle
Phase

In England the artists who represented the renaissance of the nineties were either Catholics like Francis Thompson and Henry Harland or prospective converts to Rome like Oscar Wilde, Aubrey Beardsley, Lionel Johnson, and Ernest Dowson. If Catholicism did not claim them some other form of mysticism did, and W. B. Yeats and George Russell(Æ) became Theosophists. The one who persistently hardened himself against the mystical influences of the period, John Davidson, committed suicide.

— HOLBROOK JACKSON

1

Fin De Siècle
Wilde, Beardsley, Dowson

Newman died in 1890. In a letter written shortly before his death he spoke of a vision that had ever been before him of a rising tide of infidelity and irreligion which would come on "until only the tops of the mountains would be seen like islands in the waste of waters." He had seen in the growing power of Liberalism the menace of a deluge; but he was not to witness either the Waste Land it would produce, or in what wise his work in the Catholic Church would stand against it.

The nineteenth century closed with a decade shot through with all the pathology of decadence. It was an amazing ten years, or rather five years, for most of the disquieting symptoms were packed into the first half of the decade. By 1895 most of the flaming personalities had burnt out, much of the excitement had subsided, and the new heresies were beginning to lose their shocking-power, for they were already hardening into conventions. The agony of transition was over, and the new age with its promise of a Brave New World was at hand.

The 1890's have assumed in our day many of the misty garments of fable. The history of the period has been recorded in a number of delightful volumes by matured and mellowed men who write, as only late middle age can, of a vivid and glamorous youth. "Its memory will never die," declares Holbrook Jackson in his book on the period: and George Bernard Shaw when he read the volume asked, "Did all these things happen, or did you invent them?"

They really happened, most of them at least. But not perhaps with all the romantic trimmings that Jackson, George Wyndham, Richard Le Gallienne, Osbert Burdett, and others have worked into the narrative. Maurice Baring, who was an undergraduate at Cambridge at the time and came in contact with Beardsley, Wilde, and the other personalities of the period, is an example of one who formed a different impression of the times. "When people write about the nineties now, which they often do," he says in his *Puppet Show of Memory,* "they seem to me to weave a baseless legend and to create a fantastic world of their own creation. The 'nineties were, from the point of view of art and literature, much like any other period."

This is a minority opinion and may be accepted for what it is worth. The period *was* an important one, not only in the history of the Catholic Revival, which is why we treat it here, but in the general history of contemporary culture. It was the hectic sunrise of modern times as well as the conclusive evening of the nineteenth century. *Fin de siècle* marked not only the end of the century but the end of a culture, and at the same time the beginning of what looked a new one. Something more than just the sense of tedium, manifesting itself in the general throwing off of restraint, which has marked the close of other centuries, was present here. There is no more reason, as Mr. Chesterton remarks, for being sad and riotous toward the end of a hundred years than toward the end of five hundred fortnights. This was "no mathematical autumn but a spiritual one."

The supports upon which centuries of civilization rested seemed to go down in those days, leaving at once a widespread sense of disaster and a feverish rush to build anew. What actually collapsed was the last of those compromises by which the English Church and the conservative middle class over several centuries had striven to preserve what they might of Christianity and the European tradition by entering into a loose alliance with the destructive forces which Newman designated under the name of liberalism. The last of these compromises — the Victorian — had endured longer and with more of the exterior signs of permanence than its essential hollowness justified. The resultant commercial prosperity was responsible for this; at the same time this prosperity obscured the important thing that was happening — the destruction by the apostles of evolution of the last of those reasons why men should continue to believe in the value of a formal religion and a conventional morality. And so was the awakening the more appalling.

"I wish it were *fin du globe,*" sighed Oscar Wilde's *Dorian Gray.* "Life is a great disappointment." There was a certain spiritual weariness abroad coupled with apocalyptic forebodings of the end of all good things. It was a Nietzschean spirit and is expressed in the spondaic lines of Max Nordau where he speaks of "vague qualms of the Dusk of the Nations, in which all the stars are gradually waning and mankind with all its institutions and creations is perishing in the midst of a dying world."[1] But this spirit was a restricted one and belongs rather to our own age than to the nineties. The dark prophesies of Spengler would receive wide and serious consideration only after the numerous reform movements then set on foot to build anew on the ruins of a social and artistic order had been shown to be, in the main, futile. There was an epidemic of these movements in the last decade of the century. We had the New Party, the New Age, the New Realism, the New Paganism, the New Spirit, the New Woman, the New Drama, and many others.

Virtually all of these efforts toward rehabilitation, not excluding the new Imperialism of William Ernest Henley and the socialism of Shaw, William Morris, and Wells, were brave attempts to beat a soul into nineteenth-century naturalism and to prepare it for its new function of replacing Protestantism as the religion of the masses. The enthusiasm with which the most resounding platitudes of Huxley, Tyndall, Spencer, and Darwin were received by the faithful of both sexes is almost inconceivable to us today. The future of humanity under the egis of

---

[1] Quoted from *The Eighteen Nineties,* by Holbrook Jackson.

liberalism looked as rosy to the nineties as it appears bleak and futile to the 1930's.

"The significance of the nineties," says Richard Le Gallienne, "is that they began to apply all the new ideas that had been accumulating from the disintegrating action of scientific and philosophic thought on every kind of spiritual, moral, social, and artistic convention, and all forms of authority demanding obedience merely as authority." But the significance was deeper than that. It was a middle-class manifestation. It profoundly affected that body of conservative and religious people who in former seasons of national unsteadiness could always be depended upon to restore the equilibrium. "No family," observes Holbrook Jackson, "were its record for solid British respectability on no matter how secure a basis, was immune from the new ideas; and if the bourgeoisie of the eighteen-eighties were inspired to throw their mahogany into the streets, their successors in the eighteen-nineties were barely constrained from doing the same with their most cherished principles. The staidest Non-conformist circles begot strange, pale youths with abundant hair, whose abandoned thoughts expressed themselves in 'purple patches' of prose, and whose sole aim in life was to live passionately in a succession of 'scarlet moments.' Life testing was the fashion, and the rising generation felt as though it was slipping out of the cages of convention into a freedom full of tremendous possibilities."

The most arresting of these life-testing experiments and the one which has given to the period its chief celebrity was that carried on on a grandiose scale and with a fine sense of ballyhoo by the so-called literary decadents, especially by Oscar Wilde, Aubrey Beardsley, and Ernest Dowson. So startling and so public was this display that for the brief period during which these men occupied the stage they seemed almost alone in the artistic world, eclipsing the brilliance of others then alive. Browning had died in 1889, Tennyson's theatrical "passing" was one of the memorable events of 1892. But Swinburne was still alive, and Morris, Meredith, Ruskin, Pater, as well as Huxley, Tyndall, Martineau, and Herbert Spencer. This deserves, I think, more than passing mention, because it is possible to see in the Beardsley-Wilde-Dowson phase of the decadence a vital and meaningful drama, arranged and directed by Providence for the salutary benefit of the public and those prophets of a new order who sat obscurely in the audience while young and enthusiastic actors carried their most cherished doctrines into practice and hurried themselves toward the catastrophe.

"Oscar Wilde," asserts Richard Le Gallienne, "may be said to have included Huxley and Pater and Morris and Whistler, and Mr. Bernard Shaw and Mr. Max Beerbohm in the amazing eclecticism of his extravagant personality that seems to have borrowed everything and to have made everything his own. . . . In him the period might see its own face in a glass. And it is because it did see its face in him that it first admired, then grew afraid, then destroyed him. Here, said the moralist, is where your modern ideas will lead you. . . . What serious reformers had labored for years to accomplish, Wilde did in a moment with the flash of an epigram."

Wilde's greatest drama in an era of dramatic revival was his own dramatic life. It was a tragedy, the high seriousness of which was missed by those for whom it was intended. They left after the third act; they missed the catharsis, the lesson not only of Wilde's but of Beardsley's and of Dowson's resurrection to a new life. These men had proved all the new theories to the hilt with a simple and terrifying logic. They had found they would not work, and they were brought up face to face with the modern dilemma, the choice, namely, between Christ and barbarism. What it would take others who toyed with the new evangel twenty years and the lesson of a World War to learn, they had discovered before the nineties were over.

II

Oscar Wilde's relation to the English Catholic Revival is much the same as that of Baudelaire's to the French. There are notable differences, of course. Wilde is a later manifestation. He is not a precursor of the English Revival in the same sense that Baudelaire is of the French. While the two revivals enjoyed a parallel existence it is well to note that the intellectual and ethical soil out of which they sprung was not the same. Newman, Patmore, Hawker, Faber, Hopkins were deeply religious men before their entry into the Church. The problems that most nearly concerned them and resulted in their conversions were formal theological ones arising out of the welter of the Oxford Movement. They had never sincerely tried naturalism as a way of life as had Baudelaire, Paul Verlaine, Huysmans, Maurice Barres, and Paul Bourget. Their rejection of it was not on experimental grounds. Hence we had among the early English revivalists no great penitents, no souls, heavy with the sense of sin and convinced of the emptiness of life on the naturalistic level. But with Wilde, with Dowson, with Beardsley, this element of remorse enters and remains. It is the contribution of the nineties.

This much must be said to explain why we consider Wilde a part of the Catholic Revival. He did not live the life of a Catholic. Some of his first poems, it is true, were published by Father Matthew Russell in his *Irish Monthly,* and it was this priest who told him that his only spiritual home was the Catholic Church. But having rejected the Faith, as Theodore Maynard remarks, "it was not surprising that a man of his temperament should explore every perversity in thought and art before, as a broken man, he ended where he should have begun."

Wilde's father was Sir William Wilde, a rather celebrated Irish surgeon, his mother, a poet of minor importance in the

Celtic Revival. Educated at Trinity College, Dublin, where he distinguished himself in the classics, he went to Oxford in 1874. His career of brilliant eccentricity began there, earning for him great celebrity and at the same time great unpopularity with the undergraduates who were annoyed by his languid poses, his epigrams, his artistic and somewhat feminine affectations. He was giving himself with all the enthusiasm of his extravagant personality to the art-for-art's-sake or aesthetic movement which was one of the last stands of the old Romanticism, heralding its break-up. The exalted but misty striving for political liberty and justice, moral freedom and self-expression, which had been behind the *élan* of Shelley, Byron, and Keats had all but been exhausted by the Victorian bloc against it. Consciousness of frustration and interior emptiness had given rise to a great preoccupation with the exterior qualities of art; the "cosmetic of rhetoric" was liberally used to give a hectic bloom of health to a real spiritual destitution.

At Oxford, Walter Pater was Wilde's chief source of inspiration, supplying him with the material for his *bizarrerie*. But whether this interest in the author of *Marius* was that of a disciple or that of a satirist it is difficult to say. Wilde's true inner self was always thoroughly masked by the glittering shell of his ironic exterior. Some of the stories he told about his preceptor in later life would lead one to believe he set him down from the first as something of a mystic ass. Quite the best of these is the one retailed by Richard Le Gallienne. In one of Pater's classes was a student named Sanctuary. One day he asked this individual to see him at the close of the period, an order that caused Mr. Sanctuary no little perturbation, for Pater was one of the proctors of the college and he feared he had been caught in some violation of the discipline of the place. After all had filed out of the room Pater approached the unfortunate undergraduate and said rather haltingly, "Mr. Sanctuary, I just wanted to say that I think — I think you have such a beautiful name!"

"Oscar," the artist Whistler once remarked, "has the courage of the opinions — of others." It is interesting to observe how he carried out quite blatantly all the opinions of the Neo-Romantics, many of which their originators were bold enough merely to suggest. Liberty for all men, so dear to Shelley and Byron, had come to mean "the inalienable right of a few vivid personalities to express themselves fully without regard to morality or convention." Wilde's way of popularizing this dogma was to stroll down Bond Street clad in a plum-colored velveteen knickerbocker suit. He announced that he wished "to live up to his blue-and-white china." He had satirized the whole attitude before Gilbert and Sullivan had lampooned his exposition of it in the opera *Patience.*

His method was simply a *reductio ad absurdum,* carried out in an eccentric act or epigram which might have passed for mere clowning were it not for their profound intellectual significance. Thus in his observation on the Atlantic Ocean we may see what had become of the romantic awe and worship of nature. "I am not exactly pleased with the Atlantic," he said. "It was not so majestic as I expected"; or in his dissatisfaction with Niagara Falls which deserves to be placed beside Chateaubriand's ecstasy in the presence of the same tremendous cascade: "I was disappointed with Niagara. Most people must be disappointed with Niagara. Every American bride is taken there, and the sight of the stupendous waterfall must be one of the earliest if not the keenest disappointments in American married life." The new Romantic, the aesthete, sought inspiration in the artificial rather than in the natural, in the town rather than in the country. This was a characteristic of virtually all of the men of the 90's, Arthur Symons, Whistler, Le Gallienne, John Davidson, etc. But it was Wilde who could crystallize the pose in a laughing epigram. "The first duty in life," he said, "is to be as artificial as possible — what the second duty is no one has as yet discovered."

Up to 1890 Wilde had produced little that might insure him

a permanent position in English letters. His genius had been
largely a derived, synthetic thing which had absorbed and re-
issued the intellectual contributions of others. He was a con-
summate actor, a borrower, a mimic. To Whistler who had
gotten off a good epigram he complained wistfully, "Oh, I wish
I had said that." And the artist replied, "Never mind, Oscar,
you will!" But as the 90's dawned there was evidence that he
was evolving out of this attitude into another in which his own
genius would be manifest. He had dropped the aesthetic move-
ment and had taken up the position of the French decadents.
His *Picture of Dorian Gray* is obviously an attempt to import
into England the mood of Huysmans' *A Rebours*. The theater,
however, was to give him the opportunity of expressing his
ideas and of standing on his own feet artistically. His first at-
tempt *Vera: or the Nihilists* (1883) had been unsuccessful; but
in 1893 appeared *Lady Windermere's Fan* and the following
year *Salome,* to which in the next three years were added *A
Woman of No Importance, An Ideal Husband,* and *The Im-
portance of Being Earnest,* a series of achievements which
marked him as the cleverest dramatist of his day and quite the
best England had produced for a century.

Wilde was now 41 years old and at the peak of fame and
power — rich, famous, popular. "The man who can dominate
a London dinner-table can dominate the world," he had said;
and he was dominating by his spontaneous Celtic brilliance
many of them, and rolling in luxury. Then there came out
publicly the charges of the moral perversity which had always
been a real but submerged part of the *mal romantique*. Not that
all the radical Romantics preached the sort of moral perversity
practiced by Wilde. What they preached was the superiority of
the artist to the moral law when it conflicted with what he was
pleased to call love. To this the evolutionary scientists had
added the dogma that the moral law was a convention, a deeply
established habit which man might keep or break according to
the utility involved. It was characteristic of Wilde that he

should carry all this out literally just as it was characteristic of those who proposed the doctrines to turn on him and rend him unmercifully when he brought out the disgusting character of their smug little heresy. They and the innumerable dilettantes and hangers-on who toyed with the decadence were, as Holbrook Jackson justly observes, "perhaps the only real degenerates."

Wilde's moral irregularities were suspected before the Marquis of Queensbury, whom his son, Lord Alfred Douglas, describes as a "professed and crude agnostic," began to make the open charges. He left the country temporarily but soon returned to brazen out the situation. There seemed to be a naïve assurance in his mind that a society which had supplied him with the principles upon which he had been acting would not be so hypocritical as to condemn him. He brought an action for criminal libel against the Marquis of Queensbury, lost the case, and was arrested, charged under the 11th section of the Criminal Law Amendment, and, after a memorable trial in Old Bailey, was sentenced to two years' penal servitude.

Wilde's imprisonment, like that of Verlaine's, was a personal blessing in the effect it had both on his subsequent life and upon his art. During his incarceration he wrote the series of letters addressed to Lord Alfred Douglas called *De Profundis* in which one catches glimpses of a sincerity heretofore entirely lacking in his work. After his release he wrote the *Ballad of Reading Gaol* under the pseudonym "C.3.3.," his prison number. This remains his single claim to serious recognition as a poet. "Had the *Ballad of Reading Gaol* been written a hundred years ago," remarks Jackson, "it would have been printed as a broadside and sold in the street by the ballad-mongers; it was so common as that and so great as that."

Lord Douglas in his *Autobiography* records that the day Wilde left prison he went to the Brompton Oratory and asked for one of the fathers whom he had known, apparently Father Sebastian Bowden, formerly of the Coldstream Guards. He had made up his mind to be a Catholic and wanted to be received at once. Father Bowden was not in, and he refused to see anyone else, which Douglas construes, along with other things, as evidence that Wilde did not want to be a Catholic as much as he thought he did, and that he would have resented the idea of taking instructions.

Despite the apparent sincerity of his complete penitence and desire for reform, there is evidence that during his subsequent life on the continent under the name of "Sebastian Melmoth" he did not live up to his resolutions. As to his death in poverty at Paris, November 30, 1900, and his reception into the Church, the stories told by Ross, who was at his bedside, seemed to indicate that his final penitence was far from being sincere. Ross stated that he called a priest to attend Wilde merely on the strength of his friend's statement of long standing that he wanted "to die in the Church as it was the best place to die," and that the priest administered the sacraments when Wilde was unconscious.

Lord Douglas, however, quotes the Franciscan friar who attended Wilde as asserting he assured himself that the dying man was sufficiently conscious to hear and understand all that he said to him, and although he could not speak he gave unmistakable signs of assent. "I satisfied myself," wrote the priest, "that he understood and assented," which would seem to remove the last doubt that Wilde died in the Church and as a penitent.

III

Paul Claudel has said that the only emotion the nineteenth century could experience sincerely was remorse. There was much of it in the 1890's in England. Just as the decade was running out, Smithers, the London publisher, received the following note from France:

Jesus is our Lord and Judge!
Dear Friend, I implore you to destroy all copies of Lysistrata
and bad drawings. Show this to Pollett and conjure him to do
the same. By all that is holy — all obscene drawings.

Aubrey Beardsley
In my last agony.

The drawings were not destroyed. A generation of publishers, knowing very few holy things, was beginning. And so Aubrey Beardsley died in March of the new century, and was buried in Mentone, after a Requiem High Mass in the Cathedral.

Of all the piquant personalities of the 90's none more strikingly epitomizes the spirit that gave celebrity and significance to the period than that of Aubrey Beardsley. "I belong to the Beardsley Period," declared Max Beerbohm; Osbert Burdett gives the title *The Beardsley Period* to his study of the 1890's; and Holbrook Jackson refers to him as "the unique expression of the most unique mood of the 'nineties." He stands for that double aspect of the yellow decade — decadence and renaissance; decadence in his mad attempt to live up to all the brave new theories so plentiful during this time of the old order's collapse, and renaissance, in the poignant sense of frustration that followed repentance, and the vision of a new artistic life in the Catholic Church which would never be realized.

"The appearance of Aubrey Beardsley in 1893," says Holbrook Jackson, "was the most extraordinary event in English art since the appearance of William Blake a little more than a century earlier." Blake appeared at the beginning of the Romantic Movement, Beardsley at its conclusion. Blake was little known to his generation, while Beardsley's art and astonishing personality made a brief but vivid impression upon his times.

Born at Brighton in 1872 he was from the first a delicate and precocious lad. So proficient was he in music that at the age of eleven he appeared on a London concert platform in a piano recital with his sister. By his skill with the pencil, espe-cially in caricature, he attracted attention while attending the Brighton grammar school. But his real interest was in letters, and he read incessantly. Aubrey's development was not a normal one. Indeed it was a bit forced. His sister, Mabel, worked lovingly and incessantly to bring out her brother's re-markable talents. He was permitted to read indiscriminately, and, as a boy, was something of a child-authority on Elizabeth-an drama, French classics, and modern French novels, and was an easy reader of Latin. Yet he seems to have displayed none of the unlovely mannerisms of the infant prodigy. He was liked by his schoolmates and this sweetness and charm of character never deserted him even in the hour of his prosperity.

In the late 80's Beardsley left Brighton and came to London. He found employment for a few months with an architect and later in an insurance office. He hated the work and tried to bury his boredom in books and in the study of art which he was undertaking privately. But soon even this relief was denied him. His health broke down under the double strain, and since the money he earned was sorely needed at home, he was ob-liged to abandon his art studies, even his amusements, and to conserve what little strength he had for the work he detested. These were dark days for Beardsley. He began to have pul-monary hemorrhages, death seemed imminent, and failure an accomplished fact.

Then, just as the 90's were dawning, the light broke. He had met at one of the book stalls he frequented a Mr. Evans who encouraged him to draw and later introduced him to the famous artist Burne-Jones who was impressed with some of his work; and then later to the publisher, J. M. Dent, who gave him his first commission, that of making the drawings for a new edition of *Morte d'Arthur*. Evans had shown Dent one of Beardsley's sketches, "Hail Mary," and while they were look-ing at the drawing Beardsley entered the shop. Evans merely

said, "There's your man." Beardsley was unable to believe it
was all true. "It's too good a chance," he said. "I am sure I shan't
be equal to it. I am not worthy of it." It was characteristic of
Beardsley, even after he had arrived, that any sincere tribute to
his work made him cry with joy. Richard Le Gallienne relates
that Whistler, who had originally been prejudiced against his
work, agreed to look over his advance illustrations for *The
Rape of the Lock,* and having finished, said with much deliber-
ation, "Aubrey, I have made a very great mistake — you are a
very great artist." Beardsley burst into tears.

The history of art has few examples of sudden and immediate
rises to fame such as that which overtook Beardsley. He had
deftly caught the essential spirit of the day; interest in his draw-
ings and his personality, which he exploited with a rare talent
for publicity, was widespread and enthusiastic. His black-and-
white sketches began to be in demand everywhere and he
worked hectically to supply the demand. In 1894 he was ap-
pointed art editor of *The Yellow Book* and the so-called
"Beardsley Craze" reached its peak. In addition to his artistic
work, there was now the brilliant social life which took up a
large part of his time; a figure so celebrated was accepted in
the most aristocratic circles. Twenty-two years old, a hopeless
consumptive, he was giving himself up to a routine of feverish
activity as one who knows that he has a short time to live and
has decided to spend it recklessly.

As to the moral character of his life we have little to guide
us in drawing an accurate conclusion. Some of his drawings are
certainly erotic, as were not a few of his associates. Moreover,
he was not above throwing out insinuations that he was so him-
self. But many of the decadents feigned such an attitude as a
publicity device. It was considered polite to be wicked. Of his
literary productions, the romance, *Under the Hill,* was suffi-
ciently ribald to prevent its circulation except in an expurgated
edition, and one does not risk having himself set down as a
prude to say the *Lysistrata* drawings are indecent. And yet, as

Esmé-Wingfield-Stratford has recently remarked, "this fascination of the artist by evil — may it not have been one of horror? In some pictures, *Lady Gold,* for instance, . . . the satire on the vices of the age is direct and merciless. There is a profound moral resemblance between the art of Beardsley and the prose of Mr. Aldous Huxley." Holbrook Jackson finds his drawings for Oscar Wilde's *Salome* "wickedly suggestive." We know, however, that Beardsley, despite the character of this work, never associated with Wilde, in fact, entertained an extremely low opinion of him.

Yet, curiously enough, it was Wilde's downfall that marked the turning point in Beardsley's life. During the memorable trial at Old Bailey, the newspapers reported that Wilde appeared in court with "a yellow book" under his arm. It may have been a French novel but was not, according to observers, *The Yellow Book* of which Beardsley was the art editor. Yet the trick of association had done its work, and with Wilde was also condemned, as far as the public was concerned, the magazine with which Wilde had never had any connection, not even as a contributor. It is true, *The Yellow Book* had risen to popularity by reason of the deftness with which its editors had caught the spirit of the decade. But it was not in any sense a wicked journal. One who takes the trouble to go through its files today will find it little more than a surprisingly well-edited and exquisitely decorated magazine. None the less, Lane, the publisher, and Henry Harland, the American editor, of whom more will be said later, were obliged to bow to the public decision and go through the motions of making a complete renovation. And one of the first steps was to get rid of Beardsley. He was immediately appropriated by the *Savoy,* which Arthur Symons edited.

But the affair sobered him. It was his first stinging reproof in a career that had known only adulation. It gave him an opportunity to think pertinent thoughts about himself, to turn inward the intellectual energy he had been pouring out upon a multitude of exterior things. He began to find himself, to sketch the real Aubrey Beardsley.

Among his acquaintances was a certain John Gray (the late poet and litterateur, Canon John Gray), then a young poet, convert, and priest. Gray set out to convert Beardsley. The history of his efforts and their issue is adumbrated in the series of letters the artist wrote to his friend beginning in October, 1896. On March 31, 1897, he writes to Gray: "This morning I was received by dear Father B. [Father David Bearne, S.J.,] into the Church, making my first confession with which he helped me so kindly. . . . This is a very dry account of what has been the most important step in my life."

The step, it appears, had not been taken too soon, for he had not long to live and was even then confined to his bed with the malady which three years later would be fatal. Thus on April 2, he writes again to Gray a letter that sounds more like that of a religious novice than that of a penitent. "The Blessed Sacrament was brought to me here this morning. It was a moment of profound joy, of gratitude, of emotion. I gave myself up entirely, utterly, to feelings of happiness, and even the knowledge of my unworthiness only seemed to add fuel to the flame that warmed and illuminated my heart. . . . Through all eternity I shall be unspeakably grateful to you for your brotherly concern for my spiritual welfare. . . . This afternoon I felt a little sad at the thought of my compulsory exile from Church just now; and the divine privilege of praying before the Blessed Sacrament is not permitted me. You can guess how I long to assist at Mass. . . ."

His health became rapidly worse and he was taken to Paris where he spent much of his time in the churches. Sir William Rothenstein speaks of meeting him there: "All his artifice was gone; he was gentle and affectionate and I realized how much I cared for him. . . . Perhaps some would say the old Beardsley was the true Beardsley. True as he had been to a former self,

the new Aubrey would have been truer to a finer self. I had
seen a new beauty in his face; felt a new gentleness in his ways;
and I believed them due to something other than weakness."

Beardsley did not want to die nor did he think he would. He
was already making, says Louise Guiney, hopeful plans to de-
vote his talents to devotional art. He had begun his career with
the sketch "Hail Mary." He was now engaged in illustrating
other religious subjects. But the hopes of this genius who had
"established a fair claim to rank as the greatest of all English
masters of pure line" were not to be realized, and he himself
soon came to perceive it. He died, with Viaticum, on March
16, 1900. "It is such a rest," he had written to John Gray, "to
be folded after all my wanderings."

IV

The English decadence followed, in point of time, that of
the French, and was to a certain extent its echo. This may ac-
count for the large amount of dilettantism in the British mani-
festation, which produced a pretty flock of amateur decadents
but very few genuine ones. Arthur Symons, who fairly well
represents the first class, brings out this point in the description
of one of his meetings with Ernest Dowson. It was in 1891 at
a meeting of the Rhymers' Club, held "in an upper room of the
'Cheshire Cheese' where long clay pipes lay in slim heaps on
the wooden tables between tankards of ale; and young poets,
then very young, recited their verses to one another with a des-
perate and ineffectual attempt to get in touch with the Latin
Quarter. Dowson who had enjoyed the real thing in Paris did
not, I think, go very often."

The word *enjoyed* used by Symons is hardly appropriate.
Dowson did not enjoy the decadence as did many of his con-
temporaries. It was agonizing to him because it was so real. In-
deed the wistful tragedy of his life may well be taken as illus-

trating what there was of genuine sincerity in the English *ma!
de siècle,* a state of spiritual impotence which arose from a
native philosophical and moral background. And there was
such a genuine element. Philosophically, we may find its main
tenets expressed in the conclusion of Walter Pater's *Marius, the
Epicurean,* the *locus classicus* of the philosophy of the deca-
dence. "In those days," records Richard Le Gallienne, "we were
all going about exhorting each other to burn always with the
hard, gem-like flame." What Pater had done, unwittingly per-
haps, was to supply a temporary *modus vivendi* to those who
felt keenly the bankruptcy of the Victorian ethos, and who
sensed no less vividly the inner emptiness of all the enthusiastic
plans being hatched for the construction of a new world. There
remained only art and the *nunc fluens.* Pater had written in his
Marius: "With the Cyrenaics of all ages, he would at least fill
up the measure of that present with vivid sensations, and such
intellectual apprehensions as . . . are most like sensations."
And in the "revised" conclusion: "Not the fruit of experience
but experience itself is the end. A counted number of pulses
only is given to us of a variegated, dramatic life. How may we
see in them all that is to be seen in them by the finest senses?
How shall we pass most swiftly from point to point, and be
present always at the focus where the greatest number of vital
forces unite in their purest energy? To burn always with this
hard, gem-like flame, to maintain this ecstasy, is success in life."

Dowson, as has been said, was also strongly under the in-
fluence of the French decadence. His father's health demanded
that he spend much of his time abroad, in the Riviera and in
France. The education of the son, which the parent took in his
own hands, was consequently somewhat irregular but strongly
literary, including the classics and much French, especially the
moderns. He went to Oxford but left in 1887 without taking a
degree and came to London.

It was shortly after leaving Oxford that he became a Catholic,
but what led up to it is somewhat dark. Lionel Johnson was

a contemporary and friend of his at the university (they were born in the same year), and perhaps the same influences he underwent there made themselves felt in Dowson. However, one feels sure in conjecturing that the path taken by Verlaine and Huysmans had something to do with the step. This is not an implication that there was anything insincere in his conversion. He was as thoroughly in earnest as Verlaine, and equally as unable from a moral standpoint to live out his convictions. Of his life in London we know but little. Indeed, most of what we know of his entire career is sketchy, bits from the reminiscences of others, conjectures from his lyrics, and Arthur Symons' short but interesting appreciation of him. He wrote an occasional poem for the *Century Guild Hobby Horse* and for other eccentric *fin de siècle* journals. Several of his verses appeared in the first published volume of the Rhymers' Club. His entire literary output fills but a small volume. There is a certain thinness, too, about his poetic genius. But what there is of it is genuine, and in the possession of another might have been made to yield a more abundant harvest. He was the reverse of ambitious and wrote when it pleased him to do so, and then only because he had something under his heart that cried for expression.

If we are to believe Symons, he spent a large part of his time wandering about the midnight streets of London, and might be found in any one of those strange places which the budding crop of Bohemians was just beginning to discover. "I think I may date my first impression of what one calls the 'real man,'" says Symons, "from an evening in which he first introduced me to those charming supper-houses, open all through the night, the cabmen's shelters."

It must have been shortly after he took up residence in London that he fell in love with the daughter of a French restaurant proprietor in Soho. "He used to dine every night at the little restaurant," writes Symons, "and I can always see the picture which I have so often seen through the window in passing: the narrow room with the rough tables, for the most part empty, except in the innermost corner where Dowson would sit with that singularly sweet and singularly pathetic smile on his lips . . . playing his invariable after-dinner game of cards." This affair lasted for two years, ending abruptly and with a touch of almost unbearable prose when the practical French mother chose one of the waiters as her daughter's husband.

Dowson had had his love affairs before, but this one was singularly elevated. The girl seemed to have a way of bringing to the surface the very best that was in him. He adored her as one does an ideal, as an unattainable something. But whether she returned the devotion we do not know.

This, anyway, next to his conversion to the Church was the most important event in his life. These were the two great unrealized ideals to which he turned in his later squalor and misery as to the only lights in a very dark and tearful world, and both beyond his reach. One of his most characteristic love poems, *Non sum qualis eram bonae sub regno Cynarae*, delicately records this note of frustration:

> *Last night, ah, yesternight, betwixt her lips and mine*
> *There fell thy shadow, Cynara! thy breath was shed*
> *Upon my soul between the kisses and the wine*
> *And I was desolate and sick of an old passion,*
>   *Yea, I was desolate and bowed my head;*
> *I have been faithful to thee, Cynara! in my fashion.*

*   *   *

> *I have forgot much, Cynara! gone with the wind,*
> *Flung roses, roses riotously with the throng,*
> *Dancing, to put thy pale, lost lilies out of mind:*
> *But I was desolate and sick of an old passion,*
>   *Yea, all the time, because the dance was long:*
> *I have been faithful to thee, Cynara! in my fashion.*

I cried for madder music and for stronger wine,
  But when the feast is finished and the lamps expire,
Then falls thy shadow, Cynara! the night is thine;
And I am desolate and sick of an old passion,
  Yea, hungry for the lips of my desire:
I have been faithful to thee, Cynara! in my fashion.

Dowson, like Verlaine, was morally and physically very, very weak. It would seem that all the sins and failings of a century of romantic geniuses were focused in him. But in a certain sense, his perpetual falling short of his ideals was more comprehensible than that of many of his poetic forebears. His ideals were much higher. He might be said to stand at the end of the romantic quest when the poet, haggard from the consuming search, had at last seen the blazing goal and was stunned into helplessness by the realization that he was incapable of reaching it ever; he had destroyed his moral resistance by "a life of sensations rather than of thoughts." It was the Kingdom of Heaven he saw, which suffereth violence, and he was profoundly incapable of this sort of moral effort.

If we may describe Paul Verlaine's life in Paris as a tearful and spineless oscillation between the *cabaret* and Notre Dame, the same may be said of Dowson in London. With this difference: the verse which Dowson scribbled on tables, greasy with the poisonous liquors of a pothouse, did not absorb any of the obscenity or vulgarity of this atmosphere. When he writes, as he does with rare beauty, of the Nuns of Perpetual Adoration, Benediction, Extreme Unction, or the Carthusians, the other side of his life is suggested, but with delicacy and restraint. Yet this other side was no less a real one than that of Verlaines. There was, for instance, his quest for sensation in hashish and his insane desire for strong drink and its consequences. He had also, says Symons, "that curious love of the sordid so common an affectation of the modern decadent, and with him so gen-

uine," which dragged him into "many sorry corners of life
which were never exactly gay to him."

His father had left him a dock in the East End of London,
and it was here he made his home, consorting with the rousta-
bouts of the waterfront, drinking what they drank, and mani-
festing at times "a curious disregard of personal tidiness." There
was no compromise with Dowson, it was either high spirituality
or its lowest opposite. The plane of Victorian mediocrity was
unthinkable to him. He saw clearly what he ought to be, but
his inability to reach this goal, except at times, plunged him
even deeper into the other extreme which however he did not
disguise by calling pretty names. This, I think, is the greatest
virtue of the true decadents. They call sin, sin. Their eye is clear
even when bleared with dissipation and absinthe.

"I have flung roses, roses, riotously with the throng," he cries
in *Cynara,* not in extenuation of the riot but with much beating
of the breast. And in the *Carthusians* he loves sincerely but
from a distance the monastic life of austere renunciation:

> *Ye shall prevail at last! surely ye shall prevail,*
>   *Your silence and austerity shall win at last:*
> *Desire and mirth, the world's ephemeral lights shall fail,*
>   *The sweet star of your queen is never overcast.*

*   *   *

> *We fling up flowers and laugh, we laugh across the wine:*
>   *With wine we dull our souls and careful strains of art:*
> *Our cups are polished skulls round which the roses twine:*
>   *None dares to look at Death who leers and lurks apart.*
>
> *Move on, white company, whom that has not sufficed!*
>   *Our viols cease, our wine is death, our roses fail:*
> *Pray for our heedlessness, O dwellers with the Christ!*
>   *Though the world fall apart, ye surely shall prevail.*

The source of Dowson's cry for "Madder music and stronger wine" may have been at one time or another the spurious mysticism of Walter Pater. But not for long. For he had discovered that ecstasy is not nourished by the pursuit of sensations, and that the "hard, gem-like flame" burns only for those who renounce them.

He had inherited consumption which frequently made him quite weak and helpless. On these occasions, especially toward the end of his life when the disease had progressed, he hid himself away in his dirty dock-lodgings, ate nothing, and refused to see a doctor. Friends who visited him there were even unwelcome. One day he was found, penniless and unable to walk, in a muddy outskirt of Catford, and was taken to a small cottage where he had been living with a friend. He did not realize he was going to die; he had many plans as to what he would do with a small sum he expected to receive from the sale of some property, and began the task of reading Dickens for the first time! On the last day of his life, says Symons, he sat up talking eagerly until five in the morning. He was only thirty-three when they buried him in the Catholic section of the Lewisham Cemetery.

With Dowson we may well bring this chapter on the decadent side of the 1890's to a close and turn to a more cheerful aspect of the decade and one, too, of greater importance to the Catholic Revival. Still, the decadence is not without its own peculiar importance. Artistically, it marks the end of that Romanticism which had begun so hopefully a century before. And in the lives of those who gave themselves fully to the philosophy which brought about its collapse we may see a state of soul which has projected itself into our own day, becoming the most obvious attitude of the advanced modern mind. Dowson has expressed it in a few lines from a sonnet he calls *A Last Word:*

Let us go hence; the night is now at hand;
The day is overworn, the birds all flown:
And we have reaped the crop the gods have sown:
Despair and death: deep darkness o'er the land
Broods like an owl; we cannot understand
Laughter or tears, for we have only known
Surpassing vanity: vain things alone
Have driven our perverse and aimless band.

BIBLIOGRAPHY

BEARDSLEY, AUBREY

Thought, March, 1933, p. 548. "Last Days of Aubrey Beardsley," by Isabel Clarke.

Catholic World, March, 1932, "Aubrey Beardsley — a study in Conversion," by Hugh F. Blunt.

Catholic World, Vol. 69, pp. 201–13, Louise Guiney.

Jackson, Holbrook, *The Eighteen Nineties* (New York: Knopf, 1922), pp. 91–104.

Burdett, Osbert, *The Beardsley Period* (New York: Boni & Liveright, 1925).

Last Letters of Aubrey Beardsley, edited with introduction by John Gray (1905).

DOWSON, ERNEST

Brégy, Katherine, *Poets and Pilgrims* (New York: Benziger, 1925), pp. 82–104.

Carmina, No. 11, p. 332 and October, 1930, p. 33.

Poems of Ernest Dowson, with a memoir by Arthur Symons (New York: Dodd, Mead, 1924).

WILDE, OSCAR

Jackson, Holbrook, *The Eighteen Nineties,* Chapters III, IV, and VI.

Le Gallienne, Richard, *The Romantic 90's* (New York), pp. 242–271.

Carmina No. 11 (1932), (Revised facts on Wilde's conversion by Lord Alfred Douglas).

WORKS

Poetical Works of Oscar Wilde (New York: Cromwell, 1913).

Plays of Oscar Wilde (New York: Cosmopolitan, 1914).

2

Alice Meynell

I

The concluding years of the nineteenth century were years of awakened interest in literature and the arts generally. If the result of all this bustle was not considerable in the number of masterpieces it immediately produced, its effect in another way was. The arts for better or for worse were undergoing a renovation from top to bottom. New and revolutionary ideas, affecting the very essence of expression, were filtering in from France; others just as revolutionary but long condemned to an underground existence by the Victorian self-satisfaction were coming out into the light. Energetic groups of the artistically minded, where the new doctrines were discussed and put into practice, sprang up on all sides.

"Fin de siècle was the label with something of a stigma, which was used to cover them all," says Richard Le Gallienne of these literary *cénacles* of the 1890's, "but as one looks back it is apparent that here was not so much the ending of the century as the beginning of a new one." Quite the most celebrated of these places where the literati of the period foregathered was presided over by a woman whom Le Gallienne calls, echoing a sentiment common to all who have written about her, "a veritable Egeria in the London literary world, the center of a *salon* that recalled the *salons* of pre-Revolutionary France...."

The *salon* is not a native British institution. England had had its brilliant literary women but few (almost none, we may say) who displayed either the genius or the desire of attracting to

themselves the choicest artistic spirits of the age and influencing
them all by the force of personal charm and intellectual energy.
The thing is French, and hence the necessity of going to France
for the name and for the prototype of the Palace Court draw-
ing-room of Alice Meynell during the 90's. "I may say," de-
clares Charles Lewis Hind, "that calling at that house meant ar-
riving at half-past three, staying until midnight, and meeting
in the course of the year most of the literary folk worth know-
ing." The center about which these lights of the world of letters
revolved was singularly fitted for this role. Alice Meynell was
already in the early stages of the decade, a well-known poetess,
and a master of the sort of exquisitely finished prose that most
delighted the sensibilities of the age. She was, moreover, beau-
tiful, young, a brilliant conversationalist. Her intellectual inter-
ests were the reverse of parochial. The culture of the ancient
world held her fast, yet she was at the same time what might
be called an advanced modern, a feminist, a symbolist, sympa-
thetic toward most of the new political and artistic ideas that
germinated so fast in this seminal period. Thus she was admired
and her friendship prized not only by those who belonged to
the generation that was passing such as Browning, Patmore,
Rossetti, de Vere, and George Meredith, but her presence was
also sought by many younger spirits who were preparing new
things. Her drawing-room became the *rendezvous* of the ar-
tists who gave celebrity to the period and in varying degrees
laid the foundations for most of what would become the temper
of the twentieth century. Thither came Aubrey Beardsley car-
rying with him his portfolio of sketches, William Watson,
Oscar Wilde and his brother Willie Wilde, Stephen Phillips,
Francis Thompson, Herbert Trench, Lionel Johnson, "too pale
and delicate even for speech," W. B. Yeats, and his fellow Celtic
revivalist, Katharine Tynan, and others.

The 1890's gave birth to many of these literary *cénacles* at
which apocalyptic movements were hatched and given to the
world. Most of them have been forgotten. Indeed, it is only by

"looking back," as Le Gallienne remarks, that one may dis-
tinguish those which belonged to the last flare-up of the old
Romanticism, from those which heralded the emergence of
something newer and more permanent. Retrospect reveals the
coterie of Alice Meynell as belonging to this latter class, for its
influence has reached down with progressive force to our own
days.

Under the direction of Alice Meynell it was that the Catholic
Literary Revival first took on the form of a movement. Previous
to her advent it had been scarcely more than a number of con-
vert litterateurs, of considerable importance, it is true, but more
or less isolated one from the other, or at least without a sense of
solidarity and community of purpose, except that given to them
by their common faith. Newman might have brought these
figures together had he not had many other things of greater
importance to do. Alice Meynell actually did bring them
together, and this at a time when new forces and new per-
sonalities were beginning to appear, and the old ones had not
yet passed away. To her as to a center came the surviving rep-
resentatives of the first generation such as Aubrey de Vere
and Coventry Patmore; to her also came the artists of the new
generation, such as Francis Thompson and Lionel Johnson;
the Celtic Revival had its representative there in Katharine
Tynan, a lifelong friend of Mrs. Meynell's; from America came
the poetess, Agnes Tobin. The decadent motif was there, too,
in the occasional presence of Aubrey Beardsley and Oscar
Wilde, although Mrs. Meynell was never herself connected with
the Decadent movement; in fact, she consistently refused the
importunities of Henry Harland that she write for the *Yellow
Book*. Yet she worked privately and with considerable success
to cure souls which the *maladie du siècle* had blighted.

Besides bringing together all the then existing forces of the
Catholic Revival, Alice Meynell also succeeded in impressing
upon them as a group several valuable characteristics which the
movement has never lost. This circle of hers was always a

double one. There was the outer ring composed of the acquaint-
ances and visitors, representing tendencies she never wholly
sympathized with, but which nevertheless were a part of the
contemporary scene. It was her wish that those who belonged
to the smaller and more intimate group — those, namely, who
were working for the return to English literature of the essen-
tial Catholic spirit — should not suffer from the narrowing
effect of isolation. "Let us be of the center," she used to say,
"not of the province." In her vision the Catholic tradition
stood not apart, but in the center of things, in intimate contact
with the glories of the European past and the really valuable
tendencies in the present, engaged in the work of carrying for-
ward the main stream of English letters. This mark of hers
may be seen in the Revival today.

Exquisite artist that she was, one who seemed to live wholly
for her art, she never fell into the error of imagining that an
artistic revival such as she envisioned was a task for art alone.
"Art for art's sake," the then-prevailing heresy, she saw as an
eccentric tendency. It pulled away from that center which had
nourished, and must continue to nourish, all great literature.
Her Catholic artist must be religious, characterized by a deep
personal holiness, and inspired by what Patmore called a *real*
apprehension of the mysteries of faith. She herself was such
an artist. "Never surely was a lady who carried her learning
and wore the flower of her gentle humane sanctity with such
quiet grace, with so gentle and understanding a smile. The
touch of exquisite asceticism about her seemed but to accent the
sensitive sympathy of her manner, the manner of one quite
humanly and simply in the world, with all its varied interests,
and yet not of it. There was the charm of a beautiful abbess
about her, with the added *esprit* of intellectual sophistication."
This was the impression she made upon one who did not
belong to the inner circle. For the best expression of the Cath-
olic humanism impressed by Alice Meynell upon her associates

and upon the Revival for all times, we must turn to the lines
written by Francis Thompson of her:

> *Ah! let the sweet birds of the Lord*
> *With earth's waters make accord;*
> *Teach how the crucifix may be*
> *Carven from the laurel-tree,*
> *Fruit of the Hesperides*
> *Burnish take on Eden-trees,*
> *The Muses' sacred grove be wet*
> *With the red dew of Olivet,*
> *And Sappho lay her burning brows*
> *In white Cecilia's lap of snows!*

II

Alice Meynell, as has been remarked, was a very modern
woman, and this despite the respectable Victorian background
into which she was born in 1847 and the delicacy and care with
which her parents raised her. Her father, T. J. Thompson, to
whom she owed most of her early literary education, was a man
of wide culture and refinement; her mother a musician of
talent. She had one sister, Elizabeth, who was later to become a
well-known painter of military scenes and the wife of General
Sir William Butler.

The family led a nomadic life, traveling much on the Con-
tinent, especially in Italy, where a large portion of Alice's girl-
hood was spent. Charles Dickens, who was a close friend of Mr.
Thompson, was among the literary visitors at their London
house. He saw them also at their villa in Italy, enjoying his
romps with the children. He might have been considerably
shocked had he suspected that one of them would, by her own
volition, later grow into a woman with little resemblance to the
shy and vinelike *Agnes* of his great autobiographical novel. For

Alice Thompson at an early age was not at all pleased with the place the Victorians had allotted to woman in the social scheme, as the following entry in her diary (written when she was seventeen) will indicate: ". . . Of all the crying evils in this depraved earth, ay, of all the sins of which the cry must surely come to heaven, the greatest, judged by all the laws of God and humanity, is the miserable selfishness of men that keeps women from work — work, the salvation of the world. . . . O my dream, my dream! When will you be realized to gladden my soul, to redeem my trampled and polluted sex. O my sisters, are you content to make bricks so long, sitting by your flesh-pots. Come and eat manna in the wilderness with me, and the justice of our cause will be a pillar of fire by night and a pillar of cloud by day to us, and what if we die in the wilderness — we die with the shackles off our wrists at last. O my Shelley; if you were alive you would help me to fulfill my golden dreams. . . . I must try to cultivate that rhyming faculty which I used to have, if it is not quite gone from me. But whatever I write will be melancholy and self-conscious, as are all women's poems." And so she begins to write — about autumn and roaring winds, rain and dead delights.

This little girlhood rebellion was not a passing thing with Alice Thompson. She took the sincere convictions on which it was based with her into her later and Catholic days. Indeed it was only when she was within the Church that her golden dream ceased to be a sterile, adolescent revolution and became a reality. She was able to call upon the Mother of God and the saints to witness the justice of her cause, as she did on one oc- casion when one designated as "Strephon" insisted "that a woman must lean or she would not have his chivalry." The example of St. Catherine of Siena, that medieval whirlwind of activity, who comforted the young noble on the scaffold and refused to faint at the sight of blood, was used to lay him quite low:

The light young man who was to die,
Stopped in his frolic by the State,
Aghast, beheld the world go by;
But Catherine crossed the dungeon gate.

She found his lyric courage dumb,
His stripling beauties strewn in wrecks,
His modish bravery overcome;
Small profit had he of his sex.

She prayed, she preached him innocent;
She gave him to the Sacrificed;
On her courageous breast he leant,
The breast where beat the heart of Christ.

He left it for the block, with cries
Of victory on his severed breath.
That crimson head she clasped, her eyes
Blind with the splendor of his death.

And will the man of modern years
— Stern on the Vote — withhold from thee,
Thou prop, thou cross, erect, in tears,
Catherine, the service of his knee?

With her into the Church, she also carried her girlhood admiration for Shelley, the coming of whose poetry into her life after that of Wordsworth and Tennyson made her declare breathlessly that "the whole world was changed for me thenceforth." She credited Shelley with having, in some way or another, brought her to Rome. "The Calvinist God Shelley rejected was not God," she insisted. There seems to have been very little of the emotional about her conversion. It was rather cold-blooded, based on a desire for a more rigorous moral order

which she deemed necessary to satisfy her craving for liberty
and action. Her mother had entered the Church a few years
before and "had said nothing about it." Alice followed soon
afterward, and then her sister, Elizabeth. She was about twenty
at the time, and the solemnity of the act was not lost upon her.
What were her thoughts and feelings we know from her son-
net, *The Young Neophyte,* certainly one of her very best
lyrics, and a record which the archeologist of a thousand years
hence may find of great importance in the light it throws on
the attitude of the primitive Christians in the dim twilight of
Victorian history:

> *Who knows what days I answer for today?*
> *Giving the bud I give the flower. I bow*
> *This yet unfaded and a faded brow:*
> *Bending these knees and feeble knees, I pray.*
>
> *Thoughts yet unripe in me I bend one way,*
> *Give one repose to pain I know not now,*
> *One check to joy that comes, I guess not how.*
> *I dedicate my fields when Spring is grey.*
>
> *O rash! (I smile) to pledge my hidden wheat.*
> *I fold today at altars far apart*
> *Hands trembling with what toils? In their retreat*
> *I seal my love to be, my folded art.*
> *I light the tapers at my head and feet,*
> *And lay the crucifix on this silent heart.*

Some of the "hidden wheat" she had pledged was garnered
in her first volume of poems which was published in 1875
under the title of *Preludes.* She found herself a recognized poet.
Ruskin wrote of three of the lyrics, *San Lorenzo's Mother, To
a Daisy,* and *A Letter from a Girl to Her Own Old Age,* that
they were "the finest things I have seen, or felt, in modern

verse." One of the early poems, not included in the collection, but written at this time, was later to be held up by Rossetti and others as a modern masterpiece. It is called *Renouncement* and is the touching record of her first deep affection, which had to end as it did because its object was a priest who had first encouraged her to write:

I must not think of thee; and, tired yet strong,
  I shun the thought that lurks in all delight —
  The thought of thee — and in the blue Heaven's height,
And in the sweetest passage of a song.

Oh, just beyond the fairest thoughts that throng
  This breast, the thought of thee waits, hidden yet bright;
  But it must never, never come in sight;
I must stop short of thee the whole day long.

But when sleep comes to close each difficult day,
  When night gives pause to the long watch I keep.
    And all my bonds I needs must loose apart,

Must doff my will as raiment laid away, —
  With the first dream that comes with the first sleep
    I run, I run, I am gathered to thy heart.

But Alice was not destined to pass her life in an ivory tower inditing delicate and wistful verse for the world to admire. She was to have her desire for work, hard exterior work, "the salvation of the world, the strengthener of mind and body. . . ." In 1877 she was married to Wilfrid Meynell, a young, energetic journalist who had reviewed her *Preludes* in the *Pall Mall Gazette* with such penetration of understanding and sympathy that Alice had asked to meet him. During their engagement they talked enthusiastically about the career of Catholic journalism they would enter upon together, and which would, indeed, cover the greater period of their early married lives. An early paper to be edited by Wilfrid Meynell was *The Pen*. But his longest editorship was that of the *Weekly Register,* begun in 1881 at the request of Cardinal Manning. *Merry England,* also under his editorship, was begun in 1883. It was a monthly magazine which, in the twelve years of its existence, was to exercise an important influence not only on Catholic art but upon Catholic social and political ideas. "Characteristic of one of my father's enthusiams," records Viola Meynell, "the first number had a portrait of Disraeli for frontispiece, and all the ardor of the new magazine was in support of the social revolution of the young England Movement, the revival of the peasantry, the abolition of the wrongs of the poor, the spread of art and literature."

During these eighteen years of journalism Mrs. Meynell was her overworked husband's constant helper in the weekly round of pot-boiling. "She wrote leaders, and reviewed books, and read proofs, and translated Papal encyclicals from the Italian."[1] "Sometimes I make His Holiness quote our poets," she wrote to Coventry Patmore. All this, of course, consumed time that might have been bestowed on the higher literary arts. But there was a rapidly growing family to support. It is doubtful, anyway, whether Alice Meynell would have written more poetry than she actually did even had she been able to give more time to it. It is not that her genius was thin or frugal, although it was not of the prolific variety. Alfred Noyes has perhaps best described it when he says of her that "Other poets have written sparely. . . . But in Alice Meynell the restraint was not merely negative. It was sacrificial. Her silences were a part of her music. . . . The result is that she has given to English literature now, and to the literature of the world in centuries to come, what no other poet has been able to give — a volume of a little more than a hundred pages containing only masterpieces."

The busy exterior nature of the life she was forced to lead

---

[1] *Alice Meynell: A Memoir* by Viola Meynell, p. 15.

did not, I think, injure her poetry. Rather it gave to it an objectivity, a sense of contact with reality it might otherwise have lacked had she remained cloistered in a Victorian household. For despite her seeming austere classicism she was interiorly a Romantic, a spiritual sister of her beloved Shelley and the introspective Keats. But her constant immersion in the world's work left her no time for the sort of brooding the best nineteenth-century Romantic poetry seemed to require. Nor was there any chance that in these long silences of hers she might, as Thompson feared,

> *heavened thus long,*
> *Thou shoulds't forget thy native song,*
> *And mar thy mortal melodies*
> *With broken stammer of the skies.*

There is something distinctly practical about Mrs. Meynell's mysticism. It can become subtle at times but is never vague, never given over to what must seem to the pedestrian reader a wild coursing through the ultimate region of the empyrean. Her Christ lived in the world, He was the "way" rather than the "goal":

> *Thou art the Way.*
> *Hadst Thou been nothing but the goal,*
> *I cannot say*
> *If Thou hadst ever met my soul.*

In these last decades of the nineteenth century there was growing among Catholics a fuller consciousness of Christ's presence in the world. Francis Thompson was to give the classical expression to this when, standing in the slush of the London streets he had that vision of Jacob's ladder pitched between heaven and Charing Cross, and of Christ

> *walking on the water*
> *Not of Gennesareth, but Thames!*

The Kingdom of God, Thompson had named this poem. As one engaged actively as a journalist in the work of restoring this kingdom, Alice Meynell was familiar with the intellectual and spiritual forces that were bringing it about. National Christianity was giving way before the idea of the Church as a supernational body, with the Pope, as Christ's representative, at its head and all Christians as its members. The sort of doctrinal unanimity among Catholics which made William George Ward desire a fresh papal encyclical for his British breakfast was displacing the discord of Newman's earlier days. The doctrine of the Church on the Mystical Body of Christ was beginning to be stressed and understood as it had not been for centuries. Thus at a time when outside the Church the spirit of nationalism was in crescendo, the outlook developed by Catholics was international; when class-consciousness was rife because of the enormous differences in wealth, Catholics, through the social aspects of the Mass and the Eucharist, were beginning to see how all men might be one in Christ.

Alice Meynell, especially in her Eucharistic poetry, gave expression to this new life of the Church. Thus in *The Unknown God:*

> *One of the crowd went up,*
> *And knelt before the Paten and the Cup,*
> *Received the Lord, returned in peace, and prayed*
> *Close to my side; then in my heart I said:*

> *"O Christ, in this man's life*
> *This stranger who is Thine — in all his strife,*
> *All his felicity, his good and ill,*
> *In the assaulted stronghold of his will,*

> *"I do confess Thee here,*
> *Alive within this life; I know Thee near*
> *Within this lonely conscience, closed away*
> *Within this brother's solitary day.*

"Christ in his unknown heart,
His intellect unknown — this love, this art,
This battle and this peace, this destiny
That I shall never know, look upon me!

"Christ in his numbered breath,
Christ in his beating heart and in his death,
Christ in his mystery! From that secret place
And from that separate dwelling, give me grace."

Thomas Aquinas celebrated the sacramental Christ in kingship upon the altar; Alice Meynell adored Him in the life of a brother. One chooses to emphasize, in accordance with the needs of his age, the *Person* aspect of the Eucharist; the other, in accordance with the needs of her age, the *means* or *social* aspect of the same *Corpus Domini.* "The Holy Eucharist unites us to Christ, and unites us, as well to one another, makes us 'concorporeal.'" In another poem, *A General Communion,* she sees the devout people "Fed at one holy board," separated yet united

As each asunder absorbed the multiplied,
The ever unparted whole.

I saw this people as a field of flowers,
Each grown at such a price
The sum of unimaginable powers
Did no more than suffice.

A thousand central daisies they,
A thousand and the one:
For each, the entire monopoly of day;
For each the whole of the devoted sun.

Alfred Noyes has compared Mrs. Meynell with Sappho, in the fewness of the lyrics both have left us, in the finish and perfection of each, in the passion they celebrated. "Twenty-eight lines of these (he is speaking chiefly of three sonnets of Mrs. Meynell's) outsoar everything bequeathed to us by the earlier; and when other thousands of years have gone by, these may surely still be treasured, for they embody a divine passion."

III

Toward the end of the eighties Mrs. Meynell was also beginning to be acclaimed as a writer of aristocratic prose. Her essays had been appearing in the *Pall Mall Gazette,* the *National Observer,* and other London magazines. As the nineties got under way the praise accorded to her as a master of delicate and distinguished English reached such a pitch that Max Beerbohm felt called upon to enter a good-natured protest, saying that "in a few years Mrs. Meynell will become a sort of substitute for the English sabbath." He admitted the perfection of her style but insisted that the critics were mistaken in thinking that fine English could be written in no other way. Mrs. Meynell herself, he added, "must know that there are they who can do quite as much with their flutes as she with her file."

Distinction is perhaps the word that best describes Alice Meynell's prose, distinction in thought, distinction in expression. She never permitted herself to fall into what Stevenson calls the true love of "the British pig" — "the love of the styleless, the shapeless, of the slapdash and the disorderly." The negligent, the commonplace, the mechanical was, Mrs. Meynell once said, as much out of place in letters as in prayer. One may understand the ideal, but how she managed to preserve it both in poetry and in prose is a thing that must remain hidden in the mystery of Alice Meynell's genius. For, in addition to the hurry and fatigue of the weekly round of Catholic journalism, there were other necessary duties that might have distracted her from her high artistic ideals. Not the least of these were her duties as the mother of eight children, who were at the attention-demanding age just at the period of her busiest journalistic activity. Everard, one of the children, has given us a charming picture of his mother in the act of achieving a page of her perfect prose. "At her place at the library table the 'penciling mamma' (a title given to her by George Meredith) would sit at her work, the children at scrap-books on the floor or perhaps editing a newspaper under the table. . . . I remember her, at a pause in her writing, running her pencil lightly along the curve of the young eyebrow of the child whose head came hardly higher than her table and saying 'Feather!' Blandishments we had little of; we were taken into her arms, but briefly; exquisitely fondled, but with economy, as if there were work always to be resumed."

It was at this time too, that Mrs. Meynell was presiding at her brilliant *soirées* to which the élite of literary London came, attracted as much by her beauty and intelligence as by the spectacle of the full and harmonious home life this household afforded them. It is no wonder Le Gallienne saw here not the end of a century but the beginning of a new one. Shades of George Sand, Shelley, and Byron, notorious for their scorn of domesticity! Could it be that the Bohemian litterateur had passed, that the new artist would consider himself an obedient subject and imitator of the Divine Artist?

This artist of the new dispensation was also inspiring great poetry, in Francis Thompson for instance, and an admiration verging on adoration in other litterateurs like Patmore and Meredith. For Francis Thompson she seemed to typify the Church, *Mater Artium;* she was the Beatrice of some of his best lyrics, and in her children, too, he found another prolific source of inspiration. Those who admired her most were sometimes left under the impression that their adoration was not returned with usury. She seemed distant as an ideal. To one who recited to her on an occasion some lines from Thompson's *To a*

Poet Breaking Silence she said dreamily, "I think I have heard them before; whose are they?" "What fate must my poor verses to her expect if Francis Thompson's are so soon forgotten!" exclaimed Patmore when he heard of this.

Twice during the course of her life Alice Meynell was proposed for the dignity of poet laureate, once in 1895 and again in 1914. On the last occasion it was her sex alone, it seems, which prevented her from receiving the honor — a bitter blow for so pronounced a feminist. Her life span was a long one, reaching even into the first of the post-war decades. Thus she saw every generation of the Catholic Revival from Newman to Chesterton and beyond — not only saw them but succeeded in putting her impression upon the chief figures. During the 90's she had made the Revival a movement and had preserved its continuity by uniting the writers of the first and her own generation. At the turn of the century those, then very young, who were to carry the movement down to our own times came under her sway; Hilaire Belloc, whom she considered "quite brilliant," and Gilbert Chesterton ("my Chesterton. He is mine much more really than Belloc's. If I had been a man, and large, I should have been Chesterton"); Joyce Kilmer and the poet Thomas Walsh came to her from America; and there were, among the others, Shane Leslie, Eric Gill, Theodore Maynard, and Alfred Noyes, in all of whom she inspired the same sort of enthusiastic admiration she had in the older artists.

"In her lifetime," says Noyes, "she was a tower of intellectual and spiritual strength, lifting through the mists one of the very few steadfast lights. . . . Those who were honored with her friendship find it difficult to imagine the future without that sustaining power. The memory is not one that can fade; and through her work, the living voice will still speak."

3

Lionel Johnson

I

While the Catholic Revival was not, in its origin, a manifestation of the 90's, it is quite true to say that its life was quickened, its influence augmented, either simultaneously with or as a result of the many enthusiasms let loose by the last two decades of the nineteenth century. Not a few of these enthusiasms were themselves professedly religious like the *élan* in the Church of England occasioned by the Oxford Movement; and those that were not partook of that strong mystic strain that had always been a part of the old Romanticism, now more uncompromising, more intense in this its final resurgence.

Each of these movements brought its quota of distinguished and undistinguished converts into the Church, as did also those phases of the period which seemed to be the most hostile to Christianity, such as the Decadence. Catholics, on the other hand, freely joined forces with their non-Catholic and atheistic brethren in crying for radical social reform, in exposing and alleviating the distress of the poor, in fanning the fire of romantic opposition to materialism, and in encouraging the current artistic cults strongly medieval in their sympathies. But for the most part Catholics, with some notable exceptions such as Alice Meynell in letters and Pugin in architecture, were the followers in these movements and not their leaders. Concurrently, however, with all this there was going on within the body of the Church something the existence of which was overshadowed by other and better-publicized revivals. The old religious orders had returned to England and with them new ones from foreign climes eager for apostolic work. Monastic sites, closed, in ruins, or secularized since the Great Spoliation, were repurchased and reopened; new foundations of nuns, monks, and religious priests and brothers were multiplied; and from the people themselves there came forth many public manifestations of communal spirituality, such as pilgrimages, processions, devotions to ancient saints, wells, and shrines, which declared that the ancient faith had acquired again a firm foothold in its native soil.

Time, which has a way of sifting the permanent from the passing, alone could make clear the relative importance of the many things that were going on then with the bewildering abundance of a three-ring circus. To most of the movements which seemed larger than the Church, the years have been singularly unkind. Few survived the Great War, and those that did, with not a tithe of the old promise, or unrecognizably altered for the worse intellectually. On the other hand, all the manifestations of life displayed by the Church then have increased and multiplied with that slow and certain step which has always been a characteristic of hers. Buckfast Abbey, destroyed by Henry VIII, and begun anew by the Benedictines in the last quarter of the nineteenth century was completed only yesterday, just as plans were being perfected for the cornerstone laying of the magnificent Liverpool Cathedral, the completion of which will be the work of expected generations, as the brilliant array of litterateurs, lay intellectuals, and ecclesiastical dignitaries who participated in the cornerstone ceremony declared with such splendid but not unjustified confidence.

II

There is, perhaps, no better way to see the variety and vividness of the intellectual ferment that was going on outside the Church than in the character and career of one who has been called "the most definite personality of the 'nineties." Nothing escaped the amazing intellectual awareness of Lionel Johnson. In him all the ardors, the zeals, the fanaticisms that clustered about the "new Romanticism" are focused. An excerpt from a letter written by him from Winchester, August 14, 1884 (he was seventeen years old at the time), may serve to give some insight into the mind of a somewhat typical Anglican of an upper middle-class family caught in the maelstrom of the new ideas:

"I want the mass of my brothers to feel that they are one in Christ or Shelley or Buddha or Hugo. . . . Words, mere words, till I find a means; hence I look around me and I see an ancient Church, professing Christ as the Head, with certain practical government and articled faith; with Shelley as pole-star and Whitman for pilot, I accept Bishop's tithes (a hard stumbling block), 39 articles, even Lord Penzance. . . . I have one monotone to which I will intone my life: 'I will be a priest' . . . I hope to be ordained deacon in the year 1888 or 89 . . . fellowship at Oxford for a few years and then to have a 'cure of souls.' I long for an unsophisticated parish by the dear sea. . . . To live in seclusion, writing for my bread . . . infusing beauty and the simplicity of love, the ideals of Christ and Shelley into minds fresh from God and the great sea. After that, twenty years of such work, I should wish to come in more contact with the masses of hereditary misery and want; to wear out the best of my life in our great towns. What an ambition. . . . and, Oh, to realize it." He composes this flight, as he remarks, in front of an "exquisite miniature of William of Wykeham; it prompts me to aspire to Canterbury."

We have here a cross section of very nearly all the enthusiasms, artistic, social, and religious, of the day except Catholicism and the Celtic Revival. These were to come later. The Kentish military family from which he had sprung seems to have had some Irish affiliations; but there was no Catholicism in it. Johnson describes his home life as "arid" and his school days as "lonely." How he would have had much time for social activity, granting him the desire, it is difficult to see, after one has read his *Winchester Letters* written between 1883 and 1885 while he was sixteen to eighteen years old. The reading indicated by the lavish references in them is enormous. He quotes St. Paul, Byron, Sinnett's *Esoteric Buddhism, Light of Asia,* Shakespeare, Mills' *Essay on Comte,* Plato, Swedenborg, Max Müller, Aeschylus, George Eliot, Schopenhauer, George Sand, Emerson, Newman, Dante, Thomas à Kempis, Voltaire, Catullus, Goethe, Darwin, and many others besides.

There seems to have been no plan or purpose to this wholesale gulping down of opinions. Yet one may note how the names of those like Baudelaire, Blake, Carlyle, mystics whose faces were set against the increasing materialism of Western culture, preponderate over the names of those who, like Darwin, Mill, Comte, were working toward this consummation. Johnson had a soul instinctively religious. He hated materialism because it killed beauty and idealism. The struggle that was going on in his adolescent mind arose from the spectacle, on the one hand, of the triumphs of Philistinism, and on the other, of the seeming inability of the Established Church to withstand it. So if he read the works of the proponents of a mechanical order, most of his time was spent in a frantic rush from one to another of the lurid romantic prophets in search of a synthesis that might forestall the new order and save the world for art and religion. "Combine all philosophies in one," he writes on May 26, 1884, "Christ, Buddha, Swedenborg, Kant, Fichte, Jacobi, Emerson *et hoc genus omne.* Is the little French professor [Comte] with his smattering of the sciences, a doughty dabbler in divinity, a greater man than these our fathers who gave us the hell and the death and our earth?"

Shelley seems to have been for him a more pertinent prophet in those days than He whom he was pleased to call "Christ." It was "Saint Shelley!" and for his sake he was torn between the ambition of being a priest and the desire of bursting "upon the astonished world as a poet." Toward the end of his letters, however, he is discovered turning the topmost part of his ardor to Walt Whitman. He thinks Whitman a "nobler priest" than his first idol because Shelley refused "to extend his charity to anything coarse and earthly, unrefined." The democracy of the American appealed to him, and, as could be predicted, his Romanticism becomes the more flaccid and funny.

Johnson left Winchester the finished product the English public schools aim at turning out, and he was frequently pointed to as such, learned in the ancient classics, in English, with a continental literary background, all capable of exquisite distillation in prose, verse, and speech. He, on his part, loved Winchester and its "half a thousand years" of scholarship as he loved no other place, immortalizing his affection for it in the poem that begins

To the fairest, to the noblest, to the dearest.

All of which is rather remarkable because Lord Alfred Douglas, who was a contemporary, writes of his days there, "I left Winchester neither better nor worse than my contempo- raries — that is to say, a finished young blackguard, ripe for any kind of wickedness," and W. G. Ward, who was there sometime before, "It is impossible to conceive anything more like Hell."

These Winchester letters prepare us for a step Johnson took shortly after the inception of his university career. At Oxford he naturally came under the spell of the intellectual influences predominant there, liberal theology, agnosticism, the aesthetic cults, and what remained of the Oxford Movement. There was nothing in the teaching of the most radical of these schools that was likely to shock Johnson or sweep him off his feet as it did so many others. He had by this time gone quite as far as they. He had had his romantic jag in his adolescence, where in the providence of God and according to the most solid findings of the psychologists, it properly belongs. The Oxford Move- ment, consequently, turned out to be the strongest influence, and he entered the Church.

Did his accession to Rome arise from the observation that the religious ecstasy proposed by Shelley, Pater, and the rest was founded on a philosophy no less materialistic than that of Bentham and Huxley, which he hated, and would in the end revert to this basis? Or did he merely see in the religion of the Catholic Church something that satisfied his highest artistic and moral ideals? Or did he at Oxford see what Newman and Hopkins had seen, that it was not *any* religion that would save the arts and civilization but only an authentic one? It is difficult to say. At any rate, he entered the Church, became a Catholic, and in doing so did not separate himself either from his friends or from the old intellectual idols. Very much like de Vere, he chose to focus his attention upon the undoubted element of good in Whitman, Shelley, and the rest which he now saw more clearly than ever before. His friendship and admiration for Walter Pater closed only with his death.

The next definite picture we have of Johnson is one given to us by Richard Le Gallienne on the occasion of their first meeting after he left the university: "It was a Rhymers' Club evening held at the house of Mr. G. A. Greene. Only three or four of us had as yet dropped in, and were standing about discussing some knotty question of the poetic arts, when a boy of fifteen or so, as it seemed, leaning against the fireplace . . . suddenly struck into the conversation with a mature authority and an unmistakable Oxford accent, and continued to talk with an array of learning that silenced us all. . . . His little, almost tiny, figure was so frail that it reminded one of that old Greek philosopher who was so light of weight that he filled his pockets with stones for fear the wind might blow him away. It was hard to believe that such knowledge and such intellectual force could be housed in so delicate and boyish a frame . . . his face had no little resemblance to De Quincey's, though it was finer, keener, more spiritual. When I first knew Joyce Kilmer he reminded me very much of Johnson . . . beneath his ascetic intensity, and behind that battery of learning, there was a deep and warm and very companionable humanity, as my subsequent friendship with him was to discover."

Before the end of the evening the two seemed to have known each other for years. Late that night they walked home together and as they passed Johnson's lodgings he invited Le Gallienne in for a final libation. ". . . As we mounted the stairs he made a remark that makes me smile as I write, for it was so very '1890.' 'I hope you drink absinthe, Le Gallienne, for I have nothing else to offer you.' Absinthe! I had just heard of it as a drink mysteriously sophisticated and even satanic. . . . Did not Paul Verlaine drink it all the time in Paris! — and Oscar Wilde, nightly at the Cafe Royal. So it was with a pleasant shudder that I watched it cloud in our glasses, as I drank it for the first time, there alone with Lionel Johnson, in the small hours, in a room paradoxically monkish in its scholarly austerity, with a beautiful monstrance on the mantelpiece and a silver crucifix on the wall."

Johnson was not, like Dowson, a drunkard nor, says Le Gallienne, what might be called a "drinking man." He had many qualities that separated him sharply from the typical man of the nineties both on its dilettante side and its real decadent aspect. Besides being sincerely religious he practiced his religion and was "solicitous for the spiritual welfare of his friends and anxious that they might find refuge where he himself had found it." Le Gallienne records that after Johnson's death he found in a bookstall a copy of *Religion of a Literary Man* (Johnson's personal copy of one of Le Gallienne's early works) in which he had written the following prayer: *Sancte Thomas Aquinas, per orationes tuas in ecclesiam Christi, trahe scriptorem amicum meum.*

Despite his close association with decadents, Johnson, during the critical 1890's, belonged definitely in spirit to those whose conversion had risen from the Oxford Movement and not from the Wilde-Beardsley-Dowson *milieu*. The first publication of his poems seems to have been in the 1892 *Book of Rhymers'*

Club. Among these we find a sonnet dedicated to Ernest Dowson called *Our Lady of France.* It is touching in its longing for something which "Poor France where Mary's star shines, lest her children drown," had, and London still was without:

> *Our Lady of France! dost thou inhabit here? Behold*
> *What sullen gloom invests this city strange to thee!*
> *In Seine, and pleasant Loire, thou gloriest from of old:*
> *Thou rulest rich Provence: lovest the Breton sea:*
> *What dost thou far from home? "Nay! here my children fold*
> *Their exiled hands in orison, and long for me."*

In another poem of later date he recognizes his comradeship with Robert Stephen Hawker and salutes him:

> *Oh, that from out thy Paradise thou couldst thine hand*
> *Reach forth to mine, and I might tell my love to thee*
> *For one the faith, and one the joy, of thee and me,*
> *Catholic Faith and Celtic joy: I understand. . . .*

His essay *Art of Thomas Hardy,* written in 1891 but published in 1894, established his reputation as a critic. A year later appeared his first complete volume of poems which won him recognition that was sincere but not notably wide. The same may be said of his *Ireland and Other Poems* which appeared in 1897. Johnson, indeed, was never during his lifetime a popular poet. He was unknown to the masses who adored Tennyson, and that chiefly because he made no concession to the popular taste. His diction and state of mind are distinctly classical. He wrote on occasion exquisite poems in Latin and the flavor of Latinity is strong even in his English verse. His romantic feeling for the beauty of nature was not of the gushing type which spreads itself over the landscape, but calm and restrained as we may see in his *Cadgwith, Gwynedd, In England,* and other nature poems.

Moreover, he had a pronounced interest in ideas, and he was uncompromisingly religious, although not in the sugary pious way. The absence, among his works, of verse in celebration of mundane love have caused some to regard him as too cold, too austere. But these are they who have never experienced what it is to love Him vividly who is the source of all love. They find Dante cold. One must have experienced something of this love if he is to come close to the truly incandescent spirit of Lionel Johnson.

Something needs to be said about another element in his poetry — that sense of pain, of struggle as of one who fights forces greater than himself. While Johnson cannot be called a decadent in the same sense as Dowson, Beardsley, and Wilde, he was not untouched by that strange sickness, the *maladie de siècle*. At least that is what many have chosen to call the particular spiritual malady under which he suffered, although it is quite evident that many persons of the same poetic temperament have been afflicted with a similar sickness in generations other than his own. Much of the difficulty arose from a high-strung, sensitive temperament and a physical make-up too frail to support his desire for work, which caused him at times to use strong drink as a stimulant. It would seem that this rather than the popular quest for newer and stronger sensations is the explanation of his occasional use of absinthe. For he had rejected the entire Pateresque philosophy. Yet that its beautiful despair had a strange attraction for him is unquestioned, and it was the struggle to beat down this attraction and to live up to the highest ideals of the Catholic faith that constituted the cause of the civil warfare that went on within him, leaving him at times spiritually dry and physically weak.

One gathers this from such a poem as *The Dark Angel*,

> *Dark Angel, with thine aching lust*
> *To rid the world of penitence:*
> *Malicious angel, who still dost*
> *My soul such subtle violence!*

> *Because of thee, no thought, no thing,*
> *Abides for me undesecrate:*
> *Dark Angel, ever on the wing,*
> *Who never reaches me too late!*
>
> *   *   *
>
> *Through thee, the gracious muses turn*
> *To furies, O mine Enemy!*
> *And all the things of beauty burn*
> *With flames of evil ecstasy.*

And what made the fight more bitter was the realization that on the side of the "dark Paraclete" were his romantic poetic forebears and not a few of his contemporaries and friends. Like Hopkins he fought out the lost battles of Shelley, Byron, Rossetti, and with his same spiritual armor, won. "I fight thee with the Holy Name," he says, because it was not good that a poet in gaining the world should lose his soul.

> *Do what thou wilt, thou shalt not so,*
> *Dark Angel! triumph over me:*
> *Lonely, unto the Lone I go:*
> *Divine, to the Divinity.*

In a triumph such as that of Johnson's not one but many artists triumphed. He fought the Decadence and fought it almost alone. There was nothing of the theatrical or spectacular in the fight as there was in the less successful struggles of some of his French and English contemporaries. As he remarked in *The Precept of Silence,*

> *I know you: solitary griefs,*
> *Desolate passions, aching hours!*
> *I know you: tremulous beliefs,*
> *Agonized hopes, and ashen flowers!*

The winds are sometimes sad to me;
The starry spaces, full of fear:
Mine is the sorrow of the sea,
And mine the sigh of places drear.

Some players upon plaintive strings
Publish their wistfulness abroad;
I have not spoken of these things,
Save to one man, and unto God.

IIis final years were spent alone and without publication. On September 10, 1902, he wrote to the editor of *The Academy:* "You last wrote to me sometime, I think, in the last century, and I hadn't the grace to answer. But I was in the middle of a serious illness which lasted more than a year, during the whole of which I was not in the open for even five minutes, and hopelessly crippled in hands and feet. I feel greedy for work."

His triumph over the "Dark Angel" when others of the *fin de siècle* had capitulated, had earned for him, indeed, the grace of living beyond this decade. But not far beyond. One week later he was killed, either by a fall from a high stool in a London public house or by a vehicle in the street near his Clifford's Inn lodgings. Authorities disagree. At any rate, he was picked up and taken to a hospital where he died shortly afterward.

4

Michael Field

I

So many interesting literary personalities came into prominence during the 90's, and either then or shortly afterward associated themselves with the Catholic Revival that, in a necessarily brief treatment of this kind, selection must be made. It
is a difficult business. Some of them, of course, like Henry Harland, will be spoken of later; others, John Oliver Hobbes and
Wilfrid Scawen Blunt, to mention but two, must be dismissed
with a word.

Of these latter it is to Blunt that we must give the largest
word in passing. Not that he was much the superior artist. His
slim output of verse is certainly not immortal, but is authentic
stuff for the most part, and his book of reminiscences, *My
Diaries,* critics have united in calling the most remarkable volume of its kind produced for a century. It is at least a very fascinating book. But he deserves to be mentioned here for
another reason. He was one of the few artists of the Catholic
Revival who were definitely touched with Modernism. A born
Catholic, not a convert, he had married a granddaughter of
Lord Byron, and he, indeed, united in himself many of those
qualities which made the first generation of Romantics both
admirable and unlovely. Politically, he was a fiery exponent of
liberty for small nationalities, which was all very well for poets
like Shelley and Byron, but did not precisely fit in with his
position in the British diplomatic service. His career was a
stormy one. He advocated Egyptian independence, and that not

in an abstract but a practical way; later it was the political rebellion in Ireland he aided, and for this endured a prison term. Intellectually, the conflict between faith and science, which then seemed so huge and irreconcilable, caused him considerable difficulty. He was attracted strongly toward Modernism, for, as has been stated, he belonged in spirit to the old Romanticism, and Modernism was in essence and origin a heresy of the Romantic Movement. It was under the egis of Modernism that the worst features of the Romantic resurgence (those, namely, which arose from its connection with the anti-intellectual philosophy of the late eighteenth and nineteenth centuries), threatened to enter the Catholic Church, and to the timely condemnation of it by the Church the Catholic Revival owes much in a purely literary way. This formal condemnation, much more than the wisdom of advanced critics, saved her artists from the intellectual bankruptcy and artistic ineffectiveness that was in store for those who clung to this wing of literary Romanticism.

"Tyrrell and I have both failed," Blunt once remarked sadly to Francis Thompson, speaking of the condemned Modernist, George Tyrrell. Thompson was then staying at Blunt's estate in Sussex trying to recover from the illness that resulted in his death. "As for me," Thompson replied, "I believe entirely. It is my only consolation." Deprived of much of this consolation, Blunt had others. There were his Arabian horses, his friends, his numerous political interests, and his beautiful estate where he lived the life of an English squire. There was his poetry, too, and we may quote one of his sonnets called *St. Valentine's Day* if only to show that he was not the sort of typical fox-hunting county gentleman whom Oscar Wilde immortalized in one of his epigrams as "the unspeakable in full pursuit of the uneatable."

Today, all day, I rode upon the down,
With hounds and horsemen, a brave company.
On this side in its glory lay the sea,
On that Sussex weald, a sea of brown.
The wind was light, and brightly the sun shone,
And still we galloped on from gorse to gorse.
And once, when checked, a thrush sang, and my horse
Pricked his quick ears as to a sound unknown.
I knew the Spring was come. I knew it even
Better than all by this, that through my chase
In brush and stone and hill and sea and heaven
I seemed to see and follow still your face.
Your face my quarry was. For it I rode,
My horse a thing of wings, myself a god.

II

The tenets of Modernism, however, did succeed in producing in Blunt a sort of spiritual torpor which made him less a poet than he might have been had he believed with the faith of Francis Thompson or the faith of Dowson, or Verlaine, or Bourget, or Brunetiere, or that of many others of his contemporaries who had their own peculiar ways of finding the weak points in and condemning the heresies of the age. For, excluded from the inspiration of the full Catholic spirit, he was unable to capture the temper of the only other attitude which is productive of literature — I mean the reverent and cultured paganism of the antique world. Very few, as Thompson has declared in his essay, *Paganism, Old and New,* are able to seize it in these latter days. The two women who wrote under the name of "Michael Field" may be mentioned among these few.

"There was one poet's name which was sometimes mentioned then," says Maurice Baring speaking of the 1890's. "The name has gone on being mentioned since, and will one day, I think, reach the safe harbor of lasting fame, and this was Michael Field." The fame of Katherine Bradley and Edith Cooper has not yet reached this harbor, but of all the many minor poetic voices that the end of the nineteenth century produced, none deserves it more than they. An accident and misunderstanding kept them from the recognition due them in their own day. Perhaps the renewed interest in their work occasioned by the recent publication of some of their letters and the coming publication of their journal *Works and Days* which they instructed their literary executor, T. Sturge Moore, not to open until the end of 1929, may make good the omission.

Robert Browning, who was one of the few who knew at first the secret of their collaboration under the pseudonym "Michael Field," called them his "two dear Greek Women." Katherine Bradley at the inception of their acquaintance with the poet was thirty-nine years old, the same age Elizabeth Barrett had been when he first met her. Edith Cooper was twenty-three, and seems to have been the first to enter into the correspondence with Browning which resulted in a very close friendship and warm mutual admiration. In a letter to Edith under date of May 28, 1884, he says of their first poetic drama *Callirrhöe* ". . . it is long since I have been so thoroughly impressed by indisputable poetic *genius:* a word I consider while I write, only to repeat it 'genius.' "

Miss Bradley was the aunt of the younger woman. She had reared her with the blended affection of a mother and a sister, attending personally to her poetic formation. Edith returned the affection, and so there grew up between them a friendship that endured until death. When Edith was about sixteen the two took up residence near Bristol, attending lectures in the local university and devoting much of their attention to poetry. "The aunt's taste was Greek and dramatic," says Arthur Waugh of them, "the niece's, Latin and philosophic. . . . Katherine was ruddy, buoyant, alive with the zest of life: Edith, pale, with remote grey eyes, quiet, slow to illumine, but, when aroused, capable of a rarer and more subtle effluence than her elder. Katherine was the pioneer, the fount of creative energy; Edith, the moulder, the constructor, the finished artist."

Their joint work under the name of "Michael Field" began to appear in the middle of the eighties. Critics were more than ordinarily impressed, not only by the extraordinary finish of the verse, but by the unmistakable stamp of personality they bore. The following lyric from the volume *Wild Honey* will serve to show that the judgment was not erroneous:

> *I could wish to be dead!*
> *Too quick with life were the tears I shed,*
> *Too sweet for tears is the life I led;*
> *And ah, too lonesome my marriage-bed!*
> *I could wish to be dead.*
>
> *I could wish to be dead,*
> *For just a word that rings in my head:*
> *Too dear, too dear, are the words he said,*
> *They must never be remembered,*
> *I could wish to be dead.*
>
> *I could wish to be dead;*
> *The wish to be loved is all mis-read,*
> *And to love, one learns when one is wed,*
> *Is to suffer bitter shame; instead*
> *I could wish to be dead.*

Interest in the new poet was increased by the mystery of "his" identity. There was much speculation in literary circles. On November 23, 1884, Katherine Bradley wrote to Robert Browning, who had apparently thrown out a hint that the author was of the feminine sex, asking him to guard the secret more closely: "Spinoza with his fine grasp of unity says: 'If two individuals of exactly the same nature are joined together, they

make up a single individual, doubly stronger than each alone!
— i.e., Edith and I make a *veritable Michael*. And we humbly
fear you are destroying this philosophic truth; it is said, the
Athenaeum was taught by you to use the feminine pronoun.
Again someone, named André Raffalovich, whose earnest
young praise gave me genuine pleasure, now writes in ruffled
distress 'he thought he was writing to a boy — a young man....
He has learnt on the best authority it is not so!' I am writing to
him to assure him the best authority is my work. But I write
you to beg you to set the critics on a wrong track. We each
know that you mean good to us; and are persuaded you
thought by 'our secret' we meant the dual authorship. The
revelation of *that* would mean utter ruin to us; but the report
of lady authorship will dwarf and enfeeble our work at every
turn. Like the poet Gray [Mr. Arnold] we shall never 'speak
out.' And we have many things to say that the world will not
tolerate from a woman's lips."

Her fears were correct. For when it became generally known,
as it soon did, that Michael Field was a name that covered the
identity of two women, interest in their work immediately sub-
sided. Poetry was too personal an affair to be written in col-
laboration and all the argument of Spinoza could not erase from
the mind of the reviewers that Michael Field, despite the ex-
cellence of his work, was not one but two personalities.

Arthur Waugh has said that the collaboration of Michael
Field "is one of the most remarkable examples of the fusion of
temperaments into unity ever witnessed in the history of liter-
ature. It would require all the ingenuity of Freud and Jung to
touch the hem of its garments." Perhaps this latter remark may
help *us* to appreciate their poetry, but it would not have helped
the people of the 90's.

A valuable insight into the personalities of the two has been
afforded by Mr. T. Sturge Moore's publication of some of their
letters written during the 80's and early 90's. They contain, too,
a no-less-valuable picture of the times. Browning appears fre-

quently and in relaxed attitudes, and there are some delectable bits about Herbert Spencer, Oscar Wilde, and others. But there is little in them that might prepare us for the portrait of them in their later lives which Father Vincent McNabb and Father Edwin Essex have given us. Both Miss Bradley and Miss Cooper chat interminably and delightfully about their art, their encounters with the great, the gossip and small-talk of the literary world. But there is nothing of religion.

"Paganism made us Catholics." This was their constant answer to inquiries as to what brought them into the Church. They had been Rationalists, but not, I think, of the conventional nineteenth-century type. One of their letters which describes a visit to Herbert Spencer, is illuminated by flashes of fun and gentle disdain at the pomposity, the hard utilitarianism, the artistic barrenness of the soul of the old philosopher. "On each side of the mantel-shelf hang two landscapes, for one of which he gave the highest price he had ever paid for a picture — £20. It has not the least merit, mon pere Spencer!" No, their rationalism was more that of the ancient world when men depended solely upon reason because it was the best thing they had to depend on. It was not blatant nor proud, but humble, because man was an underling. *Nos numeri sumus, fruges consumere nati.* It was beautifully wistful, too (the note runs through all their poetry of this period), because the inevitable suffering of life was unintelligible and the future dark. Father Essex is of the opinion that it was the clear and holy light which the Cross shed upon the problem of pain and sacrifice that, more than anything else, determined their entry into the Church. Once within the fold many other things came to enrich their spirits; but in the beginning it was just this.

Their poetry written after their conversion becomes definitely religious in contrast with the nonreligious character of their earlier work. Miss Bradley has expressed the change in the lines,

In the old accents I will sing, my Glory, my Delight,
In the old accents tipped with flame, before we knew the right
True way of singing with reserve. O Love with pagan might,
White in our steeds, and white too in our armour let us ride,
Immortal, white, triumphing, flashing downward side by side,
To where our friends, the argonauts, are fighting with the tide.

One is inclined to agree with Father Essex that their Catholic poetry has not the restraint, "the classical precision of expression and epithet" that marked their pagan verse. But it gains in other qualities, richness, freedom, elevation of thought, and a certain note of triumphant hope and happiness.

Naturally speaking, however, they had, after entering the Church, much less reason to be happy. The niece, Edith Cooper, developed cancer of a malignant type which caused her days and nights of anguish and enforced separation from her art. Miss Bradley suffered with her, at first from the close union of their spirits and the love she bore her; later, from the same disease. For the symptoms of cancer soon made their appearance in her too. But she said nothing, and Edith died ignorant of her aunt's physical pain.

Father Essex's acquaintance with the two women began when they came to stay in the grounds at the Dominican Priory at Hawkesyard, Staffordshire. "Miss Bradley would sit there," he says describing a visit, "almost pontifical in dignity, jealously watchful of her niece's requirements, instantly solicitous." What thoughts she had at times we may gather from one of her lyrics of this period, the full pathos of which can best be seen by placing it against a sonnet she wrote to Edith in their youthful days. It is called *Her Profile*.

> *Nought from the changing seasons can we win:*
> *I have desired that men should learn her spell*
> *As it abides, profound, perpetual,*
> *In contour from forehead to the chin;*

But there is such a tremor in the line,
Such quick beneath the chiselling — what art
The shore of her breath's egress can define?
What lips in all the world part as her's part?
Lo, if a chance, one night, she in her chair
A little from the hearth, a radiance swims
From candles lit beyond that face of hers,
So holden of a dream it never stirs,
While all its tender marge in shadow rims,
Even as a dusky pearl caresses air.

And now —

I watch the arch of her head,
As she turns away from me. . . .
I would I were with the dead,
Drowned with dead at sea,
All the waves rocking over me.
As St. Peter turned and fled
From the Lord, because of sin,
I look on that lovely head:
And its majesty doth win
Grief in my heart as for sin.

Oh, what can death have to do
With a curve that is drawn so fine,
With a curve that is drawn as true
As the mountain's crescent line?
Let me be hid where the dust falls fine!

There is another lyric from the pen of Miss Bradley which
expresses in a subtle way the pain they both had in common, as
well as the manner in which they were able to bear it and to
spiritualize it.

She is singing to thee, Domine!
Dost hear her now?
She is singing to thee from a burning throat,
And melancholy as the owl's love note:
She is singing to thee from the utmost bough
Of the tree of Golgotha, where it is bare,
And the fruit torn from it that fruited there:
She is singing.... Cans't thou stop the strain,
The homage of such pain?
Domine, stoop down to her again!

The niece was the first to die. Miss Bradley, alone in her suffering, lingered on until September, 1914, when she dropped dead while being dressed to go to Mass.

5

Francis Thompson

If Alice Meynell is the central figure of the Catholic Revival in this middle phase, Francis Thompson is its greatest figure. He belongs to the 1890's. History has definitely placed him there; all of his greatest creative work was either accomplished in or published during this last decade of the century. He was, moreover, a spiritual child of the period in that the two chief characteristics of the 90's converged in his experience. Despair, the knowledge of sin, repentance, all the solitary griefs, "agonized hopes and ashen flowers," he knew on the one hand, and on the other the exultant surge of resurrection, not partial, not momentary, as was the case with so many, but a triumphant entering into the full spirit of Catholicism out of which arose his best poetry.

But Thompson, citizen of a crazy decade that he was, had yet that genuine sort of genius which refuses wholly to be tied down by the passing marks of his age. His work is not "dated"; no one looks upon him as a *fin de siècle* poet. On the occasion of the twenty-fifth anniversary of his death two years ago, the New York *Times* said: "It is an evidence of the impression made on the literary world by Francis Thompson that the twenty-fifth anniversary of his death has evoked almost as many tributes as are commonly paid to the memory of a famous writer on his centenary. *The Times* (London), in an editorial, notes the significant fact that, while few of the favorite poets of the 80's and 90's are read today by any but the dwindling remnant of their contemporaries, Thompson has retained his hold upon the imagination of the younger generation. And this although some of the distinctive features of his verse — his wealth of classical allusion, his exotic neologisms, the deliberate richness of his diction — might be expected to jar painfully upon the susceptibilities of an age intolerant of any mannerisms but its own. He has managed to survive because his work embodies the essential qualities which everywhere and in all ages are known as the mark of true poetry. For richness of imagination, for metrical skill, and for sublimity of thought he is surpassed only by the great master poets of our language."

English letters since the 1890's have produced no poet equal in stature to Francis Thompson. And he was a product of the Catholic Revival. This is true in a double sense, for he was not a convert but a Catholic by birth; his education was Catholic, and his poetic formation (as well perhaps as his moral salvation) he owed to those most intimately connected with the Catholic literary resurgence of the time, Wilfrid Meynell, first, then his wife, Alice, and Coventry Patmore.

Thompson was a product of the second rather than of the first generation of Catholic artists. Both his mother and his father, Dr. Thompson, were converts from Anglicanism, being among the early fruits of the Oxford Movement. Shortly after Francis' birth at Preston, December 16, 1859, the family removed to a suburb of Manchester, and there his youth was spent amid the forest of smoking funnels of England's huge industrial district. The background was not a lovely one, a circumstance that Francis noted very early in life. He read much — Shakespeare, Scott, Coleridge, Macaulay's *Lays* — attending rather to the romantic atmosphere than to specific poetic qualities of these works. "I understood love in Shakespeare and Scott," he says of this period, "which I connected with the lovely, long-tressed women of F. C. Selous' illustrations to Cassell's Shakespeare, my childish introduction to the supreme poet. These girls of floating hair I loved; and admired the long-haired beautiful youths of early English history.

Shakespeare I had always tried to read for the benefit of my
sisters and the servants; both kicked against *Julius Cæsar* as
dry — though they diplomatically refrained from saying so.
Comparing the pictures of medieval women with the crino-
lined and chignoned girls of my own day, I embraced the fatal
but undoubting conviction that beauty expired somewhere
about the time of Henry VIII. I believe I connected that awful
catastrophe with the Reformation (merely because, from the
pictures, and to my taste, they seemed to have taken place
about the same time)."

Thompson's mother and father had destined him for the
priesthood, so in 1870 he was sent to Ushaw College where he
remained for seven years. He seems to have absorbed there all
the Latin and Greek offered him, but at the moral disciplines
in the curriculum he was much less apt. It was not that he was
rebellious; merely indolent, constitutionally forgetful, a
dreamer. With the best of will he could not find it in him to
get up on time in the morning. He made resolutions; he
threatened himself with such condign judgments as we find
written in huge characters in his notebook of this period:
"Thou wilt not lie abed when the last trump blows. Thy sleep
with the worms will be long enough." But the "rising bell"
which he thought he responded to not infrequently turned out
to be the dinner bell. His superiors were patient and sympathe-
tic, but in the end were convinced that one so indolent, so
hypersensitive, so slovenly in his habits would scarcely make a
good priest.

He returned to Manchester much to the disappointment of
his parents, much more so to his own. For he had wanted sin-
cerely to be a priest. His father's decision that he should be a
doctor, he accepted in silence and with an inward sense of de-
feat and frustration. It was a wistful sort of hopelessness which
had the effect of encouraging all those temperamental faults
that had blocked his path to the youthful but supreme ambition
of his life. He would not be a doctor; he knew that. But he said

nothing, only to himself he said, "If I cannot be a priest, then I will be a writer."

At Owens College, Manchester, where he now entered upon the study of medicine, Thompson had his first encounter with an education and an atmosphere that was not wholly Catholic. It did not please him. He would never have been attracted by the exact side of chemistry and biology, but there are vast concepts in the physical sciences which might have appealed to him had he not found them distorted by the materialistic cosmology of Spencer, Huxley, and Darwin. His attendance at lectures was irregular but he did succeed in picking up some scraps of scientific jargon, a little precision, perhaps, and a definite attitude toward the large claims of the preachers of the scientific evangel that in it the world might be renewed. The manner in which these savants arrogated to themselves the right of speaking dogmatically on questions outside their field was intolerable to him. "One hears much," he wrote later, "of the tyranny of the confessor. What of the tyranny of the professor?" Science had its claims to some pretensions but not these. For it was only

> *The eyeless worm, that, boring, works the soil,*
> *Making it capable for the crops of God.*

In 1879, after two years at Owens College, Francis had a serious spell of sickness during which, so it appears, laudanum was administered to him. This alone, however, would not entirely explain why upon his return to the little normal health he commonly enjoyed, he continued taking the narcotic. His mother, shortly previous to this had given him as a present (her last, as she was to die a year later) a copy of De Quincey's *The Confessions of an English Opium Eater*. The importance of this volume in explaining not only Thompson's addiction to opium but the step he was subsequently to take, can scarcely be exaggerated. His biographer, Everard Meynell, exhorts the reader to familiarize himself with the *Confessions*, "for, without the mighty initiation of that masterly prose, the gateways into the strange and tortuous landscape of dreams can hardly be forced, nor half the thickets and valleys be conquered, of the poet's intellectual history." Not only was Thompson caught by the magic of De Quincey's prose; he found in him a brother, another Manchester youth who, like him also, had spent many hours in the Manchester library, poring over the works of the Elizabethans, and who belonged to that race of romantic geniuses to whom the word *escape,* escape from the bludgeoning of a hated environment, has a thrill unexperienced by others.

His six years at Owens College culminated in his failure in the final examinations in 1884. Events went swiftly toward a crisis. His mother dead, his father faced with financial difficulties and exceedingly annoyed at this second failure, Francis was put to work with a manufacturer of surgical instruments. Two weeks of this sufficed. Burning words passed between him and his father, who charged him with being a drunkard. Francis, of course, denied it, as he well could; for it was opium, not whiskey, upon which he had been spending the parental money! But there was no staying at home now. The next morning his sister found a note on her dressing-table announcing her brother's departure. He had sold his belongings and was on the road to London with a copy of Blake's *Poems* and the plays of Aeschylus in his pocket, and the example of De Quincey before him. But no spirit of adventure surged up to sustain him. He did not want to leave home; his mood was a hopeless one, full, as he said later, "of the gloomiest forebodings."

This was in November, 1885. Francis Thompson's "midnight time" was beginning. It was to last three years in point of time, but for a lifetime as far as the memory of this man was concerned. For he could never afterwards put out of his mind the horror of the months he spent as a vagabond in "darkest London." He refrained even from speaking at length about them. Thus his experiences are known to us only in fragments. We may indicate some of them here briefly. His little money soon exhausted, and unable to receive permanent employment, he soon fell into the life of a "drifter," picking up a few pennies here and there as a newsvender, a bootblack, a sandwich-man, a carriage-caller before the theaters and restaurants, even as a common beggar. He slept where he could, in the cheap lodging house of the homeless when he had the price, and more frequently toward the end of the period in an archway or on the Embankment, standing or huddled against the protecting stones. He was weak physically, undernourished, suffering that double agony of the destitute addict whose sporadically earned sums go into the purchase of narcotics and not food.

The London underworld and the night life of huge cities was just being discovered then by the men who were to look back upon the 90's as to a fairy region of romance and adventure. Thus Richard Le Gallienne sang in one of the most popular of the *fin de siècle* lyrics.

> *London, London, our delight,*
> *Great flower that opens at night,*
> *Great city of the midnight sun,*
> *Whose day begins when day is done.*
>
> *Lamp after lamp against the sky*
> *Opens a sudden beaming eye,*
> *Leaping alight on either hand*
> *The iron lilies of the Strand.*

But there was no such magic in Thompson's London. He had seen something in Manchester of the sordid side of life in those dirty and crowded districts produced by a mad industrialism. But there he could retreat from the moral and physical filth to the sweetness and peace of his Catholic home. Not so now. He was alone, abandoned, made to feel that he was a part of the offensive atmosphere. Without any attempt to dramatize his misery as did a Dowson or a Verlaine or a Rimbaud, he

might well have called his vagabondage "a season in Hell." Of
London he said later in his review of Booth's book, *In Darkest
England,* that it is "a region whose hedgerows have set to brick,
whose soil is chilled to stone; where flowers are sold and
women; where the men wither and the stars; whose streets to
me on the most glittering days are black. For I unveil their secret
meanings. I read their human hieroglyphs. I diagnose from a
hundred occult signs the disease which perturbs their populous
pulses." This disease was a moral, not a physical one. It was sin,
and Thompson was brought up face to face with it. To him the
stench of all the other evils which affected the body of these
"gangrenous multitudes" was a small thing compared to it. "We
lament the smoke of London; it were nothing without the
fumes of congregated evil." And speaking of the children of
the district who know evil before they know good, "the boys
ruffians and profligates, the girls harlots, in their mother's
womb," he remarks that this and not their poverty was to him
"the most nightmarish idea in all the nightmares of those poor
little lives. . . ."

It never occurred to Thompson, says his biographer, that all
this experience might later be converted into the stuff of litera-
ture, that he was but serving his hard literary apprenticeship in
a placc Lamb called "the only fostering soil of genius." It was
a more serious matter than that to Thompson, and since it was,
it turned out to be the more valuable to his art. For it was a
spiritual training. During these years he learnt what sin was,
what the sons of Adam were in themselves. Later he was to
learn what God was, thus encompassing the two poles of the
spiritual life, according to the words of St. Augustine, *Noverim
me, noverim Te.* The first is as important as the second and its
necessary complement.

I have said that Thompson knew at first hand all that went
into the making of the decadence of the 90's. It is necessary,
however, to make a distinction between the manner of his
familiarity with evil and that of Wilde or Dowson or Verlaine.

They knew sin by sinning; he by a method no less experimental and productive of compunction but without the same moral guilt. He tramped the crooked streets of London as did Dante the descending spirals of Hell, knowing all sins and participating in them by the consciousness that in himself was the seed of all these *fleurs du mal*. It was this undoubtedly that enabled him later to rise to the higher terraces of the spiritual life while those who knew sin in another way remained below with only the heavy sense of guilt. Thompson in his ascent took with him this contribution of the last decades of the nineteenth century, for it is the firm foundation of all spiritual growth. It manifested itself in a fear of the just judgments of God and a holy diffidence in himself as man. This feeling stands out most starkly in his Ode to Cardinal Manning in which he pleads with the dead prelate to learn what the Book of Life may say of "One stricken from his birth, with curse of destinate verse":

> *But are his great desires*
> *Food for nether fires?*
> *Ah me,*
> *A mystery!*
>
> *Can it be his alone,*
> *To find when all is known*
> *That what*
> *He solely sought*
>
> *Is lost, and thereto lost*
> *All that its seeking cost?*
> *That he*
> *Must finally,*
>
> *Through sacrificial tears*
> *And anchoretic years*
> *Tryst*
> *With the sensualist?*

So ask; and if they tell
The secret terrible,
    Good friend,
I pray thee send

Some high gold embassage
To teach my unripe age.
    Tell!
Lest my feet walk hell.

Surrounded as he was by fleshly vices of all sorts, it is quite evident that Thompson was corrupted by none of them. Nor did he fall into the hardened, reckless attitude of those whom destitution has made enemies of society. The story is told that one of the Rothschilds coming out of his club one day gave him a florin for a paper. Thompson tried to catch him to rectify the mistake. Later when the news of the capitalist's death was read out at the Meynell's table he said: "Now I shall never be able to repay him." His one encounter with a woman (the only one we know of during this period) was a singularly sweet and beautiful episode. This woman of the streets befriended him when he was most in need of assistance. He speaks of her in *Sister Songs:*

Forlorn, and faint, and stark,
I had endured through watches of the dark
  The abashless inquisition of each star,
Yea, was the outcast mark
  Of all those heavenly passers' scrutiny:
  Stood bound and helplessly
For Time to shoot his barbèd minutes at me;
Suffered the trampling hoof of every hour
  In night's slow-wheelèd car;
  Until the tardy dawn dragged me at length

From under those dread wheels; and, bled of strength,
  I waited the inevitable last.
    Then there came past
A child; like thee, a spring flower; but a flower
Fallen from the budded coronal of Spring,
And through the city-streets blown withering.
She passed, — O, brave, sad, lovingest, tender thing!
And of her own scant pittance did she give,
    That I might eat and live:
Then fled, a swift and trackless fugitive.

Her flight, we learn, was occasioned by the news brought to
her by Thompson, after his first interview with Wilfrid Mey-
nell, that his poetry had been praised and salvation was in sight.
She refused to encumber his progress to fame, and was swal-
lowed up so perfectly by the city that Thompson was never
afterwards able to locate her, try as he did.

But the consolation of episodes of this sort did not come often
to Thompson in his London life. These were years of suffer-
ing without support except that which he got from his religion.
His narcotics gave him at times a blessed numbness and forget-
fulness, but the faith of his childhood, its prayers, its examples
of saintly heroism, its assurance that Christ was most present
to those who suffered poverty, hunger, and the world's neglect
for His sake, were there to support him when the wakeful
hours returned. He prayed, "said his Mass — always said his
Mass — at night," declared the Evangelical bootmaker, McMas-
ters, who gave Thompson one of the few examples of Christian
charity he met with during his wandering in the city which
presented to the outward eye so few of the trappings of the
Kingdom of God. But Christ was not absent to one of inward
vision. Among his papers, after his death, was found a poem
entitled "The Kingdom of God" which must date from this
period:

O world invisible, we view thee,
O world intangible, we touch thee,
O world unknowable, we know thee,
Inapprehensible, we clutch thee.

*   *   *

The angels keep their ancient places; —
Turn but a stone, and start a wing!
'Tis ye, 'tis your estrangèd faces
That miss the many-splendoured thing.

But (when so sad thou canst not sadder)
Cry; — *and upon thy so sore loss*
Shall shine the traffic of Jacob's ladder
Pitched betwixt Heaven and Charing Cross.

Yea, in the night, my Soul, my daughter,
Cry, — *clinging Heaven by the hems:*
And lo, Christ walking on the water
Not of Gennesareth, but Thames!

In February of 1888 Francis Thompson had arranged on some odds and ends of paper an essay he had been composing, *Paganism, Old and New,* two poems *Passion of Mary* and *Dream Tryst,* and had sent them to Wilfrid Meynell, editor of *Merry England.* "Kindly address your rejection to the Charing Cross Post Office," the covering note directed. The next day he spent his last halfpenny on two boxes of matches "and began the struggle for life." The greasy manuscripts lay on Meynell's desk for six months; then they were read, admired by the editor and his wife, and a fruitless attempt was made to reach the author through the Charing Cross Post Office. In the meantime "a flood-tide of misfortune had rolled over" poor Thompson, driving him to such a pitch of despair that he had attempted suicide, and was only prevented from taking the whole of a killing dose of narcotics by a vision of the poet Thomas Chatterton that came to him in his delirium in Covent Garden. Shortly afterwards his poem the *Passion of Mary* appeared in the April number of *Merry England*. The Meynells had decided upon this course as the best way of reaching him. Thompson saw it, wrote, giving as his address this time, that of the chemist-shop in Drury Lane where he bought his narcotics, and, through the mediation of the proprietor, Thompson was located and brought to the office of the editor.

A new period was opening for Thompson, although it was some time before he realized it. Shy and noncommittal, he would give no word to his rescuers of the real extent of his destitution, and consistently refused their numerous offers of hospitality. He was in a wretched condition physically. Wilfrid Meynell at length persuaded him to see a doctor, whose verdict it was that Thompson had not long to live, and that his death would be hastened by any attempt to cut down his allowance of opium. But the wiser editor had decided that Thompson should be cured of the habit, and it was *his* advice that was followed. He was sent to a private hospital and later to the Storrington Priory in Sussex. In the monastery he at length found himself, renounced narcotics, and celebrated his victory by writing the *Ode to the Setting Sun*. It was the "first conclusive sign of the splendour of his genius," notes his biographer. One finds it, perhaps, a little too splendid in execution, too gorgeous, and not a little diffuse. Still, the sign of genius was there unmistakably, most notable, I think, in the presence of that sign in which he was to triumph over difficulties that had wrecked many another poet — the Sign of the Cross. For the poem is more a hymn to the Cross than to the sun. It was begun, his memorandum tells us, "in the field of the Cross (at Storrington) and under the shadow of the Cross, at sunset." The last few months

had been agonized ones for him. He had endured many deaths
in the struggle to cut himself free from his opium habit. But on
this evening he felt the surge of victory, wherein these dyings
became as so many necessary preludes to a more complete and
fuller life; and the sun which sank only to rise again was the
symbol of all this.

There is much in the ode, as this analogy is worked out, that
any romantic poet might have been capable of. Indeed one
catches scraps of Shelley and Keats in the lines. But Thompson
goes beyond this natural symbolism of the sun as the life-giver
and the life-destroyer. He announces that he will sing

> *A song thou hast not heard in Northern day;*
> *For Rome too daring, and for Greece too dark.*

It is a song of that other Son who came "that men might have
life and have it more abundantly" through His dying and aris-
ing. The lower symbol leads him to the high reality:

> *If with exultant tread*
> *Thou foot the Eastern sea,*
> *Or like a golden bee*
> *Sting the West to angry red,*
> *Thou dost image, thou dost follow*
> *That King-Maker of Creation,*
> *Who, ere Hellas hailed Apollo,*
> *Gave thee, angel-god, thy station;*
>
> *Thou art of Him a type memorial.*
> *Like Him thou hang'st in dreadful pomp of blood*
> *Upon thy Western rood:*
> *And His stained brow did vail like thine to night,*
> *Yet lift once more Its light,*
> *And risen, again departed from our ball,*
> *But when It set on earth arose in Heaven.*
> *Thus hath He unto death His beauty given;*

The "After-Strain" which completes the ode manifests an
even higher wisdom. For the poet is not to die. He must live,
and in that life there will be pain, more than he perhaps then
realized, and of this the Storrington cross which receives the
red light of the sun is "a presaged dole."

> *Even so, O Cross! thine is the victory.*
> *Thy roots are fast within our fairest fields:*
> *Brightness may emanate in Heaven from thee,*
> *Here thy dread symbol only shadow yields.*
>
> *Of reapèd joys thou art the heavy sheaf*
> *Which must be lifted, though the reaper groan;*
> *Yea, we may cry till Heaven's great ear be deaf,*
> *But we must bear thee, and must bear alone.*

So he will bear it but not without first a prayer to the Blessed
Lady who has already made many of the better things in his
life sweet.

> *Therefore, O tender Lady, Queen Mary,*
> *Thou gentleness that dost enmoss and drape*
> *The Cross's rigorous austerity*
> *Wipe thou the blood from wounds that needs must gape.*
>
> *'Lo, though suns rise and set, but crosses stay,*
> *I leave thee ever,' saith she, 'light of cheer.'*
> *Tis so; yon sky still thinks upon the day,*
> *And showers aërial blossoms on his bier.*

"Alas for the nineteenth century," said Thompson in his essay
Moestitiae Encomium, "with so much pleasure and so little joy;
so much learning and so little wisdom; so much effort, and so
little fruition; so many philosophers, and so little philosophy;
so many seers, and so little foresight; so many teachers, and

such an infinite vortex of doubt! the only divine thing left to us is Sadness."

In February of 1890 Thompson left Storrington where

> *The hills look over on the South,*
> *And southward dreams the sea:*

and returned to London, just as the blatant decade was beginning. He spent much time with the Meynells and their children at the Palace Court House where, pacing the library floor, he composed *Love in Dian's Lap; Sister Songs* was written during the following year in Kensington Gardens but not published until 1895. The latter, scribbled in a penny exercise book, was presented to Wilfrid and Alice Meynell as a Christmas gift.

The Hound of Heaven also belongs to this period. "To be the poet of the return to nature is something," Thompson had said. "But I would rather be the poet of the return to God." He so becomes in this ode. The phrase "return to God," however, hardly describes the action of the narrative. Its spirit is not that of the Prodigal Son parable of the Gospels, but rather that of the parable of the Good Shepherd, with the lamb fleeing before the Master "across the margent of the world."

The poem occupies a rather unique and significant position among the rather large quantity of imaginative literature in which the search of the soul for God has been depicted. English poets from Spenser to Tennyson had been unanimous in conceiving this search under the analogy of the pure and hopeful knight setting out in quest for the Kingdom of God. Francis Thompson pictures it not as a quest but as a breathless flight from God. The superior realism of this conception is apparent when one recalls how often not only in the poetry but in the sober history of the past two hundred years, the European man has wandered from one glittering substitute for God to another; how under the influence of the partial philosophies and bourgeois religions of the times the Kingdom of God he sought has turned out to be a secular paradise, a humanitarian state or only a dream and there was no rest for his soul. The half-serious prophecy made by Addison in his papers on the Pleasures of the Imagination, that this "fantastik knight" would one day awake to find himself "on a barren heath or in a solitary desert" stripped of all his enchanting illusions, was on its way to fulfillment during the 1890's. London, as someone humorously remarked, was then a "city of dreadful knights." It has been called today, without a touch of humor, a Waste Land.

Wilfrid Meynell has insisted that the *Hound of Heaven* is "a purely autobiographical" poem. It is a record of Thompson's own spiritual experience. But that experience, individual as it may be, yet has such universality that many have found in it the record of their own bootless flight from the Voice that cries, "Lo, all things fly thee, for thou fliest me"; as well as their discovery that the surrender of the soul to God does not mean the loss of all the things they loved but the complete restoration of them;

> *"All which I took from thee I did but take,*
>   *Not for thy harms,*
> *But just that thou might'st seek it in My arms.*
>   *All which thy child's mistake*
> *Fancies as lost, I have stored for thee at home:*
>   *Rise, clasp My hand, and come!*
>
>   *Ah, fondest, blindest, weakest,*
>   *I am He Whom thou seekest!*
> *Thou dravest love from thee, who dravest Me."*

Oscar Wilde, on hearing the poem read for the first time, declared that it was the ode he had wanted to write. Eugene O'Neill has recently used its central theme in his modern drama of regeneration, *Days Without End*.

Francis Thompson was to find that the promise of the Voice,

> *All which thy child's mistake*
> *Fancies as lost, I have stored for thee at home*

referred not only to the reward awaiting the poet in heaven but to the hundredfold that was in store for him on earth if he should first seek the Kingdom of God and His justice. Thompson had already partly entered into this reward, as his first volume of poems published in 1892 amply demonstrated. He was now to go even further with his *Sister Songs* of 1895 and the *New Poems* of 1897.

The latter volume was written at the Capuchin Monastery, Pantasaph, Wales, where he went early in 1894 after his four-year stay with the Meynells in London. He had hoped here for a complete renewal of his art. The opulence of his poetic imagery (sometimes certainly excessive) had become displeasing to him, for he had learned, as Alice Meynell later remarked, "that these ceremonies of the imagination are chiefly ways of approach, and that there are barer realities beyond, and nearer to the center of poetry itself." These barer and higher realities he touched in his *New Poems* but without notable drift toward greater austerity of style. Verbal richness with its accompanying vices as well as virtues was a necessity of Thompson's type of genius. As much as he admired both Patmore and Mrs. Meynell, he could never write with the economy and restraint with which they wrote.

At Pantasaph, Thompson met Coventry Patmore for the first time, and during his residence of two years there, it was Patmore and the monks who introduced him to the transcendental ideas behind the Church's liturgy, thus supplying him with the philosophical and theological bases of the mystical sections of his *New Poems*. To say all that ought to be said about the poetry of this period is, of course, impossible. The genius of Thompson is not such as can be exhausted in a chapter. One can only develop briefly those phases of it he considers the most significant. So in connection with this last volume of Thompson's poetry, its chief significance, it seems to me, is caught in a statement made by the distinguished Dante-scholar, Edmund G. Gardner, writing in 1898. Of Thompson, he says, that he "would eventually stand out in the history of modern thought as the epic poet of modern Catholicity, using the term 'epic poet,' not in its more strict sense, but in that in which Shelley employed it in his *Defense of Poetry,* to distinguish Homer, Dante, and Milton: a 'poet, the series of whose creations bore a defined and intelligible relation to the knowledge and sentiment and religion of the age in which he lived, and of the ages which followed it, developing itself in correspondence with their development.'"

If we are to give to Francis Thompson the title of the "epic poet of modern Catholicity" it will be chiefly, I think, because he displays himself in the *New Poems* as the poet of liturgy; and liturgy is the unique expression of modern Catholicity.

Thompson has frequently been called "a liturgical poet," sometimes for no better reason than that he makes use of metaphors, such as "blanch-amiced clouds," "solemn thurifer," "twilight, violet-cassocked acolyte," and the like, borrowed from ecclesiastical ritual, and plastered upon the face of nature as a sort of rhetorical cosmetic. Had he done no more than this, the title would be a resounding misnomer. But despite Thompson's love of exotic imagery, it must be insisted that he did not apply the language of the liturgy to nature because it was exotic but because it was *native;* it seemed to him the most apt language in which to express the elevated position enjoyed not only by man but by infra-rational creation in the New Dispensation. In a word, he had grasped the reality behind the symbolism of the ritual, he had seen how Christ the *Pontifex,* the *bridge-builder* between heaven and earth, has raised up that which was cast down, and had united things, long disparate and warring; he had had a clear vision of a Christocentric universe. It was this that made him a liturgical poet, this and the decision to apply to all things the language of the Sacrifice which made real this surpassing unity and oneness of all things.

We have already made mention, in speaking of Alice Meynell, of how the doctrine of the Mystical Body of Christ was coming to the fore in the nineteenth century. If this doctrine made for solidarity, if it gave a new direction to Cathoiic political ideas by leveling national and racial boundaries, and to Catholic economics and social ideas by revealing the closeness and sanctity of man's relation to his fellow man, it was no less important in its influence on poetry. For the poet, too, was to find in the reality of the Mystical Body that unity of vision the Romantics had thirsted for, and which was to save him from the barrenness of materialistic monism and the disillusionment of an amorphous pantheism. In 1896 (one year before the publication of the *New Poems*) Leo XIII had "directed the modern mind to the vital doctrines of the Mystical Body, which had not been emphasized for centuries."[1] Francis Thompson could not have known that this was to be the beginning of wider interest in the so-called Liturgical Movement which with the passage of years would become the backbone of the Catholic Revival in Germany, France, England, and other countries, the essential expression of resurgent Catholicism. But at Pantasaph, just as Huysmans had at Solesmes and Chartres, he began to study the liturgy and to apply its ideas to his art.

Coventry Patmore was the person whose intellectual influence upon Thompson at this critical time was the most important. In his *Religio Poetae* this poet who looms so large in the first phase of the Revival had said: ". . . I think it must be manifest to fitly qualified observers, that religion, which to timid onlookers appears to be on a fair way to total extinction, is actually, both by tendency from without and compulsion from within . . . in the initial stage of a new development, of which the note will be *real apprehension,* whereby Christianity will acquire such a power of appeal to the pure among the Gentiles, as will cause it to appear almost like a New Dispensation, though it will truly be no more than a fulfillment of the express promises of Christ and His Apostles to the world —

[1] Ellard, Gerald, S.J., *Christian Life and Worship* (Milwaukee: Bruce Publishing Co., 1933), p. 119.

promises which in every age have been fulfilled to thousands
and thousands of individuals who have so learned the King's
secret as to have become the converts of intelligible joy." Those
in modern times who are daily discovering for the first time
the transcendent reality behind what is called liturgy do indeed
find that it appears "almost like a New Dispensation." And so
it was with Thompson in the midst of the 90's.

Of the *New Poems,* the one which most carries the impress
of the new vision is the *Orient Ode.* Just as in the case of the
Ode to the Setting Sun, of which this is an antiphonal piece,
it must be insisted that it is not a song to the sun but to Christ,
whom the language of the Church frequently designates as the
Oriens, "the one arising in the east like the sun."² "As a matter
of fact," remarks Thompson in a letter to Patmore, "it was writ-
ten soon after Easter, and was suggested by passages in the
liturgy of Holy Saturday."

> *Lo, in the sanctuaried East,*
> *Day, a dedicated priest*
> *In all his robes pontifical exprest,*
> *Lifteth slowly, lifteth sweetly,*
> *From out its Orient tabernacle drawn,*
> *Yon orbèd sacrament confest*
> *Which sprinkles benediction through the dawn;*
> *And when the grave procession's ceased,*
> *The earth with due illustrious rite*
> *Blessed, — ere the frail fingers featly*
> *Of twilight, violet-cassocked acolyte,*
> *His sacerdotal stoles unvest —*
> *Sets, for high close of the mysterious feast,*
> *The sun in august exposition meetly*
> *Within the flaming monstrance of the West.*

---

²For the explanation of passages in this poem, I have followed the exegesis of
Father Terence L. Connolly, S.J., cf. his *Poems of Francis Thompson* (New York:
Century, 1932).

> *O salutaris hostia*
> *Quae coeli pandis ostium!*
> *Through breachèd darkness' rampart, a*
> *Divine assaulter, art thou come!*
> *God whom none may live and mark!*

Although, at first sight, it may appear that the language of the liturgy is being used to glorify the sun, yet as a matter of fact the reverse of this is true. It is the sun which is being used, as in Scripture, to help us understand the liturgy. This appears quite clearly as the ode progresses. The chief idea developed is that of Christ's likeness to the sun in that He gives life, not only as Creator, the natural life, but as Redeemer, that "incredible" super-life of grace by which men are made the sons of God, and participators in the divine life.

> *Yet thy clear warranty above*
> *Augurs the wings of death too must*
> *Occult reverberations stir of love*
> *Crescent, and life incredible.*

This new life which Christ gives affects not man alone but the whole of nature. As the prayer read in the services of Holy Saturday puts it, "May the whole world experience and see that what was cast down is raised up; that which is grown old is made new; that all things may return to a perfect state through Him from whom they received their beginning, our Lord Jesus Christ, Thy Son." Ever since the equilibrium of nature was disturbed by the entrance of sin into the terrestrial order, the world, as Thompson puts it echoing the words of St. Paul, has been "leashed with terror, leashed with longing" for the advent of Him who would restore all things "to a perfect state." Christ in making the common bread and wine to participate in the Sacrament of His Body and Blood has elevated inanimate Nature to a new plane of nobility.

To thine own shape
Thou round'st the chrysolite of the grape,
Bind'st thy gold lightning in his veins;
Thou storest the white garners of the rains.
Destroyer and preserver, thou
Who medicinest sickness, and to health
Art the unthankèd marrow of its wealth:
    *   *   *

Thy proper blood dost thou not give
That Earth, the gusty Maenad, drink and dance?
Art thou not life of them that live?
Yea, in glad twinkling advent, thou dost dwell
Within our body as a tabernacle!
Thou bittest with thine ordinance
The jaws of Time, and thou dost mete
The unsustainable treading of his feet.
Thou to thy spousal universe
Art Husband, she thy Wife and Church:
    *   *   *

Thou for the life of all that life
The victim daily born and sacrificed;
To whom the pinion of this longing verse
Beats but with fire which first thyself didst give,
To thee, O Sun — or is't perchance to Christ?

It is, of course, to Christ, in whom, as St. Paul says, "all things hold together" and through the likeness of whose life-giving and unifying function to that of the sun, Thompson had attempted to give poetic expression to his own vision of a universe made one and elevated to incredible heights of perfection. But he was not entirely satisfied with the effort. He feared it lay open to unorthodox interpretations, not because it was dangerously mystical, but because it was too scientific! "The *Orient*

Ode on its scientific side," he said, "must wait at least fifty years for understanding."

The science he spoke of was, of course, not the science of the nineteenth century. It was the science he confidently envisioned for the future, when cataclysmic world events, among them very probably the World War, would blast away the last remnants of the materialistic *scientisme* of his day, and men should again find the new cosmology of Christ where he himself had found it, hidden away in the bosom of the Church.

In a poem written before his death in 1907 he speaks of the Church as the "Lily of the King" in whom are stored the King's secrets which few know or understand, but which are soon to be released by the coming of mighty happenings.

O Lily of the King! low lies thy silver wing,
    And long has been the hour of thine unqueening;
And thy scent of Paradise on the night-wind spills it sighs,
    Nor any take the secret of its meaning.
O Lily of the King! I speak a heavy thing,
    O patience, most sorrowful of daughters!
Lo, the hour is at hand for the troubling of the land,
    And red shall be the breaking of the waters.
          *   *   *
O Lily of the King! I shall not see, that sing,
    I shall not see the hour of thy queening!
But my song shall see, and wake like a flower that dawn-winds shake,
    And sigh with joy the odours of its meaning.
O Lily of the King! remember then the thing
    That this dead mouth sang; and thy daughters,
As they dance before His way, sing there on the Day
    What I sang when the Night was on the waters!

BIBLIOGRAPHY

MEYNELL, ALICE

De la Gorce, Agnes, *Francis Thompson* (London: Burns, Oates, 1933), Ch. VIII.

Noyes, Alfred, *Some Aspects of Modern Poetry* (New York: Stokes, 1924).

Dublin Review, January, 1923.

Irish Monthly, January, 1932.

Meynell, Viola, *Alice Meynell: A Memoir* (New York: Scribners, 1929).

WORKS

Essays of Alice Meynell (collected edition), (London: Burns, Oates, 1914; New York: Scribners).

Hearts of Controversy (New York: Scribner, n.d.).

Poems of Alice Meynell (collected edition), (London: Burns, Oates, 1921; New York: Scribners.)

The Second Person Singular (Oxford, n.d.).

JOHNSON, LIONEL

Brégy, Katherine, *Poets Chantry,* pp. 120–142.

Le Gallienne, Richard, *The Romantic 90's* (New York: Doubleday, Page, 1925), pp. 186–197.

America, Vol. 37, p. 212.

Catholic World, Vol. 107, p. 758.

Some Poems of Lionel Johnson, edited with introduction by Louise Guiney.

Religious Poems of Lionel Johnson, preface by Wilfrid Meynell (New York: Macmillan, 1916).

WORKS

Poetical Works of Lionel Johnson (New York: Macmillan, 1913).

Some Winchester Letters of Lionel Johnson (New York: Macmillan, 1919).

The Art of Thomas Hardy (New York: Dodd, Mead, 1928).

Post Liminium, essays & critical papers (London: Elkins Mathews, 1917).

Reviews and Critical Papers (New York: Dutton, 1921).

"MICHAEL FIELD"

Carmina, Vol. I, pp. 234–47.

Irish Monthly, Vol. 42, p. 162.

Sturgeon, M. C., *Michael Field* (New York: Macmillan, 1922).

Bookman (N.Y.), March, April, August, 1932. (Letters of Michael Field.)

WORKS

Selections from the Poems of Michael Field, preface by T. Sturge Moore (Boston: Houghton, 1925).

The Wattle-fold (unpublished poems) preface by Vincent McNabb (New York: Oxford Press, 1930).

Underneath the Bough: a Book of Verse (London: Mosher, 1898).

THOMPSON, FRANCIS

De la Gorce, Agnes, *Francis Thompson.*

Brégy, Katherine, *Poets Chantry,* pp. 142–159.

Meynell, Everard, *Life of Francis Thompson* (New York: Scribners, 1916).

Sister of Notre Dame, *The Message of Francis Thompson* (New York: Benziger, 1920).

WORKS

Connolly, Terence L., S.J., *Poems of Francis Thompson,* edited with biographical and textual notes (New York: Century, 1932).

St. Ignatius Loyola (London: Burns, Oates, 1909).

Works of Francis Thompson, Vol. III, Prose, edited by Wilfrid Meynell (New York: Scribner, 1913).

BLUNT, WILFRID S.

Colum, Padraic, *A Half-Day's Ride* (New York: Macmillan, 1932), p. 142.

Catholic World, Vol. 47, p. 370.

Commonweal, Vol. 14, p. 425.

WORKS

My Diaries (New York: Knopf, 1932).

Poems (New York: Knopf, 1923).

6

The Celtic Dawn

I

One of the friends of Alice Meynell, and a frequent visitor at her London house, was the distinguished Irish poetess Katharine Tynan. She was sometimes accompanied in these visits by her fellow revivalist, William Butler Yeats, who was destined to become the most celebrated figure of what is now known as the Irish Literary Revival. This, also, was one of the manifestations of the 90's on its renascent side — the literary emergence of Ireland — and one, too, of the first importance. The intellectual atmosphere of the times was distinctly favorable to the peculiar contribution the Celtic peoples had to offer. The rather widespread discontent with the spiritual flabbiness of nineteenth-century materialism was causing not a few pure Anglo-Saxons to look hopefully to those peoples who were less touched by this disease, less committed to this sort of culture, and who had the things of the spirit in abundance.

Says Agnes de la Gorce of the presence of this Celtic motif in the Palace Court circle: "Had not Ireland preserved intact down the centuries the old familiarity with things divine? Would not her descent upon England be to communicate to English Catholicism something of her inspiration and her dreams?" If we speak only of Katharine Tynan, both questions may be answered in the affirmative. But of the Irish Literary Revival in general only one of them may be so answered. Ireland had, indeed, kept her ancient touch with the things of God. She had kept little else. Alone among the nations of northern Europe, the great mass of her people had clung tenaciously to the Faith and had suffered the loss of culture, education, freedom — everything, rather than abandon it. She had ample cause for wishing to "descend" upon England, and at this time when the civilization which had so ruthlessly crushed her own was itself tottering, she would have wished for no more subtle or appropriate revenge than that of giving to her oppressors that which she had saved and they had flung away. It was a part she had played with distinction before. In the Dark Ages, when the old Roman civilization had collapsed and darkness was upon the nations of Europe, Ireland had for three centuries maintained the only light in the West, sending forth her saints and scholars to give to her neighbors that which afterward became the foundation of their future cultural greatness.

In the 1890's this mission was repeated only in a limited sense. We are speaking, of course, of literature and the part played in the crisis by the Irish Literary Revival. This movement did succeed in focusing the attention of the world upon Ireland, and of extracting from it the admission that she was producing artists comparable to any in Europe. It did other important things which will be mentioned later. But this significant difference is to be noted between the Ireland of the sixth and seventh centuries and the Irish Literary Revival of the 90's, that while one distinguished itself by giving to Europe something it needed and had little of, namely, Christian culture, the other made a distinguished contribution to that which existed in abundance. It involves no blindness to the real literary ability of the members of the "Celtic Twilight" group to say that much of their success, much of their inspiration was due to their having fallen in line with the "new Romanticism" which was everywhere in the ascendancy. The Irish Literary Revival of the 1890's threw the weight of its influence upon the side of this last stand of the old Romanticism, and in so doing helped enormously to multiply the type of writer of whom Herbert Cornish remarked when asked by Maurice Baring to praise a *fin de siècle* poet, "the trouble is that everyone writes so well nowadays that it is hardly worth while for any new poet to write well. All can raise the flower because all have gone to seed."

And so it turned out that when Ireland, after centuries of silence concerning the things closest to her heart, did at length become gloriously articulate, her message was scarcely distinguishable from that heard daily in the Café Royal or in the Paris Latin Quarter. Despite the deep Catholic faith of her people, on the one hand, and the crying need of all Europe for this leaven, on the other, her best literature of the period contained little of Catholicity — as neat a piece of irony, by the way, as history has to offer.

The Celtic Revival was not, then, predominantly a Catholic manifestation, although many of its founders and adherents were Catholics and wrote as such. However, with the possible exception of Katharine Tynan and Lionel Johnson (who was not Irish but English), they were by and large inferior as pure artists to those who wrote from another inspiration. The contribution of the Catholics, none the less, has, with the passage of years shown itself to have been the more wisely directed and the better calculated to achieve that which all agreed was the first aim of the Revival, namely, the building up of a genuine Irish national literature. The "Celtic Twilight" faction, falling in with the fashion of the day, put art first, above both nation and religion. The Catholic group put art in the service of patriotism and religion, and in the end won political freedom and laid the foundations of a literature which will, if present indications are not deceitful, be Irish in the full and complete sense of the term.

II

In order to see the importance of the Catholic element in this middle phase of the Irish Literary Revival, the movement must be looked at both from its early beginnings in the nineteenth century and from its present status a century later, in the twentieth. It was the aim and ideal of all connected with the early stages of the movement to produce a literature written in English, which would yet not be English but Irish. Ireland, it was pointed out, had never had such a literature. Goldsmith, Sheridan, Burke, Steele, and Swift were Irish only in birth. They lived in England and wrote as Englishmen for English audiences. It was necessary, of course, that they should so write. The rigid Anglicising methods employed for several centuries had made the ancient Gaelic almost a forgotten language. Moreover, the few to whom an education was permitted were educated as any Englishman might be trained, and as a consequence were better fitted to write for English audiences than for native.

The first half of the nineteenth century, however, brought about several changes, mostly political and having to do with the relief of oppression, which made for the production of a distinctly national literature. Around the patriot and leader Daniel O'Connell, who secured Catholic emancipation in 1829, there had gathered a group of young men who wrote well but whose first passion was not art but freedom. It was from this group called the Young Ireland Movement that Anglo-Irish literature took its origin rather than from the poet Tom Moore, who delighted English audiences with his tender and musical interpretations of Irish life, but who was not a notable patriot and lived abroad. Thus the movement was from the beginning essentially "an expression of awakened nationality." It is well to insist on this because later during the 90's Anglo-Irish literature, under the leadership of Yeats, was to take a different turn. It would be contemptuous of letters in the service of patriotism, it would put the artist in an ivory tower, it would be eager for foreign rather than for native praise.

The organ of the Young Ireland Movement was *The Nation,*

a magazine established by Charles Gavin Duffy in 1842 for the expressed purpose of stimulating the spirit of Irish nationality. And to this end he enlisted the aid of poets and scholars who might awaken an interest in the glorious but forgotten past of the nation, her sufferings, her grievances, her destiny in Europe. The response was immediate not only from those whose patriotism showed little of the refining influence of art, but also from those who were at once patriots and artists. Chief among these was James Clarence Mangan, although Thomas Davis, Thomas D'Arcy McGee, Dennis Florence MacCarthy also did some very competent work. Mangan, however, was the real genius, and with his poetry there appears "the first authentic voice of Celtic Ireland in the English tongue." He was in contact with the ancient Gaelic literature, pagan and Christian, he knew the achievements of the past, he felt the injustices of the present, he was a Catholic and a patriot. From no other background could his most famous poem, *Dark Rosaleen,* have emerged. It is based on a Gaelic lyric of the Elizabethan times, but Mangan has added to it the cumulative grievances of the centuries since then, as well as a soaring confidence in the ultimate triumph of *Dark Rosaleen,* which is, of course, Ireland.

Anglo-Irish literature grew in volume and distinctiveness as the rich treasures of the national tradition which had inspired Mangan were uncovered by successive historians and scholars. Sir Samuel Ferguson, Aubrey de Vere, and Standish O'Grady did the best work in the field of popularizing the ancient Irish legends. No less important, more so rather, as the years have shown, was the Gaelic movement begun about the same time and carried forward chiefly under the leadership of the Catholic George Sigerson and, later, Douglas Hyde. These scholars gave their attention to the work of collecting, transcribing, and translating the Gaelic songs and stories of folklore which still survived in the countryside. The true Celtic spirit was to be found here in its purity. Thus the efforts made by Sigerson and

Hyde to popularize and reduce these to English gave to the
literature of the revival a new diction and new rhythms which
have made it Anglo-Irish instead of English.

III

An important event in the history of the revival was the ap-
pearance, in 1888, of a small volume called *Poems and Ballads
of Young Ireland*. With it the first phase of the movement
ended and the second began. In the volume were contained the
poems of the young writers, Douglas Hyde, Rolleston, Yeats,
Katherine Tynan, Rose Cavanagh, and John Todhunter, all of
whom had come under the influence of the movement to re-
store national tradition as mirrored in the Gaelic sources, and
who wrote from this rather than from a purely English back-
ground. Katharine Tynan and Rose Cavanagh were the only
Catholics represented in the young group. George Sigerson, the
editor, belonged to the first generation. In 1892 more of the
character of a definite literary movement was taken on by the
formation, in London, of the Irish Literary Society and of the
Irish National Literary Society in Dublin.

It is somewhat significant that the first of these literary socie-
ties was begun in London (it was the successor of the South-
wark Irish Literary Club, founded in 1883) and in London,
too, of the 1890's. For not only did the subsequent products of
the strongest wing of the movement bear the imprint of things
English, but it bore also a large measure of the current *fin de
siècle* spirit. Several things were responsible for this. First, there
was the effort, seconded by a majority of the young writers'
group, to cut the movement free from patriotism and politics
which had been the chief source of inspiration of the Young
Ireland Movement, and to make the movement a purely liter-
ary one. It was, of course, evident that if the revival was to have
English suffrage it could not be openly rebellious after the
manner of the contributors to *The Nation*. It must find some

modus of living in harmony with the British rulers without at the same time becoming entirely English like Oscar Wilde and Bernard Shaw.

Such a device was at hand in the spirit of neo-Romanticism which was everywhere in the saddle. The canons of this Romanticism, unlike that of the earlier and healthier Romanticism, were in no way turned against the separation, however artificially, of literature from political and social conditions. Indeed, the advocacy of the principle of "art for art's sake" distinctly favored it. The literary education of not a few of the new writers, too, made their acceptance of this spirit somewhat natural and inevitable. William Butler Yeats, for instance, who very soon displayed qualities that fitted him for real leadership, had spent much time in Paris learning the art of Mallarmé and other French symbolists. So, remarks Ernest Boyd of this change manifested by the movement during the 90's, "the literature of the Revival is no longer concerned with the political revolt against England. It has lost the passionate cry of aggressive patriotism, the wail of despair, and has entered into possession of the vast field of Irish Legend."

The legends would give to the new literature its Celtic flavor. Here again the wisdom of those who desired, first of all, that the stigma of artistic inferiority should be removed from Ireland was manifest. For not all the Irish legends were to be revived, only those which had come down from the pre-Christian period. Ossian had, as a matter of fact, through the MacPherson translations, been an important element in the Romanticism of the late eighteenth and early nineteenth centuries; the wistful sadness of the early pagan bards, their vague but charming nature-worship and loose mysticism, fitted in even better with the times which saw the second revival of Romanticism. On the other hand, the definite Catholic tone of the later legends would certainly have irritated the esthetes. All this made it possible for the revivalists to cultivate the Celtic spirit and to spread a modest de-Anglicization program without molestation from the secular arm. This sort of patriotism, in a word, was acceptable because it differed in no important way from that cultivated in England. But whatever may be thought of the tone taken on by Anglo-Irish literature during the 90's, it is fairly evident that on no other grounds could it have achieved the popularity and applause it did during this period.

IV

Although the youngest of the contributors to the volume *Poems and Ballads of Young Ireland* of 1888, Katharine Tynan was, at the time, the best known. She was already the author of two books of verse, one of which, *Louise de la Valliere and other poems* (1885), had brought her great popularity in both England and Ireland. The title poem was distinctly pre-Raphaelite rather than Celtic in its inspiration. However, some of the shorter poems in the same volume were marked by the latter influence. She was in touch with the Celtic legends on which the poets of the Revival were beginning to lean so heavily, and this strain was on the increase in her *Shamrocks,* of 1887, and in her best volume *Ballads and Lyrics* which appeared in 1891.

Her literary career had commenced before she was out of her teens, and was to continue well into the twentieth century (she died in 1931 at the age of seventy). It was a career of considerable brilliance and scope, bringing her into intimate contact with the important artistic and political figures of the day, both in England and in Ireland. In England, besides her non-Catholic literary friendships, she was on terms of close intimacy with the group which constituted the Catholic Revival, with Alice Meynell, Francis Thompson, Coventry Patmore, and Gerard Hopkins; one of her children had Louise Guiney and Lionel Johnson for godparents. She was in close association, too, with the Irish revivalists, especially with "Willie Yeats" who was her particular friend. In her reminiscences she tells of abandoning him at a garden party because he insisted on pouring poetry into her ear and water down her back because of his unsteadiness with the umbrella.

It would seem, however, that the ties which united her to her English Catholic friends were stronger than those by which she was drawn to the leading poets of the Irish Revival, for these latter were frankly pagan in religion and inspiration, while she was a Catholic, and moreover a militant patriot. Thus she was necessarily out of sympathy with much that they cultivated as belonging to the true spirit of Irish literature. Yet she was not without understanding of the reason for their beautiful paganism and their wish to separate the movement from the hurly-burly of politics. They belonged to the Ascendancy, as that small but ruling class in Ireland is called — the descendants for the most part of the English Protestant land-owners who had been given grants during the religious persecutions. It was necessary that the literature of Ireland should come from this class rather than from the common people, since they constituted the majority of those who enjoyed the advantages of an education. It was somewhat natural for them, too, to deprecate the political strife and agitation for liberty, since they had no memories of evictions, official murders, starvation, and religious oppression as the vast mass of Irish people had. As for their paganism, perhaps the general break-up of Protestantism may explain this too. The "Big House," as Daniel Corkery remarks of the Ascendancy, was already then in decay in more ways than one.

The Catholic writers of the period also may be said to belong to the Ascendancy class. Their religion, however, which they possessed in common with the people, kept them from going the way of their compatriots. This may be seen most clearly in the case of Edward Martyn, who, declares Denis Gwynn, enjoyed the "peculiar position of being the only Irishman of large private means who was in full sympathy with almost every phase of the Irish Revival." He was not only the financial angel and one of the founders of the Irish Literary Theatre, but also contributed to it some of the best of its early dramas. He

was active in the Gaelic League, which was working for the
revival of the Irish language. Yet he was also an intense Cath-
olic and a fiery Nationalist. Both his Catholicism and his pa-
triotism brought him into violent disagreement with the leaders
of the Celtic Twilight faction. The artistic ideals which he
strove to maintain were the very opposite of those espoused by
George Moore, for instance, at first his protégé, later his *bête
noir*. No less than Moore did Martyn desire that Anglo-Irish
literature should be not provincial but cosmopolitan. Still he
testily rejected the idea of achieving this cosmopolitanism by
an alliance with neo-Romanticism, popular as it was in Eng-
land and the continental countries at the time. This was not,
he perceived, a continuation of the great European tradition in
terms of which his Catholicism made him think, but the de-
cadent fruit of centuries of separation from it. If he was a na-
tionalist it was because he saw that "English rule in Ireland had
cut Ireland off from the older civilizations of Europe, introduc-
ing false standards that had no relation to the ideas or religion
of the Irish people." It was one of the most significant of Mar-
tyn's achievements to have introduced the Liturgical Movement
into Ireland, with all its promise of a full international outlook.

Katharine Tynan, despite her ability to live in harmony with
the leaders of the Celtic Twilight faction, "remained undis-
turbed in her acceptation of the simple teachings of the Cath-
olic Church," and consequently her verse "voices that naïve
faith, that complete surrender to the simple emotions of wonder
and pity, which characterize the religious experiences of the
plain man."[1]

> *In a green land, without hunger and drouth*
> *God gave a gift of singing to my mouth,*
> *A little song and quiet that was heard*
> *Through the full choir of many a golden bird. . . .*

Thus she herself describes her song. Not all of it is professedly

---

[1]Boyd, E. A., *Ireland's Literary Renaissance*, p. 111.

religious. There are other notes, love, patriotism, nature, but it is always "a little song and quiet." The Catholicity to which she gives expression is that of the "plain man," the simple Irish folk of the land, rather than that of the converted esthete. We may see this in the deep feeling but rather crude theology of her poem *Maternity:*

There is no height, no depth, my own, could set us apart,
Body of mine and soul of mine: heart of my heart!

There is no sea so deep, my own, no mountain so high,
That I should not come to you if I heard you cry . . .

. . . Now you are round and soft to see, sweet as a rose,
Not a stain on my spotless one, white as the snows.

If one day you came to me heavy with sin,
I, your mother, would run to the door and let you in . . .

. . . Child, if I were in heaven one day and you were in hell —
Angels white as my spotless one stumbled and fell —

I would leave for you the fields of God and Queen Mary's feet
Straight to the heart of hell would go, seeking my sweet.

God mayhap would turn Him round at sound of the door,
Who is it goes from Me to come back no more?

Then the blessed Mother of God would say from her throne:
Son, 'tis a mother goes to hell, seeking her own.

Body of mine and soul of mine, born of me,
Thou who wert once little Jesus beside my knee.

It is like to that all mothers are made: Thou madest them so.
Body of mine and soul of mine, do I not know.

The poetry that was hidden in the heart of the Irish people was not fully explored either by Katharine Tynan or by any other poet who wrote during the middle phase. This was to be the work of the next generation. The temper of the age, for one thing, was opposed to it. The *fin de siècle* man could admire the mystical Catholicism of the French convert Huysmans or that of the English convert Ernest Dowson, but not the simple, uncultured faith of the Irish masses. Those, then, who chose to give expression to it as the source of the most authentic spirit of the nation had to remain in an obscurity unknown to those who cultivated a spirit that was less native, less living. Among these the most important, perhaps, is Moira O'Neil, who gave to the Revival its first genuine peasant poetry. Hers was not a literary folklore derived from the study of ancient texts, but the minds and hearts of the living folk of the Antrim Glens expressed in their own charming dialect. Another was Ethna Carbery, whose verse captured the hearts of her native countrymen because it sympathetically and accurately interpreted them. Yet she died at the age of thirty-five, unknown to the great world of letters. Ernest Boyd says of her, "Writing solely for popular journals, for an uncritical audience, she escaped the discipline that must go towards the making of a great artist. In short, she paid the penalty which, as Yeats had pointed out, befell all who, like the poets of *The Nation,* put intense but narrow patriotism before art."

The same criticism may be applied with justice to all the Catholic writers of this period with the possible exception of Katharine Tynan and Dora Sigerson Shorter. For the Yeats faction had something of great value to offer which these writers needed. It is true, it substituted "fairy tales" for sober "political history"; it is true it passed over the living Ireland to dwell with sadness in an ancient "dream world" that had once been a reality. But it did something more. It held up to those who may have disagreed with this aspect of the program, models of exquisite literary workmanship which, together with the fame enjoyed by the leaders, stimulated and disciplined in a remarkable way the artistic efforts of their native contemporaries and the writers of the next generation. But this it did not accomplish without injury to the idea of a literature that would be distinctly national. The elimination of the element of aggressive patriotism may have helped to create an atmosphere more favorable to the cultivation of pure art, but it also broke contact with a source of strength and robustness which the movement, considering its leanings toward the softer sort of Romanticism, certainly needed. The almost exclusive attention given to the dead pagan tradition rather than to the living Catholic tradition also proved unfortunate from a literary standpoint. It sent the revivalists to texts rather than to the people, with the consequent loss of reality and freshness. For besides their simple and resolute faith, the Irish peasant population had an important element to contribute which was minimized by these leaders until later when Synge discovered it for the drama by living among them. What this was and its value can be seen by even a cursory look at Douglas Hyde's, *Religious Songs of Connaught* — an utter absence of the *clichés* of the Romantic mode, simplicity, inevitability, a distinctive diction which is the reward of those who sing their songs far from the self-consciousness of the academies and in close touch with simple, elemental things.

Time alone was to demonstrate the superior wisdom of the Catholic writers who refused to foresake either national politics or the people in order that art might flourish. The importance of their contribution, as has been remarked, can only be appreciated by viewing it from the higher ground of the present. For while the Celtic Twilight group was accomplishing with applause the notable thing of freeing Ireland from the stigma of artistic inferiority, those who continued in obscurity the traditions of *The Nation* group were accomplishing the slightly less notable thing of freeing the nation from political serfdom and starvation. They achieved in the course of time the Free State. In the meantime the World War with its cataclysmic reversal of fashions had produced another literary attitude which was tolerantly amused at the conceits so popular in the 90's. Add to this, the fact that the Irish people and not the Ascendancy hold the reins of government and educational policy, and one will not be surprised at the movement, now quite strong, which repudiates the entire work of the pagan middle phase *in globo* as insolent and exotic and as holding up to the world a caricature of the Irish no less contemptible than the stage Irishman of an earlier period.

v

That there was to be a new direction in Anglo-Irish literature was evident as soon as the poets of the younger generation began to be heard from. The majority of these had come under the intellectual leadership of Æ (George Russell) who introduced them to the public in *New Songs,* appearing in 1904. The four most promising of these were Seumas O'Sullivan, Padraic Colum, Joseph Campbell, and James Stephens, the last named not being represented in the *New Songs.* All of them, with the exception of O'Sullivan, showed a disposition to pull away from the influence of the Celtic Twilight — that "lovely and not-to-be-regretted deception," as Seán O'Faoláin has recently called it. Of these three, only Stephens was a non-Catholic. Both Colum and Campbell found their chief inspiration in the land and the Catholic people who lived upon it. They themselves were products of this land and this people. Colum has since become one of the most important poets of the modern Irish Revival and one of its best dramatists. He is also among the first of our contemporary Catholic poets and will be treated later. Campbell, who showed just as much promise as Colum, ceased to be heard from poetically after his *Irishry* of 1914. Perhaps his recent emergence as vice-president of the Catholic Poetry Society of America is a token that his finished Celtic songs will be heard again.

To these heralds of the new direction in the Irish Revival who became known in the first decade of the twentieth century, must be added the names of three more Catholic artists. Historians of the revival are accustomed to treat Padraic Pearse, Thomas MacDonagh, and Joseph Plunkett as heroic men and geniuses, whose unfortunate participation in practical politics deprived the movement of much in the way of great literature. In their eyes they belong more to the history of Irish politics than to the history of Anglo-Irish literature. And this because in 1916, putting the *patria* before the claims of art, they stood before a British firing squad and died for the freedom of the nation. The view is somewhat contradictory. For if we accept the assertion of these same historians that the end of the revival was the production of a literature that would be distinctively Irish, then the contribution of these men must outweigh much that was given by contemporaries of a more mature art but thinner patriotism. Through their sacrifice was achieved the one thing most necessary for full national expression — political freedom, the release of the vast mass of the Irish people in whom the most valuable gifts of the Celtic spirit, as events have progressively proved, were locked up.

Padraic Pearse was one of the first of the new generation to take an active part in the recovery of the Gaelic tongue. Although a Dubliner by birth (his father was English), he learnt the language by long periods of residence in districts where it was still spoken as a living tongue. His best poems and most of his prose were written in Gaelic; what he has left us in English, too, shows the wisdom of his efforts. The ancient language has given to his English a new idiom and a new flavor as a few lines quoted from *The Wayfarer,* composed shortly before his execution, may illustrate:

The beauty of this world hath made one sad:
This beauty that will pass:
Sometimes my heart hath shaken with great joy
To see a leaping squirrel in a tree,
Or a red lady-bird upon a stalk,
Or little rabbits in a field at evening,
Lit by a staring sun.

Pearse had served on the executive committee of the flourishing Gaelic League and was editor of the *League Weekly*. It was but another of the evidences of his devotion

To the road here before me,
To the work that I see

that he resigned this position to found two secondary schools where Irish youth might receive a full and complete Celtic education from the hands not of hired pedagogues but from "the highest souls and noblest intellects of the present." It was a work he considered of great importance for the future, and he accepted its hard, obscure drudgery, its enforced separation from the field of pure literature in the spirit in which he accepted everything else he considered essential to his ideal.

I turned my back
On the dreams I had shaped,
And to this work before me
My face I turned

I set my face
To the road here before me
To the work that I see,
To the death that I shall meet.

"Padraic Pearse," says Colum, "might have been Ireland's great Catholic writer — not in the sectarian sense that the word is used in English-speaking countries, but in the philosophic sense that it is understood in Europe. Ireland had badly needed writers that would be trained in the severe Catholic philosophy and mellowed in ancient Catholic culture and would have a touch of the heroic impulse of the missionary saints." He was one of the first orators of his day; his intellectual influence on men of education was wide and profound.

A close friend of Pearse and associated with him in the educational work at the St. Enda's school, was Thomas MacDonagh. He too, had begun early the study of Gaelic and of the people who spoke it, living among the natives of the Aran Islands and the Irish-speaking districts of Munster. His first book of verse (in English), which appeared in 1903, made him the earliest of the new-generation poets to obtain recognition. His translations and adaptations from the Gaelic were declared to be superior to those of Ferguson or of any of the pioneers. He had written one play and two other books of poetry when he went to the National University in Dublin to obtain a degree and later to become an assistant professor of English literature. During this Dublin period, he, James Stephens, and Padraic Colum founded the *Irish Review*. Later young Joseph Plunkett, already the author of a book of verse, *The Circle and the Sword* (1913), and a poet of great promise, was made one of the assistant editors. Plunkett had been educated in England. He was a member of the Catholic branch of a family famous for 600 years in the history of the island. One of his forebears, Blessed Oliver Plunkett, was the last priest to be martyred in England for the Faith. MacDonagh had been assisting him in his Irish studies, and they were fast friends.

Besides being a poet, MacDonagh was also a critic of distinction. His *Literature in Ireland* still remains one of the best statements of the aims and ideals of the Irish Revival. In it he says something that may be applied to the work of all three of these men: "It is well for us that our workers are poets . . . and our poets workers. And it is well, too, that here still that cause which is identified, without underthought of commerce, with the cause of God and Right and Freedom, the cause which has been the great theme of our poetry, may one day call the poets to give their lives to the old service." That day was not far off. Perhaps MacDonagh sensed it, for in the preface to this volume (published in the second year of the World War and a few months before his death) he wrote, "the wars and their sequel may turn literature definitely into ways towards which I have looked, confirming the promise of our high destiny here."

And so it came about. On Easter Monday, April 24, 1916, shortly after noon, Padraic Pearse, poet, educationalist, and now provisional president of the Irish Republic, stood at the base of Nelson's Pillar in Dublin and proclaimed the existence of the Irish Republic; "in the name of God and of the dead generations from which she receives her old tradition of nationhood, Ireland, through us, summons her children to the flag and strikes for her freedom." The proclamation bore among its six signatures the names of Thomas MacDonagh and Joseph Plunkett. While it was being read, the insurgents took up positions in the General Post Office, Jacob's Factory, the Four Courts, and other strategic points which they proceeded to fortify.

It was a poet's rebellion. A poet, Padraic Pearse, was commander-in-chief of the rebel forces; another poet, Thomas MacDonagh, was second in command. Moreover, the cause for which they fought was from the beginning such a one as only poets can fight desperately for — a doomed one. The day before the uprising, MacNeill, commander of the volunteers, seeing that the cause was hopeless, issued an order countermanding the scheduled Easter parade. The order was rescinded by Pearse and MacDonagh, but the damage had been done. The rebellion, which according to well-matured plans was to have been a general one, was for all practical purposes confined to Dublin, and the forces there, even, were materially weakened.

The issue was never in doubt. It was only a question of how long the handful of rebels might hold out against the devastating artillery fire of the military from the streets and from a warship on the river. After five days of continuous fighting during which heroism and all the niceties of military courtesy were displayed by the rebels, Pearse issued the order for unconditional surrender. Three days later the leaders were hurriedly court-martialed. The next day Pearse, MacDonagh, and Thomas Clarke were shot at dawn. Plunkett and Pearse's brother were among the five who stood before the firing squad the following morning.

Pearse spent the interval between his condemnation and execution writing a poem which he had promised for his mother. In a letter written to her before dawn on May 3, he says: "I have just received Holy Communion. I am happy except for the great grief of parting from you. This is the death I should have asked for if God had given me the choice of all deaths — to die a soldier's death for Ireland and for freedom. We have done right. People will say hard things about us now, but later on will praise us. Do not grieve for all this but think of it as a sacrifice which God asked of me and of you."

Young Joseph Plunkett was married at midnight in Richmond Barracks and then went out calmly to stand before the firing squad. MacDonagh went to confession and Communion, made his Thanksgiving out loud, and then prayed before a crucifix until called by the guard.

Eamon de Valera, fellow poet, commander of Boland's Mill (one of the Dublin "forts" during the insurrection), and a man who shared all the ideals of the Easter Week martyrs, is, at the present writing, president of the Irish Free State. This may throw some light on the eventual political success of the rebellion. Artistically, the legacy left by these heroes and poets is no less important and can be appreciated by those who may not sympathize with the political ideals involved.

For with them there returned to the Irish Revival and to the world a new conception of what the poet should be. It was not so much a return to the patriotism of the *Nation* school, so displeasing to the esthetes, as it was the resurrection of a still more ancient ideal which supported the poets of antiquity. Horace, among others, has stated it when he declares that since Orpheus, the Bards "have founded cities, reclaimed men from vague concubinage, appointed rights for man and wife, engraved laws on tablets of wood. . . ." The poet was a man, a citizen of two cities, then a poet. But many things, most of them traceable to the philosophic whittling down of reality in the nineteenth century, had carried the artists of the West far away from the rugged realism of this ideal: the separation of art from morality, from religion, from love of *patria,* in a word, from life, has indeed brought him to the cork-lined room on the rue Huysmans where Marcel Proust wrote in isolation from everything that mattered. The example of men-poets like Pearse, Macdonagh, and Plunkett is like a breath of fresh air blown from the Irish hills into the musk-laden atmosphere not only of the Celtic Revival but of the poetry of the world.

Padraic Colum, speaking of MacDonagh, retells the ancient Irish story of how Finn, when asked to state what music he preferred, enumerated the song of the blackbird, the screaming of the eagle, the sound of the waterfall, the bay of the hounds. But when Oisinn was asked to tell what music delighted him, he replied "the music of the thing that happens." This was the music MacDonagh loved. For his own epitaph he wrote,

> His songs were a little phrase
>   Of eternal song,
> Drowned in the harping of lays
>   More loud and strong.
>
> His deed was a single word
>   Called out alone
> In a night where no echo stirred
>   To laughter or to moan.

> *But his song's new soul shall thrill*
> *The loud harps dumb,*
> *And his deeds the echoes fill*
> *When the dawn is come.*

"Life is stronger than art," says the disillusioned hero of one of Maurice Baring's stories who had put art above life and made a mess of things. Here is a dogma which may be distasteful to those who sympathize with Matthew Arnold for refusing to go out on a certain rainy night, because as he expressed it, he might get his feet wet and ruin his style. Bitter as it is, at no smaller cost may the anemic soul of art be strengthened than by following the path of those who have plunged boldly in the stream of life. There songs will be fewer, "a little phrase of the eternal song," but they will be fresher and more real; they will have that new soul that "shall thrill the loud harps dumb."

VI

The World War also cut off the promising careers of two other Catholic poets who had the very best things to offer to the revival. Both Thomas M. Kettle and Francis Ledwidge were poets and men of action after the pattern of the Easter Week martyrs whom they knew and admired, but could not follow politically. Kettle was killed in 1916, fighting in the British Army in Flanders. Ledwidge was shot down the following year in the same cause, after hard campaigning on the Eastern and Western fronts. Lord Dunsany, who discovered his rare poetic talents, said of him: "I have looked for a poet among the Irish peasants because it seemed to me that almost only amongst them there was in daily use a diction worthy of poetry, as well as an imagination capable of dealing with the great and simple things that are a poet's wares. Their thoughts

are in the spring-time and all their metaphors fresh; in London
no one makes metaphors anymore, but daily speech is strewn
thick with dead ones that their users should write upon paper
and give to their gardeners to burn." He found such a peasant
poet in young Ledwidge, trained him carefully, but not as a
hothouse plant. When the War came he subjected him to the
stern discipline of the fighting man. Ledwidge gladly followed
his patron into battle as did many another honest Irishman who
deemed it not treason but a duty to don the British uniform in
that crisis. Both Kettle and Ledwidge judged this a better way
of obtaining that which they, no less than their compatriots
of the rebellion, eagerly desired for Ireland — freedom. Among
the poems of Ledwidge written from France in 1916 we find
one to MacDonagh and another which celebrates his spiritual
kinship with the Easter Week heroes, Plunkett and Pearse.

> *And I myself, have often heard*
> *Their singing as the stars went by,*
> *For am I not of those who reared*
> *The banner of Ireland high,*
> *From Dublin town to Turkey's shores,*
> *And where the Vardar loudly roars?*

VII

There is something strange, mysterious, and seemingly per-
verse in this unquenchable desire of the best spirits in Ireland
for freedom and a culture of their own choosing. It has been
called twisted and bigoted, and many have deplored the inces-
sant political turmoil, literary divisions, and the rest, and have
wished that Irishmen would drop it all and make an effort to
get in touch with "the great European tradition." *Luke Del-
mege,* the young hero of Canon Sheehan's novel, reasoned in
this wise. The story of his gallant attempt to lift his downtrod-

den and sullen countrymen to the higher ground of messianic humanitarianism, commercial prosperity, and modern plumbing, is in many ways a parable and an explanation of the long resistance of the Irish to all attempts to impose on them the culture of the dominant European nations. They reject it, not because it is English or German, but because it is mechanical and soulless, because, in a word, it is *not* the great European tradition. Between the standards of that culture and the memory, still so strong in Ireland, of a Europe united in the possession of the highest spiritual ideals, there is essential conflict and war.

That conflict still goes on in Ireland today, with the tide, however, now definitely turned in favor of the people. The Free State has given them the power and the voice the Celtic Revival failed to give them, and they are using both to damn in its entirety the literature the world has been made to regard as "Irish." There have been popular reprisals such as the burning of Shaw's books in Galway, and the passage, in 1930, of the Censorship of Publication Law, bitterly contested by the Yeats-Russell group as a blow aimed directly at the writings of the so-called "Dublin Set." James Joyce, the most significant and talented of the products of this set, however, was as indifferent to the law as he was contemptuous of the subsequent efforts of the same group to save the situation by the hurried formation of the "Irish Academy of Letters" — a device which will probably not survive the laughter it occasioned.

The long literary dictatorship of the Ascendancy, it would seem, is now definitely at an end. Twenty years ago there would not be wanting many who might deplore the repudiation of those writers who put the island on the literary map. Today few tears are shed, even by the most intransigent, over what is obviously less the result of political tyranny than the culmination of a conviction that the group is intellectually bankrupt Its passage does not leave Ireland destitute of first-rate literary artists; the supply is abundant and growing. The most talented of these are willing to admit their indebtedness to the old writers but their faces are set toward newer and different literary ideals.

Of these, *facile princeps* is Daniel Corkery whose masterly analysis of the new direction in Anglo-Irish literature has all the force of an official manifesto. The literature of the future, he says, will be national, it will be Catholic, it will be of the land, and will come more and more to be written in Gaelic. It will cease to be Anglo-Irish literature. There will be no protests heard against this last development if the works in the new language come up to the standard of Maurice O'Sullivan's beautifully Catholic story, *Twenty Years A-Growing,* already proclaimed "the first masterpiece to be written in modern Gaelic."

BIBLIOGRAPHY

GENERAL

Boyd, E. A., *Ireland's Literary Renaissance* (New York: Lane, 1916).

Chesterton, G. K., *Irish Impressions* (London: Collins, 1919), Chs. 6 and 7.

Corkery, Daniel, *Synge and Anglo-Irish Literature* (New York: Longmans, Green, 1931), Ch. I.

Legouis-Cazamian, *History of English Literature* (London: Macmillan, 1930), pp. 1319–1328.

MacDonagh, Thomas, *Literature in Ireland* (London: Allen & Unwin, 1914).

Morris, Lloyd R., *The Celtic Dawn* (New York: Macmillan, 1917).

The Irish Rebellion of 1916, edited by Maurice Joy (New York: Devin-Adair, 1917).

———

MANGAN, JAMES CLARENCE
Selected Poems, edited with a memoir by Louise Guiney (1897).

TYNAN, KATHARINE
Bookman (New York: June, 1931), p. 373.

The Wandering Years (Boston: Houghton, 1922).
Twenty-five Years Reminiscences (New York: Devin-Adair, 1913).
WORKS
Collected Poems (New York: Macmillan, 1931).

CARBERY, ETHNA (Mrs. Seumas MacManus)
Boyd, E. A., *Ireland's Literary Renaissance*, pp. 201–203.
The Four Winds of Eirinn (collected poems), (Dublin: Gill, 1927).

SIGERSON, DORA
The Fairy Changeling, and other poems (1898).
The Sad Years (New York: Doran, 1918).
Sixteen Dead Men and other Poems of Easter Week (New York: Kennerley, 1919).

MARTYN, EDWARD
Boyd, E. A., *Ireland's Literary Renaissance*, pp. 292–308.
Gwynn, Denis, *Edward Martin and the Irish Revival* (London: Cape, 1930).
WORKS
An Enchanted Sea (1902).
Grangecolman (1912).
The Heather Field (1899).

O'NEIL, MOIRA
Boyd, E. A., *Ireland's Literary Renaissance*, pp. 199–200.
WORKS
Songs of the Glens of Antrim (New York: Macmillan, 1922).

KETTLE, THOMAS
Studies, Vol. 5, p. 503.
Studies, Vol. 20, p. 598.
WORKS
Poems and Parodies (New York: Stokes).
The Day's Burden (London: Maunsel, 1918).
Ways of War, with a memoir by Mary Kettle (New York: Scribner).

LEDWIDGE, FRANCIS
Colum, Padraic, *Road Round Ireland* (New York: Macmillan, 1926), pp. 241–244.
WORKS
Complete Poems of Francis Ledwidge, intro. by Lord Dunsany (New York: Brentano, 1919).

MACDONAGH, THOMAS
Colum, Padraic, *Road Round Ireland,* pp. 458–472.

WORKS

Poetical Works of Thomas MacDonagh (New York: Stokes, 1916).

PEARSE, PADRAIC

Colum, Padraic, *Road Round Ireland*, pp. 154–164.

Ryan, Desmond, *The Man Called Pearse* (London: Maunsel, 1919).

WORKS

Complete Works of P. H. Pearse, 5 vols. English poems in Vol. 4 (Dublin: Phoenix).

PLUNKETT, JOSEPH M.

Studies, Vol. 5, p. 536.

WORKS

Poems of Joseph M. Plunkett, foreword by Geraldine Plunkett (New York: Stokes, 1916).

7

Fin De Siècle in America

Up to the last two decades of the nineteenth century the Catholic Revival in America has no very important literary history to record. Its history even during these two decades and well beyond them is less the history of a literary movement than the individual stories of a number of isolated figures. The American-Catholic Church of the nineteenth century had almost no communal literary life, so that those litterateurs she did produce at this time, such as Louise Guiney, Maurice Francis Egan, Kate Chopin, and Agnes Repplier, or those she acquired by conversion such as Marion Crawford, Henry Harland, John Banister Tabb, and Charles Warren Stoddard, found themselves very much alone, without a Catholic audience, without leaders, without literary companionship. Some of them, notably Miss Guiney, Crawford, and Henry Harland simply left the country, went to England and the continent where Catholic intellectual and artistic life was active. Joel Chandler Harris put off his entrance into the Church until a few weeks before his death, possibly, one suspects, by way of making his isolation as brief as possible. Of those who remained at home, some attached themselves to established literary groups, while a few heroically spent themselves trying, without great success, to cultivate what Michael Williams has called the "stony and stubborn soil of Catholic literature."

The end result of this dispersion was that Miss Guiney wrote very good English poetry but little American poetry; Harland

and Crawford wrote interesting Italian novels; Kate Chopin remains one of the undiscovered members of Cable's New Orleans group, and Stoddard is lost among Bret Harte, Joaquin Miller, and other writers of the Far West. The name of Father Abram Ryan is sometimes mentioned as a war-poet of the South in literary histories which ignore the work of Father Tabb, who was infinitely superior as a poet. Almost alone among the best of these middle-phase writers Agnes Repplier seems to have achieved fame and distinction specifically as an American Catholic writer.

We must look upon this as singularly unfortunate. For between the years 1880 and 1903 American Catholicism produced a rather large and talented body of writers who might, had some force brought them together, have laid the foundations of what in the course of time would have developed into a formidable American literary movement. Moreover, new authors were in the later years of this period already beginning to appear who needed the encouragement and direction of a group. But this generation, too, was to suffer the same isolation and lack of purpose.

Unfortunate or not, what actually happened was dictated by a present necessity. The Church in America was not at this time ready for a literary revival. It had other and more pressing needs to engage the energies of those who might have been its writers and readers. Not the least pressing of these was the work of absorbing the successive tidal waves of immigrants who from the middle of the nineteenth century until well into the twentieth century poured into the country by the millions. Up to the year 1880 these newcomers were predominantly Irish and German, and of the nine millions who came during this period a large number were Catholics. The second and greatest wave, occurring during the period we treat in this chapter and, extending to 1924, reached the twenty-two million mark. These new peoples, a huge number again of which were Catholics, were of a different racial stock, Italians, Hungarians, Armenians, and other southern Europeans and Asiatics for the most part. The American Church, which up to 1840 was still a missionary Church, became progressively more so thereafter, overburdened with the work of managing the temporal and spiritual welfare of a very needy and diversified population. Such a Church had little need of litterateurs, nor could its faithful, despite their enormous number, support them. What it needed was apostles, teachers, missionaries, builders of schools, of hospitals, of orphanages — workers to establish and operate the vast spiritual and sociological apparatus necessary to Catholicize and Americanize the new people.

Divorced from these and other considerations that might be mentioned, the absence of a Catholic literature in the United States during these years is, of course, unintelligible. One would see no reason, for instance, why it did not begin simultaneously with the English revival. The conversion of Orestes Brownson in 1844, a year before that of Newman, ought to have been the occasion of a similar Romeward movement. He was a famous American figure in his day, a writer, a popular orator, something of a leader in American Romanticism. Like Emerson, he was a Unitarian minister; like Thoreau, Amos Brownson Alcott, Margaret Fuller, and others of the New England renaissance, he was a devotee of transcendental philosophy, a fervent preacher of social reform, of the superiority of mind over matter, of "bowls of sunrise for breakfast" instead of sordid commercialism — in a word, the afflatus of America's "Golden Day" was upon him when he left the movement and entered the Catholic Church.

Yet his conversion had no notable effect upon Catholic literature nor was it a signal for an exodus from the ranks of the American Romantics. American Romanticism, it may as well be remarked, was not, like the European brand, a remote preparation for entry into the Catholic Church. What little medievalism there was in it repulsed rather than attracted its exponents to the American Church which was a proletarian Church, the Church of the great unwashed and ignorant foreigners, entirely innocent of Gothic windows, incense, and gorgeous liturgy. The New England renaissance did not rise out of a disgust with a society built on human reason, a Rationalist society, but from a dissatisfaction with one built on a too rigid Puritan theology, which kept its adherents from enjoying the intellectual and artistic riches of the human spirit. What the emancipated Puritan Romantic wanted was not more religion but less of it. He felt above all the need of culture. It was America's Elizabethan period, the beginning of Protestant humanism, of an ethical rather than a religious culture, with man at the center.

Brownson lost faith in the efficacy of this movement. He said he felt the need of "an objective body of truth not growing out of human speculation," a reason for entering the Catholic Church that was far too advanced for his day to appreciate and one the least calculated to encourage followers from among the New England group. Besides the brilliant young German-American, Isaac Hecker, a Brook Farm experimentalist, there were no others of importance. The work of both of these men after their conversion was substantially different from that which engaged their efforts while in the New England group. They attempted to found no literary movement. Hecker became a religious and later founded the Paulists. Brownson threw himself into an enormous apologetic work which earned him the commendation of the American hierarchy. Of the two, Hecker's work probably had the more influence on American Catholic literature. Among other things it resulted in the founding of the *Catholic World,* a magazine which through all the lean years managed to keep alive and increase what literary activity was humanly possible under the circumstances. Its continuous volumes since 1865 give a semblance of continuity to American literary life but do not remove the fact that this life was uneven and without inner unity. It was not an organic life; it was the life of outstanding individuals whose most important contributions were not toward the building up of the whole body.

II

In Louise Imogene Guiney more, perhaps, than in any of the writers of the last part of the nineteenth century, were to be found qualities that might have fitted her for the work of bringing to a focus the scattered literary forces in the country and of molding them into a definite movement with well-defined American ideals. She was born in Boston, which in 1861 was certainly a mark of predilection. She could not boast of a long line of Puritan ancestors going back to Colonial days yet she was unquestionably an American. Her Irish-born father, Robert Patrick Guiney, was a man of education and refinement. Moreover, he had cleared the family name of the stigma of foreign origin by entering the Civil War on the Yankee side as a Major and leaving it a Major-General. The citizens of post-war Boston rewarded him with a governmental post which he held continuously until his sudden death some time later as the result of a head wound he had received in the Battle of the Wilderness.

General Guiney was a Catholic, a patriot, and a soldier; his daughter admired these qualities to such an extent that during her early years at the Sacred Heart Convent in Providence she deplored the fact that she had not been born a son, and occasionally acted as though she were one. The love of outdoor sports, by which she at times disedified the Sisters, never left her, and we find it coming to the surface again in later life, causing the natives of the country around Oxford to lift their eyebrows as they saw this American girl tramping along in the rain in mud-splattered clothes. Her inherited military spirit inspired her to pray in the poem "Knight Errant" for

> *A short life in the saddle, Lord,*
> *Not long life by the fire.*

Her love of country manifested itself in early patriotic verse, not all of which is of the flaccid sort.

Her teachers at the Providence convent had encouraged her in her desire to write, and they had the satisfaction of seeing her talents mature into authorship with *Goosequill Papers* in 1885. She was then twenty-four years old. Two years later *The White Sail,* a collection of poems, appeared, followed in 1893 by *The Roadside Harp* which made her a recognized poet. One of her biographers insists it put her in the "first class of American writers." The literati of Boston had admitted her into the magic circle even before this. To Oliver Wendell Holmes she was his "little golden guinea." There is a delightful picture, says Theodore Maynard, of her entering Holmes' study "accompanied by her St. Bernard dog and of the Autocrat getting safely behind the shelter of a table while he tried to placate the terrifying animal with 'Good doggie! Good doggie!' "

The death of General Guiney had put upon his daughter the burden of supporting her mother and an aunt. In 1894 she succeeded in obtaining an appointment as postmistress in the town of Auburndale, a suburb of Boston. The spectacle of a New England girl, youthful, pretty, and a recognized poet and essayist handing out stamps from behind barred windows was not an unlovely one to the democratic American mind. The post office became quite popular until the natives learnt that the lady was a "foreigner," an Irish Catholic in fact. Then a boycott was begun and various other minor persecutions of such a nature that anyone but the fighting daughter of General Guiney might have retreated. Louise held on, aided somewhat by the periodical press, which deplored the incident, and sustained by the philosophy of battle she expresses in "The Kings":

> *While Kings of eternal evil*
> *Yet darken the hills about,*
> *Thy part is with broken sabre*
> *To rise on the last redoubt.*

> *To fear no sensible failure,*
> *Nor covet the game at all,*
> *But fighting, fighting, fighting,*
> *Die, driven against the wall.*

She construed her reappointment to the post by President McKinley in 1897 as a token of victory, promptly resigned and took a position in the Boston Public Library.

This incident may explain why Miss Guiney did not wish to continue her literary career in the United States. But it does not tell everything. One might suppose from her early acceptance by the Boston pundits that her literary inspiration had been nourished by contact with the New England group. The reverse of this, however, is true. Intellectually she had little in common with Longfellow or Holmes or any of the other leaders of the then too prosperous Romantic school. She found cosmopolitan Boston as inane and much less exciting than provincial Auburndale. It was commercial and stodgy, an overgrown Victorian village of bourgeois litterateurs. She could not stomach Victorianism either in America or in England. Her bitterest lines are written of Queen Victoria: "That money-saving, gillie-adoring, etiquette-blinded, pudgy, plodding, unspiritual, unliterary, mercantile, dowdy, sparkless, befogged, continuous Teutonic lady, is not in one's life a necessary." None the less her inspiration was English. In 1895 appeared *A Little English Gallery* and *Nine Sonnets Written at Oxford,* the result of a walking tour in England with her biographer Alice Brown. The American critics praised the craftsmanship of the work but were not a little annoyed by the British flavor, seeing in it the progressive perversion of a promising native poet. But Louise in England had seen something she had not found in her native land, a literary cause, an aesthetic, an inspiration which called forth her complete enthusiasm; in the depths of the Bodleian Library she had seen the buried gold of the seventeenth-century poets.

at the ancient university the memory of the Oxford Movers, and in London the modern descendants of these in the midst of a revival of Catholic literature.

From then on nothing in America could hold her affection. She itched to be among those who spoke the language she spoke and shared her ideals. Amid the volumes of the Boston Public Library she sighed to be away. "Some day when I am free (i.e., moth-eaten and tame with years) I am going to emigrate to some hamlet that smells strongly of the middle ages, and put cotton-wool in my ears and swing clear of this very smart century altogether." This in a letter to the Irish poetess Dora Sigerson Shorter. Despite its nostalgia her real desire was not so much to be with the dead past as with the living present; not so much to be with Vaughan, Herbert, Donne, Crashaw, and the Oxford Movers as with their living descendants who were bringing to light the forgotten values of this past and making them active in the renovation of contemporary letters.

For twenty years after 1900 she lived almost continuously at Oxford. Before her departure she had edited the poems and written a memoir of the early Irish revivalist, James Clarence Mangan. In England she enjoyed the friendship of Katharine Tynan, Mrs. Shorter, Lionel Johnson, and others who were carrying his work forward. She wrote a memoir of Newman's co-worker, Hurrell Froude, and moved about in the society of the Alice Meynell group. She became an erudite scholar, spent much time in the Bodleian Library, and with the Jesuit, Father Geoffrey Bliss, began a huge anthology of the works of the Recusant Poets which was never published. Other studies she made in this seventeenth-century field, however, were published. "I know most seventeenth-century English writers and I know nothing else," was her slightly affected way of expressing her infatuation for the "seventeenth-centurions." It foreshadows a temper that would be widespread only in our own day which witnesses the rush of reformed Romantics to assert the superiority of pre-Romantic verse. If she now wrote less poetry, the quality of her prose made up the loss. Her criticism was just, well-informed, and balanced. She had made an integral part of herself the best spirit of the European literary renaissance. Had she returned to spread abroad the good odor of this spirit in her native land at a time when many of her co-religionists were still praising the "Catholicism" of Tennyson and proclaiming a book by William Lyons Phelps which proved conclusively that English poetry had reached its all-time high level in nineteenth-century Romanticism, she might have advanced Catholic letters in America by twenty years. But she stayed in England to die at Chipping-Camden in 1920.

It is improbable that Louise Guiney and her fellow American expatriate, Henry Harland, ever met. Yet they were both in England at the same time, Miss Guiney in scholarly seclusion at Oxford, Harland in the whirl of Bohemian life in London, editor of the *Yellow Book,* the friend and promoter of all the *fin de siècle* geniuses. Both had been born in New England and in the same year, 1861. Harland's birthplace seems to have been Norwich, Connecticut, although at a very early date we find him living in New York. Educated at the City College of New York, he had some idea of becoming a Protestant minister and spent a year in the theological department at Harvard, from which he was taken by his father and his godfather, the poet Edmund Clarence Stedman, and sent away on a European tour. These two had seen in the young man's early excursions into literary composition the promise of a career in letters which they thought should take precedence over everything else.

On the Continent Harland lived for a while in Paris, soaking up the atmosphere of the University and the Latin Quarter, chiefly, one feels, the latter, which was then in its heyday. Most of his time abroad, however, was spent in Rome where he moved about in the best social and artistic circles. On his return to America in 1885 his wife records that he was "convinced that he was a Catholic and an artist." But he did not enter the

Church. Art had become his religion and was to remain his chief passion for many years to come. He developed into something of a dilettante, ambitious, a pusher, eager for fame in letters at whatever cost, for which, I think, we may blame his father and Stedman who had encouraged this side of his character from the first to the exclusion of a truer and better side which was sincere, gentle, and genuinely religious.

Harland spent the majority of his days and energy pursuing the inconsequential, and would probably have died in this enterprise had he not at a later date emigrated to Europe where, witnessing the remorse of men like Verlaine, Wilde, and Beardsley, who had pushed this pursuit much further than he, was thus led on to follow them in taking the one entirely sincere step of his life. Had he remained in America his "conversion" might have taken the form of fleeing to the ample bosom of a middle-aged and flabby conservatism where Albert Perry, Floyd Dell, and many other minor American decadents have found surcease.

A year after his return from Rome we find Harland happily married and devoting whatever time he had left over from his position of court clerk to furious efforts at authorship. "In order to write," says his wife, "he adopted the plan of rising at four a.m. and, on a brew of coffee, of setting to work until eight. At nine he was at his office in the Surrogate Court of New York." This was in the early 80's when the second huge wave of European and Asiatic emigrants was beginning to break upon American shores, swelling the foreign colonies that existed in the seaboard cities and calling to the attention of the Native Americans the fact that exotic peoples lived in their midst. Their manner of life, their customs, their ideas, the problem of the existence of these units in the midst of a culture so different from their own, cried out loudly for exploitation at the hands of romantic and sociological novelists. Harland had heard the call and had found his material, not, as one might suppose from his Catholic predisposition, in the Irish, German, or French quarters, but in the ghetto surrounding the family house in Beckman Square.

His novel, *As It Was Written, a Jewish Musician's story,* was the first in that long series of sympathetic exposés of Hebrew life which have since made the Jews more an integral part of the American scene than either the Germans or the Irish. It was an instant success and Harland followed it with two others, all of which he wrote under the pseudonym of Sidney Luska. He grew a beard, lectured in synagogues, was seen much in Jewish circles, and rather welcomed the belief that he himself was of Hebrew extraction. The financial success of the first novel had enabled him to resign his court clerkship and to take a flying trip to Europe. He returned to find himself the object of a rather hot debate between Stedman and William Dean Howells as to whether he should continue his exploitation of emigrant life in a realistic or a romantic manner. But Harland had decided on becoming an emigrant himself. In England he had caught a glimpse of the intellectual ferment that would produce the 90's, and very soon he had packed his bags and was on his way to London and a new field of exploitation from which he would never return to his native land except as a visitor. "Harland," recalls Richard Le Gallienne, "was one of those Americans in love with Paris who seems more French than the French themselves, a slim, gesticulating, snub-nosed, lovable figure, smoking innumerable cigarettes as he galvanically pranced about the room, excitedly propounding the *dernier mot* on the build of the short-story or the art of prose. He was born to be the life of one of those *cenacles,* which from their café-tables in 'the Quarter' promulgate all those world-shaking 'new movements' in art which succeed each other with kaleidoscopic rapidity." London in the late 1880's was probably a more congenial place for such a temperament than Paris during the same period. In London Harland stood out from the crowd as a fresh phenomenon; in Paris he would have been lost. His house, if we are to believe his wife, became the center of an interesting group of litterateurs, "a brilliant coterie of men and women artists," who were responsible for "the renaissance of the 90's." They were all young, all frankly rebellious against the banal state of the arts and life.

"One foggy New Year's afternoon a little luncheon party had gathered at Harland's," so the account of the *Yellow Book's* birth very appropriately begins. Beardsley was there but what others Mrs. Harland does not say. Harland suggested that they found a quarterly which should give some sort of expression to their common ideas. The proposal was adopted with enthusiasm. A name? Beardsley suggested "Yellow Book" and so it became *The Yellow Book* with Harland as its first and only editor, more or less divinely appointed "to lead the English intelligentsia of the *fin de siècle* out of its propriety and boredom." Harland edited the magazine from the first to the last of its thirty volumes. He was a natural editor and most of the really astonishing success of the sheet must be attributed to his genius; it was he who had seen that the times were ripe for such a venture, he also who kept its contents on the thin line between the rebellious and the stimulating when the deviation of an inch might have brought ruin. His friends in America were proud of him and he was proud of himself. Another boy had made good — Whistler, Henry James, and now Henry Harland.

By 1897 Harland's promotion work in England was over. The new temper had suddenly become a very old one. *The Yellow Book* ceased publication. The virgin territory of his native America must have beckoned eloquently to him in those days. It was waiting for the spirit of the 1890's and needed only experienced promoters which it was shortly to have in Frank Harris, James Huneker, and others. But not Harland. He was through with it forever. The same year he and his wife were received into the Church at Farm Street in London.

The route that led Harland into the Catholic Church was not that taken by the penitential, sin-laden decadent. Despite his love of the Paris Latin Quarter and the imitation Bohemian life

of London, he was not a wicked young man. He might pretend
to be for the sake of fitting into the picture but in reality even
an over-frank conversation made him squirm. He belonged to
that class of hangers-on who were in many ways the real
scourge of the decadence, the triflers to whom the decadence
was a delightful entertainment. Harland finally awoke to the
insipidity of this pose. The real Harland asserted itself, the Har-
land who in his youth had preferred a career in religion rather
than in art.

He and his wife moved to Italy where, in 1897, he completed
the novel that made him famous in his own name. Previous to
that he had sought celebrity by anxiously clinging to the coat-
tails of Henry James, Edmund Gosse, Beardsley, and others.
Now he would stand on his own feet. *The Cardinal's Snuff-Box*
is certainly not a great novel, but in its own class — that of light
romantic fiction — it is something of a masterpiece. Published
in 1900, it took both England and America by storm; in less
than two years one hundred thousand copies were sold. *The
Lady Paramount* and *My Friend Prospero,* both Italian ro-
mances of the same sort, followed in 1902 and 1904, respectively.
He was at work on a fourth *The Royal End,* when he died in
1905 at San Remo, Italy, at the age of 44. The novel was com-
pleted by his wife.

What Harland might have done with his talent had he lived
longer it is impossible to say. He was not a great genius but he
had a flair for the light romance of a type the Catholic Revival
has never been particularly rich in. It is certainly unfortunate
that he had to find his material in Italian Catholic life rather
than in American Catholic life. The same may be said of F.
Marion Crawford who was very much the same sort of novelist
but a better one, I think. Crawford lived almost continually in
Italy. He had been born in Lucca in 1854, the son of an Amer-
ican sculptor, Thomas Crawford, and the nephew of Julia
Ward Howe. Educated at Cambridge, Heidelberg, and the
University of Rome, it was while studying Sanskrit at the latter

university that he became a Catholic in 1880. There followed several years of newspaper work in India from which background emerged his first successful novel, *Mr. Isaacs.* From then on almost without a break until his death in 1909 he entertained large English and American audiences with a novel a year, usually Catholic in tone. *Saracinesca, St. Illaria, Via Crucis, In the Palace of the King, The White Sister,* are among the best known. In his day he was regarded as one of America's foremost novelists and was enough of a poet to be chosen to write the National Ode for the Centennial of the American Constitution in 1887. But he couldn't write an American novel. His *The Three Fates,* a New York newspaper story, was a failure. Both Harland and Crawford did competent work in the novel but they did little to advance the cause of the Catholic Revival in America.

III

Unquestioned primacy among the poets of this period who remained at home belongs to John Banister Tabb. Unlike Harland, Guiney, and Crawford, who in the ordinary course of events should have been New Englanders, Tabb belongs to another section of American literature, that of the South, and next to Sidney Lanier is probably the best poet the *post bellum* Southland produced. He and Lanier spent the last year of the Civil War consoling each other in the Union prison at Point Lookout. Tabb was only nineteen at the time, a Virginian, born of an aristocratic Scotch-English family in 1845. He had joined the Confederate forces shortly after the outbreak of hostilities and because of weak eyesight rather than his extreme youth did not become a fighter on the land, but served as the captain's clerk on the blockade-running ship *Robert E. Lee* until its capture in 1864.

The decline in the family fortunes occasioned by the war compelled young Tabb, after his release from prison, to think seriously about the matter of earning a living. In 1866 he secured a position as instructor in St. Paul's Protestant-Episcopal School, Baltimore, where, through his intimacy with the rector, Rev. Alfred Curtis, he began to learn about the Oxford Movement. Five years later, Tabb entered the Episcopal seminary at Alexandria, Virginia, while his former rector left for England, met Newman and was baptized by him. On the latter's return in 1872 Tabb also was received into the Church and two years later began his studies for the priesthood at St. Charles College, Ellicott City, Maryland, where he was ordained in December, 1884.

From that date until his death thirty-five years later, Father Tabb remained at St. Charles College, teaching some literature and a large quantity of grammar to the seminarians, and acquiring in the course of this very exacting work a local reputation as a wit and an epigrammatist. He also began to write poetry. Father Tabb's poetry gives one the impression of something that is "also" done. Not that it is careless; quite the reverse. It is all exquisitely done, its diction and rhythm displaying much of the fine care of the *fin de siècle* "goldsmiths of words" without their conscious affectation. But it is all very brief as though achieved in the time left over from a more important work. He has given us no long-sustained flights, only a few concentrated lines of the purest poetry. The former would have demanded a leisure he did not possess, or if attempted without that leisure, might have resulted in the sort of loosely written verse Father Abram Ryan was achieving popularity with. Father Tabb certainly chose the better part.

A more detailed consideration of the work of Maurice Francis Egan, Conde Pallen, Kate Chopin, Charles Warren Stoddard, John Boyle O'Reilly, and others would be necessary to give a complete picture of American Catholic literature during this middle phase. However, nothing that might be said of these authors would alter the general outlines of the situation we have been deploring, viz., that no leader, no set of compelling circumstances appeared in those times to gather together the dispersed forces and to weld the whole into a compact group with definite aims and ideals adapted to the needs of American life. The new generation of writers who after the turn of the century began to be heard from, faced the new condition in American life in much the same disorganized fashion as their predecessors. As to these "new conditions" we speak of, much of the hard pioneering work of bringing them about was the work of two men of this middle generation, who though products of American Catholicism can hardly be called Catholics. I refer to James Huneker and William Marion Reedy. The careers of neither of these men belong to the history of the Catholic Revival; yet they throw an interesting and ironic light on that history, as showing what a Catholic Literary Revival might have accomplished in America had its best spirits applied the same energy to the work of Americanizing a truly renaissantial spirit that Huneker and Reedy devoted to Americanizing a decadent one.

It has been remarked by not a few close observers of literary history that America follows in the wake of important cultural changes in Europe, from fifty to sixty years behind France and from twenty to thirty years behind England. The accuracy of this estimate may be questioned, but none the less, that spiritual crisis, sometimes called *fin de siècle,* which followed the Franco-Prussian War in France and which convulsed England of the 1890's, did not occur in all its violence in America until shortly before the World War. True enough we did have, as Seward Collins has remarked, "an abortive 90's" of our own while the same thing was happening in England. But it didn't last. The little rebellious enthusiasm stirred up in Chicago out of intellectual eddies of the World's Fair of 1893, and a similar agitation in New York called the "Purple Cow Period" were not sufficient to begin any considerable conflagration. The first years of 1900 came on with literature still following the same established grooves.

The fact is America was not ready for the new evangel. The country was still in its Victorian period. The dominant tone of the nation's culture was still Anglo-Saxon, still Protestant, still complacently commercial. The intellectual hegemony of what has been called the "Protestant Garrison" in the eastern states had yet to be seriously questioned. "Richard Watson Gilder," records William Allen White, with all the fine confidence that the passage of years has given to Kansas, "was the literary arbiter of the times. His magazine, *The Century,* represented in the mid-eighties and nineties the heights to which American literary culture had risen. The stories he printed carefully guarded youth from contact with reality. Mr. Henry L. Alden was editor of *Harper's Magazine* in that period. He was also a sentinel of the hearthstone. From *Harper's Magazine* no raucous whine could come, no low, earthbound speech could escape to disturb the serenity of the house beautiful, the house immaculate. Mr. Burlingame of *Scribner's Magazine* held to the same high ideals of the function of literature that inspired and ennobled Mr. Gilder and Mr. Alden. They were three in one and one in three, a blessed trinity that beamed on the America of that day, kindly lights of literature and learning, beacons that shone benignly unto the perfect day." What held this society together, what gave it solidity and apparent permanence was the residue of rugged Puritan morality that still remained. The equally rugged Puritan theology upon which this morality had been founded, however, had all but evaporated under the glare of transcendentalism, Big Business, and other by-products, much in the same manner as had the Puritanism of England's middle class. "One must not mistake the philosophy of that day for a gloomy philosophy, for it was not. Hell was cooling off. The hell of the eighteenth century was pretty well crusted over. The skating was good there. . . . In the popular fiction of that day there were precious few unhappy endings. For unhappy endings would indicate that virtue was unrewarded by material counters or earthly blessings of some sort."

The scoffers who had seen or heard of the goings-on in Paris and London might foam at the mouth at the sight of such a complacent bourgeois society. But for the moment it was impregnable and forced the rebels to something like an underground existence where they gathered into small and eccentric groups, published small and eccentric magazines in which they hooted and jeered at the *status quo* and otherwise kept up their spirits while they waited for the day of deliverance. And when it at length came they sated their pent-up vengeance in what was one of the most complete literary upheavals in American history.

I have said that two American Catholics occupied patriarchal positions in this movement during its catacomb-period. James Gibbons Huneker, the better known of the two, was a Philadelphian, bore the name of America's greatest ecclesiastic, and received his early education with Maurice Francis Egan in the Catholic schools of the city. An early taste for French literature and a youthful proficiency in music sent him to Paris where in the late 1870's many things besides music were in the air. The Golden Age of Bohemianism was on, and young Huneker, fresh from the quiet of Philadelphia, enjoyed the rare privilege of witnessing most of its manifestations more or less at first hand. It was a great show. He never forgot it or permitted anyone else to forget that he was not likely to forget it. He had been a "first nighter." Had he read Verlaine? Why, he had actually spoken to Verlaine!

Back in America, Huneker taught for a time in New York's National Conservatory of Music. But after Paris, New York must have seemed unbearably tame. The city's very best social life even bored Matthew Arnold! The latter happened to be there at the time enlisting American bone and sinew in the crusade against Philistinism. Huneker had been invited to play before the distinguished guest, and in the midst of one of his favorite Chopin etudes Arnold was heard to whisper to his wife,

"My dear, we must really make the 9:30 and get out of this hole." America was literally wailing for redemption!

A beginning was made when Huneker met Vance Thompson, who was also some fifty years ahead of his countrymen by reason of a brief but concentrated visit to the Paris Left Bank, and the two with the aid of a few others brought out the fortnightly review, *M'lle New York*. It was as disdainful of American literary tastes, as abusive of solid Puritan institutions, and as indecent in a sly roguish way as the times permitted. All the elements that would at a later date so delight the country-cousins and undergraduates in the typical Menckenoid journal were present in *M'lle New York*. But it seems to have created no great stir except, as Frank Hanighen remarks, in isolated spots in the Middle Western States from which the "great rebellion" would take its origin. It lasted for a briefer period than the *Yellow Book*. Vance Thompson degenerated into a high-powered Hearst journalist, wrote some anti-booze tracts for the Y.M.C.A., and when he died at Nice, in 1924, was known only as the author of *Eat and Grow Thin*.

Huneker, however, with singular strength of character, remained faithful to his first Paris intoxication. All through the rest of the 90's and into the new century he continued to talk and write about the "wild men" of European decadence, their scarlet lives, their apocalyptic ideas. It was still the greatest show on earth to him and he never tired of reviewing it. And precisely because it was a show to him he missed whatever inner meaning there was in the decadence. He had witnessed it as a spectator, he had never entered into that genuine crucifixion of spirit behind the piquant unconventionalities that gave them something of reality, something of justification. And he passed this attitude on to his disciples, among whom the most important was H. L. Mencken.

Out in the Middle West during the same period, another Catholic, William Marion Reedy, was engaged in the same

apostolate. The son of a St. Louis police captain, graduate of a
Catholic college, Reedy had never been to Paris. But he had
read all the new books, and he had a genius for Americanizing
the decadence that Huneker's inability to forget Paris deprived
him of. His magazine, *The Mirror,* was the most powerful and
the most continuous of those "little magazines" that came and
went with such rapidity during the first years of the twentieth
century. During these early years it was the West rather than
the East that produced the greater number of rebellious spirits,
and which, moreover, began to produce a literature that was
something more than just an effort to relate what was going on
in Paris and London. The new poetry movement got under way
in Chicago with Harriet Monroe's *Poetry: a magazine of verse,*
and it was there, too, that the little theater movement was born.

Reedy had genuine talent as a writer, an editor, and as a
leader. He worked unceasingly to make the new spirit more
widespread and he left his stamp on a whole generation of
young writers. It was under his tutelage and inspiration that the
Chicagoan, Edgar Lee Masters, wrote his *Spoon River An-
thology,* the first product of the new poetry movement to get
a large American hearing. It was followed by Vachel Lindsay's
Congo, Sandburg's *Chicago Poems,* and a host of other minor
outbursts in cynical and nihilistic free verse. Theodore Dreiser's
The Genius began a vogue in the naturalistic novel, outmoded
in Europe for some time but brand new in pre-war America.
More "little magazines" sprang up; more assistance came in
from Europe — the decadent Romanticism of the Yeats-wing of
the Irish Revival, the socialism and scientific "dawnism" of
Wells and Shaw, Frank Harris with the "authentic Oscar
Wilde," boatloads of sad Russian fiction, and so on. Very nearly
all of the scientific, sociological, and artistic heresies that had
germinated in the Europe of the late nineteenth century came
over in this immigration and were naturalized with such amaz-
ing rapidity that those who began to analyze the American soul
a little later could affirm with a show of honesty that Puritan-

ism was an exotic. Large doses of the new intellectual food were being gulped down raw by farm lads and college students all over the country. They would be the writers and leaders in the complete emergence of the long suppressed forces that followed the war.

Reedy did not survive to welcome the dawn, and Huneker but briefly. But had they seen the American post-war period in all its sophomoric horrors it is improbable that they would have repented. They were working for just that. What they might have accomplished had they used their talents in the work of awakening American Catholics to the possibilities of the Revival in Europe is an unpractical speculation. They were both of the *ni pratiquant ni croyant* type of Catholicism. They had lost their faith and hence could neither understand nor appreciate the positive intellectual and artistic ideas of Catholicism. This same loss of faith made them the fittest sort of subjects to be victimized by all the negative attitudes — cynicism, revolt, despair, nihilism — that blossomed so profusely in that period of the nineteenth century when Europe discovered it had lost its faith in what there remained of the supernatural in official Protestantism. Both these men made distinguished contributions to the American *fin de siècle*. But America would have experienced it without their aid. The Protestant-Humanistic culture of the country was bound sooner or later to decay, just as that of Europe had decayed.

IV

". . . The extravagance and decadence of the so-called 'renaissance of poetry' during the last five years — a renaissance distinguished by the celebration of the queer and nasty instead of the beautiful — has made the poet seem as silly a figure to the contemporary American as he seemed to the Englishman of the eighteen-nineties when the 'aesthetic movement' was at its foolish height." Joyce Kilmer could write this way in 1918 from the battlefields of France. Seven or eight years earlier he would probably have expressed himself differently, for he was then one of the bright young people to whom the imported art and ideology of those seminal pre-war days made a strong appeal as promising great things for American letters. At the end of a year of teaching at a New Jersey preparatory school which had followed his graduation from Columbia in 1906, he had, with a few poems in his pockets, joined the caravan of youths from out-of-the-way places who were then converging upon New York, "to make their contribution to art and freedom." In the Big City he spent much of his free time cultivating the "new spirit," frequenting the haunts of the emancipated, studying and discussing the merits of socialism, and imitating in his occasional verse and frequent conversations the *fin de siècle* attitudes of Richard Le Gallienne and Bliss Carmen, men, says his biographer, "whose personalities delighted him beyond measure."

This decadent jag of Kilmer, however, was not of long duration. He had a pronounced sense of humor, and this perhaps more than any other factor except one which will be mentioned immediately, kept him from taking the movement too seriously. The other factor was his discovery, at this time, of a school of writers most of whom had been "taken in" by the decadence in their youth, had given the correct valuation to what there was of worth in it, and has passed on to something more positive. He began to read Patmore, the anti-Tennysonian friend of the pre-Raphaelites; Lionel Johnson, who had made so furious an effort to make sense out of the wild dreams of the neo-Romantics; Francis Thompson, who had in the depth of his own soul analyzed the malady of the age and had seen only a divine remedy; G. K. Chesterton who had once cultivated all the idiotic ideas that flourished at the end of the century, as he himself slyly confesses.

Robert Cortes Holliday, Kilmer's biographer, remarks that the discovery of Patmore's verse was "a finger-post" in Kilmer's life. Even the Romantics might admire Francis Thompson and Lionel Johnson but only one who had stepped entirely clear of the psychology of his age might stomach the rebellious metaphysics of Patmore. Of his poems he wrote in a letter dating from this time: "I have come to regard them with intense admiration. Have you read them? Patmore seems to me to be a greater poet than Francis Thompson. He has not the rich vocabulary, the decorative erudition, the Shelleyan enthusiasm which distinguished the 'Sister Songs' and 'The Hound of Heaven' but he has a classical simplicity, a restraint and sincerity which make his poems satisfying. . . . Of course, the 'Angel in the House' and many other of his poems are marred by Tennysonian influences. But 'The Unknown Eros' is a work of stupendous beauty. It is certainly supreme among modern religious poems. That part of it devoted to Eros and Psyche is remarkably daring and remarkably fine. . . ."

The conviction that he had outgrown the short pants of the *fin de siècle,* and the ability to look upon its sincerest manifestations as juvenile and immature were among the liberating results of his contact with the literature of the Catholic Revival. He had found a poetic faith, or rather he had found a religious faith. For he first became a Catholic and then a poet as he later remarked, "If what I write nowadays is considered poetry, then I became a poet in November, 1913" (the date of his reception into the Church).

Kilmer had already acquired some reputation as a poet through his early contributions to the "little magazines" — a reputation which after 1913 mounted steadily. Nothing, however, could have made him a great poet. He belonged to that class of authentic but minor voices in which the American as well as the English *fin de siècle* was so rich. The well-integrated ballyhoo department of the American Left Wing could have made him a "great poet" just as it made Carl Sandburg and Edgar Lee Masters "great poets," and Theodore Dreiser a "supreme novelist." But Kilmer as a Catholic had to accept the reality, and he was satisfied with it. He refused to put on the stilts of an obviously worked-up revolt or to utter loud blasphemies behind a false face of despair, or to use any of the devices minor poets employ to add cubits to their stature.

Catholic literature in America had already produced better poets than Kilmer, but none who succeeded in doing more for the Catholic Revival as an American literary movement. He almost succeeded in making it a movement. He had already read through the literature of the English and Irish revivals; he knew the French and Belgian manifestations. He saw the importance of making its positive achievement better known among American Catholics so that they too might be inspired to find in their faith the riches of expression. A man of truly amazing energy he wrote letters, gave innumerable lectures, bombarded the magazines with enthusiastic criticism. In 1914 he went to England and met most of the leading English revivalists; and what is more important, he came back again! For what Kilmer had in mind was not an English revival but an American one.

He had only, however, made a good beginning when America entered the World War. He enlisted immediately. A year later he was killed while leading an attack on a machine-gun nest that was holding up the advance of his battalion during the summer offensive of 1918. His death inflicted a great loss on American Catholic letters. Yet what he had accomplished was not lost. Moreover, he left to his fellow writers a sustaining memory of courage and self-sacrifice, of honest art and personal holiness, which during the past decade and a half has more than any other one factor operated to bring American Catholic authors into something like a unified group. In this the effect of his premature death on the Catholic Revival in America was not unlike that of Ernest Psichari on the French Revival and those of Pearse, MacDonagh, and Plunkett on the Irish Revival.

In a letter written from France a month before he was killed, Kilmer expressed the belief that American literature would learn the same lesson from the War that France was learning — "courage and self-abnegation, and love, and faith — this last not faith in some abstract goodness, but faith in God and His Son and the Holy Ghost and in the Church which God Himself founded and still rules." "I believe [he said] that America is learning the same lesson from the War and is cleansing herself of cynicism and pessimism and materialism and the lust for novelty which has so hampered our national development. I hope that our poets already see this tendency and rejoice in it — if they do not they are unworthy of their craft."

Well, they did not. The American literati who had worked hard for a real American decadence when the thing was already *passé* in Europe would not be deprived of the fruits of their labor. So we had a decadence. It is now known in literary history as "the 1920's." It followed with remarkable accuracy the course taken by the English 1890's, which is not so remarkable after all, because it was consciously modeled on it. Most of its wildest manifestations were concentrated into the first five years, and during that time its *dramatis personae* — Sherwood Anderson, Branch Cabell, F. Scott Fitzgerald, Theodore Dreiser, Eugene O'Neill, Sinclair Lewis — seemed the only authors who were writing anything that was being read. The figure of H. L. Mencken moved about through all its manifestations like a provincial Oscar Wilde. After 1925 all that the new writers had to say had been said. It was essentially a negative sort of speech — revolt, abuse, cynicism — and so there was nothing left to do but to repeat. The movement went into its crystallization stage, the stage of book-a-month clubs, popular magazines, newspaper criticism, cheap editions. A powerfully attractive force in contemporary letters as long as it remained an esoteric affair, through overpopularization it became just vulgar. By 1930 even some of the college boys were heckling it.

An interesting aspect of the American decadence was the rather large number of authors of Catholic birth who were in various degrees seduced by it, among others F. Scott Fitzgerald,

Theodore Dreiser, Eugene O'Neill, Philip Barry, Ernest Hemingway, and Will Durant. One cannot say this would not have happened had there been in existence in this country a strong and well-armed Catholic literary movement, or, in default of that, had the literature of the Catholic revivals in France and England at least been generally known and easily accessible to Catholics. However, this much may be said with safety, that the amount of excellent energy squandered in the pursuit of the asinine, the number of geniuses left stranded in philosophical blind alleys, the valuable time consumed in perfectly sterile revolt might have been considerably less. We have already seen what the discovery of the works of Patmore, Hopkins, Thompson, and Chesterton meant to a man like Joyce Kilmer. And more recently we have had occasion to see what the experience and example of these same writers is beginning to mean for those who are looking around for a way out of the impasse into which the decadence has led them. Eugene O'Neill, to mention but one instance, has found in Francis Thompson's dramatization of the mad flight from God of the men of the 90's a modern American drama and the solution of what he calls our own "hide-and-seek period."

But absolute Catholicism is still much too radical a solution for most of the celebrities of the 1920's. Some, like H. L. Mencken, have chosen to ignore the new intellectual temper that has succeeded the defunct ethos of the twenties. They remain just Liberals and, of course, ineffective. There are others, however, who, conscious of their rejection by the American middle class, have packed up their slightly tarnished evangel and have gone over to the proletariat. They have turned Communist and sing sweetly of the future of proletarian literature.

"Of course," observes Mr. V. E. Calverton in a recent blurb on this exodus, "the life of the proletariat hardly affords sufficient opportunity or leisure to encourage the development of literary talents. Proletarian writers will therefore for the most part spring from the middle class intellectuals who, like Waldo

Frank, Robert Cantwell, and William Rollins, identify their spiritual interests with those of the proletarian cause."

Of course. The masses which have been exploited into slavery by the bourgeois capitalists must now of necessity remain passive while they undergo another exploitation at the hands of the bourgeois litterateurs. Or is there another alternative? May not the masses be awakened to the fact that the ideology of these bourgeois litterateurs is substantially identical with that of the bourgeois bankers, that the promise of a Communist Utopia is just a workingman's edition of the weed-grown paradise of Science and Progress? The Catholic Church in America, which is still a proletarian church, may have something to say about this.

BIBLIOGRAPHY

BROWNSON, ORESTES
  American Ecclesiastical Review, Vol. 52, p. 406.
  Catholic Encyclopedia.
  Catholic World, Vol. 69, p. 24.
  Dublin Review, July, 1900; July, 1901.
  WORKS
  Essays and Reviews (1852).
  The Spirit Rapper: an autobiography (1854).
  The American Republic (1865).
  The Convert, or leaves from my experience (1857).
CHOPIN, KATE
  Rankin, *Kate Chopin and her Creole Stories* (biography and selected short stories), Pennsylvania University Press, 1932.
CRAWFORD, F. MARION
  American Catholic Quarterly, Vol. 17, p. 621.
  Atlantic Monthly, June, 1886, p. 850.
  Ave Maria, Vol. 51, p. 402.
  Bookman, Vol. 26, p. 121.
  Elliot, M. H., *My Cousin F. Marion Crawford* (New York: Macmillan).
  WORKS
  Mr. Isaacs (New York: Macmillan, 1882).
  A Roman Singer (New York: Macmillan, 1884).

Saracinesca (New York: Macmillan, 1887).
Marzio's Crucifix (New York: Macmillan, 1887).
Greifenstein (New York: Macmillan, 1889).
St. Illaria (New York: Macmillan, 1889).
The Ralstons (New York: Macmillan, 1895).
Via Crucis (New York: Macmillan, 1899).
In the Palace of the King (New York: Macmillan, 1900).
The White Sister (New York: Macmillan).

EGAN, MAURICE FRANCIS
America, Vol. 30, p. 348.
America, Vol. 30, p. 598.
Recollections of a Happy Life (autobiography), 1924.
WORKS
The Disappearance of John Longworthy (1890).
Studies in Literature (1899).
Everybody's St. Francis (1912).

GUINEY, LOUISE I.
America, Vol. 47, p. 550.
Brown, Alice, *Louise M. Guiney* (New York: Macmillan, 1921).
Catholic World, Vol. 90, p. 447.
Earls, Michael, S.J., *Under College Towers*, p. 68.
Letters of Louise Guiney, with preface by Agnes Repplier (New York: Harper, 1926, 2 vols.).
Tenison, *Louise M. Guiney* (New York: Macmillan, 1923).
WORKS
White Sail and other poems (Boston: Ticknor, 1893).
Patrins (Boston: Copeland and Day, 1897).
Martyrs Idyll, and shorter poems (Boston: Houghton, 1898).
Roadside Harp, a book of verse (Boston: Houghton, 1898).
Hurrell Froude (New York: Dutton, 1905).
Blessed Edmund Campion (New York: Benziger, 1908).
Happy Ending (her own selection of her poems), (Boston: Houghton, 1927).

HARLAND, HENRY
Le Gallienne, R., *The Romantic '90's*, pp. 233–238.
Irish Monthly, Vol. 39, p. 212.
Commonweal, Vol. 7, p. 103.
Bookman, Vol. 29, pp. 609–13.
WORKS
The Cardinal's Snuff-Box (New York: Lane, 1898).
The Lady Paramount (New York: Lane, 1902).

My Friend Prospero (New York: Lane, 1904).

HECKER, ISAAC
   America, Vol. 22, p. 184.
   Month, March, 1933.

HARRIS, JOEL CHANDLER
   America, Vol. 19, p. 609, and Vol. 20, p. 163.
   Bookman, Vol. 48, p. 507.
   Cambridge History of American Literature.
   Harris Julia, C., *Life and Letters of Joel Chandler Harris,* 1918.
   WORKS
   Uncle Remus, His Songs and Sayings (1881).
   Nights with Uncle Remus (1883).
   Uncle Remus and His Friends (1893).
   Mr. Rabbit at Home (1895).

LATHROP, ROSE HAWTHORNE
   Atlantic Monthly, Vol. 142, p. 372.
   Driscoll, *Convert Literary Women* (Magnificat Press, 1928).

PALLEN, CONDE
   Catholic Encyclopedia and Its Makers.
   Commonweal, Vol. 10, p. 214.
   WORKS
   As Man to Man (New York: Macmillan, 1927).
   Epochs of Literature (St. Louis: Herder, 1897).
   The Feast of Thalarchus (Boston: Small, 1901).

SPALDING, JOHN LANCASTER (BISHOP)
   America, Vol. 21, p. 598.
   Dublin Review, January, 1874, July, 1877.
   Egan, M. F., *Studies in Literature,* p. 63.
   WORKS
   Essays and Reviews (New York: 1873).

STODDARD, CHARLES WARREN
   America, Vol. 25, p. 66, and Vol. 39, p. 500.
   Catholic World, Vol. 105, p. 511.
   Lecky, *Impressions and Opinions.*
   WORKS
   Poems of Charles Warren Stoddard (Lane, 1917).
   South Sea Idylls (London: Chatto).
   The Lepers of Molokai (Notre Dame Press, 1885).
   A Troubled Heart (story of his conversion), 1885.
   A Cruise Under the Crescent (1898).
   Over the Rocky Mountains to Alaska (1899).

In the Footsteps of the Padres (1902).
Exits and Entrances (1903).
Father Damien: a sketch (1903).
Confessions of a Reformed Poet (1907).

TABB, JOHN BANISTER

Brégy, K., *Poets and Pilgrims.*
Catholic World, Vol. 73, p. 310, Vol. 80, p. 139, and Vol. 90, p. 577.
Tabb, J. M., *Father Tabb, His Life and Works* (Boston, 1921).

WORKS

A Selection from the Verse of J. B. Tabb, made by Alice Meynell
(Boston, 1907).
Poems (Boston, 1894).
Lyrics (Boston, 1897).

KILMER, JOYCE

Brégy, K., *Poets and Pilgrims.*
Daly, James J., S.J., *A Cheerful Ascetic* (Milwaukee: Bruce, 1932).

WORKS

Joyce Kilmer (poems, essays, letters) edited with a memoir by Robert
Cortes Holliday, 2 vols. (New York: Doran, 1918).
The Circus and other Essays (New York: Doran, 1921).

WALSH, THOMAS

Catholic Encyclopedia and Its Makers.
Commonweal, Vol. 12, p. 635, and Vol. 13, p. 123.

WORKS

Poems of Thomas Walsh, with appreciations by John Bunker and
Michael Williams (New York: Dial Press, 1930).

Contemporary Phase

The pitiable state of the modern world, a mere corpse of the Christian world, creates a specially ardent desire for the reinvention of a true civilization. If such a desire were to remain unfulfilled and the universal dissolution to take its course, we should still find consolation, because as the world breaks up we see the things of the spirit gather together in places in the world but not of the world. Art and poetry are among them, and metaphysics and wisdom; the charity of the saints will lead the choir. None of them has any permanent dwelling here below; each lives in casual shelters, waiting for the storm to pass. If the Spirit which floated over the waters must now hover above the ruins, what does it matter? It is sufficient if it comes. What is certain, at all events, is that we are approaching a time when any hope set below the heart of Christ is doomed to disappointment.

— JACQUES MARITAIN

1

Chesterton, Baring, Belloc

I

Among the notable exhibits at the Royal Academy in London a year or so ago was a painting by the artist H. James Gunn which attracted no little attention and comment. Popular interest in it arose chiefly from the fact that it was the portrait of three of England's most distinguished litterateurs and the principals in a celebrated literary friendship. The artist called it "Hilaire Belloc, G. K. Chesterton, and Maurice Baring: a conversation piece." It might just as accurately have been named "A picture of contemporary Catholic letters."

It was exhibited at an opportune time. Most of us were beginning, I shall not say to forget these three men (that would be impossible), but to regard them as just three among a score of other contemporary figures; they were becoming lost amid Christopher Dawson, Alfred Noyes, Ronald Knox, Eric Gill, Sheila Kaye-Smith, D. B. Wyndham Lewis, Compton Mackenzie, Sir Philip Gibbs, Evelyn Waugh, and others. Yet the importance of this trio is above that of merely belonging to the present period. They *made* the period, carved it out of a stubborn fortune, and moreover have placed their stamp on most of its manifestations.

John Sargent may be said to have painted one phase of the Catholic Revival when he drew Coventry Patmore as one of the major prophets of the Old Testament — a voice crying in the Victorian wilderness. The same artist also captured the essential spirit of the second phase in the sketch he has left us of the slim patrician figure of Alice Meynell, clad in a style of dress that belongs both to the 1890's and to our own day, the posture speaking of exquisite poise, the countenance of intelligence and spirituality. Mr. Gunn, the artist of the Royal Academy picture, has a similar achievement to his credit. He has deftly suggested the dominant note of a third phase of the revival in this painting which shows three men gathered about a table, intent on some plan, like three generals in a council of war. For the present phase differs from the other two in its marked warlike character; it is aggressive, militant, engaged in battle. What that battle is and how it has affected the tone of the entire literature of the contemporary phase will appear as we proceed. Let us first look more closely at the picture itself and its three figures.

Belloc, Baring, Chesterton, these names stand, as has been said, for a famous literary friendship, and this friendship in turn may be taken as the connecting link between the Catholic Revival of the 1890's and the contemporary period. Belloc and Chesterton were protégés of Alice Meynell who at a very early date seems to have recognized in them qualities that would fit them for leadership in the new phase of the movement. All three began their literary careers in the Yellow Decade; Chesterton in a youthful outburst against the esthetes, Belloc in rebellion against so many things that it would be tedious to mention them; Baring, characteristically enough, made his debut with an article on Anatole France in the *Yellow Book* written at the request of Henry Harland. They were all very young then, and of the three only Belloc was a Catholic.

The Baring-Belloc friendship dates from the middle of the 1890's when both were at Oxford. Baring was there preparing to take examinations for a position in the diplomatic service; his university studies had been made on the continent at Heidelberg, Hildescheim, and Florence, so he was not the thorough Oxford man that Belloc was. The latter had just finished what from several contemporary descriptions of it extant must have been a thoroughly shocking course at the ancient university.

Born in France of English and French parentage, Belloc received his early training at Newman's Oratory School at Edgbaston, where as a boy he had known the old Cardinal and had taken part in the Latin plays which Newman had made a part of the training there.

He did not go up to Oxford at once; there was an interval of two years following his graduation; and then he marched into the hallowed precincts of Balliol College fresh from a term of service in a French artillery regiment, with a history scholarship and all the foreign oaths and rough-and-tumble manners of the French gunners. "He was a devil for work and a genius at play," records one contemporary. "He read strange books, swore strange oaths and amazed his tutors by the fire and fury of his historical study." "His rooms," adds another, "were a continual focus of noise; troops of friends, song, loud laughter. . . . He found himself happy and merry beyond words . . . was a notable figure at the Union Debates, argued passionately against every conventional English tradition and attacked authority, complacence and fetishism of every kind. . . ." We may place this picture of the rebellious Belloc alongside that of the saintly, scholarly Newman who at Oriel in the early part of the century took solitary walks and wrote that he "had learned to leap (to a certain point)" and found that "the exhilaration of going quickly through the air is for my spirits very good." The contrast will prepare us for the marked difference that will be apparent between contemporary Catholic literature and that of Victorian times. Yet we detect some points of similarity in the careers of these two men at Oxford. They were both leaders, they were both rebels, they both loved the Oxford that nourished them and left it unwillingly, leaving disciples behind them. *Credo in Belloc* never became, like *Credo in Newmanum,* a consecrated rallying cry; but his corrosive *Lines to a Don* "who dared attack my Chesterton" became a favorite hymn of all worthy dons at Oxford, says Christopher Morley, who further records that "in the Oxford before the War all the

undergraduates were reading Belloc; you could hardly find a
college room that did not shelve one or two of his volumes."

Belloc was still at Oxford writing his first biography, *Danton,*
when Baring and he became acquainted. "I had met him once
before with Basil Blackwood," says the latter, "but all he had
said to me was that I would most certainly go to hell, and so I
had not thought it likely that we should ever make friends,
although I recognized the first moment I saw him that he was
a remarkable man." They soon became boon companions, how-
ever, united by a common affection for the world's literature,
vital ideas, undergraduate horseplay, and for an Oxford insti-
tution in which all of these elements were curiously mingled.
In later and maturer years, when Baring sat down to write of
these days in his *Puppet Show of Memory,* it is these nocturnal
sessions he, Belloc, and others engaged in that stand out most
clearly in his mind. And one does not wonder. "Belloc dis-
coursed of the Jewish Peril, the Catholic Church, the *Chanson
de Roland,* Ronsard and the Pyrenees with undescribable gusto
and vehemence. . . . People would come in through the win-
dows and syphons would sometimes be hurled across the
room; but nobody was ever wounded. The ham would be
slapped and butter thrown to the ceiling where it stuck. . . .
Songs were sung; port was drunk and thrown about the room.
Indeed we had a special brand of port called *throwing port* for
the purpose. And again the evening would finish in long talks,
the endless serious talk of youth, ranging over every topic from
Transubstantiation to Toggers, and from the last row with the
Junior Dean to Predestination and Free Will. We were all dis-
covering things for each other and opening for each other un-
guessed-of doors."

Friendship begun under such auspices cannot but be of the
enduring kind. The years have not deprived either of these men
of that youthfulness of spirit which is liable to erupt at any time.
Baring, for instance, almost brought international disgrace
upon himself and his government when as an under-secretary

in the English Embassy at Paris he engaged in an ink-throwing fight with a fellow secretary, staining the walls and hangings of the embassy with red and blue ink and continuing the fight out into the Rue Faubourg St. Honoré. One could have predicted that when these two at a later date would meet Gilbert Chesterton (he was studying art while Baring and Belloc were at Oxford) the same sort of friendship would spring up between them; for who in the modern world enjoys boisterous intellectual fellowship, honest fun, and the music of clashing opinions with greater gusto than he. And so E. V. Lucas in a recent book, *Reading, Writing and Remembering,* tells how he fell in with this triumvirate one day lunching in London's Café Royal. The luncheon was a memorable one for him, he remarks, because Belloc and Baring sang throughout it a number of verses and satirical ballads they had composed at Oxford, and apparently kept the concert up the remainder of the afternoon. For afterwards in a Turkish Bath in Jermyn Street Lucas was awakened from a peaceful sleep by the notes of "a deep Gallic voice"; "and there again were Belloc and Maurice recollecting more Macaronics" but this time without any clothes on.

II

It is this lifelong friendship the artist has celebrated in the Royal Academy picture; it is one of the spiritual things that more than the consummate draftsmanship of the artist has given unity and balance to the group. I say "one of the spiritual things" because there is another which must claim our attention here. For these men, now in their sixties, are united not only in a common and long-standing friendship, but in a common and long-standing battle, making us see in the group not only a council of friends but a council of war. All, despite their civilian dress, are soldiers. Belloc (ex-French artillery driver and one of England's foremost experts in military tactics) and Baring (wing-commander in the Royal Air Force) are both practical military men; Chesterton, a most impractical one but perhaps the most consistent fighter of them all. We may say of him what he has said of Belloc that "he has fought the greatest battle for the good things of any man of our times." It is this battle, the battle of ideas, of culture against culture, of civilization against barbarism, that unites these three rather than any mere rattle of steel and artillery. From the opening of the twentieth century, when the conflict began on a new basis, both Belloc and Chesterton have been in the thick of the fighting, dealing blows and taking them, and scarcely pausing for breath. For they have realized from the beginning what others are only beginning to realize today that this battle between the forces that contend for the intellectual and spiritual future of the West is the greatest struggle of our times, transcending all minor conflicts, dividing men ordinarily united into furiously antagonistic camps — and one, too, the final issue of which is still in doubt.

The world has come to know very well the parts that Belloc and Chesterton have taken in this conflict. They have been literally everywhere, on all fronts simultaneously; scattered minorities have caught the courage of their presence and have rallied, strong opponents have tasted their steel in wonder and fear. George Bernard Shaw, indeed, has contended that the two are not distinct persons at all but two heads of the same omnipresent and thoroughly dangerous monster.

The part that Maurice Baring has played in the engagement is less well known. One heard, as a matter of fact, some sharp protests against his inclusion in the Royal Academy picture from those who knew that he was an essential part of the literary friendship but couldn't see what he had to do with the council of war. The objection, to state it in another way, was that since modern Catholic letters is predominantly warlike, Baring cannot be considered a part of it, since he is neither aggressive nor polemical, but exasperatingly placid. He is, certainly, the most placid of men. One looks in vain through his writings for that sense of world-crisis, of impending catas-

trophe, which is to be found everywhere in modern Catholic
letters even in the writings of those who are in no sense
polemical. It must be admitted, too, that Baring is a rather
queer sort of soldier. During the four years of hell on the Wes-
tern Front with the Royal Air Force, he spent his spare mo-
ments re-reading Dante's *Paradiso* and Wordsworth's *Prelude*.[1]
He records the deaths of his friends Basil Blackwood and Cap-
tain Lucas simply, with pathos but no bitterness. He cannot
hate the enemy. For he remembers the culture and good-fellow-
ship of Heidelberg and the sweet simplicity of German middle-
class home life at Hildesheim, and he regrets the war that has
put at each other's throats men who should be united on the
higher things of the spirit they all love in common. And so
after the war while hatred and ill-feeling were rife and an un-
steady world was in danger of crashing about his ears, he con-
tinued to pursue his tranquil, even course, cultivating the cul-
tural riches of the European tradition in an atmosphere of pro-
found peace.

One notices that in Mr. Gunn's picture, Baring stands seem-
ing aloof in an attitude of only mild interest in the business
that absorbs the full attention of the other two, which we may
safely assume is some new offensive against those they regard
as enemies of civilization. It is not that he loves the threatened
culture of the West any less than his friends, but his method of
defending it is different. They fight for it; he cultivates it. There
is in his makeup none of the "Wild Knight" spirit of the
enormous and belligerent Chesterton; nor does he resemble
Belloc — the steel-eyed legionary smiting the barbarian on the
confines of the empire with the cry of the Roman Mark on his
lips,

> *Lift not my head from bloody ground,*
> *Bear not my body home:*
> *For all the earth is Roman earth,*
> *And I shall die in Rome.*

---

[1] Cf. Baring's *R.F.C., H.Q., 1914–1918* certainly one of the most unusual of war
memoirs.

His historical prototype, if we must have one, would be one of those clerics of the critical sixth century whom Gregory the Great reprehended for reading the odes of Horace while the civilized world was falling to pieces. Yet they, too, played their magnificent part in the making of Europe. Today, no less than in those times so like our own, the Church has its fighters who engage the barbarians hand to hand and those who in more or less quiet seclusion preserve the treasures of the great past. Baring stands for these latter and hence belongs to the picture.

An insight into Baring's temperament and his attitude toward what we have called "the great battle of our times," may be had from an incident that occurred while he was studying at Cambridge (Baring is one of the few Englishmen who can claim both universities as his alma mater). It was in the 1890's. "There was a mysterious intellectual society there [he says] called the Society of the Apostles of which Bertrand Russell and Robert Trevelyan were conspicuous members." One of the "apostles" accosted him one day and said that he was setting a bad example by going to chapel; Christianity was exploded, a thing of the past, no one really believed in it any more among the young and the advanced, but for the sake of the old-fashioned and the unregenerate he was bid to set an example of sincerity and courage and soon the world would follow suit. "I remember thinking that although I was much younger in years than these intellectuals . . ., I was none the less older than they in a particular kind of experience, the experience that has nothing to do either with the mind, or with knowledge, and that is independent of age, but takes place in the heart, and in which a child may sometimes be more rich than a grownup person. I do not mean anything sentimental. I speak of the experience that comes from having been suddenly constrained to turn around and look at life from a different point of view. So when I heard the intellectuals reason in the manner I have described, I felt for the moment an old person listening to young people. I felt young people must always have talked like that.

It was not that I had then any definite religious creed. I seldom went to chapel but that was out of laziness. While I was at Heidelberg the religious tenets which I had kept absolutely intact since childhood, without question and without shadow of doubt or difficulty, suddenly one day, without outside influence or inside crisis, just dropped away from me. I shed them as easily as a child loses a first tooth. In the winter of 1893 when I came back from Berlin someone asked me why I didn't go to Church. I said it was because I didn't believe in any Christian faith, and if I ever were to again I would be a Catholic."

One may agree that the attitude taken by young Baring in those days toward Bertrand Russell and his coterie was the proper attitude and the one which is coming to be the most common one in our own day. There is something unquestionably adolescent about the whole program of these men. But Baring's attitude is one, none the less, which, then as well as now, neglects an important aspect of the whole affair — the element, namely, of fanaticism, of crusading zeal which has characterized the exponents of the movement from the beginning. One may smile at it as a schoolboy rebellion but one cannot afford to forget that these schoolboys were "apostles," evangelical; theirs is a religion and they set out to convert the world to it. A sense of humor is perhaps the best defense a really mature mind has against it. But what of the mass of simple people who, as the years have shown, have swallowed the Bertrand Russell syncretism with amazing naïvete? What could save them but to attack these opinions of the "apostles" as serious ones.

Chesterton could never have fallen into the error of Baring in underestimating the importance of messianic atheism. For he, himself, had once been seduced by this same evangel, and he knew its force. "I freely confess," he said in 1908, "all the idiotic ambitions at the end of the nineteenth century. I did, like all other solemn little boys, try to be in advance of the age. Like them I tried to be some ten minutes in advance of truth. And

I found I was eighteen hundred years behind it." The large number of drum-thumping evangelists of the type of Wells and Shaw produced by the 1890's made Chesterton see the necessity of something more aggressive than the attitude of bored silence if Europe was to be saved from becoming a wasteland. Belloc saw the need of the same sort of offensive but from a somewhat different angle. His belligerence was a continuation of Newman's war on Liberalism as something essentially illiberal, raw, and barbaric.

And so it has come about that Chesterton and Belloc rather than Baring have determined the course Catholic literature has taken in the twentieth century. They have been the leaders. They have brought it about that the greater part of this literature should be aggressive, polemical, engaged principally in defending the good things of our culture rather than in the recollected exploration and enjoyment of them. They had determined that its novels should be problem novels, and that history, satire, and the argumentative tract should assume a greater importance than poetry and the artistic essay. They, finally, have set up as the ideal of the modern Catholic litterateur one who writes as copiously as the early Fathers of the Church, for their numbers were few in comparison with the voices of the enemy and they must cover a large battle front with a small but superactive force.

One may deplore all this as being detrimental to the interests of pure literature, and sigh for the quieter days of Alice Meynell; but one cannot ignore the fact that this new aspect is a necessity born of the times. It is well to insist that the highest art is not always struck off in the heat of battle, and that poetry of the enduring kind wells out of recollection and quiet. But when the very continuation of those things is threatened on which art more intimately depends than quiet and recollection, culture, namely, the treasures of the past, philosophy, and religion, letters can do no better service to art than to rush to the defense of these things. This is what modern Catholic literature under the leadership of Chesterton and Belloc has done. And when the history of the twentieth century comes to be written, whether by some solitary hermit near the ruins of London Bridge or by a polished litterateur in the cultural capital of a renewed Christian West, the part played by Catholic letters in the first thirty years will be one of the volume's most heroic and valuable pages.

Both Belloc and Chesterton have perhaps written more than any one man should write. Each has in the neighborhood of ninety volumes to his credit. In less critical times, or under conditions which are now beginning to prevail when many talented defenders have joined forces with them, they would probably have written much less. But it is to be doubted that they would have written any better.

The critics are continually assuring us, and rightly too, that Chesterton is primarily a poet; this insistence is usually accompanied with a note of regret that he does not retire from the clamor of controversy and devote some recollected hours to enriching the English language with more poetry of the type of *Lepanto* and *The Ballad of the White Horse*. The latter poem has been called by many critics and most recently by Charles Williams "one of the greatest of modern poems." Mr. Williams is among the very few, I think, who see that the greatness of the poem and the author's incessant fighting in the modern battle are essentially connected. He writes of battles as one engaged in them, whence arises that whiff of reality that made one critic exclaim of the *Ballad of the White Horse* that there has been no better fighting since Homer. His poems are always full of the voice of battle, they invariably deal with crises. But in reality it is only of one battle and of one crisis he writes, and that the present crisis of European civilization and the battle to save it. His poetry, by reason of this, becomes something more than just poetry. It is a proclamation, a manifesto, a challenge, a war-cry. One goes to it as he goes to Dante or to Virgil or to Homer primarily to find the living soul, the aspirations, the hopes of a people, only secondary to fill that section of his being which an arbitrary division of things has allotted to pure poetry. We may turn to it here as to the place where the essential spirit of modern Catholicity may be found.

III

Floyd Dell in a midwestern town once read to the then unknown Vachel Lindsay Chesterton's *Lepanto,* and from its "dim drums throbbing in the hills half-heard" there was born the tom-tom rhythm of *Congo.* But *Congo* is an inferior poem not only because it is an imitation but because, although more recent, it is less modern. For Chesterton has made "Lepanto" the name of a contemporary battle and not of a sixteenth-century one. He has used the historical details of this post-Reformation crisis of European civilization to make stand out clearly a present crisis. He may seem to be dealing with Pope Pius V and Don John of Austria; in reality it is with Pope Pius XI and those who, like the "last knight of Europe," have rallied about his standard for the defense of the West.

Christian knighthood, at that point in the sixteenth century to which the poem takes us, seemed definitely dead, merely waiting for the official funeral which Cervantes was shortly to give it. The Turk could have chosen no more auspicious time for his invasion of Europe, and soon "the inmost sea of all the world is shaken with his ships." Cyprus falls and the white republics up the capes of Italy are threatened. The fate of Europe is in the balance, and in the emergency Pope Pius V makes a brave attempt to rally the divided European nations to the defense of their common civilization, appealing to a spirit that had given to the West its hegemony among the nations of the world. He

Casts his arms about for agony and loss,
And calls the knights of Christendom for swords about the
cross.

But the cry goes echoless through the northern nations from which the spirit of the crusaders seems to have departed along with the spirit of Catholicism. For,

The north is full of tangled things and texts and aching eyes,
And dead is all the innocence of anger and surprise,
And Christian killeth Christian in a narrow dusty room,
And Christian dreadeth Christ that hath a newer face of doom.

The situation, naturally speaking, is quite hopeless. From such disunion there can come no defense, and one sympathizes with King Philip of Spain, who awaits the inevitable with a crystal vial of poison in his hand. It is a situation that calls for a Richard, a Raymond, a Godfrey — for one that "knows not fate" and "whose loss is laughter when he counts the wager worth." All this Pope Pius knows; he has called for a crusader, and the silence that meets his call as it goes about the western world must tell him that the age has no such spirits. Then —

In that enormous silence, tiny and unafraid,
Comes up along a winding road the noise of the crusade.

One has answered, not the cold queen of England, nor the shadow of the Valois, but "only a crownless prince on a nameless throne." Don John of Austria, illegitimate son of the Emperor Charles V, half-brother of King Philip of Spain —

The last knight of Europe takes his weapon from the wall.
The last and lingering troubador to whom the bird has sung,
That once went singing southward when all the world was
young.

* * *

Strong gangs groaning as the guns boom far,
Don John of Austria is going to the war —
Don John laughing in the brave beard curled,
Spurning of his stirrups like the thrones of all the world,
Holding his head up for a flag of all the free.
Love light of Spain — hurrah!
Death light of Africa!
Don John of Austria
Is riding to the sea.

It is the crusader resurgent, the old knight returned, sprung full-armed out of the brow of a crisis. The issue of events is no longer in question and the narrative hurries swiftly to the engagement. Out of the memorable naval engagement in the Gulf of Corinth, Chesterton has wrought one of his greatest battle pictures. It is one of sharp contrasts. The cringing fear of King Philip at home, the listless, leaden fear in the other courts of Europe, the prayer of the Pope, the despair of the Christian captives "sick and sunless" in the prison holds of the Turkish galleys. Then comes a line clear and decisive as a lightning flash —

(But Don John of Austria has burst the battle line)
Don John pounding from the slaughter-painted poop,
Purpling all the ocean like a bloody pirate's sloop,
Scarlet running over on the silvers and the golds,
Breaking of the hatches up and bursting of the holds,
Thronging of the thousands up that labor under sea,
White for bliss, and blind for sun, and stunned for liberty.
Vivat Hispania!
Domino gloria!
Don John of Austria
Has set his people free!

The poem had begun with the smile of the Sultan, who smiles an oily complacent smile because Christian knighthood is dead. It ends with the smile of the Christian warrior, Cervantes, who fought by Don John's side in the battle of Lepanto.

Cervantes on his galley sets the sword back in the sheath
(Don John of Austria rides homeward with a wreath)
And he sees across a weary land a straggling road in Spain,
Up which a lean and foolish knight for ever rides in vain,
And he smiles, but not as Sultans smile, and settles back the
*   blade. . . .*
(But Don John of Austria rides home from the Crusade)

The whole force of Chesterton's message hangs upon the smile of Cervantes. It is the smile of a Christian who in the puerile old age of Chivalry heard and responded to the call for knights. It is the smile of one who sees that while the shell of historic chivalry decays, the spirit of Christian knighthood is eternal. The smile has made the poem a modern one. For the vision of Cervantes, here, extends well beyond the straggling road in Spain — four hundred years beyond it to the end of what Berdyaev has called "the doomed world of modern history." He sees another crisis of our own civilization, the appalling disunion of Christendom, the threat of the barbarian from within and from without, the apathy of Christian men, the stoic despair of non-Christian men, and above it all the confident call of still another Pius for fighting men who know not fate.

Of Mr. Chesterton we may say that if Don John of Austria was "the last knight of Europe" in the old order, he deserves to be called the first knight of Europe in the new dispensation. I should say he especially merits this title. For he is but one of a large number of artists and literary people who as a matter of fact are devoting their best energies to the defense of the most valuable things in Western culture. The sense of conflict, of crisis, of the necessity of working while there is still light is universal among modern Catholic writers, and it has, as has been said, changed the entire face of contemporary letters. But while they for the most part are content to confront the situation in its modern and somewhat prosaic dress, Chesterton insists on investing it with all the color, pageantry, and strong-armed knighthood of historic times. The rallying cry of "typewriters about the cross" must be changed to "swords about the cross." He bitterly deplores the fact that he must, like one born out of due time, fight stoop-shouldered biologists, pale Liberals, and anemic dons instead of the strong, healthy type of barbarian that King Alfred engaged in the Dark Ages. He consoles himself by making them the lineal descendants of a once strong and vigorous race. Thus, in the *Ballad of the White Horse* he puts into King Alfred's mouth a prophecy which may stand as his own summary of the modern situation. Alfred has just driven the barbarian Danes out of his lands in a series of brilliant victories when the spirit of prophecy descends upon him in the following lines:

> *And though they scatter now and go,*
> *In some far century, sad and slow,*
> *I have a vision and I know*
> *   The heathen shall return.*
>
> *They shall not come with warships,*
> *   They shall not waste with brands,*
> *But books be all their eating,*
> *   And ink be on their hands.*
>
> *They shall come mild as monkish clerks,*
> *   With many a scroll and pen;*
> *And backward shall we turn and gaze,*
> *Desiring one of Alfred's days,*
> *   When pagans still were men.*

*   *   *

By this sign you shall know them,
The breaking of the sword,
And man no more a free knight,
That loves or hates his lord.

Yea, this shall be the sign of them,
The sign of dying fire;
And man made like a half-wit,
That knows not of his sire.

* * *

By thought a crawling ruin,
By life a leaping mire,
By a broken heart in the breast of the world,
And the end of the world's desire;

By God and man dishonored,
By death and life made vain,
Know ye the old barbarian,
The barbarian come again —

When is great talk of trend and tide,
And wisdom and destiny,
Hail the undying heathen
That is sadder than the sea.

In what wise men shall smite him,
Or the Cross stand up again,
Or charity or chivalry,
My vision saith not; and I see
No more. . . .

IV

The Ballad of the White Horse, notwithstanding its title, is an epic poem, epic in concept, epic in stature. Here again it is the same modern crisis that Chesterton celebrates under the symbolism now of the Saxon King Alfred's fight in the Dark Ages against the barbarian Danes. The poem opens with a picture of this Christian king, alone and disconsolate in the forest of Athelney. He is hiding from the triumphant invaders who have defeated him in many battles, scattered his discouraged followers and are laying waste the countryside. Nothing is left him but "shameful tears of rage" as he lies in the deep grass hardening his heart with hope in he knows not what. Of a sudden a vision is before him. It is the Mother of God, and the broken king arises and asks her for a sign of what the future may hold for him and for his Christian people.

Mary's response comes slowly. She reminds him she is not speaking to the wise of this world who demand signs and wonders, but to the brave and ignorant of Christ, who "have wars they hardly win and souls they hardly save." Then her sign, strange and seemingly ominous, that runs refrain-like throughout the entire poem:

> *I tell you naught for your comfort,*
> *   Yea naught for your desire*
> *Save that the sky grows darker yet*
> *   And the sea rises higher.*
>
> *Night shall be thrice night over you*
> *   And heaven an iron cope,*
> *Do you have joy without a cause*
> *   Yea, faith without a hope?*

She vanishes, and Alfred, alone in the forest, hears the distant sea and the marching pagans and these strange words that move him profoundly. He does not stand long.

> *Up across the windy wastes and up*
> *Went Alfred over the shaws,*
> *Shaken with the joy of giants,*
> *The joy without a cause.*

The king goes gathering once again his dispersed chiefs, coming first to the German Eldred who suspects immediately the nature of his mission and speaks his mind quite frankly:

> *"Come not to me, King Alfred,*
> *Save always for the ale;*
> *Why should my harmless hinds be slain*
> *Because the chiefs cry once again,*
> *As in all fights, that we shall gain,*
> *And in all fights we fail?*

* * *

> *"Friend, I will watch the certain things,*
> *Swine, and slow moons like silver rings,*
> *And the ripening of the plums."*

> *And Alfred answered, drinking,*
> *And gravely without blame:*
> *"Nor bear I boast of scald or king;*
> *The thing I bear is a lesser thing,*
> *But it comes in a better name.*

> *"Out of the mouth of the Mother of God,*
> *More than the doors of doom,*
> *I call the master of Wessex men,*
> *From grassy hamlet or ditch or den,*

> *To break and be broken God knows when,*
> *But I have seen for whom.*

> *"And this is the word of Mary,*
> *The word of the world's desire:*
> *'No more of comfort shall ye get,*
> *Save that the sky grows darker yet*
> *And the sea rises higher.'"*

Silence, tense and expectant, fills the farmhouse where Alfred awaits the answer to this, the strangest of messages to a defeated man. A call to fight in a hopeless fight, against odds that are admittedly too great, to die in battle, God knows when — "By God, but I know why." He watches the huge Eldred rise to his feet, his immense frame filling the room and porch and sky. He sees him turn and from a cobwebbed nail on high, unhook his heavy sword!

A greater poet than Chesterton conceivably might have told the story of how Alfred used these words of Mary to rally the broken and discouraged forces of Christianity and to defeat the Danes in the battle of Ethandune. But only a poet who is also a combatant and leader in a similar battle could have imagined *that he did use them* and that they were effective. Another might have imagined him using the noble, despairing words that Spengler gives to the modern world "as the only outlook that is worthy of us" in the impending collapse of civilization: "We are born into this time and must bravely follow the path to the destined end. There is no other way. Our duty is to hold on to the last position, without hope, without rescue, like that Roman soldier [at Pompeii] who died at his post because they forgot to relieve him."

But the greatness of the West was not built upon an attitude such as this. The primitive Christians when a little band in a vast pagan world did not know it, nor did it inspire the Christians of the Dark Ages when they laid the foundations of

Europe amid indescribable suffering and privations. It is alien
to the mind of the West which knows not fate nor iron his-
torical cycles, because it has been formed on the "mind of
Christ." Chesterton would make no such mistake. And in giv-
ing us what he intends should be not only the war-cry of Al-
fred but that which must rally the forces of Christianity today
in a crisis no less hopeless, no less critical, he has done little
more than paraphrase a lyric passage in the famous letter of
St. Paul to the Romans:

> *Who then shall separate us*
> *from the love of Christ?*
> *Shall tribulations or distress?*
> *Or famine or nakedness?*
> *Or danger or persecution*
> *Or the sword?*
> *As it is written:*
> *For thy sake we are put to death*
> *All the day long.*
> *We are accounted as sheep for the slaughter.*
> *But in all these things we overcome*
> *because of him that hath loved us.*

The contemporary Catholic literature which we shall treat in
the following chapters is, then, a literature engaged in a battle,
the magnitude and seemingly hopeless character of which is
never lost sight of by any of its exponents. It is, as Christopher
Dawson says, a contest between two orders, "between the ma-
terial organization of the world — based either on economic ex-
ploitation or an economic absolutism which absorbs the whole
of life and leaves no room for human values — and the Chris-
tian ideal of a spiritual order based on spiritual faith and ani-
mated by Charity, which is the spiritual will. The triumph of
such an ideal in a world that seems governed only by material
forces and distracted by hatred and greed may seem a fantastic

dream, but is it any more hopeless than the enterprise of a handful of unknown and uneducated men from a remote Oriental province who set out to conquer the imperial power of Rome and the intellectual culture of Hellenism? In history it is often the incredible that happens — *credo quia impossible* has been justified again and again."

BIBLIOGRAPHY

BARING, MAURICE

   Puppet Show of Memory (autobiography), (New York: Little, Brown, 1922).

   Lucas, E. V., *Reading, Writing and Remembering* (New York: Harper, 1932).

   Lost Lectures (autobiographical), (New York: Knopf, 1932).

   Bookman, Vol. 75, p. 685.

BELLOC, HILAIRE

   Mandell-Shanks, *Hilaire Belloc* (London: Methuen, 1916).

   Morley, Christopher, *Shandygaff.*

   Bookman, Vol. 74, p. 393.

CHESTERTON, G. K.

   Autobiography of G. K. Chesterton (New York: Sheed & Ward, 1936).

   Williams, Charles, *Poetry at Present* (Oxford University Press, 1932).

   Catholic Church and Conversion (autobiographical), (New York: Macmillan, 1926).

   Braybrooke, Patrick, *G. K. Chesterton* (Philadelphia: Lippincott, 1922).

   Catholic World, Vol. 95, p. 41, "Ballad of the White Horse."

   Columbia, November, 1922, "Ballad of the White Horse."

N.B. For selected works of above authors, see sections on poetry, history, satire, and novel.

2

Poetry

I

An important disadvantage in considering Catholic authors as a distinct group arises from the danger one runs of giving the impression that Catholic literature is an exotic growth, flourishing in isolation from the main stream of contemporary letters and without roots in the native soil. Attention has been called before to the danger of such a misconception. It must be insisted on again when we come to the department of poetry. For here, as a matter of fact, we find Catholic poets all huddled together in what appears to be an exclusive group. All our important poets belong either to the Catholic Poetry Society of England or to its corresponding organization in America.

Perhaps the most considerable curse under which modern poetry suffers is the multiplication of these snobbish coteries, the large number of which is symptomatic of the disparate and isolated character of the modern soul. There certainly is very little community of ideas left in our world today but what little there is these *chapelles* succeed in denying to their membership, by putting behind closed doors a group of already sufficiently eccentric spirits who batten on back-patting, exalt local obscurities of thought into profound statements, encourage mutual queernesses, and otherwise hang together by crying out against the one thing, the return of which might yet restore poetry to its old dignity and popularity — I mean the European tradition.

I shall not say that the distinguished members of the two

Catholic Poetry Societies are afflicted with none of these contemporary maladies. But their affliction is much less acute. In the first place neither of these groups could be called coteries; they are loose organizations of rather recent birth, membership in which consists for many merely in permitting their names to be placed on the roster. Further, although as they *are* banded together to encourage one another in the fuller expression of a spirit that does not belong to the whole of modern letters, that spirit, nevertheless, will be found to be one not foreign to but a continuation of the best tradition in English literature. That is the Catholic spirit. And just as today the Church is the most powerful of those few bodies left in the West that stand for the continuity of culture, so her poets are the most intelligent and outspoken defenders of the restoration of that community of ideas and beliefs whose absence from the modern scene, as John Masefield has recently complained, has separated the poet from the heart of the world.

It would be inaccurate, however, to represent contemporary Catholic poetry as blindly traditional, although, I am aware, some of it is, much to its damage. It is strongly flavored with a nostalgia for the good old days, meaning usually the prosody and diction of the mid-nineteenth century. It professes to see no value in the technical innovations of the moderns, against which its face is strongly set. But there is also plenty of the opposite attitude, which is perhaps best expressed by Evan Morgan, president of the English Catholic Poetry Society, who announces in the preface to his *City of Canals* that he has evolved out of the stage of Swinburne-worship: "the Romanticism of Keats, the philosophy of Shelley, the clangorous way of Byronic harmonies, the resounding symphonies of Browning, the organ tones of Tennyson" have lost their power of influencing him. He seems perfectly willing to drop the poetic contribution of the nineteenth century entirely out of his consciousness.

There is quite a bit of this anti-romantic temper (strongly seasoned, as is the modern brand, with Elizabethan-worship) afloat among Catholic poets. Yet it can scarcely be called the dominant attitude. I give it merely to indicate the absence of a monotonous unanimity of opinion among the membership of these societies. There is no marked drift either toward exaggerated modernism or exaggerated traditionalism. The presence of men and women of such widely divergent taste and backgrounds as Alfred Noyes, Padraic Colum, Shane Leslie, Lord Alfred Douglas, Helen Parry Eden, Maurice Baring, G. K. Chesterton, and Wilfred Childe, in the English group, and Theodore Maynard, Aline Kilmer, Joseph Campbell, and James J. Daly, S.J., in the American group, might explain this. However, I think the real explanation is the consciousness on the part of all that they have a poetic tradition of their own of almost a century's standing, modern and yet balanced, which they feel in some way obliged to continue. In that tradition which contains the positive achievement of de Vere, Patmore, Hopkins, Alice Meynell, Francis Thompson, and others, there is the determination to despise nothing in the past 3000 years of the European poetic tradition but to carry the best experience forward that it may be brought to play in the creation of the new forms that the new age demands. De Vere, for instance, did no more than preserve the tradition begun by Wordsworth (a valuable work and he has many modern followers), while Hopkins, taking the same tradition, embarked upon experiments, which perilous as they may have seemed to his age, have made him one of the most important founders of modern poetry. Tradition must grow or it becomes formalized.

There is, fortunately, as a healthy element in Catholic poetry today, the feeling that modern verse on its mechanical side is in a fluid, transitional state. It is working toward a new thing with plenty of blunders which we have agreed to call "experiments." Many, we may mention Padraic Colum and Father O'Donnell especially, have done excellent work in the new poetry. Even such an intransigent defender of the ancient meters as Alfred Noyes is experimental. Indeed, it seems to me that Noyes, despite his opposition to free verse, has a conception, clearer than any of his contemporaries of what is the primary thing needed to revive the anemic soul of contemporary poetry. The poet, he insists, must first obtain a fresh grasp on reality. Given this, the proper technique for its expression will follow spontaneously, and not in the eccentric and labored manner of those who seek first the new forms and having achieved them can only stuff them full of what is obviously old and conventional — yesterday's heresies, Victorian metaphysics, raw scientific dogmas, a dash of erudition, and the rest.

These, then, are some of the ideals and tendencies in modern Catholic poetry I propose to illustrate in this chapter. The large number of those who are today writing, I shall not say great, but certainly competent poetry, makes any detailed treatment of the whole field impossible. One can only discuss general tendencies. The two individual poets (Alfred Noyes and Padraic Colum) I have selected for consideration here have been chosen on this basis, although I think they may at the same time be taken as two of our principal poets, in which class I should also place, among others, Helen Parry Eden, the late Charles L. O'Donnell, C.S.C., Aline Kilmer, Sister Mary Madeleva, and G. K. Chesterton. As for the others I can only refer the reader to the bibliography at the end of the chapter. All the poets listed there will be found eminently worthy of consideration, some perhaps more worthy than the two to be treated here.

II

Alfred Noyes is perhaps the best known of a very small group of authentic poets who still believe that great poetry should be popular. He is, in fact, the first poet of the twentieth century to make a successful attempt to revive this tradition which began to pass from English literature sometime shortly after his birth at Wolverhampton, Staffordshire, in 1880. By the time he was ready for Oxford, Tennyson was dead in fact as well as in influence; the opinion which looked with suspicion upon poetry having a wide appeal was becoming fixed. At the University he did not distinguish himself in the sort of esoteric scholarship which might have unfitted him for anything but the versified syncretisms of Ezra Pound. He steeped himself in the literature of the vast European tradition, pulled a strong oar on the Exeter College eight, and began to write.

His first published poem was called "The Symbolist," by way of indicating, one supposes, that he was in no way touched by the theories, good or bad, of this school and never would be. In 1902 when his first volume of collected poems appeared, *The Loom of Years,* he was but twenty-two: it was hailed by George Meredith and Swinburne as the work of a new genius. Another volume, *The Flower of Old Japan,* was ready the following year, and two years later still another, *The Forest of Wild Thyme.* He was writing fast, and becoming tremendously popular. He was, in fact, earning a decent living by writing poetry, a thing no one of his generation would have thought possible, and which some who had praised his earlier work thought indecent. A still profounder shock was in store for these latter. For between the years 1906–1908 he published serially in *Blackwoods Magazine* a full-length epic poem on Sir Francis Drake. Not more than half of it had been completed before the first installment was sent to the printer! Another volume, too, *Forty Singing Seamen,* appeared during the same period. And the populace applauded. If professional poets had lost faith in the tradition that poetry should be as popular as fiction the masses evidently had not: and Noyes reaped the harvest.

The suggestion that he did this by dumping a quantity of carelessly written verse into a ready and uncritical market is not justified by the facts. Even those who most deplored his popularity could not blind themselves to his rare talents. They might deplore the fact that such gifts were wasted in an effort to revive a style of poetry they considered dead; but they had to admit that he brought to the task a mastery of rhythm which had not been seen since Swinburne, and that he told a story with Chaucerian grace.

No better examples of the modern ballad have been written in the twentieth century than his *Forty Singing Seamen, The Highwayman,* and those contained in the *Tales of the Mermaid Tavern.* They are romantic, colorful, rollicking, and simple as ballads should be. His high rank as a poet as well as his popularity is built upon these rather than upon his epic *Drake* which is turgid rather than grand, or upon his lyrics which are for the most part unsatisfactory. Some of the incidental songs sprinkled through his narrative poems are, it is true, of a high order. But exclusive of these his detached lyrics compare unfavorably with those produced by his contemporaries. He has written many of them — too many, one thinks. Some are obviously pot-boilers; but even in the majority which show careful workmanship there are observable certain defects which demonstrate the unwisdom of Noyes' refusal to see anything of value in the "new poetry." It is one thing to insist on the continuity of artistic experience, quite another to maintain that the forms of one period are the most suitable for the next because they have been tried. It is his diction which suffers most notably, most of which is of the Romantic nineteenth-century variety which has lost much of its power of stimulation through overuse. Then, too, one misses in his lyrics that element of naked sincerity: they seem just poems, exercises in versification, technically well-done. And this, I think, results from the consciousness that he is reviving a style of other days. The current distaste for the style everywhere works against him. The same criticism may be applied to his earlier narrative poems, *The Forest of Wild Thyme,* and *The Flower of Old Japan,* which abound in romantic conceits of the most offensive sort.

It is a genuine relief to pass from these to his really great narrative pieces, such, for instance, as those contained in his *Tales of the Mermaid Tavern.* We seem at once to be in another region where the effort to revive nineteenth-century poetic forms is swallowed up in the pervading reality of the narrative. Those "spacious days" of the Elizabethan revival when "Kit" Marlowe, Drayton, Lodge, and the nation's best gathered about "Will" and "Ben" at the Mermaid, come to life under Noyes' facile touch. As a piece of historical recreation one must go back to Macaulay's *Lays of Ancient Rome* or to some of Scott's best to find a worthy term of comparison. He never forgets the story, never lapses into mere poetry. His supple blank verse carries the narrative easily, and is quite sensitive to variations in mood the most diverse. Yet he varies things still more by the introduction of an amazing number of meters and rhymes from the jocund ballad measures to *terza rima* — even his lyrics in the new atmosphere take on a value undemonstrated elsewhere. Is it because he is living for the moment in Elizabethan rather than in Victorian times?

In 1913, Noyes came to the United States to give the Lowell Lectures at Harvard. His stay here was a long one (from 1913 to 1923) during the course of which he devoted the full strength of his energy and prestige to revive the waning confidence in the validity of the European tradition in literature. America saw during those pre-war years when the late-born American 1890 group was becoming formidable, no more intelligent defender of the best elements in our civilization than he. His advocacy of the ancient artistic experience was based on neither a Puritan complex nor a bourgeois sense of resistance to change. He was an opponent of the "new poetry" only insofar as it was a blind revolt against this experience and a resolution to build for the future in isolation from it. He was not an opponent of the new. He believed with Maritain that "a new world is emerging from the obscure chrysalis of history," and he welcomed it. But he insisted that "a new thing of real value is always a growth," and not a complete break after the manner of Carl Sandburg's

I sing of new cities and a new people
I tell you the past is a bucket of ashes.

He talked as one who was a genuine experimentalist, having created more new meters and variations of old ones than even the most liberated. He was the modern; it was the Bohemians who looked old-fashioned beside him. At Princeton, where he lectured on poetry for a number of years, he enjoyed great popularity with the undergraduates. E. A. Cooke writes of him: "The men who sat in Mr. Noyes' classes could find nothing bookish or esoteric in the alert, well-set-up young man who faced them. He was not a recluse: he did not pose; he did not cultivate any eccentricity in dress or manner. Just as his presence served to dispel a false awe of poetry, so did his personality convince his students that an enthusiasm for poetry and hard muscles, masculine initiative and intellectual sanity might coexist."

The cause of all the discord, intellectual, religious, and artistic in the modern world, Noyes was saying in those days, "is that our world is so highly specialized that it grows more and more difficult for us to relate our particular fragments of the truth to the whole. On every side there is a war in progress, not so much between falsehood and falsehood as between innumerable fragments of the truth." The danger was that these warring impulses might not be co-ordinated and that our civilization would perish. "It is just here," he proclaimed, "that art and letters has its great function to perform. . . . For great art, great literature, great poetry enable us once more to see all things in one." The poet must cease the work of merely holding up a mirror to the confusion; he must rebuild the world! An exalted concept, surely, of the poet's place in the cosmic economy and one not a little tinged with bombast. Yet it was sincerely, even religiously proposed, and he himself at once acted upon it.

He began an epic. Commenced in 1924, *The Torchbearers:*

an epic of science was not completed until 1930. Its place in modern literature has not yet been fixed. Some critics have thought that it merited for Noyes the title of "the Homer of Science." It is perhaps too early to place it accurately. This much, however, may be said at once; it is infinitely superior to his earlier epic *Drake,* and if with the passage of years it is not conceded a place alongside those supreme epics which have immortalized the soul of a race, it will yet remain a noteworthy epic of an individual soul.

The achievements of science it is that Noyes sings in this poem. Many have long realized that the accomplishments of man in the past 500 years in unveiling the secrets of nature was a natural theme for epic poetry. Yet the great difficulty lay in hitting upon some principle vast and sweeping which might bring about the grandeur of unity essential to an epic. Moreover, it was evident that it was these very achievements he would celebrate, which were chiefly responsible for bringing to our world the chaos of mind and uncertainty that made epic poetry impossible.

Noyes, however, clearly perceived that it was not the accomplishments themselves but the philosophy behind the scientific movement that had brought this about. It had erected science into a foreign and autonomous entity, the end-effect of whose every discovery was the destruction of that corpus of religious, philosophical, and artistic knowledge upon which the greatness of European civilization was founded. But was not science, as a matter of fact, a part of this body of knowledge, and would not its achievements if restored to the body be revealed as confirming, not destroying, the essential truth of the deposit? Noyes so thought. His principle of unity would be the European tradition, which was greater than science and to which science belonged. His aim would be to restore science to this tradition.

The Torchbearers is a long poem. But there are very few dull spots in its three volumes and these occur in the first book and arise from the difficulty Noyes always seems to be under of getting started. But once the story is under way, once he begins to exercise his supreme art of poetic narration on the lives of those who have made the history of science, the same enchantment that holds the reader in the *Tales of the Mermaid Tavern* begins to operate and never flags. Like this latter poem *The Torchbearers* would be merely a sheaf of glimpses into colorful and significant lives were it not for the central theme which binds them and makes the poem a true epic. It is contained in the title, *The Torchbearers,* under which figure the great discoverers are conceived as struggling against bigotry and ignorance to cast light on the dark places of the world, not singly but each receiving and adding to the lamp given to him by his predecessor. "If I saw farther it was because I stood on great shoulders," says Newton. Continuity is the point that is stressed.

The first book of the trilogy, *The Watchers of the Skies,* deals with those astronomers who from Copernicus to the Hershels have revealed new worlds to us and in so doing have spread great scandal among those whose faith was foolishly tied up with the images of the Ptolemaic system. This is the tragic note that is never absent from the story and which rises in crescendo until the climax in the second book is reached — the Torchbearers working to cast new light on the glories of the universe and on Him who made it all; their contemporaries mistaking the light for the fire of destruction and fleeing from it into the shadows. Noyes in his colorful treatment of Kepler, Galileo, Tycho Brahe, and the rest keeps hammering away at the ideas expressed by these great ones, that science has come not to destroy the law but to confirm it, and that this confirmation serves but to make the fundamental truths men have always believed shine out more brilliantly.

William Hazlitt in his *English Poets and Comic Writers* makes a rather dolorous remark apropos of the inevitable progress of science which is characteristic of the attitude of the sincere but muddled artist of the nineteenth and our own century: "The progress of knowledge and refinement has a tendency to

circumscribe the imagination and to clip the wings of poesy.
. . . There can never be another Jacob's ladder. Since that time
the heavens have gone farther off and grown astronomical.
They have become averse to imagination; nor will they return
to us on the squares of the distance." If Alfred Noyes had done
nothing more in this epic than to show that the revolutionary
discoverers of the past few centuries have not strapped the ar-
tistic imagination but released it, renewed it by giving it newer
and truer images and at the same time preserving intact the es-
sential human and divine verities, this one accomplishment
would deserve to make the poem a great one. He has done this
and most convincingly, I think, where he comes to treat of the
two Hershels (father and son), the musician-astronomers. They
are at the end of a long line of discoverers and with them we
witness the ancient "music of the spheres" returned to the world
but under an aspect far more sublime.

> *. . . music, all must come back*
> *To music in the end.*

Noyes' own verse here takes on the sonorous and majestic
cadence of Cicero's poetic prose in the *Somnium Scipionis*. The
old figures have indeed departed but the new ones are more
sublime. Thus he makes the sun to sing in the series of nine
lyrics on it and its planets:

> *I hear their song. They wheel about my burning!*
> *I know their orbits: but what path have I?*
> *I with all these worlds around me turning*
> *Sail, every hour, ten thousand leagues of sky?*
>
> *My planets, these live embers of my passion,*
> *And I, too, filled with music and with flame,*
> *Flung thro' the night, for the midnight to refashion,*
> *Praise and forget the Splendor whence we came.*

The second book of the trilogy, *The Book of the Earth,* which treats of physical scientists from Pythagoras to Huxley and Darwin, ends on a tragic note. The actual history of scientific achievement has issued in a tragedy and Noyes, despite his science-worship, does not blink the facts. Up to this point in the story the tragedy had been confined to the shallow hangers-on of science. But now it strikes the Torchbearers themselves who for the first time are discovered loving the darkness better than the light. Their faces are too closely pressed to the Book of the Earth to read the high scripture of its pages. They are pedants, immersed in the gathering of facts, hasty, impatient, eager to erase what has gone before. Lamarck was a Torchbearer, but of these men Noyes says with sadness that

> *. . . in their haste*
> *They flung away his fire; and, as he fell*
> *They set their heels upon it and stamped it out.*

It is the end of the Torchbearers. Henceforth there is only night and the slipping off of the race into primitive darkness.

The scene with which the final book of the trilogy, *The Last Voyage,* opens is proposed as a somewhat realistic picture of the modern man. The poet describes himself as wandering alone in the thick darkness, stumbling aimlessly through a wasteland confused and tired. The final episode of this epic of scientific achievement remains yet to be told and, it seems, it will come from the parched lips of a man completely disillusioned. The book marks a turning point not only in the story but in Noyes' own ideas and life. It is now 1930. In 1924 he had begun the epic as a non-Catholic but a believer. His first two volumes are marked by a fine sense of the supernatural, a reverence for experimental truth, a love of the noble foundations of European culture, and a clear conviction that modern scientific knowledge could and must be correlated with the other solid achievements of the West. But how? He began under the opinion that this synthesis must be achieved somewhat in the manner recommended by Matthew Arnold and our American Humanists today, a gathering together of "the best thought of the best minds" in all fields. This synthesis was to be made by poetry. "It is capable of saving us: it is a perfectly possible means of overcoming chaos." The words are those of I. A. Richards. Noyes had given expression to the idea several years in advance of this. It was a current idea — still is, as a matter of fact.

But it is precisely this idea that now breaks down, as far as Noyes is concerned. Its futility is perceived in the process of putting it into effect. It does not "work." For acutely as the warring elements in our civilization need correlation, the principle of cohesion cannot be found in these human elements themselves, taken singly or collectively. That principle, if it exists, he concludes, must be sought in something that is at once in the world and at the same time above it, that is human and in no metaphorical sense divine. The modern world appears to him like the chaos that was upon the world in its primitive beginnings, the chaos which heard the word of God and became ordered and was called good. The same Word must come again to us today and from the same source.

The poet does not see this all at once. There is only darkness at first and frustration. But, as he says in the prologue

> *— when it was darkest I came to a strong city*

It is the City of God, the Church of Christ, the same that those who had remade European civilization out of the chaos of the Dark Ages sought first and finally and all other things were added to them. Noyes entering here finds at length the principle and center of the unity he had sought. We need a "new Aquinas," he had said, to bridge the gaps in our disparate world, "a pontifex to make our sundered truth" a whole. The new Aquinas he does not find. He finds Christ, the pontifex, the bridge-builder, between God and man, as well as between man and man. It is the Sacramental Christ which had given Aquinas his center, the Sacred Host, God and man, which now becomes for him the sign and the reality of the new unity.

> *A sacramental sign, earth's common Bond;*
> *Bread of a thousand grains, compact in One —*

Thus the history of civilization's Torchbearers which had been begun among the astronomers on Mount Wilson Observatory viewing the lights of the heavens through the new 100-inch telescopic lens, ends with the poet in profound adoration before the Sacred Host, the great Torchbearer, "the light of the world."

III

Tradition and experiment — we find these two elements everywhere in modern Catholic poetry. Alfred Noyes has been used to represent those who, while modern, lean most heavily upon the former and are most concerned with the problem of carrying it forward. Padraic Colum has a claim that cannot be gainsaid to stand for the latter.

Both by early training and by affection he belongs to what is called the "new poetry." His earliest artistic associations were with those who brought to Ireland the poetic gospel according to Mallarmé and Rimbaud — "the only movement that is saying things," as Yeats declared in those days of the symbolists. His first works, both in drama and in lyric poetry, were stamped with this influence. It was his affiliation with the National Theater Movement in Dublin which brought him in contact with Lady Gregory, Yeats, and George Russell, and it was for this group he wrote and produced his first play, *Broken Soil,* in 1903 and at the age of twenty-one. He is one of the few Catholic authors who have done distinguished work in the drama.

Colum is best known, however, as a lyric poet, and it is with him in this capacity we are concerned here. With the appearance of his first book of poems, *The Wild Earth,* in 1907, there was struck, as we remarked in a previous chapter, a new note in

Anglo-Irish poetry which caused this young man to be looked
to as one of the most outstanding of those who were writing
the verse of the future. Witness the opening lines of "The
Plougher," the poem with which the *Wild Earth* collection
begins:

Sunset and silence! a man: around him earth savage, earth
   broken:
Beside him two horses — a plough!
Earth savage, earth broken, the brutes, the dawn-man there in
   the sunset,
And the Plough, that is kin to the Sword, that is founder of
   cities!

The vivid, rough impressionism, the rugged meter, the repe-
titions, the straining after the *aliquid novi,* all speak eloquently
of the New Poetry, but of a type quite removed from the soft
symbolism of the Celtic Twilight. Colum, in fact, from the be-
ginning moved deliberately in an opposite direction to the
feminine charm of this last stand of the dying Romanticism,
green twilight, neo-Platonic mysticism, and the rest. There is
something manly and robust about the glamour of his roman-
ticism, which suggest kinship with a poet like Robert Burns
whose verse combines the best in both classic and romantic at-
titudes. In "The Plougher," as in his other lyrics, we find a
freshness of perception, a delicate feeling for landscape, a
melancholy strain, mixed with a classical strength and mas-
culinity that comes from rigid concentration, absence of rhymes,
and a rhythm almost wholly quantitative.

The classical flavor which is so much a part of Colum's verse
has about it nothing of the pedantry of the modern anti-Roman-
tic coterie. It is natural, spontaneous, and not at all a reaction.
There is a line in his poem "A Poor Scholar of the Forties" that
describes it. This hedge-schoolmaster who knows his Homer
better than the Munster poets know their Ossian is asked,

> *What good to us your wisdom stores,*
> *Your Latin verse, your Grecian lore?*

and the old man replies

> *I teach these by the dim rush-light*
> *In smoky cabins night and week.*
> *But what avail my teaching slight?*
> *Years hence, in rustic speech, a phrase,*
> *As in wild earth a Grecian vase!*

It is because Colum has lived close to the wild earth of his native land, tinged as it is with the memory of Rome, that he is able to achieve these effects without suggestion of the *recherche*. Indeed, much of what strikes us as distinctly classical, that brings to the mind forgotten fragments of Homer and Hesiod, is not classical at all, except insofar as it has caught that primitive freshness of vision that was man's in the beginning, and still belongs to those who keep close to the soil. As a poet Colum lingers with the elemental things — death, birth, the wet hills, the sky, and the men who break the soil.

Of Robert Burns he has recently said that "he was the last poet of our tradition to make poetry out of his own works and days." Colum, himself, has done much to restore this tradition. As a boy in County Longford where he was born in 1881 he absorbed the folklore and popular songs because he loved them and because they were a part of his community. He believes today that these songs are about the only begetters of genuine lyric poetry. He is a communist poet in the best sense of that misunderstood term. Out of such simple communal things as the knife grinder, the ballad singers, old men complaining and maids spinning, the beggar woman, the birds, the Irish hedges, Colum has wrought great lyric poetry.

While it may seem from what has been said that there are a variety of influences at work in Colum's poetry, his inspiration is, as a matter of fact, quite simple and one. He is a Catholic; and when we have said that, we have explained why he is able to keep his Romanticism and Classicism in balanced solution, why he loves the soil, why he is a modern and an experimentalist, and yet neither shares the doubts and perplexities so much a part of the modern complex, nor is carried away by the exaggerations and eccentricities of those who intensely desire the new. He belongs to no movement, yet to all.

Colum does not wear his Catholicism on his sleeve. It is not an element in his poetry but its all-pervasive soul, which like the spirit of man is present everywhere throughout the body, giving centrality, poise, life. He does not say to himself, "Now I shall achieve a pious poem." His piety comes out with an inevitability that is its chief charm as, for instance in his poem "The Wayfarer,"

> *Christ, by thy own darkened hour,*
> *Live within me, heart and brain —*
> *Let my hands not slip the rein!*
>
> *Ah, how long ago it is*
> *Since a comrade went with me!*
> *Now a moment let me see*
>
> *Thyself, lonely in the dark.*
> *Perfect, without wound or mark!*

There is no meretricious pietism here but true emotion. Likewise in his "Cradle Song,"

> *O, men from the fields!*
> *Come gently within.*
> *Tread, softly, softly*
> *O! men coming in.*

> *Mavoureen is going*
> *From me and from you,*
> *Where Mary will fold him*
> *With mantle of blue.*

Such Catholicism is perhaps possible only to an Irishman who has taken care to be genuine in his interpretation of a people whose faith is large and ancient, and whose testimony to their affection for it is the glory and inspiration of modern Europe. Colum is not a convert, but one of these people from birth and, as such, he speaks in that wistful meditation on "The Old College of the Irish, Paris,"

> *Our order broken, they who were our brood*
> *Knew not themselves the heirs of noted masters,*
> *Of Columbanus and Erigena.*
> *We strove towards no high reach of speculation*
> *Towards no delivery of gestated dogma*
> *No resolution of age-long disputes.*
> *Only to have a priest beside the hedges,*
> *Baptizing, marrying,*
> *Offering mass within some clod-built chapel,*
> *And to the dying the last sacraments*
> *Conveying; no more we strove to do —*
> *We, all bare exiles, soldiers, scholars, priests.*

Colum's achievements in modern poetry are sufficient evidence that the Irish in striving to do no more than this have chosen the better part. Today when that hollow but glittering civilization, which has seemed during the years to have left them behind, is itself slipping, the promise of God to those who seek first the things of God is being fulfilled. Colum in name and in achievement symbolizes the important part that the Irish must play in the future of Europe. Once while on a visit to a Holy Well in Donegal one of the pilgrims inquired his name and was surprised to hear him say "Padraic Colum." That anyone should be so blessed as to bear the names of Ireland's greatest saints seemed incredible. Like Brendan, the navigator, of whom he has written exquisitely, Colum has "great saints for friends," and like him also we may say, using his own words, "he mentioned Christ to men cut off from men."

We have said nothing about Colum's incandescent patriotism which marks him off so sharply from many of his contemporaries in the Celtic Revival. It is responsible for what, in my opinion, is one of his best poems, "Odysseus," written in memory of his friend Arthur Griffith. Griffith was his youthful inspiration;

> *You had the prose of logic and of scorn*
> *And words to sledge an iron argument*
> *You were the one who knew*
> *What sacred resistance is in men*
> *That are almost broken: how, from resistance used,*
> *A strength is born, a stormy, bright-eyed strength . . .*

It was in Griffith's patriotic magazine that Colum's first poems were published at the beginning of this century. Since then his poetic output has not been notably large. He has preserved only his rarest moods for this form, supporting himself in the meantime writing prose, copiously and with distinction. Of his verse he has said,

> *I have sworn my friends shall have no parrot-speech from*
> * me:*
> *Who reads the verse I write*
> *Shall know the falcon's flight,*
> *The vision single and sure, the conquest of air and sun*

These are brave and ambitious words, but the promise they contain has been well-kept.

BIBLIOGRAPHY

NOYES, ALFRED*
  Adcock, St. John, *Gods of Modern Grub Street* (New York: Stokes, 1923).
  Brenner, Rica, *Ten Modern Poets* (New York: Harcourt, 1930).
  Carmina, November, 1930, p. 15.
  WORKS
  Collected Poems, 4 volumes (New York: Stokes).
  The Torchbearers, "Watchers of the Sky" (1922), "Book of the Earth" (1925), "The Last Voyage" (1930), (New York: Stokes).
COLUM, PADRAIC
  Carmina, June, 1931, p. 193.
  Catholic World, Vol. 127, p. 449.
  Living Authors, p. 78.
  Poetry: a magazine of Verse, Vol. 40, pp. 283–5.
  WORKS
  Collected Poems of Padraic Colum (New York: Macmillan, 1932).
CHESTERTON, GILBERT K.
  Catholic World, Vol. 95, p. 41.
  Mais, S. P., *Some Modern Authors* (London: Richards, 1923, p. 221).
  Maynard, Theodore, *Our Best Poets* (New York: Holt, 1922).
  Williams, Charles, *Poetry at Present* (New York: Oxford University Press, 1930).
  WORKS
  Collected Poems of G. K. Chesterton (New York: Dodd, Mead, 1927).
  Graybeards at Play (London: Sheed & Ward, 1930).
  Queen of the Seven Swords (London: Sheed & Ward, 1926).
BARING, MAURICE
  America, Vol. 43, p. 310.
  Kernahan, *Six Famous Living Poets* (London: Butterworth, 1922, pp. 111–156).
  WORKS
  Selected Poems of Maurice Baring (London: Heinemann, 1930).
BELLOC, HILAIRE
  Maynard, Theodore, *Our Best Poets*.
  Mendell & Shanks, *Hilaire Belloc* (London: Methuen, 1916), Ch. V.
  WORKS
  Sonnets and Verse (New York: McBride, 1924).

---

*N.B. Many of his poems have been published in separate collections all by Stokes

Verses of Hilaire Belloc, with a critical introduction by Joyce Kilmer (New York: Gome, 1916).

EDEN, HELEN PARRY

Sturgeon, Mary C., *Studies of Contemporary Poets* (New York: Dodd, 1920).

WORKS

Bread and Circuses (London: John Lane, 1914).

Coal and Candlelight (London: John Lane, 1918).

Rhyme of the Servants of Mary (London: Burns, Oates, 1919).

A String of Sapphires (New York: Kenedy, 1920).

Whistles of Silver, poems and stories (Milwaukee: Bruce, 1933).

FEENEY, LEONARD, S.J.

In Towns and Little Towns (New York: America Press, 1926).

Riddle and Revery (New York: Macmillan, 1934).

Boundaries (New York: Macmillan, 1935).

Song for a Listener (New York: Macmillan, 1936).

O'DONNELL, CHARLES L., C.S.C.

America, Vol. 28, p. 376.

America, Vol. 40, p. 115.

Carmina, No. 7 (1931).

WORKS

Cloister and Other Poems (New York: Macmillan, 1922).

A Rime of the Rood and Other Poems (New York: Longmans, 1928).

CAMPBELL, JOSEPH

Boyd, E. A., *Ireland's Literary Renaissance,* pp. 274–282.

The Month, Sept., 1915, p. 280.

WORKS

Irishry (1914).

The Mountainy Singer (Boston: Four Seas, 1919).

KILMER, ALINE

Catholic World, Vol. 119, pp. 517–23.

WORKS

Candles That Burn (New York: Doran, 1919).

Vigils (New York: Doran, 1921).

The Poor King's Daughter (New York: Doran, 1925).

Selected Poems (New York: Doubleday, Doran, 1929).

MORGAN, EVAN

America, Vol. 42, p. 116.

Prefaces to *City of Canals,* and *The Eel.*

WORKS
The Eel and Other Poems (New York: Brentano, 1927).
The City of Canals (London: Kegan Paul, 1929).

SISTER MADELEVA
Queen's Work, Nov., 1932.
WORKS
Penelope and other Poems (New York: Appleton, 1927).
Knights Errant (New York: Appleton, 1923).

QUIRK, CHARLES J., S.J.
Candles in the Wind (New York: Dial Press).
Gesture Before Farewell (New York: Dial Press).

MAYNARD, THEODORE
Catholic World, Vol. 133, pp. 129, 276, 447.
WORKS
Folly and Other Poems (London: MacDonald, 1918).
The Last Knight (New York: Stokes, 1920).
Exile and Other Poems (New York: Dial Press, 1928).
Man and Beast (New York: Longmans, 1936).

DALY, JAMES J., S.J.
Boscobel and Other Rimes (Milwaukee: Bruce, 1934).

BLUNT, HUGH FRANCIS
My Own People (1921).
Spiritual Songs (1926).

DOUGLAS, LORD ALFRED
Conversions to the Church (London: Burns, Oates, 1933).
WORKS
Lyrics and Sonnets (London: Rich & Cowan, 1936).

GRAY, JOHN
Poems (1931, 1932).

SARGENT, DANIEL
God's Ambuscade (New York: Longmans, 1935).

CLARKE, AUSTIN
Collected Poems (New York: Macmillan, 1936).

3

Satire

There is possibly some exaggeration in the statement one frequently hears that only a Catholic can be a satirist. Satire, so it is argued, demands a definite philosophic position from which the satirist may get an advantageous slant on what is going on about him, and only a Catholic today has such a position. There is, however, no exaggeration in the statement that the majority of first-rank English satirists today profess the Catholic Faith.

The emergence in our own day of an enthusiastic mob of image-breakers is a recent phenomenon in Catholic letters. There were no *ex professo* satirists among the Victorian revivalists. Newman made occasional and brilliant use of the instrument as did Patmore and one or two others. But in the nineteenth century there was little of that sort of derisive laughter, few exponents of the comprehensive curse such as we find today in men like Ronald Knox, D. B. Wyndham Lewis, Belloc, Bruce Marshall, Evelyn Waugh, J. B. Morton, Douglas Woodruff, and Chesterton. These are the men I shall treat in this chapter. And in confining myself to them I am aware that I have not exhausted the entire field. There are others. The spirit of satire among us today is quite widespread.

Many contemporary forces have focused to produce this condition. There is, in the first place, the times, which make satire in the healthy organism almost inevitable — the *difficile-est-satura -non-scribere* situation of Juvenal. I do not mean that our times are any worse than those of the nineteenth century. They are perhaps better, although Mr. Belloc seems to think that

> *. . . the hoary social curse*
> *Gets hoarier and hoarier*
> *And stinks a trifle worse*
>   *Than in*
> *The days of Queen Victoria*
>   *When*
> *They married and gave in marriage,*
> *And danced at the country Ball,*
> *And some of them kept a carriage*
> *And the flood destroyed them all.*

But the times are sufficiently bad at that, and the large number of scientific pedants, buccaneering business men, and humanitarian snobs who clutter up the landscape make it seem much worse. There is a gold mine of disrespectful laughter here for those who refuse to take these people seriously. And for those temperamentally unfitted for this attitude, the ones, namely, whom stupidity irritates immeasurably, there is that other course which has given the world quite as many brilliant satirists, viz., indignation. *Natura si negat facit indignatio versus.* Catholic satirists are of both types. For both of these, the realization that the Catholic Church, excluded from the councils of Europe, has had nothing to do with the evolution of the current mess, produces the effect of removing all barriers to the free expression of contempt. They find little in modern civilization they can defend and much they would like to dynamite. They have all the earmarks of dangerous radicals; and that they have not been handed over to the secular arm they owe to the widespread belief that their mutilation of the Great Ones is, as two eminent historians have remarked, a Good Thing.

Another element, more important perhaps than the times, must be mentioned among the causes that have given us satire. It is the growing consciousness of the new intellectual position enjoyed by Catholics, issuing in what Mr. Belloc has called the note of "triumphant irony." History has produced it. The civili-

zation so long arrayed against the Church is tottering. Gone is
enthusiastic Protestantism, gone is the firm and confident note
of the old materialism. The priests of the revamped religion of
Science and Progress still prophesy Better Things, and still
manage to keep the chosen people sullenly satisfied in the
Waste Land into which they have led them. Rebellion, how-
ever, grows especially among the young. For the scouts who
have gone ahead to explore the Promised Land have returned,
and, as Ronald Knox has observed, their reports are not at all
promising. Discredit and not a few curses have been thrown at
our most respected leaders. On the other hand, the Church,
which has been widely regarded as a corpse, has arisen and
given disquieting signs of intellectual vigor. This in itself is a
curious sort of irony of a kind which history alone is capable of.
Moreover, the numerous converts who have come into the
Church have done so with the air of those who pass from dark-
ness and superstition into light.

II

Historically, the consideration of modern Catholic satire
should begin with Belloc and Chesterton who founded it at
the beginning of the century when D. B. Wyndham Lewis and
J. B. Morton were children: yet, I think, it will not be inap-
propriate to begin with these younger men. They have dis-
tinguished themselves by a type of satire used by the Roman
Lucilius who is generally regarded as the father of satire. Like
Lucilius they both write popularly and on a wide variety of
topics; like him they both use a medley of literary forms, the
letter, dialogues, dramatic skits, verse, etc. And to both of them,
too, we may apply, if we choose, the words Horace ungraciously
used of his master Lucilius — *garrulus atque piger scribendi
ferre laborem*. They write hurriedly and with a certain smart-
ness. Their fate in the future may be that of the Roman's —
less than a hundred scattered lines left; the rest pulped. How-

ever, their contemporary value is quite precious.

Among the fragments salvaged by posterity will, I hope, be the lines of Mr. Morton's called "On Meeting a Georgian Poet," which have all the simplicity and carrying power of great epigram.

> *I know of scribblers who compose*
> *Sad verse in drunken dozes,*
> *But Mr. Tumty-tumty simply sits and Decomposes.*

Lewis has so many lapidary lines to his credit that posterity is going to be confused, and in the end do what the ages have done to the ancients, save the observations on the contemporary literati and let the rest go. So his meditations on Bloomsbury "where death holds court perpetually, and birds are songless, and the damned revolve forever in a brownish fog" will remain. There will be the line about the leader of the young intelligentsia "who takes modern letters — meaning novels written by disheveled women about incest — so seriously as almost to bleed eternally," and the description of life in those coteries of literary snobs which batten on self-admiration and insane jealousy of other groups; "as Euclid would put it, they are marvellous each to each, but to the opposite angles just like hell."

Both of these men have done most of their satirical work as newspaper columnists under the pseudonym of *Beachcomber*. Lewis began writing under this title with the *Daily Mail* of London, one of the largest papers in the world; later with the *Daily Express*. When he retired to Paris to indulge in what he calls the "luxury" of writing biography his place was taken by his friend J. B. Morton who still holds it and who has recently been called "the only satirist and about the only humorist in daily journalism."

Lewis is a convert, having entered the Church shortly after the war in which he served as an officer. His writing career began about the same time. Of the many extant estimates of him there is none, I think, more satisfactory to his admirers than the one he himself has written as the foreword to his book *A London Farrago.* "I have been asked [he says] by Mr. H. J. A. Beachcomber to write a short appreciation of this little work. It is always difficult for the writer to strike a mean between his own personal feelings and emotion on the one hand, and his duty to the public on the other. Nothing is more abhorrent and pernicious than mere slavish adulation of an author however prominent; so I will simply say that Mr. Beachcomber stands head and shoulders over his contemporaries as a writer of fine, sincere, brilliant, subtle, pure, exquisite, flexible and uplifting English, and that he is personally one of the greatest men morally, spiritually and intellectually — it has ever been my good fortune to meet."

Americans who have met him through his several published books of satire and humor recognize the accuracy of the description. His type of humor is more of the American kind than that of his successor, J. B. Morton. It is pungent and sophisticated, with a cultural background that is bewildering in its richness. "Anyone," as Stanley James observes, "unfamiliar with the *clichés* of literary circles in Paris and London might find a good deal of his writing unintelligible." But I think they will enjoy it anyway. It contains "good food for the soul, refreshment for the pensive mind and consolation against all the million charlatans and spellbinders who infest this unhappy age."

The method he uses to deflate the self-importance of the Big Wigs of Science and other Progressive Persons is simplicity itself. He describes it in the preface to that very amusing book *The Stuffed-Owl: an anthology of bad verse,* wherein he and Charles Lee have, with great industry, gathered together the poetic slips of the well-known from Cowper to Tennyson: "When some dignified headline personage, an eminent Academic, a gaitered Divine, an important Actor-Manager, a leading Thinker, a prominent Financier skids on a scrap of banana

peel and suddenly presents his western façade to the shudder-
ing stars, the impact on the sensations of a thoughtful observer
is more tremendous than if the exercise had been performed by
a nobody, some urchin, some shabby man of letters, some
threadbare saint."

But if his method is easily described, it is somewhat more
difficult to quote a characteristic example of it short enough to
fit into this necessarily sketchy treatment. He depends for his
impressions, not upon isolated lines but upon general effects.
His canvases, like those of the medieval painters, are crowded
with a medley of modern figures. Some of these persons like
Dean Inge and Wells are named; others appear under such
titles as George Bernard Bagshaw, the vegetarian, who "took
to writing plays full of nasty lines and in 1898 declared himself
the Messiah."

Meditating on the inscription in the cathedral of Siena, Italy,
"Nascimur impares, pares morimur, cinis aequat omnes" he
passes to modern England with the observation that, "the
chiselled thought I have set above is in its essence medieval and
has been superseded. As Mrs. Tonken so beautifully says in her
Life of Sir Moses Gudgeon: 'His passing was no common pass-
ing, and no one standing at that bedside and hearing the firm
unfailing voice repeating, to the very end, the Closing Prices
and Financial sayings of the Week, could have refrained from
tears — aye, and from that nobler emotion of the soul too deep
for tears. Sir Moses, as is well known, took his money with him
when he passed away. He was enabled to do so by Science.' "

I know of nothing so much like Lewis's work as that famous
fresco of Giotto's on the Last Judgment — on the one side the
damned stripped of all dignity and clothes going through all
manner of funny-paper antics, and on the other the blessed danc-
ing in a field of daisies. He is medieval like that, and his satire
strips the pundits of the rags of pretense with the completeness
and finality of the Four Last Things. There is the same use of
contrast, too. On the one side, his "hates" — the Stupid Rich,

The Lords of Big Business, Nordic Professors, Advanced Thinkers — all thoroughly damned. On the other side, his "loves" — anything Catholic, the Mendicant Orders, the Philosophy of St. Thomas ("the only philosophy worth a hoot"), disreputable poets and saints like François Villon and Benedict Joseph Labre, the Celtic peoples, the countries of "dago" culture, and so on.

The remarkable thing about all this is that it appeared in non-Catholic papers, one of them the *Daily Mail* with a circulation of two million daily. Morton still continues this tradition in which "nothing apparently, except his religion is sacred to him." The general public seems to enjoy it, a circumstance which Lewis explains by the statement that "if the pill is sufficiently gilded with humor and nonsense the public will swallow anything — even the truth!" The popularity enjoyed by both these men is a symbol of that in store for those who take advantage of what Lewis is fond of calling the "Catholic attitude." One who possesses it has a view of modern life so novel and refreshing that the masses eat it up, Catholicity and all.

How would this "Catholic attitude" fare in the United States? The question can be answered. In 1925 there came to this country on the Oxford Debating Team a young man by the name of Douglas Woodruff. He was a Catholic. His teammate, Christopher Hollis, was also a Catholic but a convert. Both were ex-presidents of the Oxford Union and both very observant young men. Returning to England they put their observations into books. Hollis called his the *American Heresy*, Woodruff, his, *Plato's American Republic*. Hollis's book sold well enough, but Woodruff's, which was pure satire, was a "sell-out." The American public liked the "Catholic attitude" to the tune of six impressions from 1926 to 1931.

Woodruff has used the Platonic dialogue with equal success in a more recent book, *Plato's Britannia,* in which his own country is amusingly measured by Hellenic standards. As an editorial writer in the *London Times* he is in touch with political and social conditions and as a Catholic he knows what ails public institutions. His satire is marked by a certain healing quality. It is sharp but never bitter.

III

Chesterton's remark about J. B. Morton, that his points of wit "are like seeds blown abroad upon a huge wind of essential and elemental laughter," is a just one, and comes from a man who, with Hilaire Belloc, first set in motion this typhoon of mirth, now so important a part of the "Catholic attitude." These two men, then very young, broke out into laughter as soon as our century began, Chesterton uproariously, Belloc with more of restraint, more of bitter derision. They laughed, as the late Stuart Sherman says of Chesterton, "at the aesthetic decadents because of their absurd hopelessness and at the scientific radicals because of their absurd hopefulness." And as the century advanced in age and stupidity their laughter increased, and others joined them to swell the crescendo until today it is really a "huge wind of essential and elemental laughter."

To understand the importance of this contribution to the Catholic attitude, we must remember that the most destructive weapon used against the Church by her enemies, from Voltaire to Bernard Shaw, has been the careless and sophisticated laugh. "*C'est le ridicule qui tue.*" This laughter depends for its effectiveness upon an attitude of cosmic seriousness on the side of religion — a sort of world-on-the-shoulders concern and heavy indignation. As long as it was present, the enemy enjoyed a position of advantage. Chesterton and Belloc, in what was a brilliant piece of strategy, demolished it. They fought laughter with laughter. Moreover, they had seen beforehand several important aspects of the modern battlefield which others, less skilled in the art of war, had neglected. The first was that the Catholic Church does not occupy an "official" position in Protestant countries; that those who belong to her either in spirit or in truth have no obligation to make apologies for contemporary society; they belong to a minority which is in rebellion against the greater part of that society. Secondly, that the attitude of the rebel and the heretic, always popular since the fall of man, has in our own century reached its apogee; the impression prevails that the heretic, the man in revolt, is always right, the defender of orthodoxy always wrong. Thirdly, that the enemies of the Church now hold the "official" position in modern society; it was theirs to defend. What the Catholic must do is to erect the supposedly heretical doctrine of the moderns into the most intolerant species of dogma (as they in fact are), insist on his position as a rebel against the rule of the pontiffs, and the burlesque is on.

For thirty years now both Chesterton and Belloc have made devastating use of this strategy, and it is good for at least thirty years more. It is scarcely ever absent from anything they write, whether the work be professedly satirical or not. We find it in Belloc's verse, his history, and his most serious prose. We find it everywhere in Chesterton. It is a permanent attitude. For instance, in his great book, *Orthodoxy,* his chief defense of orthodoxy is not that it is "orthodox" but that it is heretical, revolutionary. He says he started out to find the wildest sort of heresy for his age only to discover that it was a position held by Orthodox Christianity since the first century.

As satirists, Chesterton and Belloc differ considerably with a difference that is largely temperamental. Chesterton embarrasses his victims with uproarious laughter. His mirth is unrestrained and spontaneous; there is no malice or hatred in it. Belloc's laughter is more frequently hard and controlled — the kind that comes from deep-seated scorn and high contempt. It is the *saeva indignatio* of Juvenal. It is salted, too, at times with unmistakable hatred, especially when he speaks of the atheistic rich, as in his famous lines "To Dives" which begin,

> *Dives, when you and I go down to Hell*
> *Where scribblers end and millionaires as well —*

Chesterton shares his friend's attitude toward the rich but there is rarely in his satire the same burning sense of injustice.

I do not mind the swindle, but I deprecate the swank — he says of the polished piracy of modern bankers.

Belloc's early satire, *Lambkin's Remains,* for instance, and *Caliban's Guide to Letters* (published in 1900 and 1903, respectively) are done in a much lighter mood than his later works. He has become more bitter with the passage of years, and, I think, a better satirist. Christopher Morley has expressed the opinion that as a writer of satirical prose he ranks with Bunyan, Swift, and DeFoe. However, there is capital stuff in these two collections, one especially, the "Newdigate Prize Poems," being quite the best example of highly classical burlesque in modern English verse. It is done in heroics of the most bombastic flavor to match the sublimity of the subject chosen: "The Benefits Conferred by Science, Especially in Connection with the Electric Light." But the parody is never strained or exaggerated. He has, with the intuition of a great satirist, realized that the pretentions of the scientists have merely to be stated as accurately and as boldly as possible, and something subtly humorous is produced. The following quatrain may serve as an example:

> *Life is a veil, its paths are dark and rough*
> *Only because we do not know enough:*
> *When Science has discovered something more*
> *We shall be happier than before.*

Chesterton, too, has written well and frequently on the achievements of science and the benefits of progress, both in verse and in prose. But nowhere, I think, has he given us a lovelier picture of the devastation wrought by the Machine Age than in the autobiographical lines,

> *I am too fat to climb a tree;*
> *There are no trees to climb.*
> *Instead the factory chimneys rise*
> *Unscalable, sublime!*

Belloc has treated the same conditions in an epitaph, the stark irony of which is the more powerful when one learns that it is an authentic epitaph, uncovered by him in his historical investigations:

"Here lies N.N., an unknown, who was found perished of starvation in this Parish on the 25th of December of the year of Our Lord, 1757. Resurgam."

IV

The satire of the future will probably contain less of the burlesque humor of Chesterton and Lewis and more of the restrained manner of Belloc which depends for its effects on the simple, naïve, and clear statement of fact. For fact today has become more satiric than parody. There are modern tendencies which simply defy burlesque: the most elaborate *reductio ad absurdum* becomes a truism. Even so consummate a satirist as Ronald Knox feels that his thunder is being stolen. In his recent book, *Broadcast Minds,* he makes the following observation: "There is a melancholy difference between the fate of the prophet and that of his disreputable brother, the satirist. For the prophet, though his fortunes be ruined and his world crashes about him, has at least the gloomy satisfaction of muttering, 'I told you so.' But the satirist who has also told them so, refuses to be comforted; not only are his worst dreams realized, but they have ceased to have value as satire; there is no escape for him except the disingenuous pretense that he really meant it."

The immediate occasion for the complaint is a book by Prof. Julian Huxley called *Religion without Revelation,* which solemnly proposes (with that solemnity only a biologist speaking of theology can assume) a universal religion, in many respects the duplicate of the one Father Knox proposed some twenty years ago in the satirical tract, *Reunion All Around.* Prof. Huxley has some very amusing stuff to his credit, and it is well to remember that the crusading scientist is always a threat to the modern satirist. However, I think that Father Knox need not be immeasurably excited over the safety of his *Reunion All Around*. Posterity, which seems able somehow in spite of everything to distinguish stupidity from cleverness, will accord this book a very high place as satire.

Ronald Knox, like the greatest of English satirists, Dean Swift, is a clergyman, a Catholic priest since 1919, and previous to that a clergyman of the Church of England. It was during his Anglican period that he produced the tract, *Reunion All Around*. He has, I think, done nothing better since then. Written like most tracts to fill a contemporary situation and hurriedly, there is in it much of that quality that makes for permanence. This quality is missing from an earlier work *Absolute and Abitofhell* written in the manner of John Dryden. It is obviously dated. *Reunion All Around,* however, can be read today after twenty years with as much and even more relish than when it first appeared. The satire is directed against the liberalizing tendencies in the Church of England as its subtitle indicates: "Being a Plea for the Inclusion within the Church of England of all Mohametans, Jews, Buddists, Brahmens, Papists and Atheists submitted to the consideration of the British Peoples."

The tract, of course, is a burlesque, yet it has a delicacy of touch not very often found in work of this sort. Father Knox has never abandoned this subtle manner even though it frequently results in his being taken seriously. One of the most amusing instances of this occurred in connection with his *Studies in the Literature of Sherlock Holmes*. He was at Oxford at the time. Indeed he has never left Oxford, except to be ordained, and he returned immediately. He belongs to the place. The thing he satirized, too, then belonged to Oxford, although its original home was the German Universities. I mean the scourge of higher criticism in sacred and profane literature. He talks very seriously in the Sherlock Holmes lampoon of the "Holmes Cycle" and the "Deutero-Watson," quotes a host of German authorities, talks much of "authenticity," "internal evidence," "inconsistencies," and otherwise gleefully pins the pedants with their own jargon. Among those taken in was Sir Arthur Conan Doyle himself who wrote congratulating the author on what seemed to him a serious and scholarly work. Father Knox has used the same subtle methods in treatises on Bunyan, Tennyson's *In Memoriam,* and Boswell.

The texture of his satire is, as I have said, fine. His irony is light but certain. He rarely curses because he never seems to be very angry. Stupidity does not irritate but tickles him. Finally, he has a quality very rare in the satirist, viz., fairness. All of which qualities combine to make him most unlike his Scottish namesake, John Knox. Chesterton, with an eye for these things, has caught the contrast in his lines,

> *Mary of Holyrood may smile indeed*
> *Knowing what grim historic shade it shocks,*
> *To see wit, laughter and the Papist creed*
> *Cluster and sparkle in the name of Knox.*

v

Speaking of Scotsmen, one of the shrewdest pieces of satire in recent years has come from the chuckling typewriter of an Edinburgh accountant who lives in Paris. Bruce Marshall is a young man. He was eighteen when he entered the Church, in 1918, and the same age when he received the wound which cost him a leg while fighting on the Western Front five days before the Armistice. Like D. B. Wyndham Lewis he is drawn to Paris by the *Renouveau Catholique* which makes the French capital quite the most suitable place in the world for those who wish to curse and jeer at our best modern tendencies.

Father Malachy's Miracle is the only Catholic satire he has produced. But should he write no other this alone would entitle him to a high place in modern satire. Father Malachy is a charming old Scotch Benedictine who for the glory of God works the very modern miracle of removing a dance hall from the streets of Glascow to a position some distance away on Bass Rock. The powers of darkness are confused, it is true, but so is Father Malachy with disquieting offers from newspaper syndicates, motion-picture producers, and other exponents of that crusading faith which knows no miracles but those that are profitable. In the end he has to perform a second miracle to get out of the tangle, and the only unconfused person is the author who has the best sort of time lampooning Big Business, Liberal Churchmen, and the Scientists.

Mr. Marshall's wit is caustic and comprehensive. The same motive that causes him to sneer at those outside the Church whom greed, bigotry, and lust have blinded to her beauty and holiness makes him also rather hard on those within the fold who fail to respond in a higher degree to the message of Christ. The Scottish clergy is mildly pelted. And for this and other things his book was displeasing to a few. The other thing is an occasional lapse into what some critics thought was obscenity but which was in reality only vulgarity.

I say "only vulgarity" not in extenuation of it but by way of insisting on the very obvious distinction between these two things. Obscenity is indefensible: so, too, is vulgarity, but in a lesser degree. It is this lesser degree which today constitutes a problem to the Catholic satirists, a problem destined to become yet more acute. It is not so pressing in *Father Malachy's Miracle*. We must turn to the work of another young Catholic satirist if we wish to see it in a really serious form. The novel, *Black Mischief,* by Evelyn Waugh, appeared in 1932. The author is two years younger than Bruce Marshall, a convert of 1930, and like him somewhat *blasé* on the subject of modern civilization. He is in violent reaction against the attitude known as "post-war," and London critics, sensing the arrival of a new era, have dubbed the new alignments "pre-Waugh" and "post-Waugh."

Black Mischief is bitingly satiric in the two pictures it gives, one of modern civilization in London, the other of contemporary barbarism in the fictitious African kingdom of Azania. The story revolves about the attempt to impose the machine, birth control, and other gewgaws of Western culture on the man-eating natives. In this drama of modernization the barbarism that "smells of the forest" fights it out with the barbarism that "smells of the machine," and in an uproarious climax the primitive good sense of the Blacks asserts itself in rejecting the newer and rawer barbarism.

The idea is a capital one, and the execution . . . well, it is not as successful as it might have been had the author been less terribly serious. He is so intent on making his readers hate the pathological spots in modern life as he hates them that his details at times become messy, and detract from the satire. His irony, moreover, is of a subtle type. Those who delight in pornography liked the story and missed the satire: those who deprecate vulgarity also missed the satire and roundly condemned not only the book but the author. It was not a successful Catholic satire. Very few persons, except those who had read his previous book, *Remote People*, realized that it *was* a satire. In many ways, *Remote People* is a better satire although it is ostensibly but a book of travel. It succeeds where the novel fails, not only because there is no such fumbling of the problem of vulgarity and the consequent encouraging of the impression that the author was commercializing the popular taste for loose morality; but also because we have in it much of the full Catholic attitude, entirely absent in the novel. It is the Catholic Evelyn Waugh who compares European and African barbarism here, and bids us "just watch London knock the spots off the Dark Continent."

In Mr. Waugh's two most recent books, *Ninety-two Days* and *A Handful of Dust*, we discover him again engaged in his favorite occupation — the study of barbarians. *Ninety-two Days*, like *Remote People*, is the very stimulating account of his expedition alone into the wilds of British Guiana and Brazil. *A Handful of Dust* is a novel and the most powerful piece of satire that has appeared since Aldous Huxley's *Brave New World.* "It is in essence," declares the jacket blurb, "the story of a civilized man trapped by savages — first by the savages of modern London society who invade even the quiet of his country home, and later by those of the Brazilian jungle."

But its essence is far more pertinent than that. The "civilized man" is really the modern Liberal man, and his story, one of the most significant and characteristic of our day — the attempt, namely, of this same Liberal man to hang on to a few cultural trinkets in the face of a barbarism that is the logical *denouement* of Liberalism. Tony Last, the hero, is a pathetic and tragic figure who becomes increasingly more pathetic and tragic in stature as he struggles futilely to save his bogus but beautiful nineteenth-century world from the modernism of his wife Brenda, the chromium-plating urge of Mrs. Beaver, and the incursions of numerous other raw modern primitives. With the collapse of this dream he goes off in search of a "lost city" in Brazil where he finds awaiting him an end which for stark and pitiless irony must exceed anything in modern fiction.

Mr. Waugh's satire in this volume is profound, symbolical, and philosophic. But the story is told with such grace and humor that, like *Gulliver's Travels,* it may be read with delight even by the most simple, who, if one may judge by the enthusiastic but stupid reviews it received, are the ones who *are* reading it.

One of the elements that makes *Father Malachy's Miracle* a better satire than *Black Mischief* is the presence in it of Father Malachy, that bland old monk, the effect of whose charming holiness can best be described by words used by Mr. Waugh in *Remote People.* Speaking there of a convent in Uganda he says "it is astonishing in Central Africa — this little island of sweetness and order in an ocean of rank barbarity . . . here they are singing the office just as it had been sung in Europe when the missions were little radiant points of learning and decency in a pagan wilderness."

There is something sweetly ironic in the presence in our own wilderness of a person filled with the true Benedictine or Catholic spirit. From his point of view the antics of the modern barbarians are indeed quite funny. And he can laugh without seeming to be a mere hard and supercilious scoffer because he has something worth while to give. Bruce Marshall has produced this type of satire. It is not a new type. Mr. Chesterton has been using it for years. In his Father Brown stories, for instance, and in novels like *The Flying Inn* and *Manalive,* where the hero appears quite insane because he is the only normal spot in a thoroughly crazy background. Patrick and Boniface must have looked like that to our ancestors of the Dark Ages.

In America, a young man by the name of Myles Connolly produced such a satire and then wrote no more. His story of *Mr. Blue,* the Boston mystic who lived among the stars on a Manhattan skyscraper, still remains our best example of this type, or of any type for that matter. Ronald Knox has observed with a good deal of justice that "no country, I suppose, has a greater need of satirists than the United States of America; no country has a greater output of humor, good and bad, which is wholly devoid of any satirical quality." The appearance of Paul Horgan's novel, *The Fault of the Angels,* which was awarded the Harper's Prize in 1933, may be an indication that American Catholics have at length begun to tap the extremely rich native sources of satire.

BIBLIOGRAPHY

Hilaire Belloc
  Verse
  Verses by Belloc, introduction by Joyce Kilmer (New York: Gome, 1916).
  Ladies and Gentlemen (London: Duckworth, 1933).
  Cautionary Tales for Children (London: Duckworth).

Novels
Belinda (London: Constable).
The Man Who Made Gold (London: Arrowsmith, 1930).
Mercy of Allah (Appleton, n.d.).
The Post-Master General (London: Arrowsmith, 1932).
Prose
Caliban's Guide to Letters and Lambkins Remains (London: Duck-
    worth, 1920).
Short Talks with the Dead (New York: Harper, 1926). Cf. other
    essay-collections *passim.*

G. K. CHESTERTON
Verse
Collected Poems (London: Burns, Oates, 1927).
Novels
Manalive (New York: Dodd, Mead, 1924).
Return of Don Quixote (London: Chatto & Windus).
The Flying Inn (New York: Dodd, Mead, 1919).
The Man Who Was Thursday (New York: Dodd, Mead, 1908).
Prose
Cf. essays under "The Free Press and Its Prose."

MYLES CONNOLLY
Mr. Blue (New York: Macmillan, 1928).

RONALD KNOX
A Spiritual Æneid (London: Longmans, 1918).
La Farge, *Four Great Converts* (London: Longmans, 1919).
WORKS
Broadcast Minds (London: Sheed & Ward, 1930).
Caliban in Grubb Street (London: Sheed & Ward, 1930).
Essays in Satire (New York: Dutton, 1930).
Memories of the Future (Doran, n.d.).
Sanctions: A Frivolity (New York: Sheed & Ward, 1933).

D. B. WYNDHAM LEWIS
Ave Maria, April 28, 1928.
WORKS
A London Farrago (London: Cecil Palmer, 1922).
At the Blue Moon Again (London: Hodder and Stoughton).
At the Sign of the Green Goose (London: Hodder and Stoughton).
On Straw (New York: Coward-McCann).
The Stuffed Owl, an anthology of bad verse (New York: Coward
    McCann, 1930).
Welcome to All This (New York: Dutton, 1931).

Bruce Marshall
   Queen's Work, May, 1932.
   works
   Father Malachy's Miracle (New York: Doubleday, Doran, 1931).
J. B. Morton
   Catholic Who's Who.
   works
   1933 and Still Going Wrong (London, Eyre & Spottiswoode, 1933).
   Beachcomber's Second Omnibus (London: Sheed and Ward, 1933).
   By the Way (London: Sheed & Ward, 1931).
Douglas Woodruff
   Catholic Who's Who.
   works
   Plato's American Republic (New York: Dutton, 1926).
   Plato's Britannia (London: Sheed & Ward, 1930).
Evelyn Waugh
   Time, October 3, 1932, p. 48.
   works
   Black Mischief (New York: Farrar & Rinehart, 1932).
   Remote People (London: Duckworth, 1931).
   Ninety-two Days (New York: Farrar and Rinehart, 1934).
   A Handful of Dust (New York: Farrar and Rinehart, 1934).
Lewis, C. S.
   Pilgrim's Regress (New York: Sheed & Ward, 1935).

4

History and Biography

The professional satirist is notoriously weak at building. His proper function is wrecking, the business of blasting antique social superstructures, of leveling formalized opinions, of clearing the ground of the intellectual rubbish of centuries so that a new order may begin. History — good history, that is to say — is constructive. Consequently it was with some misgivings that one watched the passage of the three ironic and blasé young men, D. B. Wyndham Lewis, Douglas Woodruff, and J. B. Morton, from satire to history. The opening lines of Mr. Lewis' biography, *Charles of Europe,* were not hopeful. He began: "The Great Healing Dawn continually if vaguely promised humanity by more loud-mouthed soothsayers than one . . . is long in arriving." We were prepared for the worst.

But we were deceived. That refreshing experience of discovering satirists with a constructive side was ours. For these young men did not join the large and tiresome army of debunkers. Mr. Morton commences his study of John Sobieski who saved Europe from the Turks with a motto from Jacques Maritain. "I do not despair of Europe — the deep springs of her life are still there, concealed but not dried up." This note of hopefulness that Western civilization may yet be saved runs through the three biographies of D. B. Wyndham Lewis — *François Villon, King Spider, Charles of Europe* — and is the unifying principle behind the series of European biographies of which Douglas Woodruff is the editor and which includes such distinguished contributors as Algernon Cecil, Shane Leslie, Dom Bede Jarrett, and Denis Gwynn.

When these men turned to history they found awaiting them there a Catholic program of such vigor, modernity, and freshness as to permit them to be constructive without being pompous and platitudinous, and on the side of order without seeming tame snakes. Only this can explain the facility with which they made the transition. One man, Hilaire Belloc, is principally responsible for this program in our own day, although he himself has merely continued a tradition which began in the first half of the nineteenth century with John Lingard and was carried forward by Cardinal Newman, T. W. Allies, Lord Acton, W. S. Lilly, Cardinal Gasquet, and others. But Belloc has added something to the groundwork of this tradition. He has added, for one thing, the note of satire. Lingard never made use of it, despite the mastery of sarcasm displayed in his private correspondence. The times in which he wrote forbade its use. Not so the present. The events of the last several decades have shed an ironic light on history and historians, and one must give place to it. Satire, moreover, is a distinct asset to the historian in a very important phase of his work, that, namely, of correcting the numerous inaccuracies, half-truths, and lies which Whig historians in England and Puritan historians in America have placed in circulation. "After a few experiences in running down their references," says William Thomas Walsh, author of the brilliant study of Queen Isabella, in an article on Prescott, "one begins to understand the importance of Belloc's insistence that the principal task of the historian today is to shovel off the rubbish that bigots have piled on the records of past centuries and to drag out the hidden truth into the light." The contempt Lingard felt but did not express for this sort of historian, our modern workers do not scruple to make articulate. They also share his lack of awe and reverence for non-Catholic scholarship in general. Indeed under the influence of Belloc the air of confidence and urbane self-possession has become universal. The old defense attitude has completely vanished, giving place to one of attack.

There is an iconoclastic side to modern Catholic history and biography. But of far greater importance is its constructive aspect. Belloc has expressed it in the opening lines of his recent study of Napoleon: "The task before us today is the re-uniting of Europe." The pronoun "us" does not refer only to his Catholic associates, but to every man and woman of European culture. And every man and woman of European culture recognizes this as a just statement of the common problem, and is interested in hearing the solution offered, "for even the most foolish can see today that the re-union of our civilization is vital to its mere survival."

This is the essential thing to grasp if we would understand the new position of the Catholic historian. Europe is disorganized. It has been progressively so since the World War. The post-war sense of spiritual bankruptcy has lately become more acute by reason of the no less decisive economic bankruptcy. An entire culture seems to be on the rim of dissolution. Not a few observing the ominous indications of the day, such as the rise of arbitrary political dictatorship, the amazing corruption of the wealthy, the rumblings of rebellion among the masses, the collapse of moral standards, have already abandoned the ship muttering, like Spengler, dark prophecies of the impending return to savagery; others openly espouse the raw mechanical barbarism of the Soviet state; while still others, represented by Nicholas Berdyaev, author of *The End of Our Times,* look upon Bolshevism as an authentic curse of God which must purge the West of its accumulated sins before a new society can begin.

These are the few. By far the majority still hope the yet unbroken culture with its glories in art, letters, buildings, and science can be saved. The business of applying remedies began before the last gun on the Western Front was silenced. The League of Nations was one of the first essays at the restoration of unity, followed somewhat more recently by the proposal for a United States of Europe. In the arts and ethics we may mention, as being closer to us, Humanism which is a reflection of the general European effort to straighten out the disordered state of letters, and to give some solid foundation to philosophy and morals. There were many others, some so abortive as to be entirely forgotten, others still hanging on but each weary with the common disease of unsuccess. Yet the desire for unity and order still persists and daily gives birth to fresh notions, new conferences. The stage is set and waiting for anyone with a way out of the welter. The Catholic historian has a way. He has taken the stage and talks to the same sort of inquisitive, cosmopolitan audience desirous of "learning new things" that St. Paul spoke to at Athens. The new thing he gives them is the old European idea which, as D. B. Wyndham Lewis remarks, happens now to be quite modern.

To those whom fear of the next great international war has caused to pin their hopes for union on a loose political and commercial alliance, he says that the true unity of Europe is a deeper thing than abstract internationalism — a thing for which there is no historical justification. To the advocates of European unity through science and humanism he points out with Christopher Dawson that "the unity of our civilization does not rest entirely on secular culture and the material progress of the last four centuries. There are deeper traditions in Europe than these, and we must go back behind humanism and behind the superficial triumphs of modern civilization if we wish to discover the fundamental social and spiritual forces that have gone to the making of Europe."

He then presents an historical picture of a Europe that was once in a highly important sense one, "Roman in civilization and Catholic by conviction." European men were united by the consciousness of a common citizenship which transcended national ties without wholly obliterating them since it was based on a common, universal Faith, a common philosophy, a common culture, common social and moral ideals, even a common international language. This unity, this deep feeling of fellowship no longer exists today. For forces arose that broke Christendom into a collection of hostile and bigoted nations growing farther and farther apart until the most disastrous war in history united them in the conviction that something was awry. What this something is the Catholic historian hastens to point out. Europe abandoned the thing that had created and preserved this unity, "the corporate tradition," in the words of Belloc, "the core and soul of all our history for fifteen hundred years and on into the present time; the continuation of all our Pagan origins, transformed, baptized, illuminated: the matrix of such culture as we still retain." Europe lost the Faith; losing the Faith she lost her unity, her cultural treasures, her hegemony among the nations of the world. She will recover the Faith. But the recovery of the Faith is the first essential to unity. "I believe," says Christopher Dawson, "the Church that made Europe may yet save Europe."

II

Some seventy years ago Ernest Renan gave it as his opinion that historical research marked the end of the Christian religion. He was wrong. The mass of data dug up by those whom Giovanni Papini calls "the hunch-backed students" turned out to be favorable to true Christianity because it was usually accurate; and the past seventy years of actual history has so discredited the warped interpretations placed upon these findings by the dogmatic theorists that the Catholic historian has merely to put the facts in their proper order and the light appears.

The type of historian I am treating here is pre-eminently an historian of culture. His chief interest is in civilization, what made it, what threatens to destroy it. His narrative invariably begins in the present, rooted firmly in the very obvious fact that Western civilization is in danger of a complete breakdown.

The phenomenon has a cause; and it is, as Henri Massis has said, "only simple and ordinary wisdom to try to discover, at what moment and under the influence of what ideas, the deviation from its [Europe's] destiny took place; and this wisdom also requires us to go back beyond this point of historical rupture, in order to become better acquainted with the principles of civilization from which we turned away." Belloc has sketched the problem with even greater clarity: "Two historical problems are of prime importance to ourselves. To misapprehend them is to misapprehend our nature. The first of these problems is the conversion of the Roman Empire to Catholicism. . . . What made Christendom? . . . The second is the disaster of the sixteenth century. How came Christendom to suffer shipwreck?"

Both of these problems Belloc treated brilliantly and popularly in a little book, written shortly after the war, which has since become a sort of classic — *Europe and the Faith*. The idea of compressing nineteen hundred years and more of history into 260 pages was annoying to many, while others were bothered by the constant recurrence of the refrain "The Faith is Europe, and Europe is the Faith." Despite this and other objections of the same caliber the book did what it was intended to do. It inspired thousands. Most notably it gave the Catholic historian a new lease on life; it defined his status, mapped out his work; it lifted him from the old position of eye-on-the-peephole defense, and gave him a method of attack that has reversed the whole order of battle.

Mr. Belloc's influence on the rising generation of historians has been profound. Even his faults have worked beneficially. To take an example: he has a healthy distaste for footnotes, references, bibliographies, and the other accessories of exact scholarship, employed, as he says, for "ritual adornment and terror." Reaction against the undoubtedly large element of pretense in all this has led him into the error of omitting them altogether. His reputation for scholarship suffered. So his disciples, Christopher Hollis, Morton, Lewis, and Woodruff, clutter up the bottom of their pages with learned annotations in 6-point type, talk obscurely about sources, and append lengthy bibliographies.

Christopher Dawson's book, *The Making of Europe,* is fortified by a bibliography which lists some 325 works in various languages, most of them of the multi-volume variety. Co-editor of the famous *Essays in Order* series, editor of the impressive symposium, *A Monument to Saint Augustine,* author of several other solid but none the less popular books, his reputation as a scholar was secure enough without this concession to the ritual of research. The book has been widely acclaimed by both scholars and dilettantes. Yet on the large, important points it magnificently supports the thesis advanced by Belloc in *Europe and the Faith, sans* authorities, *sans* references. Dawson's sudden rise to fame has been one of the high points of the Catholic Revival. Less of a litterateur than Belloc, a more profound scholar, perhaps, his authority on cultural history is unquestioned in Europe and America. In the younger generation to which he belongs he perhaps best represents what the Catholic historian of the future will be like.

The historical problem to which Mr. Dawson in *The Making of Europe* directs his attention is the first of those two questions "of prime importance to our race": How came the pagan world to be baptized? What made Christendom? He calls the study "an introduction to the history of European unity." The period is the Dark Ages (A.D. 400–1000) which Aldous Huxley declared in a review of the book "lose their darkness and take on a form and significance. Thanks to Mr. Dawson's erudition and gift of marshalling facts we begin to have a notion of what it is all about." This period to which has been fastened the name "dark" Dawson describes in his introduction as being "the most creative of all since it created not this or that manifestation of culture but the very culture itself — the root and ground of all the subsequent cultural achievements." The various elements that went into the making of Europe are interestingly described and accurately evaluated: first the Roman Empire to which it owes its ideas of political unity and order; secondly, the Catholic Church, the source of its spiritual unity; thirdly, the Classical Tradition to which it is indebted for intellectual culture; and finally the Barbarians "who provided the human material out of which Europe has been fashioned."

It is a tribute to one of Mr. Dawson's most valuable attributes, I mean his sense of proportion, his sober and unwarped judgment, that he assigns to this last element its merited position of importance. He is not the type of historian to minimize the "obscure chaos of the barbarian world because Teutonic historians of the school of romantic nationalism have exaggerated its worth at the expense of the classical and Christian contributions." Indeed he shows more inclination to sympathize with this distorted view as having delivered the needed corrective to the equally exaggerated Latin-Christian school. He insists that the barbarian peoples supplied something more than a merely passive and negative background for the creative activity of the higher culture.

Although Mr. Dawson does not state it in so many words — he merely states the facts — one is left in no doubt as to which of these five elements had most to do with the making of Europe. Already before the break-up of the Roman Empire in the fifth century that question of such moment to the material culture of the West had been definitely settled by an institution whose interests and mission were wholly spiritual, not of this world. Would the new Christianity take holy vengeance on the Roman beast which battened on the blood of the martyrs by allowing its accomplishments in art, philosophy, building, science, and politics to perish in the impending universal ruin; or would it carry these forward for the building up of a new order? Spiritual men like Augustine, Jerome, Boethius, and Ambrose settled the question in favor of the latter alternative.

And so when the old Empire went down there occurred no break in the intellectual continuity of mankind. The Church in this age of universal ruin and destruction met the barbarians not only as the representatives of the new and liberalizing doctrines of Christ, but as the preserver of the secular culture of the past — the Greco-Roman ideal of a common civilization based on order, the primacy of intelligence, and the ennobling power of beauty. But for this, continues Mr. Dawson, our Western civilization would have been a vastly different thing than the one we know. Its religion would have been the same. But culturally it would have been no stronger in a material way than the Orient.

A capital point is here made by Mr. Dawson, in many ways the best contribution of the book because of its importance for us today. It is this: that the vast legacy of Rome and Athens with all its meaning for culture in the West was salvaged by men who thought more of the next world than of this, and precisely *because* they placed the glories of the next world before those of this.

"If that age [he says] was an age of faith, it was not merely on account of its external religious profession; still less does it mean that the men of that age were more moral or more humane or more just in their social and economic relations than the men of today. *It is rather because they had no faith in themselves or in the possibilities of human effort, but put their trust in something more than civilization and something outside history.* No doubt this attitude has much in common with that of the great oriental religions, but it differs essentially in that it did not lead to quietism or fatalism in regard to the external world but rather to an intensification of social activity. The foundations of Europe were laid in fear and weakness and suffering — in such suffering as we can hardly conceive today, even after the disasters of the last eighteen years. And yet the sense of despair and unlimited impotence and abandonment that the disasters of the time provoked were not inconsistent with a spirit of courage and self-devotion which inspired men to heroic effort and superhuman activity."

This essential conviction, *Diem hominis non desideravi*, is unintelligible to the modern "who views all things *sub specie humanitatis* and regards the 'day of man' as the only possible object of a reasonable man's devotion." Yet to understand it is to understand why the Dark Ages saved the glories of secular culture and why our own age is losing them.

This intensely interesting story of how the foundations of Europe were laid upon the ruins of the ancient world, of how amid the havoc and confusion of successive barbarian invasions from the North and East, the monks, bishops, and popes converted the new people to the doctrine of Christ and preserved the culture of the Mediterranean basin, ends roughly about A.D. 1000. The renaissance of the eleventh century is beginning. The springtime of European civilization, the Middle Ages, is at hand when the seed planted in suffering and uncertainty will come up. The work of this period will be the hardly less heroic attempt to weld into a synthesis the religious tradition of the Catholic Church, the intellectual tradition of classical learning and the national tradition of the barbarian peoples. There will be much positive achievement in these centuries. Romance will appear with the great Song of Roland; there will be troubadours and crusaders: philosophy and letters will awaken and ripen into Dante and Thomas Aquinas. Cathedrals will arise, all the arts quicken. There will be travel and exploration — much activity. And all will be enlivened by that common ideal of Christian humanism which, in the words of Etienne Gilson, "still represents, as the heir of Athens no less than of Bethlehem and of Rome, Western thought in its most complete form, determined to sacrifice nothing of whatever may give man more truth, more beauty, more love and order."

And there will be much failure. The modern Catholic historian has given us few works in glorification of the Middle Ages. Perhaps he thinks the last century of enthusiastic history of the Romantic school (for the most part non-Catholic) has done the task sufficiently well — perhaps too well. Dawson for one rises in protest against the unreality of such history and Henri Massis begs us to remember that "while nothing is more revealing in these times than that nostalgia for the Middle Ages," it is well to insist that these years were "greater for what they might have done than by what they did do and left unfinished."

D. B. Wyndham Lewis has given us two quasi-medieval studies. It is not of the young and vigorous Middle Ages rejoicing in its youth and confident in its hopes, that he writes, but of fifteenth-century Paris in the throes of transition: there is an ominous air of disaster abroad and the impending frustration of high promise. His *François Villon* is a romantic biography in the sense that it is bizarre and colorful. One does not easily forget the scene with which the book opens: "A little before nine o'clock of a bitter night in Paris, on the threshold of Christmas, 1456." The Angelus bell booming out from the tower of the Sorbonne is heard by a dark young clerk writing alone in the garret of a house called Porte Rouge, "and laying down his pen with fingers stiff with cold signs himself and begins to recite hastily, half under his breath the Salutation. . . ." The treatment is distinctly non-Romantic in the almost too-realistic picture he gives of the admirable cutthroat and poet, François Villon. Paris, too, is a medley of mud, vice, and poverty. So also in his *King Spider* the attempt is to reclaim Louis XI from the "stale stench of the theatre" which legends of melodrama have caused to lay around his name.

III

The second problem of prime importance to our race is the disaster of the sixteenth century. How came Christendom to suffer shipwreck? What made the Reformation? There is much concentration on this problem by the group of historians we are here considering. One would think that it were not the second question but the first question of prime importance. Their regard is continually fixed upon it. If they treat of the foundations of our culture in the Dark or Middle Ages as Dawson does, they look forward to it as the calamity that will rob Europe of all this painfully constructed promise. If they treat of the periods following it like Belloc in *Napoleon* and *Marie Antoinette* or like Morton in *Sobieski* they look back on it as the event from which most of our modern confusion has stemmed.

Belloc's very best work has been done in the Reformation period. Artistically his two biographies *Wolsey* and *Cranmer* are perhaps his greatest achievements; his *How the Reformation Happened* is his masterpiece of analysis. Belloc has succeeded in investing the events of the sixteenth century with an air of drama and vital contemporaneous significance that they have not heretofore had. He writes the history of the Reformation from the disasters of the present day and hence lays himself open to the charge he has so effectually used against others of "writing history backwards." But what he is really doing is writing history over again. His trick of beginning in modern time is employed merely to show that contemporary events cry loudly for a reinterpretation of the Reformation because they have given the *coup de grace* to two of the most widely accepted explanations of it. There is, first, the explanation of the Protestant historian. To him the matter was simple enough, says Belloc. The revolt of the sixteenth century was nothing but the final emergence of what had always been present below the surface, the Essential Fellow for whom the centuries were in labor, the complete man — the German, English, or American Protestant.

The skeptical or atheistical historian's explanation is above bombast of this sort. "To him the Protestantism produced by the Reformation is ridiculous and intellectually contemptible — far lower than the Catholic past." But the Catholic scheme of Europe was bound to break up. The Church is dead and it is no great loss to mankind. The interval of Bible worship, at which he smiles, is still less a loss. All this he saw as a necessary phase "in the general exodus of our race from darkness into light, a phase confused and full of contradictions . . . but suffering all these inevitably as part of a great revolution which was to end in a happy and stable society. . . . But he was all wrong. The vision of progress was in his mind alone, not in the real world. The Reformation did not continue a direct Renaissance tendency toward larger things, it deflected that tendency. It did not introduce the arts, it cramped and thwarted them. Its last effects have not led to a society happy or stable, they have led to a society we see around us today."

The puzzle of the Reformation and its interpretation by Protestant and skeptical historians is further complicated by one final circumstance, startling and exasperating in our own generation. In the midst of the double collapse of Protestantism and the dreams of the Science and Progress cult, the one positive force of importance that remains in the West is the Catholic Church, not dead but more vigorous perhaps than at any time in her career since the Middle Ages, attracting to herself and producing men whose superiority over the sort of men who wrote her obituary is markedly intellectual. It is factors such as these that fully justify Belloc in his contention that the events of the critical sixteenth century which broke with the past need re-evaluation.

This he has undertaken in four notable volumes. I say "notable" because even those who will not agree with his thesis, cannot neglect his art. Belloc never forgets he is an artist. Even in *How the Reformation Happened,* a work that treats analytically the entire European battle front of the Protestant revolt, the account reads less like a summary, which it is, than an epic; foreshadowing, suspense, climax are all employed here with that fine sense of drama that distinguishes some of his other works, and with a style nervous and swift like the "immortal rapidity" of Thucydides. He is in one of his best moods, not in the art of portraiture, not in the profound study of human emotions, but in that generalship of facts that distinguishes the historical field marshal from the historical sniper. He is *imperator et rex,* always in complete command of the situation, except where it shades off into the region where spiritual forces wrestle, where "Heaven and Hell are at work"; then he prays to the God of history and of battles.

How the Reformation Happened, is, as I have said, an analysis of the entire situation, causes, conflict, and results. For a closer and more intimate view he has given us two studies in what he aptly calls "the English Accident." "If ever there were, in all history, an event not desired by its agents: not understood by those who suffered it: coming by no design, but as the prodigious effect of comparatively small and quite incongruous causes, it was the gradual, mechanical and disastrous destruction in the English mind of that Faith which had made England." Yet it was an important accident — the withdrawal of the only ancient province of the old Roman Empire from Christian unity. But for it "what we call the Reformation would appear today in history as no more than one of the many outbreaks against the necessary discipline of our culture. . . . It was the artificial removal of the English from the main body of Europe which made the break-up of Christendom permanent."

These two studies are biographies — pictorial re-creations of the days of the disaster through the personalities of two men who may be said to stand for the two main forces that brought it about, Wolsey and Cranmer. In *Wolsey* is related the quite unlovely part played in the affair by an important official of the Church. Cardinal Wolsey, Chancellor of Henry VIII, is a symbol. He stands for that type of worldly ecclesiastic produced by the many causes responsible for the crystallization of medieval culture and the new spirit of the Renaissance.

Wolsey is a tragedy. It is the tragedy of a man who came into

power at a critical and dangerous moment in the history of
Europe. All Christendom "was in the delirium of a new, most
powerful wine." The immense flood of the Renaissance had
mounted until it had become too huge for the social framework
which had given it birth. There was danger of dissolution. Yet
there was also infinite possibility that the new thing would be
greater than the old. The Renaissance was no more than the
maturing and partial realization at some points, the falling off
at others from that ideal of Christian humanism which the
Church had carried with it when Rome fell. "The mind of
Europe had been formed under the hand of the Christian
Church, its spirit had been drawn from that one source. The
impulse of these new fires might indeed have cast it all into a
new world, enlarging the past, and producing a glorious heri-
tage of a novel kind out of the sufficiently glorious middle ages.
Had there been a sufficient control over the driving energies at
work . . . the men of our race might have been free at last
and the Christian message fulfilled. . . . With Wolsey did it
lie more than with any other man whether the good or the evil
fate should prevail. This man had it in his power, had he but
known his chances, to save our world: because he alone stood
for so many years at the helm of a united nation free from
foreign menace and with all its resources at his command. . . .
He failed. The tragedy is the tragedy of his failure. It is a trag-
edy general and particular: European and domestic. Christen-
dom made shipwreck. . . . He saw the beginnings of the
Church's ruin. His own glories ended in humiliations."

All the elements postulated by Aristotle for the high serious-
ness of tragedy are here, and Belloc neglects none of them. He
never lets the reader forget he is witnessing a tragedy. The book
is divided, not into chapters but into acts — five of them. Other
divisions are designated as "stage direction," "program," "cast
of characters." There is besides rising and falling action, climax,
everything down to the significant mistake, seemingly trivial,
which controls the subsequent action. This is Wolsey's failure

to understand, until too late, the character of Anne Boleyn and her power over Henry. Wolsey who understood men so well!

Some of Belloc's most dexterous work is to be found in the chapter called "The Cast" in which he sketches with consummate art the principal characters in the drama. Witness this excerpt from the portrait of Anne Boleyn: "As to Anne, let us get her picture. Bald above the eyes, lacking in brows, and with a stupid but very obstinate mouth, flat-chested, with a long thin neck, not too upright a carriage, she has not left a word of wit or warmth or personality whereby she may be remembered. What a wretched lanky pin on which to hang the destiny of the Christian world!"

Belloc's *Cranmer* is a notable book for many reasons. Among them not the least notable is the illustration it gives of the remarkable adaptability of his style. If his prose in *Wolsey* reminds us of Tacitus, nervous, sententious, and surprising, in *Cranmer* we have another manner which recalls the best in modern Romantic stylists like Ruskin and Stevenson. It is effortless, inevitable, and illuminated by occasional pictures that are colorful without being ornate. Men have said many and contradictory things about Belloc's ability as an historian. The final word is yet to be spoken. He makes mistakes, not large ones but the trivial sort that annoy the professionals. But his position as a master of prose is fixed, and it is a very high one. Even those whose taste runs toward the mystic type of prose in which there is much "broken stammer of the skies" concede this. But for those who have been trained on the ancient and enduring rhythms of Tacitus, Cicero (in his letters), Plato, and Thucydides, Belloc's style is the purest sort of joy. He seems to have no modern peer in the classical mode; some go back as far as Addison to find a suitable term of comparison.

In *Cranmer* he treats the character of a man who like himself was a master of the word. "He had mastery over that medium whereby the mind of man is made. He could command the word. Through this singular power he fixed the new liturgy of

the English people. . . . Cranmer is the English book of Com-
mon Prayer, and that book is at once the symbol and the cause
of a separate national religion among the English, and there-
fore of England's place apart in the disruption of Christendom."

Toward this fellow craftsman "of the despised, unlucrative
art, the trade of the Children of Apollo, who are not herds-
men nor carpenters nor practitioners of any sort of craft but
serve the Muses and the God of the Silver Bow," one would
expect Belloc to show sympathy. And so he does. He deliber-
ately contrasts him with that other type of reformer who made
permanent the "English accident" — the new millionaires, I
mean, who became fat on the loot of the Church property. The
vice of these men was greed: they despised the Church not be-
cause they hated her doctrines and the Mass but because a re-
turn to Roman and European unity meant the restitution of
their stolen fortunes to the rightful owners.

Cranmer was not greedy. His vice (and that of those he
stands for) was a higher thing, less bound to the flesh, a thing
of the mind where men sin deepest and most permanently. His
was that mysterious thing, loss of Faith, willful and cold-
blooded. For his mastery of the word Belloc bestows his sin-
cerest admiration, expressed in a style to match. But for the
man, no sympathy. He despises him, sometimes with such bit-
terness that the pages seem to crinkle under the irony. For he
has deliberately cast away a gift Belloc values more highly than
the mastery of the word; and he has used the thing Belloc
values next to the Faith, to make permanent that which he
hates the most — a lie.

Out of the many striking pictures in this biography one is
unforgettable — Cranmer's death at the stake, with which the
study abruptly closes. Every detail of that solemn scene at St.
Mary's Church, Oxford, when the old archbishop made the last
of his seven recantations of error is etched upon the memory.
The refusal of pardon, his prayers at the foot of the high altar,
his omission of the usual "Ave Maria" (Belloc would recall

that!) ; then his dramatic revocation of his recantations, and his mad rush in the rain to the stake, and death in the flames. It is a tragic scene, horrible with all the mystery of final impenitence.

IV

The rather dismal story of the "English Accident" made permanent in Elizabethan times is told by Christopher Hollis with flashes of mirth and honest irony that make the narrative much less dismal than it is. *The Monstrous Regiment* is the work of a young man; Hollis was twenty-seven when he wrote it. Since then he has produced several more stimulating books including his two most recent offerings, *John Dryden* and *Erasmus*. Son of the Anglican bishop of Taunton, he was educated at Eton and Oxford, and was received into the Church in 1924.

The Monstrous Regiment is not a work of profound historical research. It is, by design, popular, fitted to correct a vulgar misconception of the period, one taught in the schools and made more or less permanent in literature by books like Kingsley's *Westward Ho!,* which, exclaims Wyndham Lewis, wildly tearing his hair, "is still the standard gift book for innocent British youth!"

"I remember," says Hollis, "the old school-boy version of Elizabethan times — a proud Virgin Queen, lover of England, brave sea-dogs, gallant courtiers, wise statesmen, a nation which was feeling the first stirrings of its greatness, the whole world a young man's world. Put beside it another picture. A poor, weak, badgered Queen — a gang of crooks, who by a dirty trick have made themselves masters of England and the Queen, and who are playing a desperate and panicky game in order that they might be able to keep that which they have pillaged in sacrilege — the rich atheist, the poor, starving and landless — God banished from English altars, and the gallows of three counties creaking with the corpses of the last men who have died for English freedom. Is not the last picture as nearly true as the first?"

There is a dash of William Cobbett here, and a great deal of schoolboy rebellion against stupid propaganda history. It is not the picture Hollis gives us; his is more restrained: Among the interesting features of the essay may be mentioned his treatment of the rise of Protestant sanctity, epitomized in the naïve query of Sir Walter Raleigh, "Did you ever hear of men being pirates for millions?"; the religious evolution of the New Millionaires who began to prefer Calvinism to Anglicanism "because it was cheaper"; and the widespread atheism among magnates, rulers, and writers of these Elizabethan times. Of special interest, in connection with this last point, are his observations on the religious preferences of the principal Elizabethan writers. Whatever it was, he concludes, it was not Protestantism. Black magic in Marlowe, Renaissance paganism in Raleigh, Ben Jonson, and Spenser. As for Shakespeare, whether or not he died a Catholic he dismisses as a question of small importance. For one thing is quite above dispute, that he wrote always in the Catholic tradition, with a deep reverence for, if not actual belief in, the dogmas and wisdom of the Church which had built European culture on the humanism of the past. Shakespeare's poetry, as Carlyle has said, is "the last sunset glory of the Middle Ages."

The Armada victory, "the tragedy of which is not that the Spanish lost but that the Puritans won," introduces a change. "The England that spoke the language of Shakespeare was soon to fall before the England that held the faith and morals that Milton held."

The name of Milton may serve to conclude this section. He marks the end of the Renaissance in England. He inherited that ideal, conceived by the Church before the fall of Rome, treasured by her during the suffering years of the Dark Ages, and realized by her at certain points during the height of the Middle Ages and early Renaissance, the ideal, namely, that a

high and enduring type of culture might be achieved by a syn-
thesis of the best in the old Greco-Roman tradition with the
new and liberating message of Christ. Milton believed in this,
and that belief is the inspiration of *Paradise Lost.* To see how
far short not only he but the culture he stands for fell of achiev-
ing this ideal one has only to compare his work with that of
Dante, written some three centuries before. The failure is sug-
gested by the ungenerous observation of Shelley that Satan, not
Christ, is the hero. The significance is not that the ideal itself
was unattainable but that its accomplishment was possible only
by a genuine Christianity. Calvinism might attempt this syn-
thesis with pagan humanism and in some instances, such as
Paradise Lost, might achieve notable results but in the long
run it would be paganism, not Christianity, that would pre-
dominate in the fusion.

This would be the history of Christian humanism in Europe
to our day. Says Christopher Dawson, "In spite of religious dis-
union, Europe retained her cultural unity, but this was now
based on a common intellectual tradition and a common al-
legiance to the classical tradition rather than a common faith.
The Latin grammar took the place of the Latin liturgy as a
bond of intellectual unity. . . . Today Europe is faced with
the breakdown of the secular and aristocratic culture on which
the second phase of its unity was based." It is losing the Classical
Tradition even as it lost the Faith — a circumstance that gives
point to the lines of Chesterton,

> *it is only Christian men*
> *Guard even heathen things.*

v

The contemporary field of history and biography is wider
and more diversified than the treatment given here might in-
dicate. There is not, among all our writers, the same concentra-

tion on the "European Idea." Yet it is present in some degree almost universally. It is indeed the central idea, the central endeavor of Catholic history and biography of today, to throw light on the elements that have gone into the making of our civilization, to show that the neglect of these elements threatens the West with a great disaster which only a return to our cultural foundations can prevent.

The real significance of the present crisis today, says Christopher Dawson, is that the European man has lost faith, not in the old Christian European tradition, but in the secularized parody on it that has grown up since the Reformation:

"If we consider the modern movements of revolt, however hostile they may seem to be to the spiritual traditions of European culture, we shall see that they are not primarily directed against those traditions, but rather against a movement that was a revolt from them. Thus Socialism revolted against the materialism of nineteenth-century bourgeois civilization, not against the Christian social order that it never knew. Wellsian Internationalism is not an attack upon Europe, but upon the nationalism that has destroyed the European unity. And the moral rebellion of D. H. Lawrence is not directed against Christian morals, but against the post-Christian ethical compromise, which is an illegitimate substitute for them.

"The ordinary man has not consciously denied the Christian tradition; he has simply lost sight of it in his concentration on material progress. His loss of faith is due not so much to a change of belief as to a change of attention — a turning away of the mind from spiritual to temporal things which causes a blunting of the spiritual perception and a darkening of the soul."

Hence the importance of the effort to place clearly before the modern mind the outlines of that spiritual order which has been lost sight of. The epochs in which it once so successfully operated are dead and gone but the eternal principles remain, and it is these that must be brought forward to form the new age.

In illustrating this central project of modern Catholic historians, we have focused our attention on a group of English writers. We might almost as well have studied the matter through the works of American historians and biographers. For we find them, too, preoccupied with the same general problem, although under a slightly different aspect. America was discovered, explored, and settled by European men who brought to our shores an ideal of civilization that the Church has everywhere stood for. Here, as in Europe, these cultural ideals have been lost sight of; they have with the years been buried under successive strata of partial and twisted cultures imported for the most part from the Europe that had broken with the center of Christian unity. Our national development has been in a direction largely opposite to that envisioned by the early Catholic explorers and settlers, and it is only by digging through the crust of modern history that we may see that there is something more in America than Main Street.

This is what our American writers are doing, some of them in works of profound scholarship, others in popular biographies. Among the latter may be mentioned Agnes Repplier's *Pere Marquette* and *Junipero Serra,* Theodore Maynard's *De Soto,* L. V. Jacks' *La Salle,* and Joseph Gurn's *Charles Carroll of Carrollton* and *Commodore John Barry.* In Peter Guilday, of the Catholic University, American historical writers have a leader whose influence has been not unlike that of Belloc in England; he has built up a school of very competent historians, and is himself a scholar and author of the first importance. Much the same may be said of Carlton J. H. Hayes of Columbia University. Finally, to pass over others who might be mentioned, attention should be called to three men who have recently come to the notice of the American public — Louis J. A. Mercier, author of *The Challenge of Humanism,* Daniel

Sargent, author of *Thomas More,* and Ross Hoffman, author of *Restoration.* Of these only Ross Hoffman is an *ex professo* historian, but all have displayed qualities which would seem to fit them for carrying on in America the philosophico-historical work of their English contemporaries like Christopher Dawson.

BIBLIOGRAPHY

HILAIRE BELLOC
  Catholic World, Vol. 133, p. 641.
  Month, March, 1927.
  WORKS
  Europe and the Faith (New York: Paulist Press, 1920).
  Marie Antoinette (New York: Putnam, 1924).
  A Companion to Mr. Wells' "Outline of History" (London: Sheed & Ward, 1926).
  How the Reformation Happened (New York: McBride, 1928).
  James the Second (Philadelphia: Lippincott, 1928).
  Richelieu (Philadelphia: Lippincott, 1929).
  Wolsey (Philadelphia: Lippincott, 1931).
  Cranmer (Philadelphia: Lippincott, 1931).
  Napoleon (Philadelphia: Lippincott, 1932).
  Charles the First, King of England (Philadelphia: Lippincott, 1933).
  Cromwell (Philadelphia: Lippincott, 1934).
  Milton (Philadelphia: Lippincott, 1935).
G. K. CHESTERTON
  Robert Browning (New York: Macmillan, 1903).
  A Short History of England (New York: Dodd, 1917).
  William Blake (London: Duckworth, 1920).
  Charles Dickens (London: Dent, 1921).
  Robert Louis Stevenson (London: Hodder, 1928).
  William Cobbett (New York: Dodd, 1926).
  Chaucer (New York: Farrar, 1932).
CHRISTOPHER DAWSON
  Commonweal, October 27, 1933, pp. 607–609.
  WORKS
  The Making of Europe (London: Sheed & Ward, 1932).
  Essays in Order No. 1 (New York: Macmillan, 1931).
  The Modern Dilemma (New York: Sheed & Ward, 1933).
  Enquiries into Religion and Culture (London: Sheed & Ward, 1933).
  Religion and Progress (London: Sheed & Ward, 1929).

The Age of the Gods (New York: Sheed & Ward, 1933).
The Spirit of the Oxford Movement (New York: Sheed & Ward, 1933).
Religion and the Modern State (New York: Sheed & Ward, 1935).

PETER GUILDAY
John Gilmary Shea: father of American Catholic History, 1926.
Life and Times of John Carroll (New York: Encyclopedia Press, 1922).
Life and Times of John England (New York: America Press, 1927).

CHRISTOPHER HOLLIS
Catholic World, 131:401–8.
Conversions to the Church, Edited by Maurice Leahy (London: Burns, Oates, 1933).

WORKS
The American Heresy (London: Sheed & Ward, 1928).
The Monstrous Regiment (London: Sheed & Ward, 1926).
Erasmus (Milwaukee: Bruce, 1933).
Dryden (London: Duckworth, 1933).
Thomas More (Milwaukee: Bruce, 1934).

SHANE LESLIE
The End of a Chapter (autobiography). (New York: Scribner, 1917).
Downside Review, May, 1931.

WORKS
Cardinal Manning (London: Burns, Oates, 1921).
George the Fourth (Boston: Little, Brown, 1926).
The Skull of Swift (New York: Bobbs, 1928).
Studies in Sublime Failure (London: Benn, 1932).
The Oxford Movement (Milwaukee: Bruce, 1933).

D. B. WYNDHAM LEWIS
Living Authors, p. 23.

WORKS
Charles of Europe (New York: Coward McCann, 1931).
François Villon (New York: Coward McCann, 1921).
King Spider (New York: Coward McCann, 1929).

SELECTED LIST

Baring, Maurice, *Sarah Bernhardt* (New York: Appleton-Century, 1934).
―――― *In My End is My Beginning* (London: Heinemann, 1931).

Butler, Edw. Cuthbert, O.S.B., *Life and Times of Bishop Ullathorne* (London: Burns, Oates, 1927).

Bedoyère, Michael de la, *George Washington* (Philadelphia: Lippincott, 1935).

Cecil, Algernon, *Metternich* (New York: Macmillan, 1933).

────── *Six Oxford Thinkers.*

Chanler, Mrs. Winthrop, *Roman Spring* (Boston: Little, Brown, 1934).

Clifton, Violet, *The Book of Talbot* (New York: Harcourt, Brace, 1933).

Forbes, F. A., *Rafael, Cardinal Merry Del Val* (New York: Longmans, 1932).

Gleeson, J. Desmond, *The Tragedy of the Stuarts* (London: Cecil Palmer, 1930).

Gurn, Joseph, *Charles Carroll of Carrollton* (New York: Kenedy, 1932).

────── *Commodore John Barry* (New York: Kenedy, 1933).

Gwynn, Denis, *Cardinal Wiseman* (London: Burns, Oates, 1930).

────── *Daniel O'Connell* (London: Hutchinson, 1929).

────── *Life and Death of Roger Casement* (London: Cape, 1931).

────── *Pius XI* (London: Holme Press, 1932).

Howard, Esmé, *Theatre of Life* (Boston: Little, Brown, 1935).

Jacks, L. V., *LaSalle* (New York: Scribner, 1931).

────── *Xenophon, Soldier of Fortune* (New York: Scribner, 1929).

Mackenzie, Compton, *Bonnie Prince Charlie* (London: Davies, 1932).

Mackenzie, Faith Compton, *Sibyl of the North* (New York: Houghton Mifflin, 1931).

MacNutt, Francis, *A Papal Chamberlain* (New York: Longmans, 1936).

Mathew, David, *The Celtic Peoples and Renaissance Europe* (New York: Sheed & Ward, 1933).

Maynard, Theodore, *DeSoto and the Conquistadores* (New York: Longmans, 1930).

McKerlie, E. M. H., *Mary of Guise-Lorraine* (London: Sands, 1931).

Monica, Sister, *Bertram C. A. Windle: a memoir* (New York: Longmans, 1932).

Morton, J. B., *Sobieski, King of Poland* (London: Eyre, 1932).

Noyes, Alfred, *Voltaire* (New York: Sheed & Ward, 1936).

O'Shaughnessy, Edith, *Marie Adelaide* (New York: Cape, 1932).

────── *Diplomat's Wife in Mexico* (New York: Harper's, 1916).

────── *Intimate Pages of Mexican History* (New York: Doran, 1920).

Phillips, Charles, *Paderewski* (New York: Macmillan, 1934).

Pope-Hennessy, Una, *The Laird of Abbotsford* (New York: Putnam, 1932).

—— *Edgar Allan Poe* (New York: Macmillan, 1931).

Repplier, Agnes, *Pere Marquette* (New York: Doubleday, 1929).

—— *Junipero Serra* (New York: Doubleday, Doran, 1933).

Sagar, S., *Round by Repentance Tower; a study of Carlyle* (London: Burns, Oates, 1930).

Sargent, Daniel, *Thomas More* (New York: Sheed & Ward, 1933).

—— *Four Independents* (New York: Sheed and Ward, 1935).

Spalding, H. S., S.J., *Catholic Colonial Maryland* (Milwaukee: Bruce, 1931).

Steuart, R. H. J., S.J., *March Kind Comrade* (war recollections). (London: Sheed & Ward, 1931.)

Thurston, Herbert, S.J., *No Popery!* (London: Sheed & Ward, 1932.)

Trappes-Lomax, Michael, *Pugin, A Medieval Victorian* (London: Sheed & Ward, 1932).

—— *Bishop Challoner* (New York: Longmans, 1936).

Walsh, Edmund A., S.J., *Fall of the Russian Empire* (Boston: Little, Brown, 1928).

—— *The Last Stand* (Boston: Little, Brown, 1931).

Walsh, William T., *Isabella of Spain* (New York: McBride, 1930).

Ward, Maisie, *The Wilfrid Wards and the Transition* (New York: Sheed and Ward, 1934).

Yeo, Margaret, *Don John of Austria* (New York: Sheed and Ward, 1934).

—— *The Greatest of the Borgias* (Milwaukee: Bruce, 1936).

5

A Note on the Saints

I

During one of the months of 1931 the leading non-Catholic Book Club in America chose for its members a volume entitled *Mère Marie of the Ursulines*. The book was a "pious" one, the life story, that is to say, of a nun whom the Church has declared "venerable," a saint in the broad sense of the word. A decade earlier such a selection might have been taken as resoundingly significant. It caused, as a matter of fact, scarcely a ripple. The fact that its author was America's most distinguished essayist, Agnes Repplier, might explain some of this lack of astonishment. But not all. We must look to something else if we would understand not only this, but why it is possible to devote a chapter, however brief, to hagiography in a work on literature.

The saints today occupy a new position in our society. They have been recalled from a banishment of several centuries' duration, and have begun to fill the places from which they were expelled. The post-Reformation society, first with hatred and hammers, destroyed their images in the churches, and then as the new secular culture came out of the twilight of Puritanism into the expansive dawn of Progress, pitied them, called them fanatics, and handed them over to the abnormal psychologists. In the meantime new "saints" were created to take the place of the old. For saints there must always be — those who sum up in their lives the highest ideals of the society of which they are a part.

And so we had "nature's saints" like Jean Jacques Rousseau, and artistic saints like Percy Shelley ("Saint Shelley" as Lionel Johnson in his Winchester days ecstatically called him); the Puritan saint of Big Business, the Humanitarian saint, who was kind to animals, and the Scientific saint, who cut them up and erected an elaborate ritual of soothsaying on decerebrated pigeons and the warm insides of guinea pigs; and many other saints besides, all honored by appropriate statues because all with their peculiar types of asceticism were leading the faithful to a paradise of paved streets and nickel-plated plumbing.

Still the old type of sanctity persisted. It cropped up in an obscure French village or a Dublin lumberyard, and multiplied despite the increased light. So that when the ideals and direction of the new secular culture began to be called into question, when prophecy failed and disillusionment spread, when portents told of the coming end of the trumpeted "day of man" it was quite natural that nostalgic eyes should be turned upon those who promised here no lasting city.

It was the artists, I think, delicately sensitive and lacerated the most by the mechanical culture, who first sensed this change and what it implied. Baudelaire saluted the *beati* from afar and told his generation that "true civilization does not come from gas nor steam, nor yet from table turning; it lies in the diminution of original sin." And after Baudelaire many others. The new attitude toward the saints was spread by the artists to other strata of society. Today the Advanced Person affects a familiarity with St. John of the Cross and St. Teresa; the dicta of St. Thomas Aquinas are sympathetically garbled by advertising men and agnostic literati. One scarcely knows whether the saints are to be congratulated or not on this worship of the dilettantes.

But they have other and more solid triumphs to their credit in the non-Catholic world. It is impossible, for instance, for one to dismiss lightly the recent book of Henri Bergson, *Les deux sources de la morale et de la religion,* in which the eminent Jewish philosopher turns in his quest for reality from the scientists to the mystics. M. Bergson's search for that reality our post-Reformation ancestors succeeded in losing for us, has been one of the most highly interesting adventures of the last few decades. The heir of two centuries of destructive criticism of the intellect, a firm believer in the sole efficacy of empirical experience (*quelqu'un a vu, quelqu'un a touché, quelqu'un sait*) he has at length come to the conclusion that the fluidity of life, the elusive *élan vital*, can, it seems, be known by an examination of the experience of those who have plunged into the ocean of life, who have felt the throbbing of the heart of reality, the saints, in a word, *les grands mystiques,* Paul, Francis, John of the Cross, Teresa.

The historian Francis Parkman expressed the mind of his time when he says of the Venerable Mère Marie de l'Incarnation that she had been "lost in the vagaries of an insane mysticism." And Charlevoix expressed what has always been the mind of the Church when in a passage on the same nun (quoted by Miss Repplier) he says, "The human soul has a natural capacity, but no exigency and positive ability, to reach God other than by analytical knowledge. But God permits some souls to feel his sensible presence, which is mystical contemplation." Finally we may let Mr. Bergson express the modern mind, for he has helped to make it. Of these same mystics, insane to the Protestant and secular mind, saints to the Church, he makes the claim that through them alone can reality be restored, all ethics, all philosophy, all spirituality, all religion.

I have said the saints have come back. They were away and they have returned. They have come back trailing clouds of glory and in fresh garments, fashioned for them by the artists, to signalize their new position in society. Art and sanctity (if not sanctity and science entirely as yet) have indeed kissed, not on a footing of equality but on that contained in Huysman's statement that *art est la seul chose propre sur la terre après la sainteté.*

II

It would perhaps be premature to speak of hagiography in the English-speaking revival as a new literary *genre*. There has not been, as there has in France, that enthusiastic turning of a large number of novelists, biographers, dramatists, and poets to the saints as to a new and unexplored land, rich in drama, in passion the most profound, in conflict, in color and human interest beyond the inventive powers of the imagination. In France the lives of the saints have through the works of Louis Bertrand, Emile Baumann, Henri Bordeaux, Rene Bazin, and others, conquered the Academy. The effort to interpret the saints for our generation has not only given birth to popular books but to classics.

If hagiography has not in our section of the Revival as yet reached this point of excellence there are not wanting indications that it will, and that soon. This promise and the evidence of some real achievement fully justifies its treatment in a separate chapter.

As a symbol of the promise let us take two books which have recently appeared, *The Irish Way* and *The English Way*. Both are co-operative works, short impressions of saints and the near-saints by some of the principal figures in the Revivals of each country. Among the contributors to *The English Way,* for instance, one finds the names of Douglas Woodruff, G. K. Chesterton, Father Bede Jarrett, E. I. Watkin, Hilaire Belloc, Christopher Dawson, Maisie Ward, Father Martindale, Father D'Arcy, and Michael Trappes-Lomax. The cream of the English Revival is represented here, and the level of writing is correspondingly high. But what is more significant is the preponderance of the names of laymen over those of priests and religious. The English lay writer, it would seem, has discovered the saint, and for better or for worse, he it is who will produce most of our lives in the new mode. I think it will be for the better. It has been so far. What the saints lose in sanctity and in accurate interpretation they will gain in humanity and in all those qualities which endear them to the great mass of the children of men among whom it is their delight to dwell.

This indeed has been the chief characteristic and the chief value of the new hagiography everywhere. Our modern writers, both lay and clerical, are in reaction against a tradition which has insisted on making the *beati* appear as far separated from ordinary humanity as possible. The technique of the old school called for a preoccupation with bodily macerations, disciplines, hair shirts, prolonged prayer, ecstasies, astonishing miracles. Its writers consistently dwelt in the region of superlatives. They seemed, as Francis Sheed has expressed it, to feel the inadequacy of ordinary expression and to have decided to talk in falsetto. All this made a saint's life difficult reading, something for the time of retreat. It was not so much a matter of poor scholarship (there was that, too, at times) as of false stress, bad art. The result might be compared to the statues that not infrequently adorn our churches, artificial beings of affected attitudes and generally unlovely and unreal holiness. "These indeed," says Ida Coudenhove, "are no longer men, but neither are they angels — man is not meant to be an angel — they are gruesome chimaeras, arbitrarily put together, with bodies hung on them like ghostly sheaths already withered and falling, never created by God. . . ."

The book just quoted from, *The Nature of Sanctity,* contains perhaps the best statement of the ideals of the new hagiography, as well as the most vigorous expression of the freshened conception of sainthood that is abroad among those who are now rewriting the saints' lives. "We are not human enough to be saints," the author insists. ". . . We don't let our children grow up into real healthy men and women, we wish them to be simply and solely Christians — and we forget that grace needs a deep, reliable, healthy, natural ground if it is to take root and bear a hundred-fold; that otherwise supernatural remains in the air, is un-natural, a phantom without strength or life or blood, and will therefore disappear before the onslaught of a real power, springing from strong, natural roots."

That the saint is first and finally a human being, and is a saint just because and just in as much as he is a human being; that sanctity is humanity raised to the limit, the utmost possibility of one's being—this is the controlling idea of modern hagiography. There is no question here of watering down sanctity, of making the saints mere natural heroes, but of showing how those essential manifestations of a higher life, austere and unreal as they may seem in isolation, have grown out of a human nature like our own, and are indeed the manifestations of that nature perfected and completed by grace. The figure of the saint is "formed and chiseled out of the precious stone" of his humanity.

Such a task is one for an artist. It requires a profound and delicate knowledge of the psychology of character, and skill in portraying the light and shade of rich, varying personalities. It demands also piety, reverence, and faith. That is why hagiography differs from mere biography. And that, too, is the reason why in our most competent saints' lives we find that delightful "marriage of art and sweet devotion," which, let it be added, would scarcely be possible were it not for the widening realization today of the ideal of Cardinal Newman that "the devout ecclesiastic be intellectual, and the intellectual layman be devout."

The work of our contemporary ecclesiastical writers has been no less artistic than that of the lay writers, and as a general rule it is more scholarly. Father Cuthbert Butler, O.S.B., Father Bede Jarrett, O.P., Archbishop Goodier, Abbot Chapman, O.S.B., Father Bede Camm, O.S.B., Father C. C. Martindale, S.J., Father Cuthbert, O.M.Cap., Father James Brodrick, S.J., may be mentioned among those who have gracefully satisfied the demands of both art and scholarship.

Speaking of the manner in which the medieval painters represented the saints, Ida Coudenhove remarks that "they stand against the landscape of their own country 'with strong and sturdy limbs planted in firm enduring soil.'" The most outstanding work of our English writers has been in this effort to see that the saints stand against the background of their own country and generation, to integrate their lives with the secular and religious history of the day. Lifted from his *milieu* a saint — any saint — is unintelligible. It may be said that his claim to universality, to a position transcending the divisions of time, flows from his immersion in and relation to his own particular generation.

Father Martindale has given an apt illustration of this truth in his *Vocation of Aloysius Gonzaga,* a book which may be taken to represent, too, that other effort of the new hagiography — to reclaim the saints from plaster and literary caricature. St. Aloysius has suffered more perhaps from this sort of thing than any of the blessed. Hence is the triumph of Father Martindale in giving him flesh and blood the more striking. But he does not do so without considerable effort. The narrative at times impresses one as being overloaded with history and genealogies, until one wonders whether it is a saint's life he is reading or a study of the Italian society of the Renaissance through the Gonzaga line. But before long Aloysius the saint emerges from this background of exaggerated pagan culture and homicide, and it is a different Aloysius, no longer the piece of twisted iron that seems more twisted, more eccentric in the common representations of him, but that "monstrosity of a Gonzaga" — "a man who had taken all the heredity forces of that family and had turned it full against what they had always used it for — self-enrichment; self-aggrandizement; self-worship." It is only when one knows the turbulent and lascivious blood that flowed in his veins that one begins to realize that he, certainly, had need of the severest measures to turn it into other channels. And it is only, too, by catching some glimpse of the amazing immorality of his generation that one sees why this young prince who offered himself as a victim for its crimes should be held up to the universal Church as the Patron of Youth.

Much of the same effective use of history has been made by Alice Curtayne in her brilliant study of St. Catherine of Siena. Among the lay writers of saints' lives Miss Curtayne holds a place of pre-eminence. She is Irish and young, the translator of Papini's *Laborers in the Vineyard,* and the author of *A Recall to Dante,* one of the few really helpful books on the Florentine we have by English-speaking Catholics. Her large and genuine talents would seem to destine her for a career as a literary critic or a novelist—a fine feeling for prose, firm but unobtrusive scholarship, a nature delicately attuned to the poetry, the drama, the humor of life and facility in its representation. But she has chosen to bestow this genius on the saints. Most of what she has written has been in hagiography. Like Henri Gheon, the saints with her are first, the rest merely incidental. In this, too, resides her claim to pre-eminence among other English authors who write only occasionally of the saints.

But if these others write only occasionally they write well, and it is encouraging to note that more of our best novelists, poets, essayists, and biographers are joining the ranks of Agnes Repplier, Hollis, Margaret Yeo, Belloc, Alfred O'Rahilly, Chesterton, and others who have saints' lives to their credit. For this *genre* is the supreme test of the authentic spirit of the Catholic Revival. It demands, as I have said, not only the highest art but another quality much more rare and precious in our day — devotion. The particular contribution of the Revival is not so much that it has produced competent artists, but that it has given to English letters artists with faith and devotion. And hagiography supplies us with a convenient test whereby we may measure in a given artist and throughout the movement how profound and delicate is the synthesis of these two qualities so long separated in art.

BIBLIOGRAPHY

Belloc, Hilaire, *Joan of Arc* (London: Cassell, 1929).

Brown, W. E., *Bishops* (Pioneers of Christendom Series). (London: Burns, Oates, 1929.)

Blount, M. M., *God's Jester* (Fr. Pro). (New York: Longmans, 1931.)

Boyton, Neil, S.J., *Blessed Friend of Youth, John Bosco* (New York: Macmillan, 1929).

Brodrick, James, S.J., *Frederic Ozanam* (London: Burns, Oates, 1934).
—— *Robert Francis Cardinal Bellarmine*, 2 volumes (London: Burns, Oates, 1932).
—— *Saint Peter Canisius* (New York: Sheed & Ward, 1935).

Burton, H., *Life of St. Francis de Sales* (New York: Kenedy, 1927).

Caudwell, I., *Damien of Molokai* (New York: Macmillan, 1932).

Chapman, Dom John, O.S.B., *Saint Benedict and the Sixth Century* (London: Sheed & Ward, 1932).

Chesterton, G. K., *St. Francis of Assisi* (New York: Doran, 1924).
—— *St. Thomas Aquinas* (London: Sheed & Ward, 1933).

Cuthbert, Father, O.S.F.C., *Life of St. Francis* (New York: Longmans, 1925).

Clayton, Joseph, *St. Hugh of Lincoln* (London: Burns, Oates, 1932).
—— *St. Anselm* (Milwaukee: Bruce, 1933).

Curtayne, Alice, *Saint Catherine of Siena* (London: Sheed & Ward, 1929).
—— *Saint Anthony of Padua* (Chicago: Franciscan Herald Press, 1931).
—— *Saint Brigid of Ireland* (Dublin: Brown & Nolan, 1933).

Corcoran, M. J., *Our St. Rita*, 1919.

Conroy, Joseph, S.J., *Arnold Damen* (New York: Benziger, 1931).

Concannon, Mrs. H., *Saint Patrick* (New York: Longmans, 1931).

Camm, Dom Bede, O.S.B., *Nine Martyr Monks* (London: Burns, Oates, 1929).

Daly, James J., S.J., *Saint John Berchmans* (New York: Kenedy, 1921).

English Way, The, (London: Sheed & Ward, 1933).

Foley, L., *Greatest Saint of France* (Morehouse, 1932).

Fame of Blessed Thomas More (London: Sheed & Ward, 1931).

Forbes, F. A., and Cahill, M., *Scottish Knight-errant* (New York: Benziger, 1926).

Goodier, Archbishop, S.J., *Saints for Sinners* (London: Sheed & Ward, 1932).

―――― *The Public Life of Our Lord, Jesus Christ,* 2 volumes (London: Burns, Oates, 1930).

Hollis, Christopher, *Saint Ignatius* (London: Sheed & Ward, 1931).

Irish Way, The (London: Sheed & Ward, 1932).

Jarrett, Bede, O.P., *Life of St. Dominic* (New York: Benziger, 1924).

Kane, William T., S.J., *William Stanton* (St. Louis: Herder, 1918).

Kerr, C., *Life of Ven. Philip Howard* (New York: Longmans, 1926).

Lunn, Arnold, *Peter Claver: A Saint in the Slave Trade* (New York: Sheed and Ward, 1935).

MacNeill, Eoin, *St. Patrick* (New York: Sheed & Ward, 1934).

Martindale, C. C., S.J., *Vocation of Aloysius Gonzaga* (London: Sheed & Ward, 1928).

―――― *Marie Therese Couderc* (London: Burns, Oates, 1926).

―――― *What are the Saints?* (London: Sheed & Ward, 1933).

Maynard, Theodore, *The Odyssey of Francis Xavier* (New York: Longmans, 1936).

Monahan, Michael, *My Jeanne d'Arc* (New York: Century, 1928).

Monica, Sister M., *Angela Merici* (New York: Longmans, 1917).

Oxenham, John, *Saint in the Making* (New York: Longmans, 1931).

Patterson, Frances J., *White Wampum* (New York: Longmans, 1934).

O'Rahilly, Alfred, *Father William Doyle, S.J.,* (New York: Longmans, 1925).

Repplier, Agnes, *Mère Marie of the Ursulines* (New York: Doubleday, 1931).

Sargent, Daniel, *Catherine Tekakwitha* (New York: Longmans, 1936).

Smith, W. G., and H. G., *Fidelis of the Cross* (New York: Putnam, 1927).

Schwertner, T. M., *St. Albert the Great* (Milwaukee: Bruce, 1933).

Talbot, Francis, S.J., *Saint Among Savages* (New York: Harper, 1935).

Waugh, Evelyn, *Edmund Campion* (New York: Sheed & Ward, 1935).

Ward, Maisie, *Father Maturin* (New York: Longmans, 1920).

Williams, Michael, *Little Flower of Carmel* (New York: Kenedy, 1925).

―――― *Little Brother Francis of Assisi* (New York: Macmillan, 1926).

Wilby, N. M., *Story of Blessed John Fisher* (London: Burns, Oates, 1929).

Wynne, John J., S.J., *Jesuit Martyrs of North America* (New York: Universal Knowledge Foundation, 1925).

Yeo, Margaret, *Saint Francis Xavier* (London: Sheed & Ward, 1932).

6

The Novel

"Never before in the history of English literature," says
Francis Talbot, S.J., in the preface to *Fiction by Its Makers,*
"have there been so many brilliant Catholic novelists." The
statement is, I think, quite accurate, as the enumeration of
such names as those of Maurice Baring, Compton Mackenzie,
Sir Philip Gibbs, Sheila Kaye-Smith, Montgomery Carmichael,
Enid Dinnis, Peadar O'Donnell, Francis Stuart, Frank Spear-
man, Kathleen Norris, Edith O'Shaughnessy, Evelyn Waugh,
James B. Connolly will indicate. Still it must be said that the
abundance of first-rate workers in this field notwithstanding,
the status of the contemporary novel is one more of promise
than of actual achievement.

There is achievement, of course; much of it. But it bears
little proportion to the possibilities indicated by the richness of
the talent, on the one hand, and the promise of a newer and
higher type of fiction envisioned by the Catholic ideal, on the
other. For the doctrines of Christ which have so powerfully
altered human nature and life have also changed our concep-
tions of the novel which deals with life and human nature.
This must be so. And it is admitted by our most competent
artists. Many of them have never written what might be called
a Catholic novel in the full and complete sense, a novel, that
is to say, of life illuminated by Faith. But they are working
toward this goal and if many of them reach it we shall be able
to speak of classical Catholic novels as we speak of classical
Catholic poetry.

The novel has from the beginning been the weaker sister in the Revival. Rather it has been the younger sister. It began late. Two of the most important of our early novelists, Mrs. Wilfrid Ward and "Richard Dehan," died within the last two years, while another, Montgomery Carmichael, is still alive and can be reckoned as a contemporary. It is that young. Moreover the best talent in the first two phases of the Revival went into poetry. Robert Hugh Benson, Canon Sheehan, Mrs. Ward did not bring to the novel quite the same genius that Patmore, Gerard Hopkins, Francis Thompson did to poetry.

Besides starting late, the novel began under difficulties unexperienced by those who worked in poetry. One of the most notable of these, I think, was the complete absence of a guiding tradition. Patmore could and did turn for help and guidance to Dante; Thompson and Hopkins to Southwell and Crashaw. But to whom could Benson, Ayscough, Mrs. Ward turn — to what Catholic novelists? The English novel was itself a newcomer among the literary forms. It had arisen under Protestant and Humanitarian auspices. It was secular: it had never been baptized. The novelists, then, who shared with the poets the conviction that Catholic literature must embody truths, unglimpsed by others — the high and difficult truths, namely, that flow from the Incarnation, of nature elevated to the plane of grace — were pioneers and experimentalists in a more real sense than any of their fellow workers in the Revival.

Writing is a more or less recent symposium on the novel.[1] Montgomery Carmichael has given us an interesting and somewhat discouraging account of the efforts to work out this ideal:

"It is nature alone [he says] that can claim the triumphs of great fiction in the admirable pictures of such artists as Fielding and Sterne, Dickens and Thackeray, Mrs. Austin and Charlotte Brontë, Trollope and Hawthorne. In these stirring pages we find nature in her coat of many colors depicted by true master-hands. Here she is alluringly arrayed in the virtues

---

[1] *Fiction By Its Makers*, by Francis X. Talbot, S.J.

which are called after her: but here also is she intensely alive
in all her deceit and cunning, her hatred of subjection, her
loathing of contempt, her greed of lucre and her covetousness,
her love of bodily care and creature comforts, of curious and
beautiful things. . . . But of Divine Grace, with its supernatural
powers over the natural, there is not in all their fascinating
pages, so much as a vestige, and I doubt if a single one of these
great geniuses could have told us what grace really is.

"The sure hand with which nature's painters depict in
wholly unembarrassed fashion their vivid and natural pictures
is in a large measure due to their ignorance of the mystic power
which can transform nature and deify man. For it must be
admitted that the life of Grace, as a subject, is an undoubted
handicap to the writer of fiction, be his intentions as Catholic
as may be. . . . The truth is that fiction is a faulty medium in
which to convey these profound things of the spirit which
most nearly concern a Catholic. The medium would break in
the hands of even a Catholic genius who should assay the
highest."

Mr. Carmichael is one who has caught no uncertain glimpses
of the superabundant wealth of artistic material in Catholic
dogma, Catholic history, and Catholic life. But unlike many
another who has the same fullness of vision but less art, he is
under no illusion as to the difficulty of bringing this into the
novel. Perhaps he exaggerates the difficulties. Nevertheless, one
must agree that too few Catholic novelists have seen any diffi-
culty at all. They have "views of the unveiled heavens" and
they rush into expression because, as Patmore says,

> *They think they somehow should, and so they try,*
> *But (haply 'tis they screw the pitch too high.)*
> *'Tis still their fates*
> *To warble tunes that nails might draw from slates,*
> *Poor seraphim!*

While it is true the novel in the first phases did not attract to itself the artists poetry did, it would be inaccurate to say that it had no great artists. If Benson, John Oliver Hobbes, Canon Sheehan, and others do not occupy the place in the history of the English novel that some of their contemporaries do, like Hardy, Meredith, Conrad, it is not because they had no ability. They had ability. But they attempted something higher, more exalted, and the disparity between their ideals and their achievement must appear the more obvious.

Thus far in this survey, the poets have been called upon to carry the burden of the continuity. This is, I think, as it should be. For not only has the Revival accomplished its most considerable work in poetry, but the earliest of the revivalists were poets, and the development of this form has been continuous and even, supplying to each successive period those who best carried forward the central tradition and gave voice to the authentic spirit of the movement. Still, in placing this stress upon poetry something of an injustice has been done to the novel. It is obviously out of the question to give a just idea of the accomplishments of the Revival in fiction during the past half century in the brief space of a chapter. And it should be understood that convenience and the nature of the work attempted, has brought this about rather than any deficiency on the part of the early novelists themselves. The work of Benson, for instance, deserves a much lengthier treatment than can be accorded it here. The same may be said of John Oliver Hobbes, Carmichael, Mrs. Ward, John Ayscough, and others. They are as true and genuine artists as some of the poets we have treated more at length. Their work, too, is important in that it reaches into the present. They began a tradition. Others have inherited their experimental work, have profited by their errors as well as by their accomplishments. The fact that today we have novelists who can boast of positive achievement in Catholic fiction must be attributed in no small way to their work.

It is the contemporary workers to whom we must devote

our attention in this chapter. From the standpoint of number and pure ability they make a more impressive list than do the poets, the essayists, or the historians, indicating that the novel and not poetry may be our strongest department in the future. Out of this embarrassingly large group we must select some who best typify the status of the contemporary novel — accomplishment on the one hand, and great promise on the other.

II

There is a suggestion of the absurd in choosing, as those who best represent the novel on its promising side, two authors who for more than a decade have occupied undisputed places in the first rank of English novelists. No one today looks upon Compton Mackenzie or Sheila Kaye-Smith as just "promising" novelists. No one except Catholics, who do so not because they are unappreciative of their genius or unaware of the several artistic triumphs each of these converts has to his credit. Rather it is their awareness of this that makes them regard them as supremely fitted to attempt something quite different and of a higher order than they have yet undertaken.

This something is what we are pleased to call the "Catholic novel." Now I am aware there is much that is loose, much that is visionary, much that is downright unreasonable in the various expressions of the ideal that goes under this name. But at bottom it is quite sound. It would be idle to talk of Catholic literature, Catholic art, if all its canons were satisfied by the simple announcement on the part of the artists that he is a baptized and practising Catholic. The same, it seems to me, would hold if Catholic art meant nothing more than the guarantee that the works of its exponents contained nothing offensive to morality. Even this negative perfection, of course, is not to be despised, and in a certain class of fiction — the detective story, for instance, such as Mrs. Belloc Lowndes and

Elizabeth Jordan write — little more can be demanded. But in the more serious types of the novel which essay a representation of life and its meaning, something more *is* demanded, and the fact that Catholics clamor for it everywhere is evidence enough that this ideal contains something positive and different.

"The first duty of a Catholic writer of fiction," says Emile Baumann, "lies in representing life as it is, that is to say, in the way his observation dictates and his Faith reveals to him." There is nothing unreasonable or cramping to genius in the demand that life be represented "as it is." It is rather a challenge to genius to free itself from the convention which on dogmatic grounds has narrowed the real to the secular, the incomplete. "I have come," said the Divine Artist, "that you may have life, and have it more abundantly." Out of the very abundance of this life arise difficulties, it is true, but also the promise of achievement in the novel higher than any yet reached by even the masters.

Perhaps it is this that has caused Sheila Kaye-Smith to remark of Compton Mackenzie some time ago that "with his understanding of modern life, of human love, and that religious impulse which is both the synthesis of all human emotions and the unifying link with the worlds beyond it, he has it in his power to write a novel greater than any which English literature has yet produced." He has not yet written it. Perhaps he never will. But he is working toward it with capacities unequaled, perhaps, by any other modern writer.

Mr. Mackenzie belongs to that class of Catholic novelists (a very large one) who have learnt their art outside the Church. Both the advantages and disadvantages of this may be seen in his work. Born in 1883, he was educated at St. Paul's School, London, and Magdalen College, Oxford. His first novel *The Passionate Elopement,* published in 1911, was in a manner he has never returned to. It was historical — Bath in the days of Beau Nash — and was not a notable achievement. He wrote the book in the wilds of Cornwall where he had retired with his wife Faith Compton Mackenzie (also a talented writer) immediately after his university career. If thenceforth he definitely abandoned the costume novel, he did not break with his preference for writing and living in solitude. Most of his subsequent works were done far away from the London literary world which he visits but rarely, either at his villa on the Isle of Capri or at his other island home in Jethou.

His second novel, *Carnival* (1912), made him a famous and popular author. Many today still regard it as his best, especially those who find his longer works rather difficult going. What is certain is that with it he found a vein which suited his genius, and which has supplied him with most of the material and inspiration for his subsequent novels. It is an autobiographical vein. There is in it much of the business of tapping his amazingly abundant recollection of his childhood and adolescence, and of dealing with characters and phases of modern life well known to him. The theater, for instance, supplies the background for *Carnival*. Mr. Mackenzie, himself, comes from a distinguished theatrical family. Both his father and mother were noted actors and his aunt "Leah" Bateman, a tragedienne of the first order.

Carnival is theatrical in more than one sense. Its swift and tragic conclusion is indeed melodramatic, and there are in the carefully studied career of the young dancer, Jenny Raeburn, glamorous episodes such as one may find in any good (or bad) romantic novel. But it is not a romance, nor has he ever produced one, except perhaps *Plasher's Mead,* which is one of his very best novels and heightens one's suspicion that he is not a realist at all. He has also displayed marked ability in the field of humorous fiction. But both humor and romance he unfortunately seems to regard as a sideline.

Most of his novels deserve to be classed as realistic and that for two reasons. The first is his almost painful preoccupation with details — the details especially of childhood, chosen not primarily for their interest but for their bearing on the psychological development of character. He believes that only through a faithful recording of the impressions and environmental incidents of a man's early life can character accurately be given. The theory is responsible for much that is perhaps necessary but withal tiring in the opening chapters of *Carnival* and *Sylvia Scarlett;* it is responsible for the fact that the first five hundred pages of the initial volume of *Sinister Street* take us no farther with the hero, Michael Fane, than his public-school days. He wants his readers to know his characters as thoroughly as he knows them. And those who persevere certainly do. Actors born in such travail and nurtured with such infinite pains are not lightly to be abandoned. Nor does Mr. Mackenzie drop them. They turn up again in other stories.

If Mr. Mackenzie is to be classed as a realist it will be because of the first reason given. There are other elements in his books that make their kinship with the products of this school seem more marked, but which in reality separate them sharply from the sort of thing we have since Zola agreed to call realism. I refer to the utter absence of the spiritual which in some of his novels produces an atmosphere almost unbearably oppressive; his lack of reticence in matters of sex and the important part it inevitably plays; a certain insistence on the sordid. But it is not, as with the dogmatic realists, a materialist's philosophy of life that brings this about, but the kind of characters he has chosen to study. While he does not always succeed in making nature particularly alluring, the vice that appears is invariably ugly and unattractive. His attitude in this period of his career is best epitomized in the words of one of his characters, Michael Fane: "I hate free thought, free love, free verse, and yet I hate equally the stuffy people who have never contemplated their merit."

Coincident with the appearance of the second volume of *Sinister Street,* which started a vogue in the English novel, Mr. Mackenzie became a Catholic. This was in 1914. The following year he was with the British forces in the unfortunate

Dardanelles expedition, and in 1916 was invalided out of active service, made a Captain in the Royal Marines, Military Control Officer at Athens, and director of the intelligence department in Syria. This experience he subsequently made use of in several quite critical and outspoken books, one of which has recently got him into some difficulties with the British government.

His attempts after the war to introduce Catholicism into some of his novels which were sequels to *Sinister Street,* were all very unfortunate. One feels that the characters were more to blame for this than Mr. Mackenzie. Raised in another atmosphere they simply refused to take on any genuine religion. Perhaps it was a feeling of this sort on his part that made him decide to abandon them all, and to take a fresh start with characters whose chief interest *would* be in religion. *The Altar Steps* which came out in 1922 was the first volume of a trilogy recording the spiritual evolution of Mark Litterdale from Anglicanism to Catholicism. Those who deplored the absence of religion in some of his previous books were given real grounds for complaining about too much in these. Mr. Mackenzie's realistic leanings were at fault this time; his preoccupation with the minutiae of the Anglo-Catholic problem succeeded in crowding out almost every other interest. Yet the trilogy, the last volume of which was *The Heavenly Ladder* (1924), was executed in his very best manner. Even those whom the subject-matter displeased, conceded that his art in these volumes was at its highest level. His accustomed infinite pains were expended in the creation of Mark Litterdale, another character who is almost sure to come back again, and a Catholic, too, with a definite bias toward the things of the spirit. It would appear, then, that Mr. Mackenzie has, after twenty years, at length arrived at a point where a Catholic novel of real merit can be expected of him. And if it turns out to be, as Sheila Kaye-Smith thinks, "a greater novel than any which English literature has yet produced," no one will complain that the days of watching have been too long.

Miss Kaye-Smith's promise as a Catholic novelist is in so many ways similar to that of Compton Mackenzie that it needs merely to be indicated to complete the picture of some of the obstacles that stand in the way of our convert writers. Like him she has developed her art in isolation from Catholicism. By dint of long and patient observation she has become the recognized voice of a people without Catholic consciousness, and the laureate of a land which remembers only dimly the monks of Canterbury. The well-beloved Sussex of Miss Kaye-Smith, which has given to her quite as much as she has given to it, will, one feels, be the greatest obstacle in the way of her production of a Catholic novel. For, unlike poetry, the novel demands something more than that the author himself be steeped in Catholicity. It would seem to require also that the material be Catholic, that the people whose lives he interprets be firmly rooted in generations of Catholic tradition. And this is particularly true of the sort of fiction Miss Kaye-Smith writes.

She has been a Catholic for a much shorter period than Compton Mackenzie has, having entered the Church with her husband, the Rev. T. Penrose Fry, in 1929. Religion and the things of the spirit have never been absent in any of her novels, although none of them may properly be called novels of Grace. Her excellence consists in the skill with which she delineates simple nature and the fundamental emotions of people who live close to the soil. It is this that has caused many critics to predict for her works a longer life than those of other contemporaries whose talents lie in the portrayal of things less elemental and human. Not a few of her novels, notably *Joanna Godden* and *Sussex Gorse,* impress one as tremendous achievements which future generations may place side by side with the great classics. She is today certainly one of, if not the most distinguished of English women novelists. She has few equals even

among the men. Both she and Mr. Mackenzie may well stand
as representing what can be hoped for in the future if they and
others of our genuinely talented convert writers succeed in
overcoming the obstacles that lie between them and the pro-
duction of a Catholic novel in its fullest sense.[1]

These difficulties, it must be insisted again, are real. Ethel
Cook Eliot, an American convert novelist of real promise, has
in a recent statement thrown some very interesting light on
this subject. Speaking of her entry into the Church in 1925,
and the effect of the act upon her art she says: "I saw no new
fields for writing. On the contrary I felt crippled as a writer.
My whole culture was shifting, changing. The old subjective
intuitions concerning Last Things were being dissolved in the
hot, sharp, sunlight of Catholic truth. The soil of Catholic cul-
ture had need to deepen before any authentic artistic creative
impulse could stir there. . . . During this painful period of
transition I wrote six books. I made them good entertainment
and as good art as my technique could manage, and marked
time. Then I wrote *Ariel Dances,* a romantic novel. While writ-
ing this novel I found, for the first time, my Catholic conscious-
ness crowding itself in on my imagination, persistently. It took
some effort, some artificiality, perhaps, to keep Catholicism out
of the book. My reason for insisting on keeping it out was that
I was afraid my 'art' was not big enough to contain such a
strong sap. But writing the second novel, *Green Doors,* I gave

---

[1] As this book goes to press Miss Kaye-Smith is receiving unstinted praise from the
critics for her two most recent books, *Superstition Corner* and *Gallybird*. And they are
both Catholic novels, not specifically by reason of the presence in them of some Cath-
olic characters, but by reason of the realistic picture the author gives of the progressive
moral and intellectual disintegration of a family which has rejected the Faith and its
fonts of supernatural aid. The family is that of the Alards whose extinction Miss
Kaye-Smith recorded in *The End of the House of Alard* (1923). She now retraces
the early history of that family in the sixteenth and seventeenth centuries in two
historical novels that are distinguished not only by the author's accustomed art and
subtle penetration into the fundamental things of human nature, but also by an
equally subtle understanding of the relation of grace to that human nature, and of the
rank weeds of superstition, fear, and ineffectiveness which must spring up when grace
is uprooted.

up artistic pussyfooting. It was spring — a second spring in my artist's life — and the veins of *Green Doors* do run — I humbly believe it — with Catholic life."

III

Among those who have, in the face of difficulties, succeeded in producing Catholic novels, first place must, I think, be given to Maurice Baring. The judgment may be disputed. Someone, for instance, has recently taken Mr. Baring to task for his supposed failure to manifest in his works any of that militant and apostolic Catholicism of which his two bosom friends, Mr. Chesterton and Mr. Belloc, are such brilliant exponents. What this criticism overlooks is the fact that Mr. Baring is primarily a novelist and his friends are not; otherwise one might, reversing the stricture, hold up Mr. Baring's novels as the ideal and accuse both Mr. Chesterton and Mr. Belloc of excessive timidity about the things of Faith, which are rigidly excluded from most of their stories. Neither of them has written a novel with a Catholic background, a circumstance which I think may well be taken as a token of the difficulties incident to such a work. And Mr. Baring has!

The Belloc-Chesterton type of fiction manifests its Catholicism, not in a simple delineation of Catholic life, but in a vigorous exposition of Catholic opinion. They are all distinguished by the "Catholic attitude" we talked about in the section on satire even though they may contain no allusion to the Church, its priests, doctrines, and practices. The exclusion of their faith is, without doubt, deliberate, and is a concession to that queer but real kink in the mind of the modern non-Catholic and even Catholic reading public, which resents propaganda (when it is Catholic propaganda) and professes to see it where it does not exist at all. Some of our novelists, such as Owen Francis Dudley and Lucille Borden, have chosen to despise this attitude and have given us competent fiction that is frankly apologetic.

There is undoubtedly room for stories of this type but it is stupid to hold it up as the highest type of Catholic fiction, and to blast those who refuse to conform to it.

Sir Philip Gibbs is another whose work has been judged by standards of this sort and found wanting. The temptation to apply these standards to his stories is the greater because much of what he has written concerns itself with an attempt to solve the many social and moral problems presented to us as a legacy of the World War. Sir Philip belongs to that generation, the insane and flaccid liberalism of which is now being widely charged with having produced the war. He was one of the first to make the accusation and to admit the responsibility for the years of bloodshed and their devastating sequel. He witnessed the gigantic conflict on the Western Front as a correspondent, reporting the mean and glorious things in the struggle with a vividness and accuracy unreached by any other representative of the Press. Some of his dispatches have since found their way into books of literature. He was the acknowledged *doyen* of war correspondents. His country elevated him to the knighthood in recognition of his achievements, and Chesterton dubbed him, "Fleet street's ambassador at the front."

That larger and more significant war following on the peace of Versailles which today still threatens to wipe out modern civilization, has since then claimed the amazing reportorial talents of Sir Philip. His work here has been even more brilliant. It was recognized that much of his success on the Western Front was due to the fact that he was not only a journalist but a novelist and a litterateur. Unhampered now by the requirements of war dispatches and the blue pencils of censors, his wide knowledge and mature genius have been productive of essays and novels the outspoken frankness and post-war pessimism of which is illuminated by a hope that is neither banal nor forced but is based, one feels, on a deep and vivid Catholicism. Yet this Catholicism does not always appear as Catholicism. Frequently his novels do not rise above the ethical level.

Sir Philip cannot forget that he is still the chosen war and peace correspondent of a public that is largely non-Catholic. And it is to this public that he addresses himself. Consequently when his full Catholicism does appear it is by way of innuendo and through characters who play forceful but minor roles. Yet the end effect of this device is the more subtle and eloquent. No Catholic author, I think, has written a stronger novel of its kind than his *Age of Reason*. And it is a Catholic novel, not only in the quality of its devastating criticism of the high and pitiful hopes of the cult of Science and Progress, but in the supernatural solution he offers in the character of Richard Halliday. In the *Unchanging Quest* the same device is used with equal effectiveness. There is an obvious advantage in permitting a character who is indifferent to religion and has a bland confidence in all the hopeful theories which germinated in the 1890's to tell the story of the ghastly collapse of these hopes in the World War and its aftermath. Yet the very subtlety of this device is at times its greatest weakness. For it not infrequently encourages the impression that what Sir Philip is contending for is a return to the thin and conventional Christianity of the nineteenth century, a circumstance which gives a semblance of truth to the complaints not only of Catholics but of intelligent pagans. Yet he is in no sense a Victorian. A journalist of the new dispensation, someone has called him. For the stuff of his novels he has called upon his own wide and critical experience of men and events, not to extract from it the honey of romance (although he never neglects that), but to bring this experience to bear on the post-war confusion, and to propose adequate solutions for the problems.

* * *

But to return to Maurice Baring. The commonest impression about him is that he has given to our generation some of its best romances, and that he is, as a novelist, incurably romantic.

Without wishing wholly to deny the accuracy of this impression we must point out that it does not cover the whole truth about him. Mr. Baring is not a romantic novelist of the conventional sort who spins charming but unreal tales out of a glamorous fancy. His *Tinker's Leave,* to take an instance, might seem to have been done in this manner. Readers of his autobiography, *The Puppet Show of Memory,* however, could complain that Mr. Baring had given them this story before, not as fiction but as sober history. For many of the adventures of the hero, Miles Consterdine, are his own adventures lifted unblushingly and without notable alteration from the chapters that tell of his career as a war correspondent in Russia and Manchuria. Not fancy but memory is his chief artistic asset, and if his stories are romantic this is largely because his experience has been so.

The source book of all that Mr. Baring has written up to date is this autobiography, *The Puppet Show of Memory.* It explains many things about his novels. Why, for instance, they so frequently have for their background the glittering international social life of diplomatists, the nomadic rich and nobly born. This is the only life he knows, and as Frank C. Hanighen assures us, he writes about it as one who quite evidently belongs, with "none of the false gloss and snobbery for which Michael Arlen deserves the title of 'a butler in literature.'" It explains also the tireless delight his characters take in the arts, their numerous and highly diverting causeries on music, the stage, painting, ancient and modern letters. His own chief interests have lain here since childhood. Some of the most charming, illuminating, even profound of these discussions are those taken over in snatches from his autobiography. So much that is contained in his novels is to be found in the *Puppet Show* that enumeration is impossible. Let two more instances suffice. In 1897, while he was in the diplomatic service at Paris, a friend, Reggie Balfour, sent him a copy of an inscription found at Rome in the Church of St. John Lateran. *"Ci-gît Robert Peckhom, [it runs] anglais, Catholique, qui après la rupture de l'angleterre ne pouvant y vivre sans le foi et que, venu à Rome, y est mort ne pouvant y vivre sans patrie."* These brief but poignant lines Mr. Baring later expanded into his excellent historical novel, *Robert Peckham* (1930). One of his teachers at Eton, a Mr. Boucher, who, although unable to manage a division of boys, showed later his ability to do what he liked with the Bulgarians, becoming a national hero, provides the story for one of his most recent novels, *Friday's Business.*

"Memory, as someone has said, is the greatest of artists. It eliminates the unessential, and chooses with careless skill the sights and sounds and episodes that are best worth remembering and recording." So Mr. Baring begins his autobiography, and so, too, his memory has turned out to be for him the greatest artist, not only in this volume but in all his novels and most of his delightful essays. His first novel of importance did not appear until 1921 when he was 47 years old. Memory must be mellowed by time — another rule of his art to which he adheres so rigidly that all the experiences he has so far used belong to his pre-war period, that of his youth and early manhood. The possibilities of his war experiences, glamorous as their skeletonized recital makes them, have not yet been tapped except briefly as in *The Coat Without Seam* (1929).

Time seems to be just as important to his art as memory. His best material is that farthest away. The section of his *Puppet Show* that is the most charmingly done is that describing his babyhood and youth. And it is brief, almost too brief, one feels. Compton Mackenzie once remarked that if he were to put down all he remembered of his early days he would not yet be past his fifth year. In the diverse uses each of these men makes of the faculty of recall, we may see why one is known as a realistic, the other as a romantic novelist. Mr. Mackenzie's memory is photographic, accurate, comprehensive;

that of Mr. Baring lacks entirely this camera-like quality: it resembles more the eye and imagination of the painter, selecting, choosing with "careless skill."

He records that, as a boy, his favorite chapters in Lane Fleury's French History were those which began in this manner: *"Jean II, dit le bon, commença son regne par un assassinat,"* a predilection for homicide and the violent the years have stripped him of. In his novels he follows the advice given to Rene Bazin, "young man, never kill anyone!" Mr. Baring never kills anyone — except for love. The strength of this passion is such as sometimes to end in the death of his characters. But whether it issues in death or not it is almost inevitably the source of his best tragedy. We may see this in *Cat's Cradle,* his most finished novel, and at the same time that which most aptly illustrates what is meant by the statement that his stories have a Catholic background. Spontaneity and naturalness are the qualities of this Catholic element not only where it is found in Italian and Russian but also in its English manifestations. *Cat's Cradle,* moreover, has a Catholic moral, one based on a passage from Cervantes: "Love is too strong to be overcome by anything except flight, no mortal creature ought to be so presumptive as to stand the encounter, since there is need of something more than human, and indeed a heavenly force, to confront and vanquish that human passion." The Catholicism which the heroine, *Blanche Clifford,* finds after her tragic Italian marriage, supplies her with the "heavenly force" which enables her to confront and almost vanquish this and other human passions.

Mr. Baring's faith illuminates and inspires all that he has done. In happier days than our own his novels would be generally regarded as approximating closely the ideal in Catholic romantic fiction. But the critics clamor for propaganda, and Mr. Baring, they say, touches none of our pressing modern problems. No, the agony of world crisis finds little place in his stories. His Catholicism and that of his characters is serene, tranquil, uncombative — secure in the possession of centuries of culture, undismayed by the present, and of the future unafraid. He does not preach; but he teaches, discharging the function Aristophanes says belongs to the poets.

IV

Enid Dinnis, Francis Stuart, Viola Meynell, Cecily Hallack, Aodh de Blacam, Margaret Yeo, James B. Connolly, Frank Spearman, Edith O'Shaughnessy, Julian and Anne Green, Peadar O'Donnell, Helen C. White — the works of each of these at least would demand separate and detailed treatment in any summary of the modern Catholic novel aiming at completeness. Little more can be done here than to mention their names — a poor gesture at best. The novel deserves not a chapter but an entire book.

NOVELIST'S BIBLIOGRAPHY
Founders

JOHN OLIVER HOBBES (MRS. P. M. CRAIGIE) 1867–1906.
Thought, Vol. 6, pp. 282–295. Isabel Clarke.
WORKS
A School for Saints (New York: Stokes).
Robert Orange (New York: Stokes).
MRS. WILFRID WARD (1864–1932).
America — March 18, 1933, by Alfred Noyes.
Catholic World — 83:282–292.
Month — May, 1899 (contrasted with Mrs. Humphrey Ward).
WORKS
Not Known Here (Hutchinson).
One Poor Scruple (New York: Longmans).
The Job Secretary (New York: Longmans).
The Shadow of Mussolini (New York: Sheed & Ward).
Tudor Sunset (New York: Longmans, 1932).
ROBERT HUGH BENSON (1871–1914)
Benson, A. C., *Memoirs of a Brother* (London: Smith, Elden, 1915).
Martindale, C. C., S.J., *Life of R. H. Benson,* 2 volumes (New York: Longmans, 1916).
Month, December, 1918. (Compared with Huysmans.)

Month, September, 1915. (His works.)

Shuster, G. N., *Catholic Spirit in Modern English Literature,* Chapter XII (New York: Macmillan, 1922).

WORKS

By What Authority? (New York: Benziger.)
Initiation (New York: Kenedy).
Lord of the World (New York: Dodd, Mead).
Oddsfish (New York: Kenedy).
Richard Raynal (St. Louis: Herder).
The Coward (St. Louis: Herder).

MONTGOMERY CARMICHAEL

Catholic World, Vol. 103, p. 360.
American Catholic Quarterly, Vol. 47, p. 130.

WORKS

Christopher & Cressida (New York: Macmillan).
John William Walshe (New York: Dutton).

JOHN AYSCOUGH (MSGR. FRANCIS BICKERSTAFFE-DREW), 1858–1928.

America, August 11, 1928.

Braybrooke, P., *Some Catholic Novelists* (London: Burns, Oates, 1931), pp. 75–113.

WORKS

Fernando (New York: Kenedy).
Gracechurch (New York: Longmans).
Marotz (New York: Putnam).
San Celestino (New York: Putnam).

ERNEST J. OLDMEADOW

WORKS

Antonio (New York: Century).
Coggin (New York: Century).
The Hare (New York: Century).
Wildfang (London: Grant Richards).

SHEEHAN, CANON

Heuser, H. J., *Canon Sheehan of Doneraile* (New York: Longmans, 1918).

WORKS

Luke Delmege (New York: Longmans).
My New Curate (London: Art and Book Co.)
The Triumph of Failure (London: Burns, Oates).

Contemporary

SIR PHILIP GIBBS

Bookman, May, 1919 (Vol. XLIX), pp. 257–262.

Braybrooke, *Some Catholic Novelists.*
Living Authors (New York: Wilson), p. 146.
WORKS
Darkened Rooms (New York: Doubleday, Doran, 1929).
Heirs Apparent (New York: Doubleday, Doran).
The Age of Reason (New York: Doubleday, Doran, 1928).
The Cross of Peace (New York: Doubleday, Doran, 1934).
The Unchanging Quest (New York: Doubleday, Doran, 1926).
ENID DINNIS
America, 38:115.
WORKS
God's Fairy Tales (St. Louis: Herder, 1916).
Mr. Coleman, Gent. (New York: Kenedy, 1919).
The Anchorhold (St. Louis: Herder, 1922).
MARGARET YEO
WORKS
A King of Shadows (New York: Macmillan).
Uncertain Glory (London: Sheed & Ward).
FRANCIS STUART
Authors of Yesterday and Today.
WORKS
Pigeon Irish (New York: Macmillan, 1932).
CECILY HALLACK
WORKS
Mirror for Toby (London: Burns, Oates).
The Sunny Wall (London: Burns, Oates).
The Sword Blade of Michael (St. Louis: Herder).
PEADAR O'DONNELL
Living Authors, p. 303.
WORKS
Adrigoole (New York: Putnam).
The Way it Was With Them (New York: Putnam).
AODH DE BLACAM
WORKS
Holy Romans (Dublin: Maunsell).
The Flying Cromlech (New York: Century).
KATHLEEN NORRIS
Living Authors, p. 299.
WORKS
Certain People of Importance (New York: Doubleday, Doran).
Little Ships (New York: Doubleday, Doran).

Lucky Lawrences (New York: Doubleday, Doran).
Mother (New York: Macmillan).
JAMES B. CONNOLLY
  Queen's Work, January, 1933.
  WORKS
  Gloustermen (New York: Scribners).
  Coaster Captain (New York: Macy Masius).
  Out of Glouster (New York: Scribners).
  Tide Rips (New York: Scribners).
FRANK SPEARMAN
  Catholic Daily Tribune, February 12, 1933.
  Queen's Work, May, 1931.
  WORKS
  Nan of Music Mountain (New York: Grosset).
  Robert Kimberley (New York: Scribner).
  Spanish Lover (New York: Scribners, 1930).
  Whispering Smith (New York: Grosset).
EDITH O'SHAUGHNESSY
  WORKS
  A Viennese Medley (New York: Harcourt).
  Married Life (New York: Harcourt).
  Other Ways and Other Flesh (New York: Harcourt).
MAURICE BARING
  Bookman, August, 1932, p. 321.
  Commonweal, 10:386.
  Puppet Show of Memory (Little, Brown, 1922).
  WORKS
  Cat's Cradle (New York: Doubleday, 1926).
  Coat Without Seam (New York: Knopf, 1929).
  Passing By (London: Secker, 1921).
  Robert Peckham (New York: Knopf, 1930).
  Tinker's Leave (New York: Doubleday, 1927).
  When They Love (New York: Doubleday, 1928).
COMPTON MACKENZIE
  Bookman, 62:391–95.
  Bookman, 74:268.
  Catholic World, 115:733.
  WORKS
  Plasher's Mead (New York: Harper, 1915).
  The Altar Steps (New York: Doubleday, Doran, 1922).
  Parson's Progress (New York: Doubleday, Doran, 1923).

Heavenly Ladder (New York: Doubleday, Doran, 1924).
Rich Relatives (New York: Harper, 1921).
For Sale (New York: Doubleday, Doran, 1931).
Water on the Brain (New York: Doubleday, Doran, 1933).

SHEILA KAYE-SMITH
America, 44:339.
Johnson, R. B., *Some Contemporary Novelists* (women). (London: Parsons, 1920.)
Thought, 6:108–19.

WORKS
Sussex Gorse (New York: Dutton, 1916).
Tamarisk Town (New York: Dutton, 1919).
Joanna Godden (New York: Dutton, 1922).
The End of the House of Alard (New York: Dutton, 1923).
Shepherds in Sackcloth (New York: Dutton, 1930).
Summer Holiday (New York: Dutton, 1932).
Superstition Corner (New York: Harper, 1934).
Gallybird (New York: Harper, 1934).

OWEN FRANCIS DUDLEY
Queen's Work.

WORKS
Pageant of Life (New York: Longmans).
The Masterful Monk (New York: Longmans).
The Shadow on the Earth (New York: Longmans).

ETHEL COOK ELIOT
Queen's Work, November, 1933.

WORKS
Ariel Dances (New York: Little, Brown, 1931).
Green Doors (New York: Little, Brown, 1933).
Her Soul to Keep (New York: Macmillan, 1934).
Angels' Mirth (New York: Sheed & Ward, 1936).

CORKERY, DANIEL
WORKS
A Munster Twilight (Dublin: Talbot Press).
The Hounds of Banba (London: Fischer Unwin).
The Threshold of Quiet (Dublin: Talbot Press).

WHITE, HELEN C.
WORKS
A Watch in the Night (New York: Macmillan, 1934).
Not Built With Hands (New York: Macmillan, 1935).

7

Foreign Influences

I

The consideration of such co-operative works as the *Essays in Order* series or the *Monument to Saint Augustine* opens up an interesting and highly important phase of the Catholic Revival in English-speaking lands. Edited in England by Christopher Dawson and T. F. Burns, the *Essays in Order,* since their first appearance in 1931, have drawn chiefly for contributions on the leaders of thought and the arts in continental countries. We find such savants as Jacques Maritain (a Frenchman but now largely an international figure), the Germans, Peter Wust and Karl Schmidt, the Russian critic of culture, Nicholas Berdyaev, the Austrians, Rudolph Allers and Ida Coudenhove, appearing side by side with English writers like E. I. Watkin, Michael de la Bedoyère, and Christopher Dawson in an extended symposium on vital intellectual problems of the day. National boundaries and language barriers are leveled and one is given a glance at the mind of the Western Church at work, a cross section of the Catholic intellectual renaissance in Europe.

Several circumstances have co-operated in modern times to increase to an unprecedented point the influence of foreign thought on native letters. There is, for instance, the augmented sense of a community of interests and problems among the peoples of Western culture, induced largely by the war and the various international efforts at reconstruction that followed it. Scarcely less important is the facility with which translations are made and quickly printed and distributed throughout the world. The latest works of a Nobel Prize winning novelist like Sinclair Lewis or Sigrid Undset are published simultaneously in six or seven modern languages. Books like Papini's *Life of Christ* or Remarque's *All Quiet On the Western Front* become best sellers in lands where little Italian or German is spoken. No country today exists entirely on native literature — a statement which is truer perhaps of America than of any other nation.

This literary internationalism has been singularly beneficial to the English-speaking revival. It has swelled its products and increased its influence by distinguished contributions from foreign lands. The Catholic artistic and intellectual renaissance is, itself, an international and not a purely national phenomenon. It enjoys a healthy life in all European countries, in some of which, notably France, it is in a much more advanced and influential stage than in England. Thus the quest of domestic publishers for significant foreign books has resulted in the popularization of many Catholic artists who otherwise would have been known only to those with a mastery of several languages. From the Scandinavian countries have come Johannes Jörgensen and Sigrid Undset, from Germany Karl Adam, Gertrude Von le Fort, Erich Przywara, S.J., Romano Guardini, Waldemar Gurian; Enrica von Handel-Mazzetti from Austria, Papini from Italy, Martinez-Sierra from Spain; and from France, Paul Claudel, Maurice Blondel, François Mauriac, Etienne Gilson, Paul Bourget, Henri Bordeaux, and many others.

It should be pointed out that most of this popularization has been done by non-Catholic publishers — a disinterested tribute, if one is needed, to the distinguished caliber of the work produced by the foreign revivals. Among exclusively Catholic publishers Burns, Oates and Washbourne and Sheed & Ward have easily led the field in the quality of their foreign importations. The latter house deserves special mention. From its inception in 1926 it has caught the idea that the Catholic Revival is an international affair, and has presented it as such. We may instance a recent work, *A Monument to Saint Augustine,* in which Martin D'Arcy, S.J., Maurice Blondel, Christopher Dawson, Etienne Gilson, Jacques Maritain, C. C. Martindale, S.J., Erich Przywara, S.J., John Baptist Reeves, O.P., B. Roland-Gosselin, and E. I. Watkin unite in honoring St. Augustine on the fifteenth centenary of his death. Some of the best minds in Europe are here, philosophers, historians, theologians, litterateurs, lay and cleric. Seventy-five years ago such a symposium would have been impossible or if possible marred by sterile unanimity or complete disagreement and suspicion. Paris in the Middle Ages might have produced it or Oxford or Bologna in that healthy atmosphere of scholarly and free discussion that Newman longed for. Indeed to read one of the several symposia of this house is to return to that state of European society when all the West was one, united by a common language, a common religion, a common culture, and predominant over the rest of the world because of the excellence of that culture and its real and solid unity amid stimulating differences. Or rather let us say it is to go forward to that future state of the West when such conditions shall again prevail. For this is the common ideal of all Catholic artists and thinkers that unites them despite national and lingual differences — a united Christendom.

II

Although it would be possible to give a summary account of the Catholic renaissance in all of the major continental countries, stressing the principal writers of each, yet it seems advisable for several reasons to concentrate on the movement in France. In the first place, the revival there is unquestionably the most outstanding literary and intellectual event of our times; secondly, its influence on the English Revival has been the most profound; and finally its significance for all of Western civilization is such that it deserves a somewhat more lengthy treatment. For it must never be forgotten that the

French have a peculiar genius for spreading their ideas over the world and making them prevail; Paris is still the intellectual and artistic capital of the world. A strong Catholic renaissance in France means sooner or later a strong Catholic renaissance throughout the whole of Europe.

The Revival in France is, in another way, linked historically with that of England. It was on the evening of October 9, 1845, that Newman was received into the Church at Littlemore. Three days earlier — so runs the legend perpetuated in verse by Lionel Johnson — Ernest Renan left the seminary of Saint Sulpice to begin his career of poisoned apostasy. Both of these men founded Catholic revivals. Newman's conversion was the first in a long line of English litterateurs who have since turned to the Faith. And Renan's apostasy an ironic Providence turned into a reaction in favor of the Church which has been more fruitful of literary conversions than even Newman's entrance into the Fold. The historian of literature finds difficulty in explaining why from causes so diverse the same result should emerge. He can only say that, after many years of separation from the Church, it seemed to be the desire of God that in these latter days the artist should return home.

The fortunes of the Catholic Church reached perhaps their lowest level during the middle decades of the nineteenth century. Goethe, who was a wise man, did not see how she could survive the century. And nowhere did her plight seem more desperate than in the France of the Second Empire, the France of Ernest Renan, of Hippolyte Taine, of Flaubert, of Leconte de Lisle. Artists like Flaubert and Leconte de Lisle blasphemed her and wished to destroy her because, as they averred, she had destroyed the cult of Beauty. Scientists like Renan and Taine looked upon her as already dead, her doctrines discredited by scientific discoveries, her phase in the evolutionary cycle eclipsed by the new secularism which had explained away the supernatural and freed men from the tyranny of mystery. No book perhaps expressed more accurately the new dominant spirit than Renan's *L'Avenir de la Science.* Science was the new religion which was to replace Christianity and Renan its high priest who summed up in himself all the forces arrayed against the Church — an intellectual, an artist, a scientist, an apostle with a childlike belief in all the dogmas of the evolutionary hypothesis.

The principal cause of the Catholic Revival not only in France but throughout Europe was the death of this *scientisme.* It died first and most conclusively in France, not under the blows of Catholic apologists, but from the dissatisfaction and remorse of those who had accepted the new faith and had found it wanting. To a poet belongs the distinction of having sounded the first and most famous notes of revolt. Charles Baudelaire was not a Catholic, but in his veins coursed the blood of Christian France. He had tasted the fruit of human iniquity and he knew that it was bitter beyond the power of all the sugared platitudes of science to make it sweet. He knew that sin was a reality, the great reality, the last answer to the promise of a paradise here on earth. Disgusted with his own degradation and the stupidity of his generation, he sang in his *Les Fleurs du Mal* of things that men had superficially forgotten, of God and of His fatherly love for His children, of His willingness to forgive them their trespasses; of the transiency of earthly joy, of the hope of heaven and its many mansions waiting and prepared. It was an accent of humility that stood out in the chorus of haughty voices, a song touched with some love and confidence that found an echo in many another disillusioned soul. France stopped to listen. *"Baudelaire,"* says Paul Claudel, *"a chanté la seule passion que le dix-neuvième siècle pût éprouver avec sincérité, le remords."*

Baudelaire's reaction gave birth to a generation of *nostalgiques* who wandered aimlessly, but not without a certain grace, in search of relief from the intolerable boredom of their *milieux.* They had lost faith in Science and their wavering admiration for the Church was a thing almost entirely aesthetic.

But with the new generation, the generation of Coppée, of Verlaine, of Huysmans, of Brunetière, of Retté, of Bourget, of Léon Bloy, the tide definitely turned and turned to the Church.

The armies of Prussia had in the meantime swept down upon a demoralized France, captured Paris, and imposed a humiliating treaty on the French. Men began to ask what had brought about this deterioration in the national fiber. Among those who sought out the cause in a scientific way was a comparatively young man named Paul Bourget. Trained in a cold, objective method of investigation, a psychologist, a medical man, Bourget was well qualified to conduct a vigorous and impartial examination. Using the technique of a doctor in the presence of a very sick patient, he probed here and there in the body civic of France until he had found the cause of the universal relaxation of morals. His diagnosis was that it lay in the widespread acceptance and practice of the theories of the intellectual and artistic leaders of France during the decades immediately preceding the war with Prussia. He dealt with these men — Renan, Taine, Flaubert, Leconte de Lisle, Dumas *fils* — in a volume of criticism called *Essais de Psychologie Contemporaine*. Six years later, in 1889, appeared his powerful novel *Le Disciple*. Its thesis, boldly stated and vigorously exemplified, is that a writer or a teacher is responsible for the moral effect on his readers of his scientific and philosophical doctrines. For the first time the omnipotence of science and its right to the unrestricted promulgation of raw theories was challenged on a basis no Frenchman could ignore and by one who was both a scientist and an artist. Taine, who together with Renan had influenced Bourget's youth, was surprised and pained to find himself publicly censured in the character of *Adrian Sixte*. Talk was heard of the bankruptcy of science which increased as Bourget elaborated his thesis in a series of corrosive novels which have made him the foremost exponent of the *roman à thèse* of the day.

Among artists of a somewhat different type than Bourget who were won over to the Church, were Joris Karl Huysmans

and Paul Verlaine. Both of these men in their temperaments
and in the quality of their art are key-figures in nineteenth-cen-
tury literature. These mark the end of the old and the begin-
ning of the new. They are our first moderns. We have already
seen how "Science" dominated French thought during the
middle decades of the nineteenth century. Its influence on liter-
ature resulted in the birth of Naturalism and later in the found-
ing of the *école Parnassienne.* Huysmans was in some respects
more representative of the movement than even Zola. Indeed
in his *A Rebours* he outstripped in starkness and brutality any-
thing Naturalism had before or has since produced. He had
pushed the tenets of Naturalism to their ultimates, and Barbey
d'Aurevilly summed up the impasse with the remark that after
such a book nothing remains for the author except either to
blow out his brains or cast himself at the foot of the cross. Huys-
mans chose the latter alternative and to the scandal of the es-
thetes entered the Church. Across the dreary wastes of Natural-
ism his restless soul had sought for a Beauty which had always
escaped him. Now he found it in the plain chant, the liturgy,
the architecture, the monastic observances of the historic
Church of his fathers. To a disillusioned generation in which
spontaneous song was failing he opened up new possibilities
of beauty.

No less important in its effect on the renewal of artistic in-
spiration was the conversion, sincere but wavering, of Paul Ver-
laine. Nothing, it seemed, could kill the poetry in his soul, not
drunkenness, nor crime, nor debauch — he was guilty of all —
not even the *esthetique Parnassienne,* to which he adhered and
whose barren principles he observed in his early poetry. But as
he lay in prison for the attempted murder of his friend and
"dark angel," Arthur Rimbaud, and while the turgid vapors
of sin and absinthe lifted momentarily, leaving his vision free,
he composed the greatest French Catholic poem of the century.
In *la Sagesse* poetry joined hands with prayer and found its
soul again.

While the artists were exploring their newly discovered sanctuary, one of the most prominent intellectuals of the day was finding another door to the Church. Ferdinand Brunetière, editor of the authoritative *Revue de deux mondes* and distinguished critic, after a long journey, in the course of which he could say with Newman that he had never sinned against the light, became a militant convert and spent a good portion of the years remaining to him doing battle for the Church and developing a productive Catholic criticism. Brunetière, Bourget, Huysmans, Verlaine, and their associates bear the same relation to the French renaissance that Newman, Patmore, Hopkins, and de Vere do to the English. They are its founders. Interesting as they may be as converts they have a far greater significance as being the first to open the wall that separated the Church from the artist and the thinker and who laid the foundations for a literary movement of the first importance. We may, by way of concluding this rather bald enumeration of converts and founders, mention just one more figure who will bring us to the contemporary field.

More thoroughly than anyone else, Ernest Psichari symbolizes the changes that have taken place in France. He was the grandson of Ernest Renan, bore his name, and was raised in the master's own household where every effort was made to educate him according to the new evangel. Jacques Maritain has described how together they went to the *lycée* and later to the Sorbonne, mastering the ideas made popular by Renan and Taine. Psichari, with his unusual gifts of mind and heart, should have been the perfect realization of the Renanian ideal. But he was not. Fearful of the moral degradation toward which he was tending, he left the university without taking a degree, and fled to the army in search of a hard discipline which alone might save his manhood and self-respect. He found something else. During the silent night watches in the deserts of Africa he discovered in profound meditation the God whom his famous forebear had lost.

A year before the war he became a Catholic. He was filled
with a desire to repair the blasphemy of his grandfather and to
do homage to the God who had renewed his youth. It was a
beautiful but brief career. Like his friend Charles Péguy he was
shot down in the early weeks of the war. He had, as he says of
a character in his *l'Appel des Armes* taken "the part of his
fathers against his father," the part of ancient Catholic France
— a phrase which may be applied to the entire generation of
which he is the symbol.

III

The authoritative historian of the *Renouveau Catholique,*
the Abbé J. Calvet, has said that, taking into account certain
exceptions, notable but rare, there are today in France just two
types of literature — "the sensual literature, established for in-
dustrial exploitation, and Catholic literature, which has the
honor of representing art." The revolution in letters effected by
the revival, he adds, has been more complete than that of Ro-
manticism and more profound than the realistic revolution or
the symbolistic revolution. Despite the prolific nature of its out-
put it maintains a high level of art. Moreover, its art is Cath-
olic art as we may see from a summary examination of its work
in the various fields.

The French Catholic novel, as understood by a Bourget, a
Bazin, a Baumann, a Bordeaux, a Mauriac, represents an en-
tirely new and quite lofty concept of realism in fiction. Realism,
it will be remembered, was the dominant note in French liter-
ature during the greater part of the last century. Its ideal was
ostensibly "to see life steadily and to see it whole"; but in the
hands of a Zola, a Flaubert, a de Maupassant it not infrequently
became a myopic, truncated realism which saw life steadily
enough, but failed to see it whole. The baseness of mankind
was there — sin and pollution, epilepsy, disease, and running
sores — but the angel in man was not. Logically it had to be so,

for the iron dogmas of materialism excluded the spiritual and made man a beast.

Freed from these restraints Catholic novelists have aspired to a complete realism in which no real aspect of life and human nature would be neglected. They see in man an animal nature with real propensities toward bestiality, but they also perceive an element which is above the animal and destined to dominate it. Furthermore, to put it quite simply, the complete realist recognizes in man a creature redeemed by the blood of Christ, a child of God, living a supernatural life of grace and destined for beatitude, a being, human and divine. "Infinity itself," observes Emile Baumann, "converges towards the puny spark of our life. . . ."

The debate, sometimes heard in America, about the possibility of the specifically Catholic novel has been silenced here once and for all: Baumann's *l' Immolé,* Mauriac's *Mystère Frontenac,* the *Lazarine* of Bourget, almost the whole of the late René Bazin's work, the novels of Brillant, Renaudin, Cazin, and others place beyond doubt not only the possibility of a Catholic novel but its inherent artistic greatness.

Although the French can point to several contemporary masterpieces, still much of the work in the field of Catholic fiction must be regarded as experimental. The slow and sometimes exasperating evolution of François Mauriac, whose most recent books, *le Noeud de Viperes* and *le Mystère Frontenac* stamp him as one of the greatest of French novelists, is a good example. Most of his earlier work is not Catholic at all, and some of it morally dangerous to any but hardened readers. The work of pioneering has not progressed calmly, and the problems growing out of the treatment of human passion have been the cause of much bitter controversy. While the final word on this point has not yet been uttered, it is not too much to say that most of the pioneering work is over, and that the future of the French Catholic novel is assured.

After the novel, biography holds the attention of contem-

porary readers. Without attempting to survey the whole field
we may mention as outstanding the imposing collection,
Grands Coeurs, the more recent *Les Maîtres d'une generation*
and the *Chefs de file.* In the first have appeared Bazin's *Pie X,*
Geraud's *Bossuet,* Dies' *Platon,* the *Thomas d'Aquin* of Sertil-
langes, Goyau's *d'Ozanam,* Weygand's *Turenne,* and others of
equal note. The *Maîtres d'une generation* is still in its infancy.
Already have appeared the biographies of the great bishop and
promoter of international peace, Monsignor Julien, and of
George Fonsegrive, a philosopher too little known outside of
France. The Canon Alleaume and Paul Archambault are the
respective authors. Among the other "masters" whom the edi-
tors intend to commemorate are Victor Delbos, Ollé-Laprune,
Léon Harmel, Monsignor Batiffol, and Henri Lorin. Only one
volume has appeared in the newest collection *Chefs de file,*
Victor Geraud's *Ferdinand Brunetière.* It sets a high standard.

Without wishing to minimize the importance of this phase
of French biography there is another of greater importance —
an achievement unique in the history of letters — I mean the
popularization of the lives of the saints. The saints, of course,
have had biographers before, devout men who set down the
facts in their lives for the edification of the faithful or the en-
richment of history. Never before, however, have litterateurs in
considerable numbers attempted to catch the sublime beauty of
these lives and to represent it with the same mastery of the art
they have exhibited in secular departments. The painters and
the sculptors have done this in the past but not the men of
letters. Why this source of literary inspiration has been neg-
lected for so long it is impossible to say, for the stuff of great
literature is certainly there. We must be content with the fact.
A number of first-rate writers, seeking to rejuvenate a jaded
literature rapidly losing all sense of the heroic, discovered the
saints. Louis Bertrand, the recognized master of the *genre,* con-
tributed two classics in *Saint Augustin* and *Sainte Thérèse,*
Baumann wrote a penetrating study of St. Paul, Paul Renaudin

gave us his *Saint Vincent de Paul,* Bernoville, his *Sainte Thé-
rèse de l'Enfant-Jesus,* and André Bellessort, his *Saint François
Xavier;* a group of Catholic academicians paid homage to the
national heroine St. Jeanne d'Arc, in addition to such other in-
dividual efforts as Bordeaux's *Saint François de Sales* and Baz-
in's *Charles de Foucauld.* The saints have truly, as Paul Don-
coeur put it, conquered the French Academy. Eight years,
roughly speaking, have passed since the new hagiography made
its appearance. Since that time there have come from the presses
of France a constant stream of saints' lives. We are perhaps too
close to the phenomenon to analyze accurately the influence of
the new hagiography on contemporary literature. We may
safely say, however, that modern biography has gained in
beauty and that the idea of the heroic has been temporarily
salvaged.

IV

Since the early and romantic part of the nineteenth century,
there has never been totally absent from French poetry a Chris-
tian note. Too often, however, this accent has been artificial
and merely decorative, the homage of a dilettante or dreamer
to a beauty not completely understood. That Catholicism was
a source of artistic inspiration, Chateaubriand had shown to
a generation still influenced by Voltaire; but in his demonstra-
tion this great Romantic had attached himself to surface beau-
ties, neglecting the richer realities that grow out of Christianity
taken as a philosophy of life.

The Catholics of the modern renaissance have progressed far
past the dilettantism of Chateaubriand and other Romantics.
The poets, and what is true of the poets is also to be predicated
of the workers in other departments, have learnt the first lesson
of the Catholic revival everywhere, that in order to hymn the
beauties of the Christian order one must live as a Christian and
a Catholic, not partially or spasmodically but continually and

Catholic Literary Revival

completely, in full union with the soul of the Church by participation in her sacramental life. The result, as far as poetry is concerned, has been that productive union of prayer and poetry foreshadowed by Verlaine's *La Sagesse*. One finds it in Paul Claudel, in Maurice Brillant, in Louis le Cardonnel, in Marie Noël, in Camille Melloy, in Francis Jammes, in Henriette Charasson. It is the characteristic note of the new poetry.

If one must select the poet who realizes most completely in his work the ideal of the French renaissance, that man would be Paul Claudel. Despite his enigmatic utterance — Claudel was early in life initiated into the secrets of symbolism by Mallarmé himself — he has caught the all-prevailing sense of the supernatural as has no other French poet with the possible exception of Louis le Cardonnel. A reader unacquainted with Catholicism finds him more obscure than a sibyl and as tantalizing; even intelligent Catholics are frequently unable completely to penetrate the double veil of profound content and eccentric technique: but no reader however unsympathetic or unbelieving fails to feel that in reading Claudel he is close to the essential mystery of life. His lyrical dramas have enjoyed a wide popularity in America principally among non-Catholics. In the face of much adverse criticism Claudel has remained doggedly faithful to his Christian symbolism. Outside France he is perhaps the best known of all modern French poets; and at home his example has been widely followed. Prominent among his disciples are Germaine Maillet, Serge Barrault, and Henriette Charasson, whose *Heures du Foyer*, done in Claudelian *versets*, is a beautiful and highly original revelation of a Christian mother's soul.

Poetic output has been abundant, but for the most part it falls short of classic greatness. Only two or three poets have thus far shown that sustained power essential to the classic. Claudel, Jammes, and Marie Noël, among the living poets, will certainly find a place in the future histories of literature. Our generation is notoriously unsympathetic to poetry. The wonder is that we have poets at all and those we have perhaps do best to speak, like Claudel, in parables.

This lack of sympathy is the chief reason why there has not been a brilliant renaissance of Catholic drama. The writers are there in force, Poizat, Des Granges, Claudel, Montier, Alibout, and the delightful and irrepressible Henri Ghéon, their desks covered with plays — Ghéon has written forty or more — but the large theaters, with one or two notable exceptions, will not produce them. They have their reasons, none of which have anything to do with the question of art. The most important is that the modern theater is a commercial enterprise, entirely dependent on the caprice of a public which must be amused or shocked. As long as this highly conventional situation exists, a Catholic drama is impossible.

Meanwhile the Catholic dramatists are doing their best under the adverse circumstances — in schools and parishes their plays are presented before small but select audiences. Recently, however, a new play of Ghéon's, *Le Mystère de l'Invention de la Croix,* was given at Tancrimont in Belgium, a famous spot of pilgrimage, before a crowd of six thousand. The spiritual effect on the audience was described as immense. Sometime later, three presentations were given at Brussels before an audience composed of the city's élite, and with the same effect as that obtained before the pilgrims. During Easter week of 1933 the *Vie Catholique* sponsored three performances of two new plays by René Jacquet and on each occasion the hall was filled. After several more such ventures the theaters of Paris may be induced to experiment with the new Catholic drama.

They will find it Catholic indeed. The lives of the saints, legends current in the provinces, Catholic history and dogma, provide the material. The treatment is characterized by deep reverence and vivid faith, joined with a delicate and unobtrusive art. The effect on the spectator, on whose part a certain reverence is also required, is spiritual and profound. It is not inconceivable that the new Christian theater, as understood by

Ghéon especially, may not only save the dying drama but also become a decisive factor in winning the masses to Christ.

v

No literary movement, at least in the beginning, can dispense with criticism. The way that leads to mediocrity is so easy, the temptation to pander to the instincts of the crowd so seductive, the tendency to excess in one form or another so prevalent that a high level of art cannot be maintained without the discipline of a healthy and articulate aesthetic.

Beginning with Paul Bourget's *Essais de Psychologie Contemporaine* we can trace the evolution of a modern Catholic critical movement which has grown tremendously since the war. Today it represents the most powerful and independent body of thought in France. Restricting ourselves to literary criticism, we find in the first rank, the late Henri Brémond, Paul Archambault, Louis de Mondadon, Alphonse de Parvillez, Henri Massis, René Johannet, J. Calvet, Pierre Dumaine, Maurice Brillant, and Jacques Maritain. The list might easily be extended, but this partial enumeration will give some idea of the richness and variety of the field.

The chant that arises from this chorus of critics is not one of unanimous praise and benediction. Criticism of this sort seems inevitable in a closely knit literary movement. But France has avoided it. The sharp differences in individual judgment are so frequent and marked as occasionally to hide the fundamental philosophical unity that is certainly there. Maritain and Massis, for instance, are violently anti-Romantic, while the dicta of Brémond and Archambault are quoted throughout Europe on the side of the much-bated Romantics.

Calvet in his *d'une Critique Catholique* gives as the two outstanding qualities of this criticism, probity of spirit and courage. In it we find no vacillating subjectivism, impotent alike to appraise or judge, no obsequious gyrations in the presence of publishers or popular writers or fellow Catholics. Paul Archambault did not hesitate to censure Maritain in *Jeunes Maîtres,* although Maritain was a popular figure, a Catholic, and a friend. Criticism of this sort is criticism in the best sense of the Horatian definition, and perfectly invaluable to individual writers and the whole movement.

It is owing in no small degree to the vigor of the Catholic philosophical revival in France that this body of criticism has been made possible. Back of the literary critics, stand the philosophers. In the pronouncements of Henri Massis we discover the ideas of Maritain, in the work of Archambault we see the influence of Maurice Blondel. The abundance and variety which characterize the criticism is a reflection of the abundance and variety of contemporary philosophic thought. There is Maritain in the direct line of the strict Thomistic tradition, Blondel more open to modern contributions, Sertillanges and Chevalier, absorbed in the problems of knowledge, not convinced that St. Thomas has spoken the last word, and Mareschal, student of mysticism and Kant, Gilson, the great historian, honored by the Sorbonne with the newly created chair of medieval philosophy for his pioneering work in this field. Many others there are, too, whose concerted action has made Scholasticism a popular philosophy, realizing the dream of Leo XIII scarcely thirty years after his death.

Nothing has yet been said of the work of Monsignor Batiffol and Léonce de Grandmaison in the field of comparative religion, of Goyau's efforts in sociology, of Brémond's brilliant accomplishments in history, or the work of men like Charles Le Nôtre and Louis Madelin. We must pass over, too, the various reviews and organizations, so characteristic of the *Renouveau Catholique,* which solidify the effort and give it corporate unity.

Belloc has somewhere said that the course which Western civilization will take after the post-war crisis has passed depends to a large extent on developments in France. "For it is

an invariable rule in the history of our race that the spiritual
direction of the Gauls should be an index of general move-
ments outside its boundaries." It is this that gives a vital and
dramatic interest to the contemporary French renaissance, not
only in letters and philosophy, but in every department of life.
What the future may hold no one can tell. But the promise
that the Church and civilization may yet triumph is great.

BIBLIOGRAPHY*

BAZIN, RENÉ
America, October 8, 1932.
WORKS
Davidée Birot (New York: Scribner, 1912).
Those of His Own Household (New York: Devin-Adair, 1914).
The Barrier (New York: Benziger, 1919).
Children of Alsace (New York: Brentano, 1915).
Pierre and Joseph (New York: Harper, 1920).
The Nun (New York: Scribner, 1908).
Redemption (New York: Scribner, 1909).
A Blot of Ink (New York: Cassell).
Juniper Farm (New York: Macmillan, 1928).
Magnificat (London: Burns, Oates, 1932).
Pius X (London: Sands, 1928).
Charles Foucauld: hermit and explorer (New York: Benziger, 1931).
BORDEAUX, HENRY
Catholic World, Vol. 110, pp. 471–5.
WORKS
The Woolen Dress (New York: Duffield, 1912).
Footprints Beneath the Snow (New York: Duffield, 1913).
Fear of Living (New York: Dutton, 1913).
The House (New York: Duffield, 1914).
The Awakening (New York: Dutton, 1914).
The House That Died (New York: Harper, 1922).
Which was the Greater Love (New York: Como Publishing Co.,
    1930).
Georges Guynemer (New Haven: Yale University Press, 1918).
Palestine (New York: Brentano, 1928).
St. Francis de Sales (New York: Longmans, 1929).
The Gardens of Omar (New York: Dutton, 1924).

*Only English translations of foreign works are listed here.

BOURGET, PAUL
Bookman (New York), Vol. 73, pp. 273–83.
Living Age, Vol. 304, pp. 301–2.
WORKS
The Night Cometh (New York: Putnam, 1914).
The Gaol (New York: Brentano, 1924).
BRÉMOND, HENRI
Saturday Review of Literature, June 28, 1924, pp. 661–2.
Dublin Review, Vol. 183, pp. 161–75.
Commonweal, November 17, 1933, p. 70.
WORKS
Prayer and Poetry (London: Burns, Oates, 1927).
Sir Thomas More (London: Duckworth, 1904).
A Literary History of Religious Thought in France (2 vols.) (New York: Macmillan, 1928–30.)
The Thundering Abbot (New York: Sheed & Ward, 1930).
CLAUDEL, PAUL
Living Authors, p. 71.
The Living Age, November, 1932, p. 225.
Madaule, Jacques, *Paul Claudel* (New York: Sheed & Ward, 1932).
WORKS
The Tidings Brought to Mary (drama). (London: Chatto, 1916.)
The Hostage: a drama (New Haven: Yale University Press, 1917).
Tête-d'or: a play (New Haven: Yale University Press, 1919).
The City: a play (New Haven: Yale University Press, 1920).
The Book of Christopher Columbus: a lyrical drama (New Haven: Yale University Press, 1930).
The Satin Slipper (drama). (New York: Sheed & Ward, 1931.)
Three Poems of the War (New Haven: Yale University Press, 1919).
Letters to a Doubter (New York: Boni, 1927).
Ways and Crossways (collected essays). (New York: Sheed & Ward, 1933.)
GHÉON, HENRI
Catholic World, Vol. 130, pp. 1–12.
WORKS
The Marvellous History of St. Bernard (play). (New York: Sheed & Ward, 1924.)
The Marriage of St. Francis (play). (New York: Sheed and Ward.)
The Comedian (play). (New York: Sheed & Ward, 1927.)
The Secret of the Curé d'Ars (New York: Sheed & Ward, 1929).
The Secret of the Little Flower (New York: Sheed & Ward, 1934).

St. Germaine of the Wolf Country (New York: Sheed & Ward, 1933).

MARITAIN, JACQUES

Bookman, September, 1929, pp. 1–14.

Living Authors, p. 251.

WORKS

Three Reformers (New York: Sheed & Ward, 1928).

Prayer and Intelligence (with Raissa Maritain). (New York: Sheed, 1928.)

Art and Scholasticism (New York: Sheed & Ward, 1930).

The Things That Are Not Caesars (New York: Sheed & Ward, 1930).

Religion and Culture (New York: Sheed & Ward, 1931).

The Angelic Doctor (New York: Sheed & Ward, 1931).

Theonas: conversations of a sage (New York: Sheed & Ward, 1933).

PSICHARI, ERNEST

WORKS

Soldier's Pilgrimage, with introduction by Paul Bourget (London: Melrose, 1927).

MAURIAC, FRANÇOIS

America, September 2, 1933, p. 519.

Bookman, January, 1931, p. 466.

Living Authors, p. 258.

WORKS

Maundy Thursday (London: Burns, Oates, 1932).

The Family (New York: Covici, 1930).

Viper's Tangle (New York: Sheed & Ward, 1933).

JÖRGENSEN, JOHANNES

Ave Maria, Vol. 30, pp. 225–8.

Missionary, Vol. 44, pp. 331–3.

WORKS

Jörgensen: an autobiography (2 vols.). (New York: Sheed & Ward, 1929.)

Lourdes (New York: Longmans, 1914).

Saint Francis of Assisi (New York: Longmans, 1912).

War Pilgrim (New York: Longmans, 1917).

Don Bosco (London: Burns, Oates, 1934).

UNDSET, SIGRID

American Review, January, 1934, p. 316.

Living Authors, p. 410.

WORKS

Kristin Lavransdatter: The Bridal Wreath, The Mistress of Husaby, The Cross (New York: Knopf, 1927).

Master of Hestviken: The Ax, The Snake Pit, In the Wilderness, The
Son Avenger (New York: Knopf, 1928–30).
The Wild Orchid (New York: Knopf, 1931).
The Burning Bush (New York: Knopf, 1932).
Christmas and Twelfth Night (New York: Longmans, 1932).
Stages on the Road (New York: Knopf, 1934).

PAPINI, GIOVANNI
Living Authors, p. 314.
WORKS
Gog (New York: Harcourt, 1930).
Laborers in the Vineyard (New York: Sheed & Ward, 1930).
Life and Myself (New York: Brentano, 1930).
Life of Christ (New York: Harcourt, 1923).
Saint Augustine (New York: Harcourt, 1930).

ADAM, KARL
Catholic World, September, 1933, pp. 658–666.
WORKS
The Spirit of Catholicism (New York: Macmillan, 1930).
Christ and the Western Mind (New York: Sheed & Ward, 1930).
Christ, Our Brother (New York: Sheed & Ward, 1931).
Saint Augustine (New York: Sheed & Ward, 1932).
The Son of God (New York: Sheed & Ward, 1933).

GUARDINI, ROMANO
Catholic World, September, 1933, pp. 658–666.
WORKS
The Spirit of the Liturgy (New York: Sheed & Ward, 1929).
Sacred Signs (New York: Sheed & Ward, 1930).

* * *

Baumann, Emile, *Saint Paul* (New York: Harcourt, 1929).
Bernoville, Gaetan, *Guy de Fontgalland* (London: Burns, Oates, 1934).
Bertrand, Louis, *Saint Augustine* (New York: Appleton, 1914).
——— *Louis XIV* (New York: Longmans, 1928).
Bibesco, Princess Marthe, *Crusade for the Anemone* (New York: Macmillan, 1932).
Chevalier, Jacques, *Pascal* (New York: Sheed & Ward, 1930).
Dimnet, Ernest, *The Art of Thinking* (New York: Simon & Schuster, 1928).
——— *What We Live By* (New York: Simon & Schuster, 1932).
Franc-Nohain, *Life's an Art* (New York: Holt, 1930).

For Joan of Arc, an act of homage by nine members of the French Academy (London: Sheed, 1930).

Gasquet, Marie, *Nais* (New York: Sheed & Ward, 1929).

Goyau, Georges, *Cardinal Mercier* (New York: Longmans, 1926).

Gurian, Waldemar, *Bolshevism, Theory and Practice* (New York: Sheed & Ward, 1932).

Handel-Mazzetti, Enrica von, *Jesse and Maria* (New York: Holt, 1931).

Klein, Abbe Felix, *Diary of a French Army Chaplain* (London: Melrose, 1919).

—— *Madeline Semer* (New York: Macmillan, 1927).

—— *Jesus and His Apostles* (New York: Longmans, 1932).

Kuhnelt-Leddihn, Erik M. R. von, *Gates of Hell* (New York: Sheed & Ward, 1934).

Lavedan, Henri, *Heroic Life of St. Vincent de Paul* (New York: Longmans, 1929).

Le Fort, Gertrude von, *The Veil of Veronica* (New York: Sheed & Ward, 1932).

—— *The Song of the Scaffold* (New York: Holt, 1933).

—— *The Pope from the Ghetto* (New York: Sheed and Ward, 1934).

Monceau, Paul, *St. Jerome* (New York: Sheed & Ward, 1933).

Massis, Henri, *Defense of the West* (New York: Harcourt, 1928).

Martinez-Sierra, G., *The Cradle Song and Other Plays* (New York: Dutton, 1929).

Ponelle, Louis, *St. Philip Neri* (New York: Sheed & Ward, 1932).

The Life of the Church: Rousselot, Huby, Grandmaison, D'Arcy (New York: Sheed & Ward, 1932).

Silvestre, Charles, *Aimee Villard, Daughter of France* (New York: Macmillan, 1928).

Verkade, D. W., *Yesterdays of An Artist Monk* (New York: Kenedy, 1930).

A Monument to Saint Augustine, ed. by Christopher Dawson (New York: Sheed & Ward, 1931).

The Essays in Order series includes the following books all published by Sheed & Ward: *Religion and Culture,* by Jacques Maritain; *Crisis in the West,* by Peter Wust; *Christianity and the New Age,* by Christopher Dawson; *The Russian Revolution,* by Nicholas Berdyaev; *The Necessity of Politics,* by Karl Schmidt; *The Drift of Democracy,* by Michael de la Bedoyère; *The Bow in the Clouds,* by E. I. Watkin; *The Modern Dilemma,* by Christopher Dawson; *The Nature of Sanctity,* by Ida Coudenhove; *The New Psychologies,* by Rudolph Allers; *Form in Modern Poetry,* by Herbert Read; *Paul Claudel,* by Jacques Madaule; and *Virgil, the Father of the West,* by Theodor Haecker.

8

The Free Press and its Prose
Conclusion

I

There is no department of Catholic literature that labors under a wider misunderstanding than journalism. It is not appreciated, because it is not understood. And a sign of that misunderstanding is this: that the Catholic young man or woman in this country who wishes to appear advanced and emancipated beyond his fellows, affects to be a close reader of the *New Republic* or the *New Masses,* rarely of *Commonweal* or *America.* He may tell you he finds the first two journals better edited and better written than the latter two. Perhaps he does. But that he gives this as his reason for preferring one to the other shows that he does not even appreciate the *New Republic* and the *New Masses* at their true worth, and that he has a profound misunderstanding of the value and function of the Free Press, to which class all four journals belong.

The term "Free Press" is here used to designate a type of journalism which has been called in a book of that title "the most important intellectual phenomenon of our time." This little book or pamphlet (for such it is) first appeared in 1918. It is a classic of its kind. No clearer or more intelligent statement of the case for the Free Press has since appeared. Anyone wishing to understand the place in the social economy not only of the Catholic Free Press, but of the Jewish, Communistic, Socialistic as well, must consult it. It is a radical book and daring: not specifically by reason of the language it uses in damn-

375

ing the modern Capitalist Press — that may be heard daily in
any of those places where journalists congregate — but in this,
that its author, Hilaire Belloc, has dared to put these common-
places into print.

"I propose to discuss in what follows," he says, "the evils of
the great modern Capitalist Press, its function in vitiating and
misinforming opinions and in putting power into ignoble
hands; its correction by the formation of small independent or-
gans, and the probably increasing effect of these last."

The author first gives a brief historical account of the origin
of modern journalism which, he insists, was concurrent with
the rise of modern Capitalism and Finance, "the domination
of the State by private capitalists, who, taking advantage of the
necessities of the State, fix an increasing mortgage on the State
and work perpetually for fluidity, anonymity, and irresponsibil-
ity in their arrangements." Not only did journalism grow up
with these two forces but it has served them.

As an historian he must point out certain evils inherent in
the nature of the press even in its primitive state and before its
control by the capitalists. It was a substitute for the oral testi-
mony to the truth of an event, and as such made a man rely
for his news on one rather than a number of independent oral
witnesses. Moreover the opinions it disseminated were presented
"in a sort of impersonal manner that impresses with peculiar
power because it bears a sort of detachment, as though it came
from some authority too secure and superior to be questioned."
In the early press, say, of the eighteenth century, these evils
were counteracted by the existence of a number of such organs
representing diverse interests whose news and opinions could
be balanced one against the other and a fair measure of accuracy
obtained.

But with the development of Capitalism in the nineteenth
century these disadvantages were accentuated. For "the devel-
opment of Capitalism meant that a smaller and yet a smaller

number of men commanded the means of production and distribution whereby could be printed and set before a large circle a news sheet fuller than the old model." This, of course, meant a decrease in the number of independent journals, which tendency was still further accentuated by the entrance of another important element, also Capitalistic in origin — *"subsidy through advertisement."* Revenue from this source made it possible for a man to print a paper at a cost of two cents and sell it for one cent at a substantial profit. The value of a newspaper or journal as a medium for advertisement and the rate it might charge for its space, depended upon the number of people it reached. Circulation was the thing. And since it cost money to build up a large circulation and maintain it, journalism came to be more and more what it is today, a hazardous commercial enterprise, involving great expense, great risk, but also great gain. It tended to fall into the hands of a very few rich men, not a few of whom were of base origins and capacities, plungers and financial gamblers. The old type of poor but fighting journalist disappears and in his room come men who look upon journalism as a business enterprise to be operated not for the commonweal but for profits.

Another result was the control exercised by the advertisers over the proprietors. They support the paper, hence they might demand, at the penalty of refusing their ads to the journal that failed to obey, that no opinions or news offensive to Capitalism or their particular industry be printed. Belloc is of the opinion this was not so important an element since the newspaper proprietors, being themselves capitalists and frequently holding stock in the legitimate or illegitimate enterprises advertised, would not be inclined to print such news or opinion anyway.

The most important result was the increasing impossibility, on an economic basis, of an independent, non-capitalist press, since the public had been educated to expect for one cent what it cost two cents to make — the difference being made up by ad-

vertising subsidy. And from this the growing control of all
sources of news by one class — those who had money for such
an enterprise — the capitalists.

Now, the dangers of such a monopoly are obvious. Politically
it tends to put a disproportionate amount of power in the hands
of a very few men, and these rich men, whose influence in a
democratic society is always too great. Belloc contends that the
"top-heavy plutocracy" of England is ruled by a few wealthy
newspaper-owning families, who actually govern the politi-
cians by their control over vast areas of public opinion, and
govern abominably. No such general statement can be pred-
icated of conditions in the United States. Yet all the evils of the
Capitalist Press are present here and at work. If our large news-
papers and magazines do not actually govern the nation, they
set its moral tone and set it quite low. In the mad scramble for
circulation and the increased advertising rates this involves,
there are few things in sex presentation or crime exploitation
that they have not stooped to, short of what would exclude
them from the mails.

In general, however, it is true to say that we have seen in
this country only in restricted districts the major disadvantages
of the Capitalist Press. They are waiting for us in the future
in tendencies, such as the merger orgy, that are on the increase
today. For instance, it is evident to all observers that the old
type of independent, fearless organ of public opinion, small
but powerful in its sincerity, run by a man of journalistic rather
than commercial antecedents, has all but disappeared from
among us. Its place has been taken by a smooth-running, effi-
cient news-gathering machine, operated by those whose chief
interest is in the business office where the real power resides. Old
journalists wax sentimental over this change that has occurred
in their lifetimes. The young ones accept it sullenly. Those of
them who are prudent do not trouble their souls about what
seems to them something inevitable. They settle down to work
for the new thing as they would for any other public-utility

corporation. But there are those to whom this debased position of the journalist is a constant source of irritation. These — and they are in the minority — make their dissatisfaction known in a cynical attitude, which, I think, is nowhere better expressed than in that ironic masterpiece of Cecil Chesterton's, "The Ballade of Professional Pride":

You ask me how I manage to consume
So many beers and whiskeys multiplied;
Why I can stand as rigid as a broom
  While others gently sway from side to side;
Why from the phrase "Ferriferous Vermicide"
My tongue, all unembarrassed, does not shrink?
— Hear then my city's boast, my calling's pride:
It was in Fleet Street that I learnt to drink.

Not mine the glory. From the narrow tomb
Call the strong voices of dead men that plied
Their starving trade along the Street of Doom,
And on its heedless walls were crucified:
Yet grasped a little laughter ere they died
Drowned deep in dole and debt and printer's ink,
And with proud note above their torments cried:
"It was in Fleet Street that I learnt to drink."

ENVOI
(To a newspaper proprietor):

Prince, you have taken bribes, blackmailed, and lied.
Your horrid vices to the heavens stink.
Yet by this thing our craft is justified —
It was in Fleet Street that I learnt to drink.

II

Belloc's pamphlet is something more than just a thorough-going damnation of the Capitalist Press. He speaks hopefully of a widespread reaction to its abuses. "Now to every human evil of a political sort that has appeared in history there comes a term and reaction." There has arisen side by side with the Capitalist Press a certain force called the "Free Press," which, he says, after surveying its progress in England, France, and America, seems to him "the chief intellectual phenomenon of our times."

Belloc speaks not only of the Catholic Free Press but of the Communist, the Socialist, the Jewish, and all other manifestations of this effort to apply a corrective to the misinformation and stereotyped opinions of the official press. Perhaps I should turn this statement about and say that he speaks not only of the Jewish, Communist, and Socialist Free Press but of the Catholic as well. For there are not a few who will consider a Socialist weekly an important intellectual phenomenon, but who will see no such significance in a Catholic weekly. And why? They do not understand the specific value of the Free Press; and they invariably betray this misunderstanding by giving the wrong reason for preferring the Socialist weekly to the Catholic weekly, viz., that one is better edited than the other. Now, it is well to remark that the man who says this sort of thing is more frequently than not deficient in journalistic taste. The fact is, the best Catholic journals are in no way inferior in this respect to other representatives of the Free Press, and both are, as a rule, below the level of the best capitalist organs.

But there are cases where his judgment is true. Even here, however, he has given the wrong reason for his preference. If he understood the nature of the Free Press, its function, the particular value of that function as well as the difficulties under which it labors in the discharge of it, the inferior journalism of the one would make him prefer it to the other. It would keep continually before him the source of this deficiency, the grave economic handicap, namely, that comes from lack of advertising subsidy. Frequently ads are refused it because of the opinions it holds and expresses. More frequently because of its lack of circulation, which is itself an impediment arising from the nature of its fight against the Capitalist Press. For, as has been pointed out, the Capitalist Press by reason of its huge revenue from advertising is able to sell cheaply what it cost much more to make, and it has educated the public to expect this sort of "donation." As long as the public continues to set a higher value on "journalism" than upon that other thing which it is the peculiar function of the Free Press to give, this situation will persist.

That other thing is truth. The Free Press everywhere has arisen as a protest against either distortion or active boycott of certain types of news and opinions. Hence the first and most fundamental reason that must be given for supporting it, is that it supplies the needed corrective to this sort of misinformation. It gives truth.

The driving force behind this protest has been, in the main, religious, but also, Belloc adds, "certain racial enthusiasms or political doctrines which by their sincerity and readiness for sacrifice have all the force of religions. Great bodies of men who cared intensely for a definite creed found that expression for it was lacking." Sometimes they found, as did those pioneers of the Catholic Press in the United States, that the Official Press actively attacked their doctrines and gave space to malignant untruths against Catholicism. This condition has given way to another which we find today. The great papers refuse to talk about things that matter in religion. They take for granted a sort of "invertebrate common opinion" which they feed on only the "vaguest ethical platitudes." They do this at their best. At their worst they sometimes distort important news; and they continually act as the germ carriers of our most stupid and destructive doctrines on economics, morals, and religion. The Catholic who daily gulps down all this misinformation and raw opinion without the salt of the Free Press is in danger of spiritual indigestion.

One may get some idea of how widespread this danger is from the fact that the Catholic Press weekly of the largest circulation in the United States can boast of only thirty thousand subscribers in a Catholic population of over twenty million. For twenty-five years this weekly, *America,* has done distinguished work in the most important department of the Free Press, viz., that of correcting the propaganda of the Capitalist Press. Yet relatively few Catholics have considered it an "important intellectual phenomenon."

Non-Catholic groups also have resorted to the Free Press as a measure of defense against the evils of a top-heavy plutocracy. They have found boycott and active misrepresentation of their interests and beliefs in the Capitalist Press, and they have been willing to support journals that may correct this, even though these journals must be, from the very nature of the situation, inferior in all the externals of journalism. This very inferiority, however, becomes a badge of honor and a banner to rally the loyal.

Michael Williams, in his very interesting autobiography *The High Romance,* has made some acute observations on the superior loyalty manifested by anti-Christian groups in supporting their Free Press. He is in a position to compare their enthusiasm with that of Catholics because, although now editor of *Commonweal,* he was once associated with those obscure and eccentric groups that engineered the revolution in American thought that burst upon us in the 1920's. Of these Mr. Williams says that they are "usually more actively apostolical, in the sense of desiring and seeking to convert others to their way of thinking than lay Catholics are. Decidedly they are more zealous in their service of their beliefs. . . ." In the days before 1920 while Catholics were generously supporting the Capitalist Press and neglecting their own because of its inferiority, these "apostles" were giving whole-hearted support to their organs which in many cases were more cranky and carelessly edited than the Catholic journals. And in the long run their loyalty and spirit of sacrifice was fittingly rewarded. On such sacrifices are the triumphs of the Free Press built.

There is among Catholics very little of that party spirit which is found in other and smaller groups and which accounts for their greater influence in this country. In one sense this is a good thing, in another quite harmful. It works a distinct hardship, for instance, on the Catholic Free Press. The Capitalist Press in America has no more loyal supporters or more careful readers than the twenty million Catholics, many of whom swallow its most banal pronouncements as blandly as any gum-chewing atheist. They are, on the other hand, the severest critics of the Catholic Press, just as they are as a body wholly unwilling to make those sacrifices which are essential if the crudities they deplore are to be removed.

Not only does the Catholic body in this country generously support the Capitalist Press by buying and reading it, but perhaps more than any other single group it has given and still gives to it a large number of its most distinguished and undistinguished writers. I do not wholly deplore either of these facts. What I deplore is that so small a proportion of this money and talent should be given to the Catholic Free Press. This at least is deplorable. Some of its results are far from being good. Its full effects have never been accurately estimated. They are profound. One has already been touched upon. The danger, namely, that the Catholic body may become intellectually what others who consistently and without antidote feed on the cant of our great newspapers and magazines actually are, flabby and superstitious, putty in the hands of Brisbanes and callow editorial weather men. Another is the amazing emptiness of the Catholic mind that is unnourished by contact with the active Church. Let me add one more to these.

For the Catholic, as for the average American, the ordinary approach to a literary career is through what is called "experience" on a metropolitan daily. It looks like the best approach, yet, I think, more promising writers are lost to the Church by this means than by any other: and not only to the Church but to literature. A young man, fresh from a Catholic college and filled with the desire to make a name for himself as a Catholic writer, succeeds in getting a berth on a newspaper. The years go by, and one of the first things he learns is the character of the organization he is working for. It is not, frequently, an evil or iniquitous thing; but it is also not the noble, crusading institution he may have imagined it to be. It is a public-service corporation, a little less soulless, perhaps, than the local electric-light or telephone company, but still a corporation operated primarily for profits and not for sweet virtue's sake. The policy of the sheet may contain planks that conflict with his own ideas of social and economic justice. He may even be called upon to do things his better nature opposes. Yet he does them, not as one wholly reprobate, but by way of carrying on. He says to himself, "When I am city or managing editor I'll put a stop to this. . . ."

I recall a certain quiet night in the local room of a daily when the young city editor strode out of the managing editor's office, pounded on his desk and announced arrogantly to the whole room that he was "damned tired of being the managing editor's telephone boy." Everyone secretly applauded his independence of spirit, and sympathized with his action in resigning, the next day, to look for another battery of telephones and another managing editor. Everyone knew, too, that his tirade against the "boss" was eminently unjust, for what was the managing editor but the "telephone boy" of the publisher? Journalists learn these things sooner or later and quietly resign themselves to the task of "turning the crank that increases the balance in somebody's bank." It is not their show. They have talent but no capital: they have families to support.

Again, let me say, I am not wholly deploring this situation. Modern journalism, after all, is a legitimate means of support, and is just as clean and wholesome perhaps as any other commercial occupation. One even finds at times newspapers where the old tradition still prevails and the journalist is a gentleman and not just an employee. But even as an employee a Catholic can earn a modest living, which is all any journalist asks, and may achieve some measure of fame as the late Frank Ward O'Malley, Floyd Gibbons, and others have.

My point is that his fame will not be founded on the expression of that which lies closest to his heart — the essential Catholic spirit. The restrictions placed upon him by the very nature of the Capitalist Press, its preoccupation with claptrap instead of truth, will prevent this. Only a few succeed in breaking through these restrictions, and they only partially. The vast majority are simply lost, swallowed up by the huge secularizing machinery. They make a burnt offering of their talents and enthusiasm and are rewarded with a living.

For some, such a reward is an ample one. But there are others for whom a living is an insufficient thing. They need something else, and that thing is a *cause,* some ideal or enterprise of sufficient loftiness to draw from them the best they have in energy and sacrifice. Lacking this they are half-men. This type of man frequently finds no such cause on the metropolitan daily of his choice, or in the secular weekly or monthly journals to which he submits his more literary extra-work. He feels that his inspiration, his genius is strapped by the restrictions imposed by these organs, becomes vastly cynical over his own unsuccess and the debased position of the modern journalist. Yet in the midst of this the Free Press never occurs to him as a remedy. It is the one institution that may restore the profession of journalism to its ancient dignity. It is the one atmosphere wherein his highest ideals may have full play. He does not look upon it as a way out because he has a huge contempt for what he calls its "inferior journalism," and thus he pays the penalty of those who think more of the exterior of journalism than they do of its soul.

III

Belloc has well stated the problem: "To release the truth against whatever odds . . . is a necessity for the soul. We [the journalists of the Free Press] have this consolation, that those who leave us and attach themselves for fear or greed to the stronger party of dissemblers gradually lose thereby their chance for fame in letters. Sound writing cannot survive in an air of mechanical hypocrisy. They with their enormous modern audiences are the hacks doomed to oblivion. We, under the modern silences, are the inheritors of those who build up the political greatness of England upon a foundation of free speech, and of the prose which it begets."

To read the sparkling commentaries on current events in *G. K.'s Weekly,* for instance, not only by Belloc, Chesterton, and G. C. Heseltine but by J. Desmond Gleeson, Gregory Macdonald, F. Keston Clarke, and others besides, is indeed to be "in another world from the sludge and grind of the Official Weekly." It is this new atmosphere, the consciousness of a cause, and the freedom of speech it must have, that produces what Padraic Colum calls "the prose of logic and of scorn." And produces it everywhere, in England, in Ireland, and in America where the *Commonweal* and *America* maintain as high a level of journalism as any Free Press weekly in the field. Our monthly and quarterly journals, too, show not less aptitude in sounding the cultured and confident note of the Catholic Revival; in England, *Blackfriars, Dublin Review, The Month, Colosseum, Downside Review;* in America, *Catholic World, The Sign, Thought;* in Ireland, *Studies* and *Irish Monthly.*

The qualities I have been describing as belonging to the modern resurgence of Catholic thought and letters are all to be found reflected in these publications, in the distinction and modernity of their formats; in the justice and lack of commercial blurbing in their general comments on books and men, in the scholarship behind their articles on religion, economics, history, and science, in the high quality of their incidental poetry, in the clarity and distinction of style, in the note of triumphant irony, in the air of confidence and poise. There are exceptions, of course, to this, such as are inevitable in the hurly-burly of journalism. But one finds consistently in our best weekly, monthly, and quarterly journals an authentic cross section of the Catholic renaissance. In one sense it may be said that the Free Press has arisen out of the spirit behind the movement, in another that the Free Press has actually created the spirit and is actively engaged in the work of making its manifestations more just, more polished, more widespread. The part it plays in the movement is an immensely important one. To follow it is to follow the revival.

This is particularly true in the field of the detached essay. Most of the examples of this type that are later collected in book form have first appeared in one or another of our Catholic journals. We may read in *Catholic World* the contributions of Katherine Brégy, Montgomery Carmichael, James Gillis, Seumas MacManus, Joseph J. Reilly; in *Studies,* Christopher Dawson and Denis Gwynn; in *Commonweal,* Michael Williams, George Shuster, Padraic Colum; in *The Month,* Stanley James, Herbert Thurston, James Brodrick, C. C. Martindale; in *America,* Agnes Repplier, Margaret Mackenzie, Theodore Maynard, Wilfrid Parsons; and so on, through the rest.

Our essayists also write for other Free Press and capitalist organs, but it is in the Catholic journals, I think, that their best work, with some notable exceptions, has appeared. The atmosphere such as they alone supply seems necessary for the releasing of the best prose. In this air there is today little of that crankiness so characteristic of all Free Press organs. Gone, too, is the old note of apology and defense. In its place there is the consciousness on the part of editors and contributors that the Catholic program in economics, science, and letters is not for Catholics alone but for the world; that it is not a queer program or an inferior one, but the only consistent hope for the salvation of our culture.

The numerous forces which today threaten Western civilization with extinction have given to our journals a prestige among non-Catholics they have never before had. Not only has this modern crisis widened their audiences, but it has brought to them the literary contributions of distinguished men who, although not Catholics, find that this section of the Free Press alone stands for the cultural things they consider valuable and worth fighting for. A few Catholic magazines have worked their way to positions of leadership in various intellectual fields, they have become the center, that is to say, about which many thinkers who sympathize intellectually with the Church rally. This situation has, moreover, given birth to a new type of journal of which the *English Review* is the most outstanding example. Its editor, Douglas Jerrold is a Catholic as are many of its contributors; but the magazine differs somewhat from the journals we have been considering. It is the organ of a group of men and women whose views on economics, politics, and the arts are so close to without being wholly identical with those of the Church, that it has become a medium wherein these differences may be threshed out and a strong united front be presented against the organized forces of dissolution.

In America a somewhat similar position is occupied by the new *American Review,* successor to the *Bookman.* Its editor, Seward Collins, is not a Catholic, but the platform of the magazine places it on record as espousing the Distributist program of Chesterton and Belloc, and scholastic philosophy. "The magazine," says Collins, "is a response to the widespread and growing feeling that the forces and principles which have produced the modern chaos are incapable of yielding any solution; that the only hope is a return to fundamentals and tested principles which have been largely pushed aside." It aims at providing a forum for what Collins calls the "Radicals of the Right" or "Revolutionary Conservatives."

Whatever may be the future of magazines of the type of the *English Review* and the *American Review* they are highly symbolic of the new position held today by Catholic thought in the intellectual world. We shall probably have more magazines of this sort. They answer the present pressing need for solidarity on the part of all those, independent of religious beliefs, who are working to preserve the most valuable elements in our culture. But they will not take the place of the Catholic Free Press. They will supplement it but not supplant it. And if a reason must be given it is this: The radicalism they of necessity must stand for is not radical enough. Only pure and uncompromising Catholicism is. The effort to formulate a common creed that may satisfy the divergent beliefs of all concerned not infrequently results in extracting from the Christian message all its explosive content. Christianity loses its supernatural character, becomes a mere social, economic, or artistic philosophy — it becomes a bourgeois Christianity with which the world is so justly disgusted. Indeed there is not a little danger that Catholicism may be involved in the general damnation that is being hurled at this sort of Christianity from all sides. The function of the Catholic Free Press in averting this danger is an important one, and it can only be discharged by a policy of uncompromising supernaturalism, by refusing, for whatever reason, to water down the essentially radical character of the Gospels.

For the organ that adopts a policy of this kind there is a promising future. We have recently seen in America a striking exemplification of this in the phenomenal growth of *The Cath-*

olic Worker. Begun in New York by Miss Dorothy Day and Peter Maurin as a modest effort sheet to counteract the influence of Capitalist and Communist propaganda among the workers, it has in a year and a half become a magazine of a hundred thousand circulation. Its triumph is a triumph for the Free Press, for all the elements that make the Free Press an "important intellectual phenomenon" were present at its birth and presided over its growth. Its editor, Dorothy Day, launched it without capital and has continued to support it without the aid of advertising subsidy. She and her associate Peter Maurin (a man certainly of unusual genius) both have unlimited contempt for all the brave and expensive apparatus on which the world depends. They have placed their faith in the simple promises of Christ to the poor in spirit and to those who shall seek first the Kingdom of God and His justice. This faith has given them the liberty and joy of the children of God, and has made *The Catholic Worker* a paper one may read without having his intelligence insulted by the formulae of a Christianity that squints.

The same may be said for another new addition to the Catholic Free Press — the English quarterly journal *Colosseum.* "We believe," says its editor Bernard Wall in a statement that aptly sums up the position of Catholics today, "that men in our time are summoned to an integral restoration of Christian values, to a universal reinvention of order. They must expel from their minds all barbarism, both Capitalist and Communist, of the naturalist and atheist world. To the Liberals we say: The age of compromise is over and done with. It is a war *à l'outrance* between integral materialism (Marxism) and integral Christianity (Catholicism) — take your choice. To the Communists we say: Be honest and don't be sentimental — work out your integral materialism to its logical conclusion or chuck it. . . . To the Christians we say: Be Christians, apply the Gospels uncompromisingly to social injustice and you will have secretly achieved the second Christian revolution."

BIBLIOGRAPHY — ESSAYS

BARING, MAURICE
WORKS
Dead Letters (New York: Doubleday, 1925).
Lost Diaries (Boston: Houghton, 1913).
Punch and Judy and Other Essays (New York: Doubleday, 1924).
Hildesheim (London: Heinemann, 1924).
Lost Lectures (New York: Knopf, 1932).

COLUM, PADRAIC
WORKS
The Road Round Ireland (New York: Macmillan, 1926).
Cross Roads in Ireland (New York: Macmillan, 1930).
A Half-Day's Ride (New York: Macmillan, 1932).

NOYES, ALFRED
WORKS
New Essays and American Impressions (New York: Holt, 1927)
Some Aspects of Modern Poetry (New York: Stokes, 1924).
Opalescent Parrot (London: Sheed, 1929).
The Unknown God (New York: Sheed & Ward, 1933).

BRÉGY, KATHERINE
WORKS
From Dante to Jeanne D'Arc (Milwaukee: Bruce, 1933).
Poets' Chantry (New York: Benziger, 1925).
Poets and Pilgrims (New York: Benziger, 1925).

BELLOC, HILAIRE
WORKS
This and That (London: Methuen, 1912).
On Nothing (London: Methuen, 1908).
On (London: Methuen, 1923).
On Anything (London: Constable, 1910).
Cruise of the Nona (Boston: Houghton, 1925).
Survivals and New Arrivals (London: Sheed, 1929).
Short Talks with the Dead (New York: Harper, 1926).
Path to Rome (New York: Putnam, 1915).
Essays of a Catholic (London: Sheed, 1931).
The Free Press (London: Allen & Unwin, 1918).
Conversation with an Angel (London: Cape, 1928).

CHESTERTON, G. K.

WORKS

Heretics (New York: Lane, 1905).
Orthodoxy (New York: Lane, 1908).
All is Grist (London: Methuen, 1931).
Charles Dickens (New York: Dutton, 1921).
Catholic Church and Conversion (New York: Macmillan, 1926).
Eugenics and Other Evils (New York: Dodd, 1927).
The Everlasting Man (New York: Dodd, 1925).
The Resurrection of Rome (New York: Dodd, 1930).
Sidelights (London: Sheed, 1932).
The Thing (London: Sheed, 1931).

D'ARCY, MARTIN, S.J.

The Mass and the Redemption (London: Burns, Oates, 1926).
The Nature of Belief (New York: Sheed & Ward, 1931).

GIBBS, SIR PHILIP

WORKS

More That Must Be Told (New York: Harper, 1921).
Ten Years After (New York: Doran, 1925).
Now It Can Be Told (New York: Harper, 1927).
Since Then (New York: Harper, 1930).
The Way of Escape (New York: Harper, 1933).

O'SHAUGHNESSY, EDITH

WORKS

Alsace in Rust and Gold (1920).
My Lorraine Journal (New York: Harper, 1918).
Other Ways and Other Flesh (Boston: Harcourt, 1929).

LUNN, ARNOLD

Sign, January, 1934.

WORKS

Now I See (New York: Sheed & Ward, 1934).
Within That City (New York: Sheed & Ward, 1936).
The Flight From Reason (New York: Dial Press, 1931).

REPPLIER, AGNES

America, 31:138.
Commonweal, August 18, 1933.
Schelling, *Appraisments and Asperities,* pp. 21–26.

WORKS

Books and Men (Boston: Houghton, 1888).
Essays in Idleness (Boston: Houghton, 1893).

Essays in Miniature (Boston: Houghton, 1893).
A Happy Half-Century (Boston: Houghton, 1908).
In Our Convent Days (Boston: Houghton, 1905).
Points of View (Boston: Houghton, 1891).
Points of Friction (Boston: Houghton, 1920).
To Think of Tea (Boston: Houghton, 1932).
WILLIAMS, MICHAEL
WORKS
The High Romance, autobiography (New York: Macmillan, 1924).
Catholicism and the Modern Mind (New York: Dial Press, 1928).
The Shadow of the Pope (New York: Dial Press, 1932).
GILL, ERIC
Commonweal, July 14, 1933, p. 285.
WORKS
Art Nonsense and Other Essays (London: Cassell, 1929).
Beauty Looks After Herself (New York: Sheed & Ward, 1933).

* * *

Carmichael, Montgomery, *In Tuscany* (New York: Dutton, 1905).
Curtayne, Alice, *A Recall to Dante* (London: Sheed, 1932).
Daly, James, J., S.J., *A Cheerful Ascetic* (Milwaukee: Bruce, 1932).
Earls, Michael, S.J., *Under College Towers* (New York: Macmillan, 1927).
Gibbons, John, *Tramping to Lourdes* (New York: Dutton, 1932).
——— *London to Sarajevo* (New York: Dutton, 1931).
Gillis, James, C.S.P., *False Prophets* (New York: Macmillan, 1925).
Kilmer, Aline, *Hunting a Hair Shirt* (New York: Doran, 1923).
Knox, Ronald, *An Open-Air Pulpit* (London: Constable, 1926).
——— *On Getting There* (London: Methuen, 1929).
Mackenzie, Compton, *Unconsidered Trifles* (London: Secker, 1933).
Maynard, Theodore, *Our Best Poets* (New York: Holt, 1922).
——— *Carven From the Laurel Tree* (New York: McBride, 1922).
Musser, Benjamin, *Straws on the Wind* (New York: Bozart Press, 1932).
——— *Franciscan Poets* (New York: Macmillan, 1933).
Reilly, Joseph J., *Dear Prue's Husband* (New York: Macmillan, 1932).
Shuster, George, *Catholic Spirit in America* (New York: Dial, 1927).
——— *The Germans* (New York: Dial, 1932).

* * *

SELECTED LIST OF MAGAZINES

Weekly

America, 329 West 108th Street, New York ($4 a year).
Commonweal, Grand Central Terminal, New York ($5 a year).
G.K.'s Weekly, 2 Little Essex Street, London, W.C.2 (28s a year).
Tablet, 6 Adams Street, Adelphi, London, W.C.1. (30s a year.)

Monthly

Catholic World, 411 West 59th Street, New York.
Columbia, New Haven, Connecticut ($1 a year).
Downside Review, 31 Paternoster Row, London, E.C.4.
The Month, 31 Farm Street, Berkeley Square, London, W.1.
The Sign, Union City, New Jersey ($2 a year).
Blackfriars, 40 Broadstreet, Oxford, England ($3 a year).
Queen's Work, 3742 West Pine Boulevard, St. Louis, Missouri (50 cents
  a year).
Irish Monthly, Rathfarnham Castle, Co. Dublin (8s a year).
The Catholic Worker, 436 E. 15th Street, New York (1 cent a copy).

Quarterly

Dublin Review, 43 Newgate Street, London, E.C.1 (15s a year).
Studies, Educational Company of Ireland, Dublin (15s a year).
Thought, 329 W. 108th Street, New York ($5 a year).
Spirit (Catholic Poetry Society Publication), 327 W. 108th Street, New
  York, $2.
Colosseum, John Miles Ltd., Amen Corner, London E.C.4 (8s a year).

English Review, 6 Great New Street, London, W.C.1 (monthly).
American Review, 386 Fourth Avenue, New York (monthly), $4 a yea

Index

Index

397